deviant BEHAVIOR

occupational
and organizational
bases

deviant behavior

occupational and organizational bases

Clifton D. Bryant
Virginia Polytechnic Institute
and State University

Rand McNally
College Publishing Company Chicago

*This Volume is Affectionately
Dedicated to my Mother–
Helen Bryant*

Preface

Work is a fertile contextual matrix for the various processes attendant to the social enterprise. Many of these work-related social processes have been explored in considerable detail by sociologists, and in fact, a number of them have become constituent elements in the conceptual frameworks which have been applied to the sociological analysis of occupations and work systems. Not the least of these work-related social processes is deviancy. Curiously, the relationship between work and deviant behavior, while by no means ignored, has, perhaps, not received the enthusiastic attention or treatment which I feel it deserves. It is quite evident, for example, that we are shaped and regulated by our work in terms of attitudinal posture, routine, and life-style. However, it is less evident that our normative transgressions, pathologies, abberations, and/or behavioral illegalities may often derive rather directly from our work and the millieu in which it is conducted.

The overly-energetic worker, motivated by the Protestant Ethic and visions of modest financial affluence, may well find himself classified as deviant, if not pariah, by virtue of the norms of work restriction imposed by fellow industrial workers. The alcoholic career military man or addicted physician is surely just as much a product of his work and its concommitant sub-cultural strains as is Cottrells' overly time conscious railroader, or Hughes' professionals who become indifferent to clientele emergency. The white collar criminal learns to steal via occupational socialization, in a manner not unlike that of an attorney who acquires insights into appropriate courtroom demeanor and strategies. The medium who spuriously summons up the spirits of the departed, or the "professional" hustler, could find themselves on a wanted poster in spite of an occupational routine that is structurally quite similar in some ways, to other more conventional occupational specialties, but by virtue of an exploitive occupational intent that transcends the threshold of community tolerance, these people may find themselves engaged in criminal activities.

This anthology seeks to explore the parameters of work-deviant behavior relationships, and in this connection the various essays and articles scrutinize both a number of deviant behavioral configurations and a variety of occupational and organizational examples ranging from strippers to physicians, and from abortion mills to the U.S. military. More than half of the articles were either written expressively for this volume or had not been previously published, and some of the previously published material has come from journals and periodicals less seminal to the mainstream of sociology and accordingly less well known. I believe the reader will find each to be both cogent and insightful. Hopefully, such readings, along with the editorial material, will be both illuminating and sensitizing, and will stimulate further interest in the occupational and organizational bases of deviant behavior.

I am indebted to my colleagues at various institutions, Fuad Baali, Louis M. Beck, H. Dirk Dansereau, and William E. Snizek who provided helpful suggestions and comments during the development of the manuscript. And to my secretary, Mrs. Karen Bass, whose clerical assistance in preparing the manuscript for publication proved invaluable.

CLIFTON D. BRYANT

Blacksburg, Virginia
June, 1974

Contents

List of Contributors

Dr. H. Eugene Hodges
Department of Sociology and Anthropology
University of Rhode Island

Dr. Donald F. Roy
Department of Sociology
Duke University

Dr. Wiliam E. Snizek
Department of Sociology
Virginia Polytechnic Institute and State University

Dr. H. Kirk Dansereau
Department of Sociology and Anthropology
Western Kentucky University

Dr. Paul M. Roman
Department of Sociology
Tulane University

Dr. Clifton D. Bryant
Department of Sociology
Virginia Polytechnic Institute and State University

Dr. Richard M. Hessler
Section of Behavioral Science
University of Missouri

Dr. Charles H. McCaghy   and   Dr. James K. Skipper, Jr.
Department of Sociology   Department of Social Medicine
Bowling Green State University   Medical College of Ohio, Toledo

Dr. Donald R. South   and   Dr. Donald J. Shoemaker
Department of Sociology   Department of Sociology
University of Southern Mississippi   Virginia Polytechnic Institute
                                      and State University

James Boyd

Dr. Ellwyn Stoddard
Department of Sociology and Anthropology
University of Texas at El Paso

Charles Gillespie

Dr. Charlotte R. Tatro

Dr. Julian B. Roebuck   and   Dr. Robert Bruce Hunter
Department of Sociology   Department of Sociology
Mississippi State University   University of Colorado

Dr. Jacqueline Boles   and   Dr. A. P. Garbin
Department of Sociology   Department of Sociology
Georgia State University   University of Georgia

Dr. Patrick C. Easto   and   Dr. Marcello Truzzi
Department of Sociology   Division of Social Sciences
Eastern Michigan University   New College

John L. Gordon, Jr.
Department of Anthropology
Harvard University

Mary Riege Laner
Department of Sociology
Virginia Polytechnic Institute and State University

Nicholas Pileggi

Dr. Donald W. Ball
Department of Sociology
University of Victoria (British Columbia)

WORK AND DEVIANT BEHAVIOR

A Conceptual Introduction

The topic of work and deviant behavior has been a long time, albeit relatively peripheral, object of sociological interest. The pioneering researchers of the "Chicago School," for example, examined a wide variety of occupational activities that were concomitantly criminal in nature, such as jack-rollers, and "professional" thieves, as well as practioners of other deviant pursuits such as taxi dancers and hobos. The Mayo studies had of course pointed out the existence of worker-established informal normative systems and the eventuality of individual violation of such norms, but without emphasizing the deviant aspect of such behavior. More recently, of course, this point has been well developed by Don Roy, Melville Dalton, Joseph Bensman, Israel Gerver, and others. In 1939 Edwin H. Sutherland suggested the concept of white-collar crime in describing structured criminality in white-collar and commercial work systems. Somewhat later other researchers have articulated additional forms of occupational criminality, including blue-collar crime, blue-coat crime, and khaki-collar crime.[1] The contemporary resurgence of ethnomethodological urban studies (reminiscent of the earlier "Chicago studies") has focused attention on a number of deviant and sometimes illegal occupational enterprises such as stripping, topless waitresses, faith healers, exploitive carnival concessionaires, proprietors of underground movie houses and massage parlors.

The mass media today has tended to make us all more aware of consumer frauds by commercial enterprises, the invasion of legitimate businesses by criminal elements, and the almost endemic nature of political corruption. Similarly, in recent years as our attention has been focused on social problems involving human addictive behavior, the fact has not escaped us that alcoholism and narcotic usage tend to be more prevalent in some occupational settings than in others. Curiously, writers of sociological textbooks about occupations and work did not until recently generally concern themselves either with deviant occupations or occupational deviancy. Notable examples are Elliott A. Krause's text[2] which includes the former, and George

---

[1] These studies are examined in considerable detail later in this volume.

[2] Elliott A. Krause, *The Sociology of Occupations* (Boston, Little, Brown, 1971), especially Chapter 11.

3

Ritzer's volume[3] which treats the latter. Deviancy does not occur in a social vacuum; it takes place as part of the on-going processes attendant to our major social institutions and their behavioral configurations. Such a central institution is that of work. A very significant proportion of deviant behavior occurs within, concomitant to, or as a result of, work and occupational specialty. Inasmuch as work organization involves both formal and informal normative structure, violations of these work norms, such as "rate-busting," quota restriction, the use of forbidden procedures, such as a shortcut technique or to cover up mistakes or shoddy workmanship, and unethical professional behavior, are in fact deviant behavior. Because certain kinds of work engenders specific routines, pressures, stresses, and problems, some occupational structures and cultures appear to induce, facilitate, and harbor particular kinds of pathological behavior such as alcoholism, narcotic addiction, or homosexuality. Similarly, the structure and culture of some conventionally legal work and occupational systems seem to be conducive to characteristic forms of illegal activities. Such work systems apparently possess singular opportunity structures for crime as well as unique milieus that contribute to the individual motivation for such illicit behavior. Some occupational specialties, while not always defined as illegal, do often transcend the boundaries of propriety and community acceptance, either because of intent or the nature of the service rendered, and can accordingly be classified as deviant. A great many other occupational pursuits are clearly in violation of legal statute even though they provide genuine occupational and career opportunities for the practitioners and are thus deviant also. To gain insight and understanding, these various configurations of work and deviant behavior may be examined from several perspectives.

WORK CULTURE

To cope with their environment, provide for their needs and wants, and accomplish their social goals societies develop distinctive patterns of behavior and attendant material artifacts and accessories. So too do smaller social structures, including work organizations. The totality of these behavioral and material configurations is labeled *culture.*

An entire occupational system or whole industry may have a distinctive work culture, as may a small work system or component of a larger unit with membership of only a few workers. Culture, as John J. Honigmann has pointed out, is basically a way of coping with problems.[4] Work culture, then,

---

[3] George Ritzer, *Man and His Work: Conflict and Change* (New York, Appleton-Century-Crofts, 1972), especially Chapter 2.

[4] John J. Honigmann, *Understanding Culture* (New York, Harper & Row, 1963), pp. 24–25.

represents an elaborate way of coping with the problems of work, including getting the job accomplished; making the process endurable, if not rewarding, for those involved; and developing a social justification and individual rationalization requisite to the continued existence of the work system.

The culture of a society or a work organization is the collective product of the individuals who are or have been members; but just as culture is the product of man, so too is man the product of his culture. The culture of a work organization may, for example, define the appropriate routine and tempo of work for the workers. In time they will internalize these norms and values and thus be shaped by the culture of their work. For example, because of the necessity of precise timing for the running of trains, the railroader becomes obsessed with time.[5] By company mandate he carries a precision watch to which he refers with great frequency, and time becomes a critical dimension of his existence. Frequently organizing his life around a precise routine, meals must be served on an exact schedule; and a promise to meet at a given time must not be broken even by a variation of a few minutes. Such a preoccupation with time becomes ingrained in the railroader's personality and is not diminished even with retirement.

Man becomes a victim, so to speak, of habit and custom and thus of culture, even work culture. In the military, for example, everything that is thrown on the ground must be picked up, or "policed up." Accordingly, newcomers quickly learn to "field strip" cigarette butts (tearing them open to scatter the tobacco, tearing the paper into small pieces, and rolling the pieces into little balls that will be invisible on the ground). Once this operation has been internalized as a mechanical skill, it becomes unconscious and reflexive. After an individual has been discharged from the armed services, he may well continue to "field strip" his cigarettes for weeks or months, even though there is no longer constraint to do so.

An individual is subject to more than the influence of work routine, tempo, or procedure, however. Work culture also defines social conformity and thus, to an extent, morality in that it provides reason and rationalization for certain kinds of job-related behavior as well as clarifying, obscuring, or modifying the individual's perspective of social control and sanction. Work cultures provide elaborate myth systems that in turn may initiate, support, sustain, and perpetuate various kinds of deviant behavior attendant to the occupational efforts.

The collective disaffection of work-related travel may, for example, give rise to the myth of "overworked and underpaid" traveling employees who in turn may routinely "pad" their expense account in a rationalized effort

---

[5] W. F. Cottrell, "Of Time and the Railroader," *American Sociological Review,* Vol. 4, No. 2 (April 1939), pp. 190–98.

to compensate themselves for their perceived privations. The same traveling man, who in his home community would never dream of being unfaithful, may easily be convinced by circumstances and co-workers that when "on the road" he is entitled to a little "messing around" with a cocktail waitress, especially since "what the little woman back home doesn't know won't hurt her!" Taking home "samples" may become defined as an informal fringe benefit, and small items deliberately stolen will "never be missed," especially because the victim is a large and affluent corporation.

All work has inherent physical, mental, or social strains. In some instances the strains are redefined or modified so as to ameliorate them or make them more tolerable. In the absence of such redefinitional mechanisms, however, the work culture, either formally or informally, may define effective and appropriate buffering agents. Both semi-formally and informally, the military traditionally has relied on alcohol for between-combat respites or to dull the edge of garrison duty monotony. But in recent years, especially in Vietnam, the informal culture dictated marijuana as the preferred relaxant, although it is sternly forbidden by formal military regulation. In addition to being readily accessible in Vietnam, marijuana is in a sense a "protest" drug and symbolic of the counterculture. Because the many young draftees were making a significant input to informal military culture, they were incorporating into it something of the youth counterculture, including "dew," or "pot."

For a bureaucratic executive, the three-martini lunch, called for by business tradition, hopefully raises the business conference to the level of conviviality, theoretically facilitating negotiations and transactions and rendering more bearable the existential strains of executive life. A physician may not imbibe alcohol, except on rare occasions when he will not be called by patients or unless he drinks vodka, the "breathless" potable. The telltale smell of alcohol would be immediately discernable and might erode the medical image and thus interfere with the treatment process. The physician must cope with the stresses of occupational routine, however. Within his material culture are many chemical aids that can assist him to stay awake or go to sleep, provide pep or afford relaxation and release of tension. His work culture also supplies him with the expertise necessary for the knowledgeable use of these drugs. Although "officially" frowned upon, there is tacit toleration of such drug usage by colleagues who hold a sympathetic perspective of the stresses that motivate it.

Work culture may also define the appropriate image of, and value stance toward, customers or clientele. The stripper may originally be attracted to her vocation by the lure of "show biz," the attendant glamour, and the anticipated accolades and admiration of audiences. Once she really encounters the audiences, however, and discovers the real pathological depth of their viewing appreciation, she may become disenchanted with them and males in general. Reinforced by similar attitudes held by other strippers, she may reject male companionship as "exploitive" and depraved and seek the intimacies of lesbian relationships instead, especially if there is subcultural pressure to do so, finding them more satisfying and compensating for the dissatisfactions of her work.

Very few varieties of work exist outside a rationalizing milieu. Almost invariably the myth system operates to justify and reassure the practitioner. If the young neophyte prostitute had any misgivings about the unsavory flavor of her vocation, she soon loses them, once she is told and "learns for herself" and comes to believe that she is doing what all women do. Even married women, prostitutes rationalize, give sex and receive financial support in return. The professional confidence man seldom has trouble sleeping nights because he well knows, as a result of his subcultural indoctrination, that his victims could not be victimized if in fact they did not have larceny in their hearts and did not intend exploiting him. One learns relatively early in the carnival business that the clientele are "suckers," "marks" or "apes." Conceptualized in such a derogatory fashion, there is little compunction about attempting to "separate the mark from his money."

Work culture may define an appropriate means for workers to deal with the boredom of their work. The diversion may be as innocuous as simple games constructed out of variations in the routine of the work itself. It may, however, take more reprehensible forms, such as frequent and intense amorous and sexual liaisons with employees of the opposite sex, and even involve atrocity behavior, where soldiers, in an attempt to alleviate the personal strain of war, may while away their spare hours sniping at isolated civilians or seeking to rape and plunder the indigenous population. The work culture may also take into account the stresses involved in working with persons of the opposite sex, where circumspect comportment is called for, and may dictate an appropriate escape mechanism in the form of the annual Christmas office party or spring picnic where one can drink to intoxication, engage in open flirtation and mild intimacies, and in general overlook the need for sexual comportment.

At a formal level work culture may identify an expected level of work performance, but at an informal level it may articulate the means by which the members of the work system may appropriately and successfully evade or subvert the formal norms. Informal work culture may also impose an alternate set of work-level expectations and also specify the sanctions for violators of the norm.

Because work culture defines for the individual much of his perspective of reality and thus shapes his existential experience, it in effect provides him with an awareness of opportunities for deviant behavior within his work and a motivation and justification or rationalization for engaging in such behavior.

OPPORTUNITY STRUCTURE

Participation in crime or deviant behavior is not solely a function of volition alone. The ways and means must also be available. Merely to want to be an embezzler is not sufficient, for example. It would be extremely difficult, if not impossible, to embezzle if one were not strategically located in a work system, perhaps as a bookkeeper or purchasing agent. A would-be confidence man needs confidence and salesmanship, just as those who would engrave counterfeit plates need artistic ability. A successful "society" jewel thief would obviously need "society" contacts and a degree of *savoir faire*. To "crack" a safe takes skill, and one can hardly steal atomic secrets if one has no access to such secrets. Similarly, an unknowledgable middle-class house-wife who wished to "sample" marijuana might have to pass up the experiment since she might not know where to obtain the "pot."

As suggested in past research, persons learn to commit crimes and thus to become criminals. They learn the necessary skills and attitudes, and they learn to identify the opportunity to commit crime, if it exists. They also have to learn how to avoid being detected and arrested. An aspiring prostitute who had not learned to recognize a disguised member of the vice squad would not remain "on the street" long. The prostitute must also learn how to attract clients and negotiate with them as well as to render the required services efficiently with the requisite "bedside manner" to satisfy the customer and generate "repeat" business. Prostitution flourishes best where the law enforcement apparatus is tolerant of commercialized sex or amenable to payoffs and protection. It also is more prevalent in places that are con-ducive to making contact with clients, such as an abundance of bars and lounges, or resort areas with many hotels and motels, especially those with a clientele seeking the services of prostitutes.

The successful commission of many kinds of crimes requires the acquisition of social as well as technical skills. Similarly, persons usually have to learn how to engage in other forms of deviant behavior. Alcoholism is often cultivated, as it were, over a long period of time as an individual learns how, what, and when to drink. Howard Becker has told us that one must learn to smoke marijuana, in the sense of learning to recognize and appreciate its effects.[6] An individual could undertake to "mainline" heroin

---

[6] Howard S. Becker, "Becoming a Marihuana User," *American Journal of Sociology,* Vol. 59, No. 3 (November 1953), pp. 235–42.

only with assistance if he lacked experience. To use marijuana or heroin one must be able to obtain a supply and hopefully be able to indulge in their use with minimal fear of apprehension by the authorities. Even homosexual behavior must be learned, in the sense that the subtle nuances of social contact and sensory appreciation are usually cultivated over a period of time. Again, community permissiveness, the presence of a homosexual subculture, and opportunities to make contact with other homosexuals facilitate homosexual activities.

Work often provides the opportunity structure for deviant behavior. This opportunity structure may include, for example, access to the vehicle of deviance. The physician or nurse has physical and professional access to narcotics and access to the skills to use them. It is relatively easy, therefore, to divert the narcotics for their professional use. The jazz musician, because of the work milieu in which he operates, has similar easy access to marijuana and to the knowledge of how to use it effectively. One must have an expense account to "pad" and the "know-how" as well. Usually only politicians and public officials are in the strategic position to let public contracts, influence legislation, or grant political favors. They are also accessible to receive kickbacks and graft. The knowledge of graft, in a sense, "goes with the office." Because police have the power to arrest (or the illicit prerogative not to), they also have the opportunity to take payoffs. Similarly, when a police officer who is alone or with a single companion has occasion to inspect the interior of a retail establishment, in the dark of night, it may be much like the fantasy of the kid locked in the candy store all night. The goods are there for the taking, and a few "samples" will "never be missed." The blue-collar worker could not easily pilfer if he did not come into daily contact with mountainous amounts of the items he misappropriates. When bank tellers elect to commit economic crimes, they are more likely to embezzle than to perpetrate burglaries. The soldier could not loot if he was not in a combat or occupied area where there is little or no effective social control to prevent it. War, in a sense, opens the doors for behavior that probably would not and could not occur otherwise.

Few occupational specialties, even of a criminal variety, could operate in the absence of public demand and thus a degree of tacit societal toleration, if not acceptance. The medical "quack" can offer his spurious nostrums only because there are those who either cannot or will not patronize legitimate physicians, or having obtained an unpalatable and thus unsatisfactory opinion from a physician, seek another opinion more amenable to their own predilection. Ours is a health- and body-oriented society, and the abundance of hypochondriacs and those who seek hope where there is none make it easy for the quack to practice his "trade." Strippers can sell raw views of themselves only where there is an ample supply of persons who like to watch naked women. (Interestingly enough, carnivals often have to feature two strip shows to meet the demand when they travel in the presumably erotically deprived Pennsylvania Dutch country and the isolated provinces of the Southern "Bible Belt.") It is also possible only where the local authorities will tolerate such types of entertainment for the sake of tourism or promoting business in general. Hustlers could not hustle without persons who enjoy gambling and like to hustle themselves. Most exploitive occupations are dependent on access to an abundant supply of persons ready and willing to be exploited. Further, such a practitioner must not only have a potential clientele, he must have the additional opportunity of a facilitative economic and social climate.

Prostitutes enjoy an especially lucrative business around mining camps, military posts, and boom towns where there is an imbalance of the sex ratio. An overabundance of unattached males is likely to produce an attitude of sexual permissiveness conducive to commercialized sex. Prostitutes also find business to be especially good just after payday or at other times when money is in abundance. Car theft became a major crime only after the automobile was widely owned by the American population. Moonshine continues to enjoy a considerable following among culturally and economically deprived populations who lack the social discernment to reject it because of quality or aesthetic characteristics, but can fully appreciate its "bargain" qualities. Office romances tend to flourish best where there are workers of the opposite sex who are willing and available to become involved and where the general office culture is tolerant, if not facilitative, of such activities. Various kinds of theft become especially prevalent in the face of economic affluence and an abundance of material goods owned by some segments of the population. Before the recent liberalization of state abortion laws the criminal abortionist clearly could not have operated if there had not been pregnant females who sought to terminate their condition and professional colleagues as well as legal authorities who were willing to tolerate his presence to some degree. Many illegal abortionists derived their clientele via referrals from legal practitioners. District attorneys sometimes avoided trying to prosecute an abortionist because they may have felt he performed a needed and valuable service to the community.

The occupational opportunity structure offers absorption or concealment of deviance, avoidance of stigma, or neutralization of guilt as well as opportunity for the commission of the deviance itself. The alcoholic can operate successfully within the occupational framework of the carnival because a relatively low level of work efficiency will be tolerated there, and there also is a strong respect for personal privacy. The alcoholic laborer will be "carried" by his carnival co-workers. The physician who is a drug addict may go on almost indefinitely without being reported by a colleague because other physicians generally hold sympathetic attitudes concerning the strains and problems of medical practice and private life. Furthermore, when discovered, the physician may not be arrested or prosecuted. Many physician addicts who have lost their license to practice have had it restored after treatment. Even legal officials apparently believe that a doctor can "do no wrong" (at least not much anyway).

Moonshiners may be able to maintain a low profile *vis-a-vis* law enforcement personnel because of the supportive milieu in which they operate and the reluctance of the community to cooperate with the law. The executive may be able to conceal his alcoholism. His "business drinking" can be routine and innocent appearing enough to disguise the fact that he is dependent on the alcohol he consumes. From the public viewpoint, however, successful businessmen are never "drunks" or alcoholics. They simply overindulge or are viewed as hard fisted and hard drinking executives on the cocktail circuit. A person of lesser status would more readily be labeled as a deviant.

The high prestige of public office may well cushion the public impact of scandal and corruption, and corporate fraud never seems to be exactly like "genuine" theft. All traveling employees are expected to inflate their expenses somewhat as a matter of shrewdness. Policemen, as public servants and enforcers of the public will, are often believed to be beyond reproach in their actions. A soldier operating far away from domestic scrutiny may well discover a freedom from most social controls that he never experienced previously. More important, the danger he faces and the mission he attends may well outweigh the fact that he indulges in particularly reprehensible behavior. A man who fights and bleeds for his country can well be excused for various "excesses" which he perpetrates in time of war.

The amateur deviant may begin his career by the infortuitous accident of opportunity. The keys left in the ignition may make possible an illicit joy ride, and the unattended counter may motivate initial shoplifting. Addiction may arise out of a chance attendance at a pot party and the offer to experiment, just as the casual sexual encounter between a married executive and clerical worker may grow out of the chance facilitative circumstances of being intoxicated at the Christmas office party. For ongoing commission of deviant behavior, the individual must be able to acquire the necessary expertise, be strategically located to indulge in the behavior, be able to successfully disguise his actions and evade detection and sanction, encounter sympathetic and tolerant agents of social control, identify willing clients, victims, or co-perpetrators, and even if exposed, be able to enjoy a cushion for the resultant stigma and sanction. He must, in short, have an opportunity structure for deviant behavior, such as that often offered by his occupational specialty or the organizational work system in which he operates.

OCCUPATION-RELATED STRESS

Individuals neither live nor work in a state of tranquility or equilibrium. Rather, they are subjected to a variety of disruptive stresses, conflicts, and disaffections. Particular kinds of occupational specialties and work systems may expose their member practitioners to characteristic configurations of such stresses and disruptions. The disequilibrium may be both chronic and unique to the particular work setting. The attempt on the part of the individual to evade, ameliorate, cope with, or compensate for these strains may take the form of pathological or deviant behavior, either antisocial or self-destructive. The hazards, dilemmas, and discomforts of a job are as much a part of the fabric of work as are the benefits, affections, and satisfactions that accompany the occupation.

The monotony and stultifying dehumanization of factory assembly work may drive a worker to pilfer from his employer systematically or to seek diversion in sexual dalliance with female employees. An individual pressed into a military role against his will may aggressively react to his dilemma by deliberately attempting to "sabotage" his work role. The professional role may call for circumspect comportment, but professional persons, being human, have economic and other drives they may not be able to satisfy within the constraints of professional ethics. Fee-splitting and ambulance chasing may be the result.

Some work roles are almost beyond the ability of some persons to accomplish satisfactorily. To perform their job may require a crutch to enable them effectively to discharge their responsibilities. The harried executive may need the three-martini lunch to make it through the day; and the physician, in experiencing almost inhuman demands on his physical and mental reserves, may have to turn to drugs as the only means of enduring the stresses of his routine. The work of war and the disaffection of military life may require a means of dulling the realities of existence. The stripper seeks the sexual embraces of other women, because she is daily confronted with the depths of depravity in her lustful clientele. The stress or alienation in some occupations becomes unendurable, and suicide offers the only release. The underpaid and frustrated corporate employee may find that white-collar crime is a means of maintaining the dignity and status attendant to his position, but it simultaneously generates the economic resources necessary to enjoy the affluent lifestyle to which he and his family aspire. The policeman, physically endangered by the offenders he arrests, underpaid, largely unappreciated, and subject to a circumspect set of expectations concerning his personal behavior and his work performance, may become embittered and cynical in his frustration, turn to brutality in the discharge of his responsibilities, and be amenable to bribes and corruption. The public official makes an enormous investment financially, socially, and personally in attaining public office and serves his constituency with the knowledge that his occupancy of the position may be short lived because of the vicissitudes of political life. Faced with the ephemeral nature of his office and its structured opportunities for graft and the near-incessant importuning of those seeking favors and offering profit in return, the politician may elect to violate his public trust and become corrupt against the possibility of a "rainy day." War is a dehumanizing experience where, because of the exigencies of combat survival, expediency becomes sufficiently crucial that an individual can willingly commit atrocities to stay alive and to accomplish his mission.

Even the would-be thief who strives to avoid larceny may find it difficult when he experiences the constant temptation of suckers "being born every minute" and who literally beseech him to take advantage of them. Confronted by a poor soul who trembles in fear of hell and damnation, how can the religious huckster do otherwise than provide comfort, assurance, and hope—for a price—and how can the medical quack deny relief to the hypochondriac or hope to the hopeless? For the young girl of economic, educational, and cultural deprivation and with few career alternatives, there are tremendous pressures both personal and social to exploit the few assets she may possess—even in the nude—if it leads her to the seeming glamour and relative affluence of "show biz."

Persons do not always pursue illicit careers out of pure economic motivation, nor is simple intrinsic satisfaction from the job the entire answer. Criminal careers attract individuals on the same complex motivational basis as do conventional occupational pursuits. The isolated Appalachian moonshiner is better able to support his family through illegal whiskey, but his monotonous existence also impels him to seek the diversion and excitement he finds in evading the federal revenue agents. He also has a need to excell and to create which he handily accomplishes in trying to turn out the best "shine" in the region and thus obtain recognition and self-realization. The doctors who performed illegal abortions no doubt enjoyed the economic rewards, but many articulated supposed humanitarian or altruistic motivations as major factors that led them into their illicit specialty. Some abortionists also spoke of their need to obtain expertise and perfection. The inept surgeon-turned-abortionist may well have taken real professional pride in the fact that he performed literally thousands of such illicit operations, never losing the mother and never getting caught.

Even prostitutes are not lured into a life of vice for entirely economic reasons. Like all women, they experience culturally defined pressures and individual needs to be admired and desired. For some, commercialized sex is the most expeditious means of relating to men and thus overcoming self-doubts and inadequacies. They also experience pride in craftsmanship, perhaps not otherwise attainable, in giving a satisfied customer his money's worth and providing services in an expert professional manner.

SUMMARY

This volume is addressed to various aspects of the interrelationship of work and behavior. The selections are focused on a range of work-related deviant behavior varying from simple inappropriate behavior while at work to patterns of "professional" crime. The contributors pursue the thesis that a number of occupational factors are involved in such configurations of deviant behavior. The deviant patterns may, for example, be encouraged and supported by the occupational subculture with the result that conformity to occupational norms may place one in violation of societal norms. Work may also offer unique circumstances and opportunities for the commission of various deviant acts. Some occupational specialties and work systems provide singular kinds of inducements and motivations for the violation of both formal and informal social expectations on a recurring basis. An examination of the intricacy of the deviant dimension of work should yield new insights into the influence of work on social behavior and afford a new perspective on the motivation and concommitants of work-related social deviancy.

I

INAPPROPRIATE OCCUPATIONAL BEHAVIOR

The Violations of Social Norms at Work

Work, like other social behavior, is structured and is therefore performed according to specific social rules. Its practitioners are related to superiors, colleagues, co-workers, clientele, and others in a prescribed method of constrained cooperation. Work takes place within socially approved contexts, is often integrated with other activities labeled as work, and is subject to monitoring and control during and after its occurrence. As structured behavior work is usually compartmentalized to permit ease of learning as well as performance. The basic structural compartment of work is status, with its accompanying social role specifying the details of task performance and articulating the systemic linkages with other related work statuses. The compartmentalization of work into individual social statuses with their accompanying roles facilitates the socialization of work skills and norms and the enactment of work by the persons who practice it. Work-role performance can be better monitored and appropriate social control effected through this individual compartmentalization. Thus occupational or work systems constitute networks of interrelated work statuses frequently linked together in a symbiotic way that permits the individuals to perform their specialized roles and to accomplish a set of work tasks in concert, subject to social control.

Work behavior is therefore subject to a variety of controls including legal codes, formalized expectations, customary standards, and informal social norms.[1] Some of these controls are external to the occupation or work system. Examples are the standards and regulations attendant to some kinds of work imposed by various government agencies and bureaus and the influence of labor unions or occupational organizations. The impact of public sentiment on rate-board and licensing-board decisions, the pressure of Better Business Bureaus, and the wishes of clients or customers all constitute forms of external work control. Some of these controls are severely sanctioned, and violations of government agency norms, for example, may engender heavy fines, loss of license, or injunctive prohibition of continuation of work. Violations of informal controls may result in the loss of clientele or impediments to the performance of work.

---

[1] For a detailed treatment of occupational controls, see Edward Gross, *Work and Society* (New York, Thomas Y. Crowell, 1958), especially pp. 134–39.

Work frequently is subject to control by the formal organization within which it occurs. The firm or organization may impose work rules on its employees. Even self-employed professionals such as physicians must submit to the formalized norms and procedures imposed by the hospitals and clinics where they practice. Professionals are bound by the codes of ethics established by their colleagueal associations, and deviations from standards may mean censure, the withholding of referrals and recognition, or even expulsion from the profession. Some work systems are so specific in their prescriptions for work behavior and so severe in their sanctions for violations that the offender who deviates from expected standards may face a long prison term, disgrace, or even death. In the military sleeping on guard duty, insubordination, or desertion in the face of the enemy may all call for extremely severe punishment.

At an informal level work groups often develop elaborate systems of norms in an effort to exert control over the nature of their work and the conditions and circumstances surrounding it. Work crews may establish norms or quotas that influence the tempo of their work and the quantity of their output. They may also reach informal concensus concerning their own informal division of labor and the techniques they employ in their work. Deviants from these norms may be sanctioned by group pressure involving ridicule, ostracism, the withholding of assistance and information, and even sabotage of the offender's own work or tools.

The expectations regarding some work roles are relatively unspecific or vague, while other individual work roles may require extremely circumspect job behavior. All work roles are subject to some degree of specificity and control, and violation of these expectations constitutes deviance, although such behavior may not attract the same interest and concern as other varieties of deviance.

WORK-ROLE SABOTAGE

Many persons fail in the performance of their work or occupational roles. Some fail because of personal ineptness and others because of role inadequacy, where they are not sufficiently prepared to be able to conform to the work-role expectations.[2] Still other individuals deviate from the requirements of their role as the result of role frustration that arises because of facilities or resources insufficient or inappropriate to the task of effective work performance. A small percentage of persons purposely misplay or sabotage the role. William Crain, in documenting such behavior among delinquent

---

[2] Deviation as a result of various kinds of role stresses is discussed in Alvin L. Bertrand, *Basic Sociology: An Introduction to Theory and Method* (New York, Appleton-Century-Crofts, 1967), pp. 232–35.

children in a treatment camp, labeled the perpetrators of such role sabotage as "chronic mess-ups" or "dings" and suggested that such inappropriate behavior becomes a kind of deviant role itself.[3] According to Crain, the "mess-ups" or "dings" in the camp were "forever playing, ignoring staff demands, or screaming with real and put-on pain," and they "all played and clowned, [and] did foolish spur-of-the-moment things." Children in this camp were electing to sabotage their conventional roles by substituting inappropriate or "fool" behavior as an adaptive mechanism.[4]

Role sabotage in the form of "fool" behavior which occurs in connection with occupational statuses and roles may also represent an adaptive pattern and can be functional to a degree. Daniels and Daniels, for example, relate the account of a group of recruits in Air Force basic training during World War II and their experiences with one member of their flight who because of his "fool" role performance frequently kept the other members of the unit in difficulties with their superiors.[5] This individual's role sabotage, however, was also functional to the men in the flight in that the "fool" often acted as a buffer between them and the depredations of their superiors. His behavior demonstrated the vulnerability of the military system, and thus he stood for the men as a symbol of individualism, albeit irrational individualism, in the face of regimentation. This fool's behavior also represented a form of boundary maintenance and helped spell out the limits of tolerated deviance for the others.

Fool behavior may not always be functional to the group and it may not always be based on personal awkwardness. It may serve as a device for attacking discomforting institutional control over the occupational members. In the first essay in Part I, "A Sociological Analysis of Dud Behavior in the United States Army," H. Eugene Hodges examines a variety of role sabotage where the violation of role requirements represents a deviant form of adaptive mechanism for coping with unwelcome and uncomfortable regimentation and restrictions on individualism. The army is viewed as a total institution, and the "dud" is a kind of rebel who sabotages his work role by emulating the inept. Nonconformity to army norms concerning work role behavior is severely sanctioned if identified and defined as deliberate. Insubordination, dereliction of duty, incapacitating oneself for duty, or malingering may all call for harsh punishments including imprisonment or less than honorable discharge. "Dud" behavior violates the role norms but

---

[3] William Crain, "The Chronic 'Mess-Up' and His Changing Character," *Federal Probation,* Vol. XXVIII, No. 2 (June 1964), pp. 50–56.

[4] For an elaborate discussion of "fool" behavior, see Orrin E. Klapp, *Heroes, Villains and Fools* (Englewood Cliffs, N.J., Prentice-Hall, 1962), especially Chapter 3, "Fools," pp. 68–91.

[5] Arlene K. Daniels and Richard R. Daniels, "The Social Function of the Career Fool," *Psychiatry,* Vol. 27, No. 3 (August 1964), pp. 219–29.

in such a manner as to evade the sanctions for deviance. The disguise of ineptness provides a high degree of immunity from the formal processes of social control. It may be a means of striking back at a work system for the enforced occupancy of a work status and may also constitute an effective vehicle for evasion of the norms pertaining to work performance. As a *de facto* violation of social work norms, however, such deviancy represents inappropriate occupational behavior.

THE SUBVERSION OF SEXUAL COMPORTMENT

Work frequently throws persons of the opposite sex together. A male worker, for example, may have one or more females as subordinates, peers, or even superiors. Some mixed-sex dyadic arrangements are quite institutionalized. The male executive and his female secretary, the male physician and his female nurse, and the male artist and his female model, for example, are all traditional mixed-sex work relationships. Additionally, many occupational practitioners interact (perhaps intimately) with a clientele of the opposite sex in the course of their work. The physician, for example, may physically handle the most intimate parts of his female patients' anatomy in the course of a physical examination, and the male hair stylist or dance instructor may also have extensive physical contact with their female clientele. The painter, photographer, or dress designer may see his female co-worker unclothed, and the male actor may have to simulate scenes of affection or sexual intimacy with his female leading lady. Male and female co-workers may have to work physically isolated from others for extended periods.

Male–female interaction at work could lead to a variety of difficulties dysfunctional to work performance including sexual self-consciousness, over-concern with appearance, time-consuming flirtation, emotional involvements, disruptive jealousies, misunderstood behavior, and sexual alliances.

Cognizant of the disruptive elements latent in a mixed-sex work force or in a mixed-sex practitioner–clientele relationship, many work organizations and occupational systems have effected appropriate work norms relevant to decorous sexual comportment on the job and thus attempt to apply an element of social control. Such norms of sexual propriety, especially in regard to the practitioner–clientele relationship, are often professionally institutionalized and sometimes codified into law. For example, a physician performing a pelvic examination on a female patient should have a female nurse or assistant in attendance. In some states this is required by law because the situation could lose its depersonalized definition. In his novel *Guard of Honor* James Gould Cozzens has a group of WAC officers complain to the base commander that some of their female personnel have been offended by the behavior of one of the base medical officers when he was giving them pelvic examinations. The officer, it seems, "often made coarse remarks to them [the WACs] and sometimes treated them with undue familiarity." The females also complain that male enlisted medical personnel at the hospital make little holes in the dressing room walls for the purpose of peeping at the WACs getting undressed prior to a medical examination.[6]

In spite of the norms of sexual propriety operant in most work settings, violations do occur, and such deviations from the norms can be both disruptive to the ongoing work processes and also a source of friction and disaffection among the workers and in their family lives. In a study conducted several decades ago J. O. Reinemann pointed out that the husband or wife employed in one of the war industries sometimes began to associate with a fellow employee of the opposite sex, and these associations occasionally led to extramarital relationships and ultimate divorce.[7] Although the sample was small, Reinemann concluded that marriages of longer duration or where the age difference in the spouses was greater than usual or the husband was over 30 tended to be overrepresented in the extramarital activity group. The problem has not abated in recent years as the percentage and number of married women in the labor force has increased. A psychiatric social worker I know in a small town community health clinic claims that a significant proportion of his case load is female industrial employees whose romantic flirtations and entanglements at work have produced strains and difficulties in their own marital relationships.

In spite of its more dignified and decorous atmosphere, the office has also been the scene of improprietous flirtations and sexual activities. The office setting may present both partners in their best light—the important, aggressive, distinguished executive and the pert, well-coiffured and stylish, young, understanding secretary. Propinquity breeds familiarity, relaxed interaction, and ultimately, intimacy. The affair between the boss and his secretary and the office romance are firmly ingrained in American fact and fiction, and accounts of such liaisons are legion. The movie *The Apartment,* starring Jack Lemmon, was such an account of office romances. For a variety of motivations, office romances do often develop into full-blown sexual affairs. As Lawrence Lipton describes it:

> From the standpoint of the secretary, in particular, an unenduring but exceptionally rewarding form of office wife relationship is that of the female sex novice and the sex-wise older boss. It might be described as a

[6] James Gould Cozzens, *Guard of Honor* (New York, Harcourt, Brace, 1948), pp. 213–18.

[7] J. O. Reinemann, "Extra-Marital Relations with Fellow Employees in War Industry as a Factor in Disruption of Family Life," *American Sociological Review,* Vol. X, No. 3 (June 1945), pp. 399–404.

one man college of sexual knowledge with only one matriculated student.
    As a form of on-the-job training the school for sex with its one-to-one teacher-student relationship and the office for a campus is perhaps the most successful educational institution in the country.[8]

Firms are less tolerant today of office affairs and flirtations because such activities are distracting and disruptive and are costly to business.[9] (In this connection many firms have in recent years discontinued the practice of having Christmas parties.) Office flirtations, romances, and sexual affairs can be equally disruptive and dysfunctional to the marriage and family life of those involved. There are often sanctions invoked, however, for such deviant behavior. The firm may fire the secretary or, if the affair has become scandalous, perhaps even the executive. In any event, the office norms usually call for extremely circumspect behavior, but propinquity and the relaxed setting in which a working relationship places individuals may precipitate violations of the norms. Deviance of this sort may be socially costly, however; equally important, perhaps, is the fact that love is difficult to integrate with a supervisor–employee relationship.

Norms effecting proprietous sex-role comportment in a work setting are functional to the work system and insulative to individual temptations. Subversion or violation of these norms represents a disruptive and thus potentially serious type of work deviance. Sanctions, if invoked, may portend equally serious repercussions for the offenders.

The factory is the setting where the largest number of individuals of opposite sexes work closely. Donald Roy gives an account of "Sex in the Factory." Drawing on field notes gathered through observations, informants, and experiences as a factory employee, Roy details the interactional specifics of various romances and sexual indulgences of a group of blue-collar employees both in and out of the factory. Despite controls imposed by management and spouses, sexual banter and intimacies do occur, sometimes with disruption and dysfunction to the production schedule, the erosion of work-group cohesion, and personal and familial strain.

NONCONFORMITY TO CO-WORKER CODES

Work is also subject to normative control imposed by the work group itself. Students often try to interpose their own collective interpretation of term paper length upon the general requirements specified by the instructor and thus protect themselves from homework perceived as excessive. In a similar

[8] Lawrence Lipton, *The Erotic Revolution* (Los Angeles, Sherbourne Press, 1965), p. 60.
    [9] For an interesting account of love at the office, see Stephen Birmingham, "What's Happened to Office Romances?" *Cosmopolitan*, Vol. 159, No. 6 (December 1965), pp. 64–67.

manner, co-workers often also attempt to interpose their conceptions of the tempo and quality of work on (or in opposition to) the general guidelines laid down by management. Such informal control represents an attempt to establish a counterbalance or check to formal control.

Because the success of the work system in accomplishing its goals depends in large measure on the cooperation of the members, any informal handicap or resistance collectively imposed on the system is often quite effective. The story is told, for example, that postal employees in China at one time sought a salary raise but were not granted one. They were also forbidden to strike. They informally solved the problem, however, by the simple expedient of processing and delivering the mail without appropriate postage, thereby threatening to bankrupt the postal system. They got their raise.

Formal authority may define the general but not the specific parameters of work in a given system. The codes and norms established informally by members of work systems may supplement and complement the formal rules by augmenting the general guidelines with specific details for procedures and participation. The informal norms may also serve as subterfuge to evade the formal norms.

In the military there are frequent equipment inspections to ensure an appropriate inventory level and the proper maintenance of the equipment. Equipment shortage and equipment deterioration are endemic to many military units, so supply personnel often meet the challenge by "pooling" their equipment, with each borrowing whatever is needed for the inspection. When the inspecting officer leaves via the front door and goes toward the next unit, supply personnel leave via the back door bringing the equipment to the next unit to be inspected.

The more rigid the formal controls, the more intense the efforts appear to be to effect informal social controls. If prison populations may be considered as work groups, the inmate social systems may be taken as examples of strong co-worker control. Inmates of correctional facilities develop elaborate systems of informal mores and demand intense conformity to these norms. As Harry Wilmer describes it:

> The inmates of a prison live by what is known as the "inmate code." It demands a high degree of group loyalty; it forbids any close liaison with custody; it incorporates the attitudes of the outside criminals, such as high value on violence, strength, exploitive sexual attitudes, a predatory attitude toward money and property, distrust of all but a few friends, and a suspiciousness often becoming paranoid to the extent that men boast of their tight-lipped behavior as the honored way of "doing one's own time."[10]

[10] Harry A. Wilmer, "The Role of the 'Rat' in the Prison," *Federal Probation,* Vol. XXIX, No. 1 (March 1965), p. 45.

Violations of these codes are severely sanctioned and offenders of the more serious norms such as "informing" or turning "rat" or "stool pigeon" do so at the peril of their lives.

In Chapter 3 William E. Snizek provides an overview of informal norm violation among blue-collar workers. Surveying some of the "classic" literature on the subject, including the research reports of Roy, Homans, Dalton, and others, he articulates several forms of blue-collar conformity to co-worker codes such as output restriction and the use of forbidden tools and procedures. Such acts are deviant, but are on occasion functional to the worker group. Violations of co-worker codes do occur, however, but are usually sanctioned by the group. Violators, according to Snizek, usually possess a "rugged individualism" mentality.

DEVIATION FROM COLLEAGUEAL EXPECTATIONS

The professions stand as the elite of occupations. The rigorousness of their training, the extent and depth of their professional knowledge, the intensity of their personal obligation to their art, the degree of their personality involvement, and the essential nature of the services they render to society all combine to place them in a unique and superior occupational category.[11]

Professionals (and semi-professionals) stand apart from other occupational groups and thus they must stand together. Theirs is a special mission, and accordingly, they have collective concerns about who may accomplish the mission, when, and under what circumstances. These concerns often manifest themselves in normative specificity regarding admission qualifications and a detailing of the conditions under which professional practice may be accomplished. The trappings of these normative specificities are the degrees, examinations, boards, certificates, and licenses requisite to occupational admission and continued practice. As a means of strengthening their control over such matters, professional groups often enlist the aid of the polity and its legal apparatus. In this way the restrictions on entrance and professional practice can receive the legitimatization of public support, and their enforcement is made relatively efficient by government process. Paramount in almost all professional endeavors, however, is the necessity for maintaining public faith and trust in the believed omnipotent quality of professional services. All professions, in spite of their lengthy and rigorous training, are at best imperfect sciences and tend to be arts; and their practitioners, in spite of their erudition, are mere mortals given to human frailties and defects. Such frailties and defects, however, must not be allowed

---

[11] My comments of professions here are drawn heavily from Gross, op. cit., especially pp. 77–82, and some of the writings of Everett C. Hughes.

to erode or dilute the faith of the clientele. Anything that might shake or diminish this faith is to be resisted or avoided. Morton Thompson, in his medical novel *Not as a Stranger,* has the young idealistic physician hero go to the chairman of his County Medical Board to denounce a colleague whom he deems incompetent and who, in his opinion, is responsible for the death of a patient as a result of that incompetence. The older physician pragmatically points out:

> ... we [physicians] are all made of meat, Dr. Marsh [the young hero], we are all human, none of us is beyond error, we must make mistakes before we die—something for which your fellows could have denounced you, denounced you publically—and which they did not, but closed around you protectively, keeping it in the family, knowing we are all made of meat, knowing the thousands you would save? The error you would not commit again?[12]

The Chairman of the County Board refuses to entertain the charges of malpractice brought by the young doctor. The privileges and immunities of professionalism serve, among other things, to protect the practitioner and his craft from his own mistakes and misjudgments. Without the immunity to make mistakes, no professional would ever take the risks, and the clientele could not be effectively served.

Such power, privilege, and immunity dictates equally stringent countercontrols. In addition to formal controls, the clientele is able to exert pressure and thus control on the professional to some degree by withdrawing or minimizing his patronage. The professional can usually counter the threat of such economic reprisals, however, through a variety of manipulative devices. He uses his knowledge and the client's ignorance to neutralize most of the control the client might be able to exert.

Professionals also seek to effect their own controls in their own self-interest and for the protection of their craft and its privileges and immunities. The greatest danger to the professional is the loss of business to other occupational groups and especially charlatans. Since the charlatan does not operate "by the rules," he is a particularly dangerous competitor. Such loss of business can occur in either of two principal ways: through the erosion of public confidence and faith in the professional and through uncontrolled competition within the professional ranks that may cause dissension and hostility among colleagues and may in turn allow the outside competitor unobtrusively to capture some of the business. Therefore, controls effected by professionals themselves are, directly or indirectly, aimed primarily at

[12] Morton Thompson, *Not as a Stranger* (New York, Charles Scribner's Sons, 1954), p. 648.

maintaining public confidence in the profession and preventing uncontrolled competition. As Gross puts it:

> One type of action that can easily create antagonism, cleavages, and even a loss of the market to charlatans is *uncontrolled competition.* Consequently every occupation (even that of private business) tries to regulate competition by securing consensus on the "rules of the game." The most celebrated form that such controls take are professional "ethics," . . .[13]

A profession cannot tolerate uncontrolled competition without exposing itself to risk. The physician or attorney may not ethically, for example, advertise, give "cut-rate" services to attract business, actively solicit clientele, or in any way aggressively seek new business. Professionals do not ethically denigrate their colleagues in front of clientele, especially for the purpose of courting new business. Regardless of the economic exigencies facing the professional, he must passively await business rather than actively pursuing it. Deviations from colleagueal expectations do, however, occur. Some professionals do actively pursue business as in the case of attorneys who are "ambulance chasers"[14] and physicians who manage to "advertise" informally. Some physicians, on the very borderline of ethical if not legal tolerance, may, for example, develop a reputation for their heavy reliance on narcotics in treatment. Such a physician may find himself inundated with patients who are drug users seeking a legal supply. As Richard Quinney has also pointed out, business goals and professional ethics do not always mix. In his study of pharmacists he found that professional deviance in the form of prescription violation tended to occur with greatest frequency among those pharmacists with a strong orientation to their businessman role.[15] Unethical behavior is seldom tolerated for long, and such deviant behavior usually draws the formal wrath and sanctions of the profession and the informal pressures and retaliations of colleagues.

In the last article in this part, "Unethical Behavior: Professional Deviance," H. Kirk Dansereau attempts to provide an overview of this variety of work deviance and surveys a wide range of materials and information relevant to the subject. He concludes that as long as professional attention "is poorly balanced" in regard to "the dollar" and "service," "a favorable climate for professional deviancy exists."

[13] Gross, op. cit., p. 230.
[14] See, for example, Kenneth J. Reichstein, "Ambulance Chasing: A Case Study of Deviation and Control Within the Legal Profession," *Social Problems,* Vol. 13, No. 1 (Summer 1969), pp. 3–17.
[15] Richard Quinney, "Occupational Structure and Criminal Behavior: Prescription Violation by Retail Pharmacists," *Social Problems,* Vol. 11, No. 2 (Fall 1963), pp. 180–85.

1. A Sociological Analysis of Dud Behavior in the United States Army

H. EUGENE HODGES

"You know, sometimes I don't think the captain is very smart. He claims that he would like to see all criminals in prison and all drunks in a hospital. But if all the criminals were in prison, who'd run the government? And if all the drunks were put in a hospital, what would we do for a national defense program?" Zero—one dud who is also a composite protagonist—made this comment after a preliminary court-martial hearing in Germany, 1959.

This paper is a descriptive study of a special kind of deviant behavior found in the peacetime American army during the period from 1957 to 1959. The type of behavior discussed falls under what the military establishment classifies "dud behavior." The term *dud* when used to refer to military ordnance, is a shell, cartridge, or piece of equipment that does not work. Applied to an individual, the label means not only that the person will not work but that he will probably muddle the assigned task. This makes a dud something different from the malingerer. Whenever the situation permits, he becomes a saboteur.

Several types of persons participate in dud behavior, but this paper is focused on one of these types and is an attempt to formalize some of the rules of interaction that enable the dud to remain as a deviant in a total institution that is uniquely equipped to punish or weed out deviance of any kind.

Goffman's outstanding contribution to sociology in *Asylums* was to perceive that there is a basic similarity between dissimilar institutions such as homes for the blind, concentration camps, boarding schools, the army, and monasteries.[1] Goffman groups them all under "total institutions," which he defines as "a place of residence and work where a large number of like-situated individuals, cut off from the wider society for an appreciable period of time, together lead an enclosed, formally administered round of life."[2] He lists five rough groupings into which the total institutions of our society may be placed.[3] The following discussion has relevance to only the fourth of these: the institutions purportedly established to facilitate some worklike task and justified only on these instrumental grounds. He places ships, work camps, colonial compounds, and army barracks in this grouping.

As Goffman expands on the concept of total institution, the reader begins to get the impression that the total institution is total not only in the sense that it fullfills all the needs of its members, but total also in its control over the behavior of its members. For example:

> The surveillance nature and the system of differential punishment is such that each offense results in an almost immediate corresponding punishment to fit the seriousness of the offense. The more frequent the offense, the more severe the punishment will be, even if the offense is not generally considered to be serious.
>
> Counter to the punishment system is the reward system. The reward system gives to the conformer certain privileges which the non-conformer is conspiciously denied.
>
> If the members of the total institution are recruited from society-at-large, then initially, the same types of deviates are found in both. But because of the surveillance nature of the total institution most deviates are promptly discovered. Once identified as a deviate the individual is either reformed or excluded from the social situation.[4]

But Goffman tempers this "total" aspect of the institutional control by allowing for some types of deviant behavior that may occur at night when the surveillance system is not operating, such as the thief in the military, and also allowing for secondary adjustments which are practices that do not directly challenge staff but allow inmates to obtain forbidden satisfactions or to obtain permitted ones by forbidden means.[5]

Goffman lists several types of adjustments that an inmate may make to the total institution.[6] He considers these types of adaptations in which an

---

[1] Erving Goffman, *Asylums: Essays on the Social Situation of Mental Patients and Other Inmates* (Chicago, Aldine, 1962), pp. 4, 5.

[2] Ibid., p. xiii.

[3] Ibid., pp. 4, 5.

[4] Ibid.

[5] Ibid., p. 54.

[6] Ibid., pp. 61–64.

inmate may choose one or the other or a combination of them during different periods of his career. Only two of these modes of adaptation—conversion and intrasigency—are relevant to this discussion, and the point I wish to make is that in a task-oriented total institution a person can make an adaptation that is a combination of these two and maintain a continued degree of intrasigency throughout his military career.

Goffman describes conversion as that point at which the inmate appears to take over the official or staff view of himself and tries to act out the role of the *perfect* inmate. The issue I take with this is that in a task-oriented total institution, the inmates are not only "stuck" with having to remain for a period of time in the total institution, but the total institution is to a degree "stuck" with having to retain and accomplish their allocated tasks with the types of inmates with which they are presented. Some of the inmates may be totally unacceptable, and in due course they are weeded out. But the vast majority of inmates fall somewhere on a continuum between being somewhat less than perfect and stop short of being totally unacceptable. In the military the staff's view of its privates are many and varied, certainly not just one category of "perfect soldier."

Because the army is a task-oriented total institution, its privates can be placed into three general categories on the basis of work performance. The first is the person who excells in his task performance. Initially this is considered undesirable. The private's peers see him as a pace setter, and his immediate superior, the corporal, perceives him as a threat, perhaps a future competitor for rank. In any case it is less than a desirable category even though in certain areas excelling is acceptable. For example, to excel in personal appearance seems to be acceptable in basic training, or after the training period, one can excel in a specialized job, such as mechanic. The second is the average producer who does the minimum acceptable to get by. This is where the vast majority of privates fall, the average soldier. The third is the nonperformer or "dud." Several types of individuals fall within this category. There is the inept—the soldier who tries too hard, the person of low mentality, or the egghead—who remains in the dud category generally throughout his army career. A *visitor* to this category of nonproducers would be classified as an average soldier who for some reason such as a hangover from a long weekend, a family problem, or some other problem that results in general depression, becomes a nonproducer for a period of time. Within these categories many individuals move up and down. The third type in this category is the malingerer, the rebel, or conscious dud; the saboteur, the insurgent, or the intransigent.

Goffman describes the "intransigent line" of adaptation as one in which the inmate intentionally challenges the institution by flagrantly refusing to cooperate with the staff.[7] They are the "open rebels" who do not attempt to avoid the consequences of their actions. These individuals may be characterized as saying, "I am not going to do it, and to hell with you sergeant!" As Goffman points out, they are quickly detected and weeded out.

A second group of individuals take the intransigent line of adaptation, but without flagrantly refusing to do anything. This paper is focused mainly on this group. They are implacably opposed to the organizational goals of the total institution; but unlike the "open rebel," they attempt to avoid the total institutional consequences of their actions. One of the primary methods of doing this is emulating the inept.

Both the military and the inept are caught in a very peculiar position. The military has to accept the inept, for if a person could be discharged for this reason, it could become a method of exit for those who wish to avoid the military service. If a serious penalty such as a dishonorable discharge or being sent to the stockade was conferred upon them simply for muddling a task, there would be such a large proportion of our population having a dishonorable discharge or prison experience that the penalty would lose its stigma. And since some of the inept are eggheads, it is conceivable that such a discharge could even become a letter of recommendation in the intellectual world.

While the inept are generally outside the reward system, they are also outside the system of severe punishment. The allocation of severe punishment too liberally reflects upon the leadership abilities of the commanding officer. I was present when a company commander was called to task by a regimental commander when it was discovered that 12 percent of his company had been court-martialed. In addition, there are tasks to be performed and only a limited number of personnel with which to do them, and these tasks cannot be accomplished when a large number of privates are in the stockade.

Perhaps as significant a factor as any of those mentioned is that the average soldier may for some reason or other become inept for a period of time or inept at a particular task. If the private knew that a severe punishment awaited him the moment he ceased performing at a certain level, the degree of stress and feeling of insecurity would, perhaps, make him inept.

Given the fact that the military has approached a high degree of technological complexity and the fact that the enlisted man is a member of a heterogeneous mass (not a particular personality type), he must be given "rights." These rights set bounds within which he can operate with a degree of psychological security and therefore perform rather complex tasks. Military organizations give certain legal protections to its enlisted personnel not out

[7] Ibid., p. 62.

of an innate sense of decency, but because these legal protections are functional to the institution. So, while the staff can make frequent assaults on an enlisted man's self and, almost at will, remove him from the privilege system, the staff is nevertheless limited in its ability to allocate the severe punishments.

THE DUD GROUP

Because the development of the career of the dud has to be viewed as a process, I must select a point in time to do the analysis. One year from the time the recruits were inducted into the army is a useful point because by this time the dud group was indeed a group and no longer only an aggregate of individuals. And by this time there were 12 permanent members from the same company and five honorary members from other companies in the battalion. This dud group was unusual because they met after duty hours daily and at the same place. This seems to be an exception, because dud groups in other companies collected only at irregular intervals. This group met at a customary table in the enlisted men's beer parlor, and during duty hours many of the dud group were placed together by the NCOs to "perform" undesirable details. The group was known to nonmembers as "the dud group," but the members themselves preferred to call the group "The Buena Vista Country Club." When a number of the members assembled in the beer parlor, a member would pound on the table and call the meeting to order.

The group is difficult to describe because of the extreme variation in the individuals who were members and because it was unique from other groups not so much in what it was, but in what it wasn't. The need for group membership brought an aggregate of harassed intransigents together and a common identity developed.

Two traits characterized the group and both were instrumental in the group's existence: The first was a negativistic philosophy about the army and the tasks the members were assigned to perform, but no one discussed the army in general, and seldom did anyone refer to his particular job. I believe the combination of the surveillance nature of the army and the fact that no one could assume that secrecy could be maintained within the group would have made a group with a positive philosophy of insurrection impossible. The negativistic philosophy did not have great organizational potential, but each member possessed it. I designated this philosophy the "philosophy of no!" "No, I won't do it short of prison. I won't do it unless you stand over me, and if you turn your back, I shall screw the job up. If I do it, you shall have to make me. If it will break, I'll drop it. If it will rust, I'll wet it."

The "philosophy of no" is not a philosophy of *planned action* or one that requires a stated purpose or direction or even a sense of morality or a sense of justice. It is simply something that says, *"No!"* There is no attempt to offer anything in the place of what it is resisting; there is no attempt at formalizing a justification for the behavior it requires. It requires no degree of sophistication to practice. To attempt to direct it is like trying to push a wet noodle in a straight line. The philosophy is there. You either ride with it or get off. There is no potential for its manipulation into anything else.

There is no justification for it, just as there is no defense from it. It is not so much a philosophy as it is the absence of one, but like a philosophical system, it permeates the individual's thought pattern. It is an attitude, but it is more. It approaches being a "world view," but unlike a "world view," it is much more transitive. It is a tendency to act in a destructive manner when the opportunity is available, a tendency not to perform at all when the opportunity is not available. Only when the individual is faced with severe sanctions will he move toward task accomplishment, and when such a situation presents itself, he moves toward task accomplishment with the same degree of enthusiasm and zeal he would if he was trying to destroy an $85,000 motor.

The dud group's membership ranged from sociopathic personality types and confirmed criminals through devout Baptists to ideological rebels. A rule existed, something on the order of the hippy concept that "everyone has his own 'bag,' and he should be allowed to have it." This concept would seem to be anti-organizational in that, if you can't open another person's "bag," you cannot build a unifying philosophy. But it allowed this diversified collection of individuals to remain as a group. A humorous comment answered any attempt on the part of a member to get the conversation onto a serious topic, and a member's reason for rebellion was never discussed. If the reasons were openly discussed, the chances were that they would be totally unacceptable to the other members, and the speaker would be admitting that he was an insurgent.

They had a common bond—"I ain't going to do it, but I don't want to go to prison"—which the individual members recognized independently before the group formed, and they perceived their situation as the same. While these "cohesive" factors didn't build for within-group "trust," their sense of common destiny allowed for self-sacrifice for other individuals in the group when the situation called for it. This commitment to "not doing it" was so compelling that the duds almost daily face constant attacks on the self, complete removal from the privilege system, the possibility of spending considerable time in prison, and on occasions even death. For example, once a dud who was an ex-howitzer loader asked me, "Did you know that if you drop a live, fixed, High-Explosive, 105 mm. howitzer shell on an iron floor, they won't let you load the howitzer anymore?" "But," he added, "if it doesn't hit exactly on its side, it may go off."

The philosophy of no does not separate this dud from the open rebel, but the second characteristic does. He attempts to avoid paying the full institutional consequences of his actions. The group functioned to socialize its members on how to emulate the inept and to reinforce the dud aspect of the members' behavior. Socialization was accomplished by a constant flow of humorous examples of dud behavior. Humor was the *form* of conversation. With a continued humorous flow of conversation someone described how Sgt. X got so mad at Dud B and how Dud C washed the motor of a jeep for 20 minutes with a water hose and scrubbed it clean with detergent. The content of conversation performed the "demonstration effect" of showing the others in the group where the bounds were between the stockade and the staff's definition of inept. In the process of listening, the dud improved on his methods of emulation and became more invulnerable to the staff's attack on the "self." More invulnerable, because the staff's definition of the dud and the group's definition of its members was the same: "We aren't worth a good goddamn." And this was what the humor of the conversation was all about. The constant flow of the content of discussion, of past and present experiences, functioned to reinforce this one identity. No one ever talked about successes. This became the dud's greatest protection against the mortification process, *he had bought the institutional identity of himself,* but the institutional identity he bought is just short of being totally undesirable to the institution.

DUD BEHAVIOR

I have observed a dud tank driver turn his lead tank broadside on a bridge during an alert that sent the battalion rushing to predetermined locations around the border. Other duds, seeing what had happened, jumped out of their vehicles and started cursing the driver, who got out of his tank and seemed almost to be getting into a fight with them. An officer jumped into the fracus and cursed the dud driver who was then struck to the point of tears and started to tell the officer that he had hit an icy spot in the road, but that he shouldn't call "my mother that." The officer, seeing that he had stepped out of line (he shouldn't curse a private), became flustered, and the other duds told the driver, "Say, did you hear what the captain called your mother man?" "Say, Zero, the captain called Bob's mother a whore." Zero asked, "Say, Captain, did you ever know Bob's mother? Hell, Captain, I never knew you were ever in Kansas." The duds were playing Bob as well as the captain, and Bob rose to the bait. The end product was that the battalion was late getting to its destination, and the battalion staff again failed an exercise.

One member of the dud group, who was a surveyor, was accused by the company commander of purposefully sighting all the howitzers incorrectly during an important battery exercise, which the company failed miserably. During the same day another member of the dud group directed a company of tanks into a swamp for camouflage purposes. When confronted with this act, the private responded, "All they told me was that they wanted the tanks camouflaged. Hell, I don't know what they were so angry about; after the tanks were parked there for 10 minutes, all you could see was their turrets." It took three days to get the tanks out of the swamp.

The problems of the staff discerning what is purposeful and what is due to "ineptness" also becomes a problem in the participant observation of dud behavior even when the observer is a member of the dud group. The rule of "never coming off the game" even within the dud group left a lot of the dud's behavior open to interpretation. One example, however, where a dud came off the game in anger, bears repeating. Jim was angry because Bob had made pfc. twice and even though Bob was a private at the time, Jim was upset about never making it even once. Jim said angrily, "I am going to tear the fucking motors out of my howitzer until they make me pfc." Jim kept true to his word and tore up three howitzer motors before he made the rank. This is insurgency on a rather high level because the motors of an armored howitzer cost $85,000 each.

The threat of physical violence always hung over the dud. One dud's answer to this was somewhat unique. He carried a *Bible* with him most of the time and made a point of reading or pretending he was reading when he had a few minutes break. But he only did this when he was away from the details composed mainly of duds. He mentioned to me one day that "That fucking Sergeant Smith apologized to me in front of the whole detail today for saying goddamn." The point is that this adaptation seemed to be a satisfactory justification for the dud's ineptiness to the average soldier and the staff, so that the dud was not subjected to physical abuse.

That two NCOs could call a dud away from the detail to a spot where they could not be observed and beat the dud was always a possibility. If the dud would say anything about it, the NCOs could say that the dud struck the first blow and have him court-martialed for it. I have only heard of a few instances of this happening, but it is a threat. But the average soldier is the dud's worst enemy from the period of induction to about one year after induction. After that, the average soldier sees the dud as not causing the harassment that he is getting but, in fact, is demonstrating how he can get back at the staff.

The dud seems to be unusually equipped to handle himself in case a fight is forced upon him. I observed a dud group socializing its members on the technology of how to fight. After filtering through the humor of the conversation and the irrelevancies the following rules emerged: Don't fight from anger; fight from fear. Don't hit when you are angry; you can't control your expression and the opponent will know when the punch is coming. Back down all the way until he thinks he has missed the expected fight. By this time he has become brave and has said things to you such that no court-martial in the world will convict you for whipping him. When the point comes to hit him, you must hit him first, have your weight shifted to your right leg, and have your left shoulder to him. Never hit him full on in the face; always hit him on the side of the face. The reasons for this is that he has all the bone reinforcement straight on his face. "You'll mark him, but you'll also make him angry." If you hit him straight-on, you'll knock him backwards and you'll have to run 15 feet to hit him again. He could recover by the time you come up to hit him again. So always hit him on the side of the face. This suddenly throws his whole head sideways, and he will be dizzy for a second. Then lay on the punches with both hands as hard and as fast as possible. Try to put him on the ground, because the rule is *"you don't want to have to fight him tomorrow."* You have to beat him good. If you get him down, *try to step on his hand.* "If you step on his hand you ain't going to have to fight him for a month or so." "Give him time to time about it." This rule became institutionalized to the point that when two duds met after one was in a fight, the immediate question was, "Say man, did you walk on him?"

The rule about a knife being pulled by an opponent in a fight was simply "the only place a smart man gets cut with a knife is on the back of the heel."

In cases where there were no witnesses, the rule was "throw something in his face to blind him, and hit him with something heavy." Or when there was more than one opponent, "put your belt around something heavy. There is no way to block it once it is swung. If he holds his hand up, the belt will bend and the coke bottle will hit him in the head for "the pause that refreshes."

The rules are obviously an aspect of the lower-class technology which is little known, and after several demonstrations of his technology, few average soldiers or NCOs are anxious to invite the dud "out back."

I seldom observed a dud referring to a task he had muddled. If questioned about why Sergeant X had sent him to the CO, the dud would reply simply, "Aw, I dropped a battery out of one of those tanks and broke it." But he may add something like, "Did you know those batteries cost $150 each?" But since a number of duds were generally on the same detail together, a dud's muddling of a task would generally be observed by the others. When the dud group met, there would be a humorous account of how Roberts got Sergeant Harris so angry with him that he dragged Roberts bodily out of the motor pool.

One of the dud rules was "never come off the game." If a dud did admit that he took pleasure in his deviance, he would be saying, "I am not inept; I am a rebel." The identity of "not being worth a good goddamn" is one that the dud must maintain even in the dud group. This was the common identity of the group, and the dud knows that secrecy can never be assumed, so what he says can always get back to the staff. The dud may still be suffering from recent penalties he received for muddling the task. But by the time the incident has been rephrased in a humorous manner and everyone has had a good laugh about it, his spirits are up and his identity has been reestablished by the group.

A unique aspect of the group was that the pecking order was reversed. The members with less group prestige pecked on members with more prestige. For example, if a challenge about the validity of a humorous story concerning something that happened "back home" was made, it would be made by one lower in prestige than the speaker. The speaker could choose to answer the challenge or ignore it, but he would not attack the underling.

At the beginning of the evening most of the members would start off "talking trash" or "telling lies," as the discourse was referred to. But as the interaction continued, the underlings would restrict their conversation to harassing comments or supporting statements.

I believe this was why the average soldier could not sit at the table for more than a few minutes. He was forced to acknowledge the comments of a person whom during duty hours he could totally discount.

This reversal of the pecking order should not be surprising in a group whose members were harassed continually during the duty hours. Perhaps the requirements for leadership were that the person could take and handle more harassment than the others and that to move up in prestige in a group requires the underling to better adapt himself to take harassment—to demand more harassment from the staff. The more harassment a dud took during duty hours, the more he would become the subject of conversation in the dud group.

During duty hours the same reversed order existed. For example, on one occasion in which a sergeant attacked a dud underling, a dud leader interrupted the sergeant at the height of his attack and asked, "Sergeant, would you mind if I go to the toilet?" The sergeant, who was angry at the interruption said, "No." The dud leader then interrupted again and asked, "Sergeant, could I have permission to go see the captain?" The sergeant angrily asked, "Why?" "Because you won't let me go to the toilet." This time the sergeant's attack fell upon the dud leader who is by now asking to see the Inspector General to report the sergeant for denying him permission to see the commanding officer.

When the attack is on one of the leaders, the other duds join in the battle, some interrupting the sergeant by also attacking the leader. "Zero, why didn't you just pull down your pants and take a dump here in the middle of the motor pool? You didn't have to bug the sergeant like that." Some of the other duds started wandering off from the work area. Someone else lets out a loud fart, and everyone laughs.

The sergeant suddenly perceives that he has lost control of the detail and breaks off his attack on the leader and starts attacking the group, attempting to regain control. This takes time, and the sergeant is responsible to his superiors for getting the task completed. The dud knows this and uses it as a kind of blackmail; it becomes a power base for dealing with his immediate superiors. He also knows the limitations of the sergeant's power. When the sergeant later got back to confronting the dud leader with his behavior, the dud sets the sergeant up against the chaplain, the medical officer, and the Inspector General with the statement, "Sergeant, I have diarrhea; when I have to go, I have to go. Now you can raise all the hell you want to, but it won't change that."

The significance of this example is that the duds with prestige seem to be saying to the staff, "Don't peck on him, I am the leader, peck on me."

Let me add, in passing, on the statement by the officer with combat experience about the "dud being your best fighting man." It is repeated so often that it can be said to be "institutionalized." I believe it is true for the following reasons: While the average soldier is participating in regular barracks behavior, the dud is learning to come to terms with a situation fraught with anxiety and perils that could be almost equal to a combat situation. He is capable of initiating spontaneous and unplanned action and knows that without a word he will have a group following him. As studies of the German Army have shown, a soldier fights well, not because of abstract ideological principals or mother's homemade pie, *but because of loyalty to his group*.[8] The dud has a loyalty to his group that is unsurpassed by any average soldier's loyalty to a group, and the dud is capable of self-sacrifice to defend the group's members.

But the dud in a combat situation will define the "enemy" in rather broader terms than the military would wish. Like Yousarian in *Catch 22*, he will define the enemy not only as the "people on the other side who are

   [8] Edward A. Shils and Morris Janowitz, "Cohesion and Disintegration in the Wehrmacht in World War II," *Public Opinion Quarterly* 12 (Summer 1948), pp. 280–315.

shooting at him," but will also include the staff who forces him to get there to get shot at.[9] For example, during a political crisis in which everyone was saying, "There is going to be a war," a special Troop Information session was called to re-explain what "we are fighting for." The company's 1st sergeant, who had two wars behind him and who had been giving "Old Zero" a particularly rough time, said in an unusual joking manner, "Zero, if there is a war, I guess I'll be the first one you kill." Zero didn't answer, but the sergeant continued, "That's right, isn't it Zero?" Zero broke a dud rule, but said in a joking manner, "No sergeant, rank has its privileges, I'd kill the captain first. You would have to be second." Everyone laughed except Zero and the 1st sergeant. He later stopped the harassment of Zero.

Another example of this occurred well after the period of one year at which this analysis has been focused, but since it has relevance to the dud's definition of the enemy, I shall give it out of context of the time sequence of the analysis. After the dud group had been formed for about six months, a number of close friendships began to form within the dud group. But these friendships were just between *two* members, and on no occasion did it include a group of three close friends. It allowed for open discussion of things with this one person with whom a degree of "trust" had been built without fearing legal consequences for his statements, because that requires *two* witnesses. I placed "trust" in quotations because they both have information that would get the other in trouble with the authorities.

I was friends with a dud I shall call "Bud." Bud, myself, and several other members of the dud group had been placed as security guards around a criptographic machine (an instrument used to decode messages) while the regiment was on maneuvers around the Czechoslovakian border. Even though it is the kind of detail that is extremely important, it is the kind on which the dud is frequently placed, because in the mid-winter it is an extremely unpleasant task and if the dud is caught sleeping on duty, he goes to the stockade.

Bud woke me early in the morning, saying, "God almighty, I had a chance to kill a general a while ago. He was walking through the woods about 3 o'clock in the morning and walked right into the security area and as he passed by the light I could see the star on his shoulder. He was a little drunk and, man, there was not a soul around. I could have killed that son-of-a-bitch, I could have shot him dead." I asked, "Well, why didn't you?" He answered, "Because that fucking Zero has lost all the bullets to the guns." After cursing Zero for his ineptness I went back to sleep.

The dud carries his struggle on at the lowest level possible, in task-oriented activity systems, and his opponent is generally the NCO. The

[9] Joseph Heller, *Catch 22* (New York, Simon & Schuster, 1961).

NCO who finds himself with a group of duds is in an uncomfortable situation. The officers are aware that the dud will work only if completely supervised, and the dud acknowledges this by working only when completely supervised. This is no more than the officers are prepared and willing to provide, since the NCO's job is to supervise. If he turns his back for a minute, the dud stops working or breaks a shovel, and then the NCO has not performed his task correctly, and to a degree he is responsible to his superiors for it.

If the dud is referred to a higher authority for disciplinary action, he becomes the inept private, but he attempts to avoid an encounter with the officers. This is the level at which the so-called "shithouse lawyer"—the dud who has acquired some legal information in the dud group—operates, but he usually loses in such a confrontation. The dud's main defense is an appeal to the decency of the CO and a form of mild blackmail.

The group's greatest organizational assets would be considered liabilities in any other setting. Its loose organization, its lack of planning, the lack of formalized rules, the absence of serious discussion, and the constant flow of humorous examples of rebellion enabled the members to avoid the institution's proscriptions against mutiny, malingering, and sabotage. The group members' sense of common identity and common destiny brought this diversified assortment of human material into a cohesive group whenever one of its members was assaulted by the staff and with a degree of spontaneity that all the planning possible could not accomplish. The humorous discourse established, maintained, and reinforced the dud's identity as a task muddler. The content of the discourse gave him the methods of insurgency and provided the demonstration effect by showing him where the boundaries lay in the system of differential punishments. The characteristics of the philosophy of no and the desire to avoid the severe institutional consequences of their actions placed them in a position of being continuing insurgents but without any belief system that could be grasped by the staff as a unifying force of insurgency.

The dud presents the authorities with a special problem. They are required to draw a line between ineptness, inefficiency, extenuating circumstances that would affect the completion of a task and the purposeful intent towards incompletion and gross incompetence. This must be done in many cases without any objective act being performed.

AN ATTEMPT AT FORMALIZING THE DUD RULES

From my observations in the peacetime army, I would think that any attempt by privates to build a positive philosophy of action to resist the military authorities would be quickly discovered and harshly dealt with.

To build a group with a positive philosophy requires a degree of discussion, argumentation, and a kind of conversion experience of the new members that is observable by the staff. Of all the things the dud learned, the most salient was to avoid the statement of rebellion, a statement of a position that transcends the task-oriented situation. One such statement was made by a private who was something of an ideological rebel. During a conversation about the army the private said, "I hate the army, and I am not going to do a goddamn thing for them. *I am not even going to put salt on their food.*"

This latter statement is an example of breaking a dud rule. The private put his whole approach to the army in one sentence, a sentence that was clever, well phrased, and bears repeating. Since secrecy is almost impossible to maintain, such cleverly expressed sentences eventually get to the staff. When this happens and the private is identified as a rebel, in Goffman's words, "the institution shows as much special devotion to the rebel as he has shown to it."[10]

Zero broke this rule when he threatened the life of the CO and the 1st sergeant in the presence of the company and not only got away with it but to a degree benefitted from it. This says something about general rules as boundary-setting mechanisms. One plays by the rules when he can't trust his feeling about the social situation! But within the general context of these rules, each situation has its own rules; with each NCO or officer the game was adapted to his characteristic response pattern.

Another dud rule was "watch out for the intermediary, the person who is between the privates and the staff." This is sometimes the corporal who has not fully left his former pfc. status and is not fully at ease with sergeants. But it is also the private who forms a friendship tie with the NCOs or the private, such as the company clerk, who occupies a coveted position in the institution. They are the carriers of information, of statements; but perhaps even more significantly, they are the carriers of impressions and interpretations of what is going on in the community of privates in which they live, and they name the persons they *feel* are causing it. If a private was a friend of a corporal, the duds constantly harassed him with statements like, "Say, I hear you are screwing Corporal X's wife." Or, "What are you doing in the EM club, I thought you would be drinking with Corporal X in the NCO club."

While the clever statement about taking a rebellious stand was breaking a dud rule, the clever, or certainly precise, statement was considered a dud's best verbal defense when he was referred for punishment to the company

---

[10] Erving Goffman, *Asylums: Essays on the Social Situation of Mental Patients and Other Inmates* (Chicago: Aldine, 1962), p. 62.

commander. The rule is: Avoid an elaborate discussion or explanation to explain why you have done something or why you haven't. Select and reiterate the statement that places you outside the severe punishment system and attempt to settle for an attack on the self or further removal from the reward system. An example of this was a dud who had gotten into a drunken brawl with an NCO. In the preliminary court-martial hearing after the statement is read that "anything you say may be held against you" and when the CO asks, "Private what do you have to say in your defense?" the private answered, "I want to press charges against the sergeant, because he hit me."

"But Private, you cursed him."

"But Sir, the sergeant hit me."

"You cursed him first."

"But I didn't hit him first, Sir, a sergeant shouldn't hit a private."

"You put the sergeant in the hospital."

"Sir, he shouldn't have hit me."

It was this one statement that was the difference between the stockade and suffering company discipline. Any further explanation would have only gotten in the way of the main point. The private would have gone to jail if the sergeant hadn't hit him, but to get the private, the CO would also have had to court-martial the sergeant. Added to this was the problem of conflicting reports from the witnesses, because some of them were part of the core dud group.

A case of the carefully worded statement that reeks of "ineptness" was one when a dud was referred to the CO for discipline for calling an Italian sergeant a "Wop." The dud's defense was, "But sir, that is what he is—a "Wop."

The CO responded, "Don't you know not to call an Italian a 'Wop'?"

"Sir, the first time I ever saw one was when my daddy carried me to Tampa, and we met this funny talking man, and I said, daddy, who was that?" and he said, "Why, that's a 'Wop,' son." And sir, that's what the sergeant is, sir; he's a 'Wop'."

This kind of defense gives the company commander a feeling that he is persecuting an inept private. The statement, "But, sir, that is what he is, sir, a Wop" brings forth a desire to educate, not punish. But also behind the statement is a threat of blackmail, because to bring such a case before a summary court-martial on a battalion level would, to a degree, open up the company to inspection by the CO's superiors. If a suspicion of persecuting an inept private arises in his own mind, it may arise in his superior's mind.

The dud's greatest weapon is "blackmail," and the army can be characterized as an institution of perpetual blackmail. The dud knows that the system is a lot looser than it seems, and he also knows that the professional soldier generally violates as many regulations as he thinks he can get by with. And the dud watches for his superiors' violations.

If the dud wants to "get at" a superior, he generally has to do so through his superior's decency." Whenever the superior opens himself up to the dud, the superior is vulnerable. For example, a sergeant had recently spent a pleasant Sunday afternoon playing poker with some of the privates. Several days later he was taking a dud to the CO for muddling a task, and when they got out of earshot of the others, the dud said, "Sergeant, you are angry with me because you think I am going to tell the other guys that you were cheating at poker the other day. Well, Sergeant, I ain't going to tell anyone, I ain't even going to tell the CO. So there ain't no need to be angry with me." (Experience tells the dud to cover the overt threat, so he follows it with as much "trash" as he can.) The dud continues, "My granddaddy taught me to play poker back in Alabama, and he taught me every trick in the book. He was a professional poker player, and the railroads used to hire him to keep the section gangs broke so they wouldn't quit work and go home, but he began to drink a lot. . . ."

The fact that the dud is dependent on the "decent" side of the staff necessitates another rule and it is as basic to his survival as any other. This is: Never game call. Never confide in anyone what the game is, because once you have described your interactional pattern to others and the rules by which you are playing, you have done one of two things: You have "killed the game" or you have certainly changed it by making it visible. You may have killed it because you have created expectations in others about your performance, and you are stuck with it because you know they are watching. For example, the private who said "I don't want to put salt on their food" was game calling. When others know the game, the game caller can no longer maintain the flexibility required, and he is forced to embrace the game and play it even when he would be better off out of the game.

Even within the dud group there was no "game calling." Dud rules were never discussed between individual duds or in the group. They were unspoken rules communicated by the never-ending examples of what the duds did during duty hours. When "game calling" occurs and the staff gets word of it, the dud's protection collapses.

When the game is even suspected by the staff and a particular dud comes under attack, the legal knowledge he has picked up in the dud group becomes instrumental. The staff may set up a situation in which the dud has a task to do and witnesses are present to testify that he was malingering. One Sunday afternoon the dud group was sitting in the EM Club. An NCO came in and walked up to a dud whom the CO had recently promised would be in the stockade within a month. The NCO, who was basically a very unfriendly sort, placed a friendly hand on the shoulder of the dud and said, "Jim, Sergeant Jones and I have a little job we are going to have to do, so come along and give us a hand. It is not going to be hard." Jim said, "Be glad to help you, Sergeant." The two NCOs got in the front of a truck, Jim jumped in the back, and they drove to the coal pile. Sergeant Jones said to Jim, "Jim, you don't have to work too hard, but this is a direct order, load the truck with coal." Jim shoveled coal as hard and as fast as humanly possible, until he filled the truck to overflowing. They returned to the company area to unload the coal and Sergeant Jones went to report to the CO's office. With the witness gone, Jim began to have trouble unloading the coal. The sergeant eventually decided he would rather do it himself than spend his Sunday afternoon watching Jim drop his shovel.

When he is under duress and threat of court-martial, the dud can become a producer to protect himself. If the period of duress is a long one, he can even move up to the category of "average producer" for a period. But he doesn't leave the dud group. Once the pressure is off and the CO is attempting to put another dud in the stockade "within a month," the dud will return to his pattern of dud behavior. With this adaptation he has achieved a degree of efficacy, a feeling of having an effect on his environment, and a feeling of control that the total institution of the army has denied those of his station.

2.   Sex in the Factory:

Informal Heterosexual Relations
between Supervisors and Work Groups

DONALD ROY

Sex is a commonly overlooked aspect of informal social organization in the lower reaches of factory life. I don't mean sex as a dichotomous variable to be used in the explanation of differences in work behavior, as one might employ the variables of age, race, education, occupational status, and so forth. I mean sex as sexual activity, copulation, plus the various and sundry male gallantries and female coquetries leading up to it. I have observed the interference, so to speak, of amatory behavior with kinds of social interaction more clearly relevant to generally recognized purposes of factory management.

This may surprise some people, including those whose conception of human relations in industry is confined to geometric images of formal organization charts or work-flow diagrams. Even those most centrally involved in our current sexual revolution may raise eyebrows. Sex is considered not only functionally inappropriate for industrial activity but also out of place, in a very literal sense, in regard to general layout and material furnishings of the typical factory. Industrial management may here and there show a diffuse sort of indulgence toward the premarital or extramarital achievements of employees, but it is unlikely that benignity extends to approval of mating maneuvers on company time. Machine crew members are not expected to pair off, unless work operations necessitate such subgroupings, and then only to carry on the kind of coordinated activity that furthers organizational demands for better production or lower costs. To my knowledge, our sexual revolution has not yet led to the institution of anything on the order of the "fornication break" in American workshops.

In the perspective of the late Edward Sapir, we maintain a "spurious culture," as distinct from a "genuine" one; and a major requisite for attaining spuriousness is to compartmentalize our activities.[1] Work, recreation, art, religion, family life must be kept separate in time and place. For instance, one wouldn't hesitate a moment for prayer while tightening a nut on the assembly line. At least one wouldn't kneel and bow his head or otherwise make a time-consuming ceremony out of it. During his hours on the job, an employee would normally resist his religious impulses, postponing their expression until Sunday's hour in church. He would likewise put off bowling, fishing, getting drunk, or seducing women until the time came for him to doff his work hat and don one representing another activity.

Of course, we know that it isn't quite that neat, that industry hasn't become completely rationalized, that society hasn't become totally spurious, that the worker doesn't keep his nose to the grindstone for the entire period between time clock punches. Researchers have described for us various kinds of activities besides work that go on in our factories. We have learned that operatives engage in fun and fooling and otherwise "horse around" on the shop floor. We are aware, almost insouciantly so, that workmen waste production time in too-lengthy exchanges of banter or trivial information at soft drink dispensaries. They make bets on ball games and other events of doubtful outcome, and they sometimes conspire to restrict output. Sex, we know, is not a taboo topic of social intercourse in the blue-collar world of work. As long as interaction is conducted on a strictly verbal plane, discouragement of expression seems to be minimal. Restraints imposed by supervisors or other monitors of employee behavior would be directed at duration rather than moral laxity of conversation. We have heard that many workmen find occasional humorous references to amatory matters a suitable alternative to sports as an antidote to tedium.

Perhaps it is not so well known that in rare instances worker inspiration and managerial permissiveness may stretch to more vivid symbolic representations of sex in the form of pantomime. I recall a factory job in my early work experience in which the massive boredom of performing simple repetitive operations as a member of a cooky-machine crew was alleviated by the lewd antics of a moronic operative whose job it was to feed our trays of stamped out cooky dough into the revolving shelves of a large oven. This mentally but not sexually deficient fellow would rescue the rest of us from our pit of painful boredom at intervals by flashing an erection and whirling back and forth with it, to and from the oven, quite gracefully in fact, and by responding to the cheers, laughter, and obscene suggestions of his workmates by imbecilic grinning. Lest it be wondered how such high jinks escaped the watchful eye of management, I report that our first-line super-

[1] David G. Mendelhaum (ed.), *Selected Writings of Edward Sapir in Language, Culture, and Personality* (Berkeley: University of California Press, 1949).

visor, a man of misanthropic stare, ready profanity, and all 'round disheartening personality, was an occasional witness, but his watching involved no move toward restoration of cooky-baking decorum. Perhaps observing the phallic drolleries made his own problems more bearable; he would appear in the background for an appreciative moment, a smile breaking out beneath glowering brows, like an indulgent gorilla watching its offspring at play.

Under certain circumstances, chief of which is the presence of both males and females in the work group, sex in the factory may progress considerably beyond mere exchanges of verbal indelicacies or audience appreciation of bawdy pantomime. When the situation is one of men and women working side by side or sharing a task that calls for team work, Eros may infiltrate the production line to evoke attachments of various qualities and durations of affection, ranging from the protracted attentions of true love to ephemeral ardencies of the opportune moment.

Passion for a machine tender of the opposite sex, chronic or evanescent, may carry consequences that are merely personal, not to any appreciable extent organizational. Those who engage in *folies à deux* may be the sole beneficiaries of the relationship or they may be the only ones who suffer. Reciprocated affinities may bring fulfillment; they may also bring "troubles" of one sort or another, such as those connected with deterioration of relationship with spouse, with paramour's spouse, or with each other. Positive or negative consequences may also include the organization. Case materials to be examined here indicate that in its early stages of development an *affaire d'amour* between two members of a work crew may be good for the company that employs them. Salutary effects on group morale and machine output may accompany the euphoria of a loving pair. In widening circles of good fortune the benefits of "heing-and-sheing" may spread from couple to work group to industrial organization. Relations between the work crew and its supervisors may reach highs in congeniality, as managerial benediction follows swiftly upon the rise in production.

However, in a reversal of fortune these organizational benefits may and do turn to liabilities. At first compatible, Eros and Vulcan draw apart. As romance continues, the work group disintegrates, production collapses, and blessings from the bossmen shrivel. Thus in cyclical sequence, from the impulsion of sexual magnetism, social cohesion and machine output may rise then fall. Such a cycle may be understandable in some aspects, puzzling in others. It is easy to see the connections between improved performances of the work team, company welfare, and the superintendant's amiability; but why should the mutual attraction of two members of a work group engender an appreciably greater productivity of the whole? And why, as love endures, should the team effort suddenly faint and fail? It is here, in probationary examination of the cyclical effects of the injection of sex into manufacturing processes, that the central interest of this paper lies.

In this inquiry I refer to observations gleaned primarily from one work situation. I single out a pseudo-named department of a pseudo-named factory and describe the behavior of pseudo-named employees. These observations are by no means recent; so the loving couples of yesteryear are insulated from possible identification by a blanket of time. More recent observations and conversations with other observers of the industrial scene indicate to me that this exhumation from my files will not be a portrayal of the life and customs of a bygone age. Rather, the more up-to-date revelations point to maintenance, if not acceleration, of the tendency of workmates to become bedmates.

I have labeled the technique of field study employed in this research "continuous observation and interviewing in context." It involved frequent visits to the factory and several years' cultivation, sometimes friendship, of both workers and management, and it enabled me to keep in touch with many situational developments. "Interviews" were for the most part informal conversations; they involved discussion of current and past events and future likelihoods and possibilities. The diverse subject matters varied in depth, length, and seriousness of treatment. There were issues of abiding interest and importance that ran as discursive threads binding months and years. Some topics flashed in the stream of conversation as items of ephemeral attention, perishing with the passing moment, save in my field notes. Sex was not one of the major preoccupations, but it was a constantly recurring topic of comment and discussion that centered mainly on the development of various intrashop alliances.

When I say "observations" I do not mean that any embrace, tender or passionate, came within my range of vision. This was no Johnson and Masters type of study. My reporting is based on the accounts of associates of those directly involved, sometimes on the confessions or claims of male participants. I did observe facial expressions and other nonverbal gestures as workers told of the sex experiences of their associates and admitted their own. In general, the pattern of "finding out" was one of telling about the other fellow followed by admitting that what had been told was about oneself. It was as if my respondent were saying to himself, "Well, he's heard all about it anyhow; so I might as well talk about it." I did have some observational checks on the information offered in conversation about the personal and organizational consequences of the various romantic attachments. There were posted production records, physical evidence of absenteeism or turnover, and the behavior at work of machine-crew members. I feel that however sketchy or distorted my cognizance of the nature of sexual activity in the factory studies, my casual conversation technique of eliciting information produced a closer approximation to the facts than could have been achieved by formal techniques, such as the interview schedule or questionnaire. I am sure that if I had appeared too interested in the sexual behavior of my respondents and their associates, resistances to the dissemination of information would have been built up.

Of course, I cannot claim that this single factory situation is "representative." In fact, some of my managerial respondents looked upon the situation as extraordinarily high in incidence of sexual hanky-panky. In their experience, no other workshop was comparable in number of affairs. When one psychologist who joined me for a few months to conduct a special investigation described the situation to her research director, the latter's was the wry acknowledgement, "It looks like all they make in that factory is each other." Yet the plant manager, who had spent his early years at low-status levels of the work force, saw the situation as not at all unusual.

More importantly, in regard to the determination of circumstances that foster the development of sexual alliances at work and the ascertaining of the organizational consequences of such collaborations, my judgements of relationship between fornication and other behaviors cannot be based on anything but tentative inferences. Their weakness lies mainly in the fact that the work situation investigated was a melange of happenings, with influences other than sex to be considered in trying to account for vagaries in production and turnover. Temporal entwinings of romance with other possible impediments to organizational efficiency such as "mechanical troubles," would make definitive conclusions quite dependent upon carefully devised controls. Eros and Vulcan may join hands only under certain conditions, but what the contingencies may be beyond the presence of both sexes on the work floor, I cannot say. Age may be a factor, of course. In my observations pairing off seemed to be limited to the relatively young and vigorous, those under 40. Marital status seemed to be of possible contingency, too. One detached observer pointed to a tendency of the company to hire women who were divorced or otherwise separated from husbands. However, I did note the reputed involvement of a few young single women. Male participants were for the most part anchored in what appeared to be stable marriages. At least, they spoke of their spouses with devotion.

I also suggest that a facilitating, though not necessary, condition for the formation of sexual alliances in the factory would be shared membership in a small work group, with intimacy resulting from the long hours of association in work. In general, pairings were maintained with a constancy characteristic of the lover–mistress relationship. Affairs tended to be "for the duration," meaning until one of the partners, commonly the woman, terminated employment. The role of the mistress bore resemblance to that of "office wife" noted by sociologists whose focus of research centers on white-collar circles. Here it was "factory wife," with an otherwise unattached female forming a sort of polygamous alliance with a married co-worker of somewhat higher status and seniority. There were exceptions, of course. Some attachments were of the moment, or they crossed work-group lines, or they involved married women living with their husbands. In a category that I would provisionally label "miscellaneous philandering," I would include prostitution and a few instances of casual "race mixing."

I choose the following excerpt from my field notes to indicate the quality of the more stable kind of extramarital alliances established by married men of the work force. The two men involved in the extended conversation, Roger and Hank, were skilled workmen of approximately 40 years of age. They had been employed by the company for several years. The third man, Harry, nearing 40, served as machine operator, or "leadman," over a crew of seven or eight employees, the majority of whom were women. The girl with him was a young married crew member with whom he had started an affair. According to my notes:

> At the corner of St. George and Hoop, Roger and I started to turn the corner to go on down Hoop Street, but Hank started across the street. Roger stopped him, took him by the elbow, and brought him back to the curb. Hank said that he would go on over to the St. George Tavern and not bother Harry, because Harry had a woman with him. Roger argued, "What difference does it make?" and pulled Hank along with us.
>
> Roger said, as we walked along, that he never tried to hide the fact that he was going with a girl at the plant. He said it didn't do any good to hide it anyhow, and if he didn't attempt concealment, he wouldn't be embarrassed when he ran into friends at some tavern.
>
> "It isn't anybody's business what a man does after work hours, anyhow," he said to Hank.
>
> Sure enough, Harry was sitting at a small booth with Wilma when we arrived. I noticed that Wilma was drinking a mixed drink, and Harry a beer. Roger walked up to greet the pair, and took the initiative to ask them what they wanted to drink. Harry insisted that he had to leave, and Wilma said she had to get home right away, too.
>
> After greeting Harry and Wilma, Hank sat up at the bar. Roger joined him and ordered the first round of drinks, beer for the four of us and a mixed drink for Wilma.
>
> I asked Hank then what was the matter with him tonight. He said that he was "just tired." I attempted to kid him a little then, suggesting that he was worried because he had bungled a makeready today. Hank insisted that he wasn't worried about any makeready, that he "just wasn't feeling good."
>
> Hank left to go to the lavatory. When he left, Roger said to me, "You want to know what's the matter with him? He had a fight with his girl today!"
>
> Roger went on to say that Hank had been for some time the way Harry was now getting in his relations with Wilma—"serious."
>
> I expressed incredulity that Harry was serious about Wilma.

"I tell you it is getting serious!" said Roger, "She's getting crazy about him! Why do you suppose he takes her out and spends money on her if he isn't serious? I know that guy! Money used to be his god! He wouldn't even buy his buddies a beer, and now he's buying her whisky! He won't even take his wife out, but he's out with this girl every night!"

Roger said that Harry had been "making" Wilma. He offered to bet me ten to one on it. I, of course, refused.

"And I don't blame him for it. I'd do it myself if I had the chance. She's got a nice ass on her!" said Roger.

After Harry and Wilma left, Hank came back. Roger told him that we had been talking about Harry and Wilma and that I didn't believe that the affair was serious.

"He doesn't act serious about it," I said.

"Can't you see? He's just putting on an act!" said Roger.

Hank agreed with Roger that Harry was putting on an act.

"Remember how tight he used to be?" Roger asked Hank. "He wouldn't buy a beer, and now he buys her drinks every night! And he buys her whisky. Not beer! Whisky!"

Hank agreed that Harry used to be tight, and that he had changed recently. He said that the other night at a tavern Harry was waving money around and saying, "What's money! Money isn't anything!" Hank said that Harry was spending freely, insisting on paying for drinks.

"Where do you think those two are going now?" Roger asked me.

I said that they were going over to Dorton and Hoop to pick up Harry's package, then Harry would go home and Wilma would go home.

"She lives around here close," I said.

"Yes. She lives near here. I know where she lives," said Roger, "but Harry isn't going home. He's going home with her and lay her after they have a few drinks."

"To her home!" I exclaimed. "But she's got a husband!"

"He works nights," said Roger.

Roger went on to say that Harry was plenty worried about the situation. His wife was bound to get suspicious, if she was not already so; and she might likely divorce Harry if she found out what was going on. Harry's leaving his dirty work clothes at the tavern was plenty to worry about. That was something not easily explained.

"He doesn't dare come home with any lipstick on his shirts." said Roger.

Roger then contrasted Harry's home situation with his own. He said he didn't have to dodge around because his wife already knew that he was chasing around with other women. If she had been going to divorce him she would have done so already. Roger said that his wife didn't step out with other men herself; as far as he knew, he was the only man who had ever had sexual relations with her.

Roger said that there was always danger of having the girl one stepped out with get fond of you and deliberately try to break up your home. He said that if any girl he took out threatened to phone his wife, he could challenge her to "go ahead and phone! She knows about it already!"

"I suppose you know who my girl is," said Roger.

I said that I had heard it was the glue machine feeder. Roger nodded.

"She's nothing to look at," he said. "She's skinny and she's got a big nose. They call her the cherry-picker because she could hang on a limb by her nose and pick cherries with both hands. Why do you suppose I go out with her? Because she's better fucking than my wife. . . . She can give me all I want, but my wife can't stand much. I'm oversexed."

Roger said he went out with the cherry-picker three times before he "got it." Now he tells her that the reason he's buying her drinks is that he expects to get it before the evening is over, and if she doesn't intend to come through he isn't going to spend his money on drinks.

Roger said that he would like to have two or three girls on the string at the plant, instead of just one.

Roger got loud on one occasion: In an exclamation he used the word *fucking*. The bartender stepped over and in a nice way cautioned him to be careful about his language. He held up the palm of one hand, pointed to a woman nearby with the other, and shook his head. He was smiling as he made these gestures. Roger said "I'm sorry," and lowered his voice.

Roger and I got to talking about love in general. Roger asked me for a definition of love, and while I was trying to think of one, he said facetiously that it was "a tickling feeling around your heart."

I said that it wasn't a feeling around the heart, but one in a person's guts, a sickening feeling in the guts when you had to be parted from the object of your affections. I said you couldn't tell whether it was love or not until you had to separate. If it hurt when you had to separate it was love; you were on the "downward path."

I noted that Hank was all ears now and made my description slant toward getting him to talk.

Roger insisted again that love was sex, then Hank entered the conversation to protest that it wasn't. Sex didn't have anything to do with it.

"I've been going with a girl at the plant now for six months. I suppose you know who it is."

"Sure, that English girl," I said.

Roger laughed. "You mean to tell me that you don't know who Hank's girl friend is?"

"I thought it was that English girl," I said, "Everybody is teamed up but her; so I assumed she was the one."

"She isn't going with anybody yet, but she isn't the one," said Roger. He looked at Hank to see if Hank minded if he told me the name of the girl. Hank indicated that he didn't mind, and Roger told me the girl was Mabel.

"Oh, I know who you mean. She's short. . . ."

"She's short and she's fat," said Roger.

"She isn't good-looking," said Hank, "but that doesn't make any difference. And I haven't been going with her for sex, either."

"Come on now, Hank!" said Roger, with a reproving smile.

Hank then admitted that he had been taking Mabel to hotels from time to time, but insisted that that wasn't what he was talking about. He said his fondness for Mabel didn't have anything to do with that.

Roger argued that it was the underlying basis of it, then let Hank go ahead and tell me his story.

"I tell you I'm going to pieces!" said Hank. "I don't know what to do or which way to turn. I've been going to pieces since last August, for three months now, and it's getting worse all the time. Mabel can't hold a candle to my wife, and I wouldn't think of giving up my wife and family for her, but I don't know what to do!"

Roger said to Hank that he could go on laying Mabel as he had been doing and keep his family. Hank shook his head.

"I can't go on doing this to her!" he said. "She isn't trying to break up my home. As a matter of fact she tells me that if I ever lose those kids she will beat me over the head. But I can't go on doing this to her. It isn't fair to her. Every time we go up to a hotel now she cries, and I can't stand it!"

"You know what's going to happen to you if you keep this up," I said to Hank. "You're going to lose your wife and kids!"

Hank said he realized that, and it was worrying him. He said he didn't think his wife would divorce him if she found out, but she would never be the same toward him again. Now she trusted him, and he wanted to keep her trust. He said he thought she was already getting a little suspicious, as she had suggested that he quit National Products and move back to West Virginia.

"I've thought of that, but what could I do down there?" said Hank. "Nothing there but the coal mines." ...

I remarked that I had noticed that Hank has been glum the last few months, that he used to be quite a kidder, one of the jolliest fellows in the plant. But lately I had sensed that something was wrong I said that I had thought it was Hank's health.

Hank admitted that he used to be one of the jolliest fellows in the plant. Roger agreed that this was so. ...

Roger then told Hank that the only solution was to "fuck them all," and your emotions wouldn't get tangled up with any one of them. Hank rejected this solution.

Roger suggested to Hank that he would feel different about Mabel if he knew that she was fucking someone else. He said that he would take it upon himself to fuck Mabel for Hank.

"Would that make you feel any differently toward me if I did?" asked Roger.

"I wouldn't like it," said Hank.

Roger then said that he was giving Hank fair warning that he was going to try to. He said he was going to try to make Wilma, too.

"If this was your wife, I wouldn't talk like this!" he said to Hank.

"I don't like the idea, but you can't make it anyhow," said Hank. ...

I told the boys that they should listen to Ed Grover, and they wouldn't get into trouble. This got the rise that I expected. Roger said that Ed was worse than anybody in the plant. He didn't even phone his wife when he was out all night, and his wife had finally given him his last chance.

Roger said that Chuck Dashiell was the only wise one in the plant. He didn't let anyone know whom he was stepping out with; he didn't even let anyone know he was stepping out.

Joe Kranz's name came up, linked with Dorothy. Roger said that Dorothy was crazy about Joe, but Joe "kicked her around." He said that Joe would take Dorothy out *before* he went bowling; thus he could get home fairly early and get away with telling his wife that he had just stayed over for a few drinks with the boys.

Roger said that Ed Grover was after Stella, of the box partition department.

The factory provides a place for working-class people to meet each other, to develop the ties of friendship and courtship. Where youth has its schoolhouses and street corners, the more mature boys and girls have their jobs. As students of working class marital behavior have pointed out, young wives tend to cling to their mothers' apron strings after marriage while young husbands persist in their male peer-group attachments. Examination of the peergroup activities of such aging pace-setters in impulse gratification as Ed Grover and Roger Wells, quickens curiosity along various lines of questioning. For instance, just what do the boys do, in their companionship, and how long in the life cycle do such sharings last?

Excerpts from my field notes show Harry and Hank discussing the peer-group activities of fellow oldsters Ed and Roger:

Harry spoke of the night that Ed had stayed out without going home at all. He was with one of the girls from the plant and went back to work with her for the three o'clock shift. His wife was alarmed in the morning and called Harry's wife. Harry had tried to cover up for Ed by saying that he probably had to work overtime, but Mrs. Grover phoned the plant to find out that Ed did not work overtime. Harry had to say then that Ed was probably out with the boys. Before it was all over Mrs. Grover had phoned the police, thinking that perhaps something had happened to Ed.

Harry spoke of Ed's interest in feeling the girls' legs after he had had a beer or two. Hank spoke of the way Ed's mouth used to be smeared with lipstick by morning after a night of drinking. Hank told with a laugh of the time Ed got sore at him when he [Ed] was kissing a girl in the booth while Hank was running his hand up and down her leg.

Roger's behavior next came up for discussion, and comments were made on his crudeness in asking a girl for sexual favors as soon as the group sat down to drink. According to Hank, Roger would come out immediately with the statement to the girl, even before they had time to drink a little and get acquainted, that he was laying his cards on the table and that what he wanted was a fuck. Hank told of the time that he was with Roger in The Grill, and the blonde [feeder who formerly worked at Finished Board] walked out on Roger at the start of the evening. Hank had stepped away from the booth, and when he returned the blonde was gone. Roger swore that he hadn't said anything out of the way, that this was the first time a girl had walked out on him. Hank said he knew better than that; he knew that Roger had insulted her. Harry and Hank both deplored Roger's crudeness; Harry remarked that girls expected a few drinks before you started to get familiar and that even then the matter could be handled more politely.

Hank remarked that he had never seen such a place where the girls went for the fellows like they did at Finished Board. He made the comment that everybody was "fixed up" with a girl there but Chuck Dashiell. Harry and Hank then speculated on who was going with whom. Harry asked Hank whom little Marie was going with; Hank said that she was going with Godowsky. Harry suggested that Kranz's girl was Dorothy; Hank said that Joe used to go with Dorothy, but no more; of late he had been stepping out with Gladys.

On another convivial occasion Ed Grover joined conferers Hank and Harry in a discussion on their relations with Finished Board girls:

Ed kidded Harry about one of the box partition girls who had come to the tavern with them one night. He said that Harry had told him that his girls were "pure," that they didn't drink, swear, or smoke, and that he shouldn't make any passes at them.

"This one girl sat up at the bar, and when the bartender asked her what she wanted she said 'Gimme a shot of Old Taylor. Gimme a double shot.' Oh, she was pure, all right! Never drinks! Never smokes! Goes up to the bar and says, 'Gimme a shot of Old Taylor!' "

Hank and Ed laughed, to Harry's discomfiture. Harry then claimed that they couldn't get any girls from the press department [their department]; he had to bring girls from his department [box partition] for them.

"Ed comes in and orders a couple of beers! He doesn't give the girl a chance to say what she wants! He orders beer for her!" accused Harry. "He wants to get a piece of ass for about 50 cents...."

Ed's rebuttal was to the effect that what was the use of buying a girl drinks if you didn't expect something out of it? Harry came back with the same accusation, that Ed didn't want to pay any more than 50 cents for it, and the argument went on and on, louder and louder.

Jack Patman, assistant operator on O'Keefe's laminator crew, a man long on seniority, keen in observation, and heavy with disgust at what he heard and saw, provided an occasional smoking booth comment concerning the teeming sex life at Finished Board. Patman made it clear that he entertained no illusions as to the "purity" of his female co-workers:

"They're just a bunch of bums," he said. "A fellow is better off to pick up the bums on Water Street. You can forget them the next day!"

He said that he had heard that Marie, the buck-toothed press feeder, in an argument with another woman worker, had said "If you had had as many dicks in you as I've had in me, you wouldn't be able to get around!"

Patman said that the foulest-mouthed girl in the place was the little short girl who was now feeding on the gluer, a girl by the name of Daisy. He said that Daisy had said one day, "I need a good prickin!"

Negro men shared the jobs of lesser skill with white women at Finished Board. Black women were not accepted for employment because members of management feared the development of a "real mess" if they were introduced into the work force. A chance street corner conversation with Gertie, disgruntled ex-employee of the box partition department, was one source of information on the casual "race mixing," practiced by black males and white females. Gertie was also outspoken in reporting the use of plant facilities for quickie romance, both mixed and unmixed.

Gertie explained that the girls in the box partition department had framed her to force her off the job. She said that she was the only member of the crew who was minding her own business. She said her only interest down there was her work, and though she knew that the other girls were "screwing around with the Niggers," she paid no attention to them and said nothing. She said that Dolly and Martha were screwing various Negroes, and that she once caught Mabel [Hank's girl] in the act with Jackson, but the two did not know that she saw them. The storerooms beneath the fibre house were used for clandestine meetings, and couples would disappear for various periods to go down there. Gertie said that she also caught Pete Moon [box partition leadman] with Dolly. Mabel, she said, was screwing the Negroes for money.

The frameup was as follows: One of the girls approached her to ask if she knew that Mabel was screwing the Negroes. Gertie replied, "Sure, I know it." Gertie said that she had not attempted to spread this information; the girl had asked her if she knew, and she told her she did. But then this girl told everybody that Gertie had said that Mabel was screwing the Negroes, and the trouble started.

"Those sons-of-bitches framed me to get rid of me!" said Gertie, now highly wrought up. She used *sons-of-bitches* and *screwing* loudly and freely, accompanied by waving arms to emphasize her points, and I was somewhat embarrassed when passers-by stopped to look at us.

Members of management were aware that blacks and whites were forming sexual relationships. Foreman Chester Schaefer was an interested observer.

Chester then made the statement that he knew everyone on the floor now—who was going with whom, etc.

"I can predict just what trouble is coming up in the future. For instance, Dolly and Kathy are going out with three colored fellows. Daisy, Kathy, and Martha Sellers, who used to work on box partitions, spent an entire weekend with Ronnie Wilson, Jones, and Massey [Negroes] in a West Side hotel.

"But Martha doesn't work here any more," I said.

"But she still runs around with Daisy and Kathy," said Chester. "Others are doing the same thing. Even the union president."

Ralph Tetley, Director of Personnel for Finished Board, at first carried a *laissez-faire* attitude toward the sexual entanglements of the plant's employees.

> Ralph asked me if I had heard about the recent trouble in the box partition department. I knew he was talking about Pete Moon and his relations with Dolly, and said that I had ... I remarked that Finished Board was a kind of sex tangle anyhow, a sort of group marriage situation with a complexity of relationships.
>
> Ralph then said that what the employees did after work hours was none of the company's business, unless entanglements affected the work situation.
>
> "It's only natural that when you have men and women working together, women that are fairly good-looking, and a group of young and good-looking men that they're going to get interested in each other," said Ralph.

Six months later, under the influence of researcher Ruth Grossman, Tetley had second thoughts. Ruth, a psychologist whom I had introduced into the plant to give close attention to social interaction involving female employees, had directed part of her attention to sexual alliances. Tetley now began to show concern over the "problem."

> Ruth expressed bewilderment and exasperation regarding the problem of the relationship between men and women employees of Finished Board. ...
>
> Ralph spoke up then to say that this problem has been bothering him. Just how far was he responsible for this situation? He said he realized the company didn't have any business butting into what the employees did after they punched their cards out, but still he had feelings of guilt that perhaps he could have done something to prevent the development of the situation. He said he had been wondering just how far he should go. Should he have spoken words of warning to the girls when they were first hired? Should he have told them that they were going to work with married men who had families and that the company didn't intend to put up with any behavior with these family men that might tend to disrupt their family relationships? Perhaps he could have advised them that going out with single men was all right but that if the company heard any reports or rumors about their going out with the married men they would be fired.

"I thought at the time that the thing to do was to fire Pete Moon, and the girls involved with him, but others didn't agree with me," said Ralph. "That might have done some good." ...

Ruth spoke up to say that she was inclined to agree with Ralph, that something should have been done about it by management a long time ago. Pete should have been fired; that would have thrown a scare into the others.

I commented that sex in this factory might be affecting production.

"It does affect production!" said Ruth. She pointed out that those involved in these extramarital relations were under tension all the time and their tensions had a definite effect on production.

"And turnover," I said.

"It definitely affects turnover," said Ralph.... "We should have called them into the office at the very beginning and got tough with them. We should have told them that if we heard any more of this monkey business going on, they would be fired!"

Ruth came up with solutions to the "sex problem" that would stop immorality at the front gate, so to speak—in the hiring process. She offered her conclusions to Richard, Ralph's assistant, and Richard passed them on to Ralph and me.

Richard spoke up to say that Ruth had made an observation about their hiring procedure that he had not himself noticed before but which he recognized as true. He said that Ruth pointed out that whenever one of the girls left, personnel hired another girl with general characteristics just like her. He said that Ruth had pointed out that they kept hiring the same type, divorcees or women who had separated from their husbands and who had one or two children.

Ralph remarked that it was this type who seemed to be most stable on the type of job offered women in Finished Board.

Richard then pointed out that she might be stable, but she was of a type to get involved in sex tangles with the men employees.

Ruth also discussed the "problem" with observant Chester Schaefer, countering his defeatism with her "stop it at the gate" solution. Chester's considered opinion was that "nothing could be done about it—not with a union in the plant."

"I'm for having a union here," said Chester, to me, "but the fact remains that after a worker has been here 30 days and joins the union, there isn't a thing we can do about him. We've got exactly 30 days to find out about him and either keep him or get rid of him.... After that we can't do a thing. After 30 days all we can do is get in and drive them...."

Ruth then spoke up to say that Dolly should have been "caught" during the hiring interview and should never been hired at all. Chester quickly agreed. Ruth went on to tell me that while she was waiting in the outer personnel office to be interviewed, Dolly sat there holding hands with a man. She told Mary [personnel assistant] later in the interview that she was married, and Mary assumed that she was holding hands with her husband. She referred to this man as Dolly's husband, and Dolly corrected her to say that it wasn't her husband; she had never seen him before in her life.

THE CASE OF HARRY AND PETE

The following case study suggests a cyclical relationship between the wenching of work-group leaders and the efficiency of their crews. An initial rise in production may well be caused by imitation of the leader's exhibiting the rapture of new love by heightened hustle in work performance. This case also suggests that a sudden drop to low levels of production may be largely accounted for by a decline in the morale of crew members who find themselves outside the "enchanted circle." Group efficiency is difficult to maintain because loss of enthusiasm is accompanied by absenteeism. It may collapse completely as the unattended and resentful quit.

Leadmen Harry and Pete were in charge of rotating crews that operated two box-carton machines. Before accepting their box-carton assignments both men had become habituated to the goldbricking practices that permeated the production lines of their company. Yet, for approximately a year these two confirmed loafers gave each other stiff and unrelenting competition to set production records for daily output. For many months they battled for production through a seemingly endless succession of machine breakdowns and other mechanical troubles. The honor of holding production records seesawed, only to have "woman troubles" slow them both to levels considerably below reasonable potential.

I watched the struggle with fascination. Management also watched—with mixed feelings but always with timely moves to renew crews when group cohesion collapsed.

In early May, when the box-carton partition machines had been in operation for only three months, the crew leaders of the three shifts were Harry, Pete, and Bob. Production records showed that Harry's crew had been taking the lead; Bob and Pete's crews were in close competition with each other but lagged behind Harry's. The supervisor said that each crew was trying to beat the others, "but it may level off later when they find out what they can do." Because I knew how the three operators had behaved on their previous jobs in the plant, I expected them to come swiftly to some kind of output quota agreement that would reduce the stress of competition. But the struggle for ascendancy continued.

A month later Harry's crew was still in the lead. A female member of his crew attributed their success to Harry's ability to keep the machines running. "When the machine stops, we lose production. They all run the same when they're running." Later Harry gave credit to the "feeder" of the one hand-fed machine.

But the machines did not run steadily. There were many stops, delays, machine breakdowns. The superintendent regarded Harry as the best operator, Pete the least effective because "He changes things around too much." Pete seemed to be trying to compensate for Harry's mechanical ability by speeding up the machines; under the higher speed they broke down. The "trouble" was analyzed by a member of Bob's crew: "They're trying for 750 bundles. It's better to try for 640, and a [machine] speed of 5 is about right for steady performance."

One Monday afternoon in late August Harry declared that he was "sick of the job."

> That's a hell of a job. It's hard on a man. Too much running back and forth from one machine to another. By the time you get one machine running the other one is down again. All an operator should have to handle is just one machine. Then when he gets that running he should sit on his ass and take it easy.

Harry was beginning to sound like his old self again. But then I discovered a plausible reason for Harry's sudden discontent.

Pete had established a new production record, and several days later he broke his own record. From my notes:

> Pete walked up, smiled at me, and seemed eager to announce that he had already got 550 bundles so far in the shift [with less than an hour to go]. "That's a new record," he said proudly.
>
> Pete went back to the machine, and Ada came up to sit in the booth. I commented on the speed that the machine was going, and she agreed that it was running very fast. "They ought to change feeders once in a while and give that girl a rest," she said. "That's hard for one feeder to stand there all day and feed at that speed."
>
> Ada was referring to Myrtle Zuchinski, and Myrtle looked tired. She stood by her machine with her eyes half closed, just her hands and arms moving. The knife kept going up and down like a trip-hammer. I studied the dial to see what the speed was. It registered a shade less than 8 on the dial.

When Pete stopped the machine he had beaten his record by 76 bundles.

Harry, coming in for the second shift was less than elated when I told him that Pete had set a new record. He insisted he was going to follow management's orders not to set the machines too fast. He further remarked that he had not paid any attention to production records and had slowed his production so as not to surpass Pete's. Now Pete had upped his production so Harry would be forced to match it.

> Why do you suppose they leave this production book out here? They've got all the figures in the office when they want to look at them! They leave them out here so we can look at them! Do you notice how the first thing the girls do when they come on shift is to gather around this book to see what the other crews have done?

Harry was told that Pete had to work during lunch hour (20 minutes) and rest period to make his record. Harry said that he would keep going for rest periods, but he was going to stop for lunch. "I'm not going to try to break any records."

In early September Pete held the record on both machines. A union steward suggested that the reason for Pete's success was that he had the two best feeders. He was referring to Myrtle Zuchinski and an attractive young woman named Dolly.

A few days later I found Harry in good humor again. He had set a new record for the two machines on one shift. By then Bob's shift had been dropped, and the two competitors, Pete and Harry, remained. The following week Harry was elated. From my notes:

> Harry seemed unusually full of pep and unusually cheerful. I wondered what had come over him. He fairly danced around with his arms flailing, laughing as if he didn't have a care in the world. I wondered for a minute if he had been drinking but didn't smell any alcohol, and he talked coherently in his serious moments. "My 924 is still high," he announced with glee. "It hasn't been beaten yet!"

Harry had been surpassing Pete's production by wide margins for nearly a week.

> When I started to bring up the subject of a record again Harry waved his hand negatively. "I'm not interested in any record," he said. "There's my Queen of Spades [points at Stella], and there's my Queen of Hearts [points at Gertie]."
>
> Harry complimented Beulah on her "light touch" in jogging the partitions. "That's it, Beulah!" he shouted. "You've got the touch! Nice work, Beulah!"

Later that afternoon Harry described his "new system" of "keeping the girls happy."

> The idea is to kid them along, pay them compliments. They like it. For instance, Stella wore some perfume the other day. I said I like it and

was going to get my wife some of it. Then I moved up on a stool and sat down beside her at the machine. I said that I just wanted to sit there and smell that perfume.

Harry mentioned other things that he did to keep the place livened up. He said that he put up a little cardboard box with a sign: "Help the operator with contributions to his beer fund." The girls got a kick out of that and put pennies in the box; he had eight cents at the end of the day. He said he had gotten the idea of kidding the girls along to make them happy just before he went on vacation. "I was getting to be a nervous wreck. I knew I couldn't go on like that, so when I came back I started the new system." Harry said that his new system was better than the drive system Pete used and he had formerly used.

In looking over my notes I was drawn to two items concerning the institution of the new system: Harry's vacation had ended approximately a month and a half before there was any sign of the new system, and the arrival of Wilma coincided with my first awareness of a new system. Wilma was 22 and very pretty, even prettier than Dolly, Pete's star feeder.

A few days later Harry told me there was trouble on Pete's shift. He said that Myrtle had threatened to quit if she was not transferred to his (Harry's) shift because Pete was discriminating against her in favor of Dolly.

> "Pete's been taking Dolly out, and he favors her over Myrtle," said Harry. "Now that's what I heard. I don't know for sure. But Myrtle says that when both machines are down Pete rushes over to fix Dolly's first. And when Dolly's machine is down Pete has her work on the floor instead of relieving Myrtle. So Myrtle has to stay there all day without relief."
>
> Harry went on to say that Myrtle had told Irene [Pete's wife who was also an employee of the company] about his stepping out with Dolly, and today Pete, Irene, and Dolly were called into Lenny Davis' [foreman] office. Harry did not know what happened in the meeting, just that there was one and that Pete was in trouble.
>
> "A man should never fuck around with the women where he works," said Harry. "I never do it. I take them out for a glass of beer, but that's all. I never step out with women around my own neighborhood. If I want a strange piece of ass I get clear out of my district."

The following week Pete regained his position as record holder with 928 bundles, four more bundles than Harry had been able to achieve on one shift. However, Myrtle had asked for and received a transfer from Pete's to Harry's crew. Within a few days Harry's group recaptured the record with 989 bundles. That evening only two of Pete's crew showed up at the start of the shift, but later two more women arrived.

The superintendent extolled Harry's work to me and called him "the best operator in that department." He further confided his plans for elevating Harry to assistant foreman over both glue machines and box-carton partition machines on second shift.

> He's done a good job mechanically since he was put on the box-carton machines, and he's done a good job handling his crew. I figure he'll put pressure on the other glue operators just as he's put pressure on the other operators in the box-partition department. Harry is a driver!

Production laurels changed hands twice more within a week. Pete raised the record to 1,012 bundles, and five days later Harry increased it to 1,031.

Rating his feeders to me, Harry listed Stella as the best, Myrtle second, and Gertie third. That evening he met Wilma and Gertie in a tavern on the south side of town and got home at 2 A.M. A few days later Harry confided in me that he had been visiting taverns with Wilma far away from their respective homes. Also, he expressed puzzlement over the new absenteeism of Stella; she had rarely been absent before this.

Then Pete's crew added 20 bundles to the record set by Harry earlier in the month. Interpreting Pete's success, Harry pointed out that Pete set the machine speed higher and worked his feeders without relief. He also said that in running fast Pete turned out a lot of "junk."

> He bundles up everything. Stuff that we would throw in the hay wagon, he ties it up and shoots it in. We throw the crumpled partitions away, but Pete doesn't throw anything away.... You know, I've attended a couple of those union–management meetings, and I take this business of quality seriously. I try to get good quality because I know it's important.

In November Harry made more complaints about being shorthanded. "My girls are absent all the time." However, the cartoons and pictures kept going up on the wall until there was hardly room for another clipping or sign in the favored area behind the smoking booth. Gertie was the biggest contributor to the collection.

During November Harry and Wilma were a twosome in the local bars.

One day in mid-December I found Harry tired and angry and faced with, in his words, "nothing but trouble." He complained that he needed an assistant operator to handle one machine breakdown while he was working on another, and "Those feeders are getting too damned independent." At that moment one of the machines broke down; he cursed feeder Myrtle under his breath and said something disagreeable to her. Her face darkened. She sat in her feeding station while Harry worked on her machine with an angry disgusted expression.

By mid-January both Myrtle and Gertie left Harry's crew by voluntary termination of their employment. There were several replacements, and the crew broke Pete's long-standing record with a total of 1,088 bundles for one shift. Early in February he pushed it up to 1,196, approximately 90 percent efficiency, according to the foreman.

The next day I commented to Pete, "One of these days you'll break 1,200!"

"I will if I get the chance and feel like it," he said.

> I stopped to watch Dolly. . . . The machine was hammering away at an amazing clip—the dial registered 10! And Dolly was keeping up with the machine, though occasionally she had to stop to allow Pete to clear away jams. Martha, at a jogging station, was frowning and looking generally sour. She was having a time of it to keep up with the jogging, even with a girl across the jogging table to help her.

During this time Pete appeared to be out-producing Harry each day. When I referred Harry to the recent production figures and suggested that he would have to jack up his machine speed to 10 to keep up with Pete he replied:

> "No, I won't! Pete's crazy! He's beating himself out just for a few lousy bundles, running back and forth from one machine to another. He doesn't walk, he runs! You know, the faster you run these machines, the more work you have to do—changing rolls sooner and keeping the feeders supplied with primaries!" Harry informed me that one of Pete's girls, Martha, had walked off the job the day before because of the high speed.

In discussing feeders Harry told me that Dolly was the best of all groups, though Ethel, Pete's second feeder, was good too. Two days later I heard at a union meeting that Martha and Ethel had walked out.

> Ethel had complained to Foreman Chester that Pete had been showing favoritism to Dolly over all the others; she had told both Chester and Irene [Pete's wife] about Pete's carrying on with Dolly. Tom said Dolly and Pete would probably be fired tomorrow. Dolly and Pete were caught *flagrant delicto* in the plant.

Pete did remain on the job, though only three girls, including Ethel, who came back when Dolly quit, remained on his crew.

> Harry spoke laughingly of Pete. . . . He said he went up to Pete, slapped him on the back, and shouted, "Hi, Romeo!" loud enough for everyone to hear. Harry said that Pete looked pretty sick these days. He'd come in with his head down and not speak to anyone.

Harry seemed to take pleasure in Pete's discomfiture.

A week later Pete's crew was reinforced, but he estimated that it would take three months to break them in. Pete spent the month of March at lowered production while breaking in his new crew. In one conversation with Harry I remarked that he seemed to keep the same crew month after month. "Yes, I've got a pretty steady crew," he said. "I can't help it," he added with a smile, "if they like to work for me and won't quit."

But early in March Wilma did not come back to work. Harry did not know what had happened to her. At the end of the month she visited the plant with one of her small daughters. She was pregnant and was going back to her home state to be with her mother and other children. She was divorcing her husband. He refused to claim the child as his own, saying that it couldn't be his. Gossip was starting that Harry was the child's father.

Early in April Harry informed me that Wilma was now with her mother and children in Tennessee. I asked Harry if he missed her.

> He said that he did, and went on to say that she was a good worker and was a lot of fun. He said that Wilma had quite a sense of humor, and that they were always cutting up on the floor. He said he would give Wilma a slap across the buttocks on occasion, and she used to put paper shavings down his back.
>
> I remarked that he and Wilma appeared to be a nice couple. Harry put in quickly that he would never leave his wife for her. He said he was satisfied with his wife and family, and got along all right at home. He said that his wife was a good cook and took care of the kids, everything that a wife should do.
>
> "But it's natural to want to step out with somebody else once in a while," said Harry.
>
> Harry said that the trouble with his relations with Wilma was that the other girls on the crew got jealous.
>
> Harry said that Alberta didn't like Wilma; she was jealous of her and accused Harry recently of favoritism. He had a little fight with Alberta the other day. She threatened to complain to the boss about his favoritism. He advised her to keep her mouth shut unless she could prove what she said. . . .
>
> "Alberta is a troublemaker," said Harry, "I wish she'd leave!"
>
> "Didn't you used to go out with Alberta?" I asked.
>
> "I did a few times, but no more," he said.

By mid-April Pete had brought his new crew up to production that approximated that of Harry's crew. There were days when one crew or another would achieve 1,000 bundles, but Pete's record of 1,196 was not threatened. Pete kept complaining about his feeders. Not only did it take time to develop them, but they didn't have the natural ability that Dolly had had.

Harry was now in trouble. A woman had phoned his wife, telling her about his affair with Wilma, and now Harry was "sweating it out." Harry told me that he didn't know who made the call, but sooner or later he would find out.

Then I heard that Wilma had had a self-abortion and nearly died. It had happened at the time Harry was telling me that she had gone home to her mother.

A week later Harry was still looking forward to finding out who had phoned his wife. He had asked Alberta if she knew anything about it, and she replied that she didn't. She acted as though she were telling the truth.

> Harry spoke to me on the walkway outside the box-partition room, saying that he was staying out of that room as much as he could now. "I don't talk to them any more," he said. "I used to kid around with them at first, but no more of that."
>
> Ruth [my research assistant] told me that Wilma was coming back to work within a week and that she didn't think the girls on Harry's crew were going to like it. Ada had asked . . . for a transfer to Pete's shift. She said that she would quit if she were not transferred; she would not work with Wilma. Stella and Alberta were going to ask for transfers to Pete's shift too.
>
> I remarked that it would be tough for Harry, and Ruth told me that Harry had been giving the girls miserable treatment lately. He wouldn't speak to them at all, save to bawl them out.
>
> I said that Harry probably felt that one of the girls on his shift had been the one who phoned his wife. "Yes, and he doesn't know who; so he's taking it out on all of them!" said Ruth.

Wilma did return to work within a week. A third shift had been added again, and except for Wilma, Harry's present crew was inexperienced. His old crew, under a new operator, Mike, turned out 450 bundles on the night shift. Mike was said to have remarked that the job was enough to drive a man crazy.

A few days later Harry seemed to be his old self. He gave me a report on production.

> I asked Harry if he was using his system on his new crew. He said that he wasn't. . . . He said his relations with them were "friendly," that he spoke to them in friendly fashion, but relations were "strictly business." He said that there would be no more "cutting up" on the floor, no more drinking with any of the girls, not even Wilma.

By the second week in June Harry and Pete were getting 800 and 900 bundles a day. Mike's crew was running third. "Any time we get over 800, it's good production," said Harry.

I was gone for the summer. When I returned in September I heard about the trouble Harry got into during the summer.

Wilma's husband had twice come to the plant looking for Harry and had once caught him outside after work. Hemrich said that the reports were that the husband had pulled a knife on Harry...and Harry had run up the street. Hemrich said with a laugh that reports varied on just what Harry did; some said he ran; others said that he merely walked fast. I could use my own imagination.

Wilma was gone; competition for 1,200 bundles a day was over; and Harry never got promoted to assistant foreman.

3.   Deviant Behavior among Blue-Collar Workers-Employees: Work-Norm Violation in the Factory

WILLIAM E. SNIZEK

The term *deviant* is virtually meaningless without a referent. Since deviant behavior is generally viewed by sociologists as behavior that violates a given set of norms or rules of conduct, thereby transgressing certain specified role expectations, an accurate delineation of the exact norms that have been violated assumes paramount importance. Only after individuals' behaviors have been viewed within the context of a specified normative system can a valid and accurate assessment be made of the deviant nature of such behavior or of its perpetrators. Shoplifting is considered a criminal (deviant) act by society in that it violates its laws (institutionalized norms). However, for certain adolescent groups within which shoplifting is both a valued and accepted (normative) form of behavior, one's reluctance or failure to engage in such behavior is labeled deviant by group members.

Operating within a framework of relative deviance, the discussion that follows is focused upon blue-collar personnel as both *workers* and *employees*. When examining the deviant work practices of blue-collar workers, the referent will be that of the *work group* or *informal organization*. In analyzing the deviant behavior of blue-collar employees the referent will center upon the various role requirements set forth by the *formal organization*. Given the frequently documented conflict between informal and formal organizational norms, such a distinction will aid in better understanding and categorizing deviance in blue-collar behavior.

FORMS OF DEVIANCE

Before discussing the various forms of blue-collar deviance, some mention should be made of the extent to which deviance from the viewpoint of both workers and employees has been reported in the literature. The vast majority of studies dealing with the subject of blue-collar deviance are focused primarily upon employee deviance. The principal emphasis has been to center

67

upon those informal work practices that violate the formally instituted work demands of the organization. This emphasis is quite understandable in the light of the generally accepted view among managerial personnel concerning what they feel to be the antithetical, and thus deviant, purposes of these practices. Since investigators generally found it necessary to elicit the cooperation of management, whether monetary or otherwise, in order to engage in intraplant research, such views were given considerable attention.

Though generally neglected, however, some references to worker deviance do appear in literature. In commenting upon worker violations of informally set output restrictions, Roethlisberger and Dickson noted the following of bank wiring room personnel:

> They shared a common body of sentiments. A person should not turn out too much work. If he did, he was a "rate buster." ... On the other hand, a person should not turn out too little work. If he did, he was a "chiseler;" that is, he was getting paid for work he did not do. A person should say nothing which would injure a fellow member of the group. If he did, he was a "squealer."[1]

Apart from the derogatory labels attached by fellow workers to those among them who had deviated from informally set levels of output, mention was also made of various sanctions and methods of enforcement which might be levied against the deviant.

> If one of the employees did something which was not considered quite proper, one of his fellow workers had the right to "bing" him. Binging consisted of hitting him a stiff blow on the upper arm. The person who was struck usually took the blow without protest and did not strike back. ... Other practices which naturally served the same end were sarcasm and the use of invectives. If a person turned out too much work, he was called names such as "Speed King" or "The Slave."[2]

Similar social mechanisms of enforcement were observed to exist among drill-press operators in a machine shop studied by Collins, Dalton, and Roy.[3] In those situations in which workers refused to restrict their outputs within informally agreed limits, such nonconformists were often subject to threats of injury, ridicule, hidden tools, and ostracism. Ostracism was a particularly potent sanction of the work group. In addition to its psychological impact

---

[1] George C. Homans, "The Western Electric Researches," in Schuyler Dean Hoslett, ed., *Human Factors in Management* (New York, Harper & Bros., 1951), p. 235.

[2] Ibid., p. 236.

[3] Orvis Collins, Melville Dalton, and Donald Roy, "Restriction of Output and Social Cleavage in Industry," *Applied Anthropology* 5 (Summer 1946), pp. 1–14.

upon the individual, it carried with it the added penalty of depriving one of certain "trade secrets" needed to become a proficient operator.

The violation of informally agreed upon production rates represents only one form of worker deviance. Others include, for example, squealing on co-workers, the use or misuse of another's tools, and wearing "street clothes" while at work. Workers commonly label certain tools or machinery as their own, regardless of whether such implements are owned by the company. By means of initials or other distinctive markings, laborers lay claim to shovels, painters to ladders, and machinists to drills. To use another's personal tools is to run the risk of immediate, and in some cases severe, reprisal, because such an act is often seen as an indirect threat to one's livelihood.

The informal organization among blue-collar workers often sets acceptable standards of work attire. Generally, work clothes are simple and unpretentious, thereby reflecting the theme of the "dignity" in hard work. Should a worker attempt to work while smartly dressed, or in what are referred to as "street clothes," he is likely to be chided by fellow workers as perhaps having a heavy date after work, aspiring to enter management, or just being queer. If persistently worn, work attire adjudged to be deviant may unfortunately result in a number of dirty industrial "accidents" for its wearer.

Accounts of blue-collar deviance also have generally tended to be focused upon informal group violations of officially instituted work rules and procedures—employee deviance. This type of deviance encompasses such things as simply wasting time on the job, calculated restriction of output, intentional absenteeism, strikes, and employee sabotage.

There exist in the literature few accounts of "talking, fun, and fooling" among blue-collar personnel that surpass those reported by Donald Roy in an article aptly entitled "Banana-Time: Job Satisfaction and Informal Interaction." According to Roy, the small group of factory workers he studied were observed to enter into verbal interplay based upon several predictable "themes" (for example, taxes, better jobs, property ownership) to engage in ritualistic horseplay, and to avail themselves of numerous unofficial work breaks.

> Most of the breaks in the daily series were designated as "times" in the parlance of the clicker operators, and they featured the consumption of food or drink of one sort or another. There was coffee time, peach time, banana time, fish time, coke time, and of course, lunch time. Other interruptions which formed part of the series but were not verbally recognized as times, were window time, pickup time, and the staggered quitting times of Sammy and Ike.[4]

[4] Donald Roy, "Banana Time: Job Satisfaction and Informal Interaction," *Human Organization* 18 (Winter 1959), p. 47.

Employee deviance in the forms of output restriction and purposive absenteeism have been most notably examined by proponents of what has come to be known in personnel relations as the "human relations approach." By focusing on the work plant as an ongoing social system rather than as a mere technical organization, researchers such as Elton Mayo,[5] Fritz J. Roethlisberger and William J. Dickson,[6] William F. Whyte,[7] Donald Roy,[8] and others were able to explain those forms of employee deviance that had hitherto escaped the logic of "scientific management."

In studies conducted among machine operators, for example, Roy found the practice of "soldiering," or output restriction, to be of two major types. The first, "quota restriction" referred to "a limitation of effort on 'gravy' jobs in order not to exceed set maximums." A second type of output restriction, associated with "stinker" jobs is that of "goldbricking," centered upon the "holding-back" or failure to release effort, when a close approach to the quota seems unattainable."[9] Both types of output restrictions on the part of the operators were heavily dependent upon informal group categorizations of jobs as either "gravy" or "stinker" jobs. Similarly, various manifestations of the informal social organizations among employees were shown to have had considerable influence on output restriction in Roethlisberger and Dickson's bank wiring room[10] and Whyte's restaurant[11] and for absenteeism in Mayo and Lombard's aircraft plant.[12]

Strikes and industrial sabotage, perhaps more than any of the aforementioned forms of employee deviance, are most often viewed as tactics of labor unions. While certainly true in some instances, such actions may also be the result of the informal work organization operative within the work plant

[5] Elton Mayo, *The Social Problems of an Industrial Civilization* (Cambridge, Mass., Harvard University Press, 1946).

[6] Fritz J. Roethlisberger and William J. Dickson, *Management and the Worker* (Cambridge, Mass., Harvard University Press, 1939).

[7] William F. Whyte, "Who Goes Union and Why," *Personnel Journal* 23 (December 1944), pp. 215–30; *Human Relations and the Restaurant Industry* (New York, McGraw-Hill, 1948).

[8] Donald Roy, "Quota Restriction and Goldbricking in a Machine Shop," *American Journal of Sociology* 57 (March 1952), 427–42; "Work Satisfaction and Social Reward in Quota Achievement: An Analysis of Piecework Incentive," *American Sociological Review* 18 (October 1953), pp. 507–14; "Efficiency and the 'Fix': Informal Intergroup Relations in a Piecework Machine Shop," *American Journal of Sociology* 60 (1954), pp. 255–66; "Banana Time: Job Satisfaction and Informal Interaction," *Human Organization* 18 (Winter 1959), pp. 158–68.

[9] Roy, "Banana Time," op. cit., p. 429.

[10] Roethlisberger and Dickson, op. cit.

[11] Whyte, *Human Relations in the Restaurant Industry*, op. cit.

[12] Elton Mayo and George F. Lombard, *Teamwork and Labor Turnover in the Aircraft Industry of Southern California* (Boston, Harvard Graduate School of Business Administration, 1940).

or factory, quite apart from any union. In view of this distinction, Ross notes that in those situations where the informal work organization initiates actions contrary to the desires of the official work organization, such actions are generally spontaneous and of a violent nature. Thus, informally sponsored strikes are most often of a "wildcat" variety, while sabotage includes acts such as arson and theft. Union-initiated strikes are, however, considerably more orderly and painstakingly planned so as to gain specific concessions from management. When violence does occur in the form of sabotage, it is often linked to the actions of a radical few who have become impatient with their leaders, management, or both.

SOCIAL PROFILE OF THE DEVIANT

Although the behavior of both blue-collar worker deviants and employee deviants has been shown to take many forms, research devoted to describing their social characteristics usually has centered upon the act of output restriction. Thus researchers have contrasted the characteristics of indivuals who conformed with those who refused to conform to informally agreed upon production rates.

In studies conducted among machinists working under a wage incentive system, Collins and his associates found that worker deviants generally were of rural American ethnic background, were more conservative politically, and held less strongly pro-union attitudes than those who conformed to worker norms. By contrast, those who conformed to informal group demands concerning the restriction of output were shown to have urban backgrounds, to argue in favor of the New Deal, to be strongly pro-union, and generally to be of second- or third-generation European ethnic ancestry.[13] Numerous studies of trade union members have indicated that such individuals closely approximate employee deviants on the characteristics of residence, ethnic background, and political ideology. Similarly, nonunion workers or apathetic union members have been shown to have characteristics similar to worker deviants.[14]

At this point, one may inquire as to the etiological factors associated with both worker and employee deviance with respect to output restriction. As concerns the deviant worker or nonconformer, Collins made the following observations:

[13] Collins et al., op. cit.
[14] See William Spinard, "Correlates of Trade Union Participation: A Summary of the Literature," *American Sociological Review* 25 (1960), pp. 237–44; and Daisy L. Tagliacozzo and Joel Seidman, "A Typology of Rank and File Union Members," *American Journal of Sociology* 61 (May 1956), pp. 546–53.

Transplanted to an urban environment he [the deviant worker] continues to adhere to rural American attitudes concerning property rights, free enterprise, individual opportunity, *laissez-faire* government. To him it is incomprehensible that workmen should allow themselves to be formed into tightly organized groups for the purpose of restricting the activities of one another. Beyond being economically unjust to both employer and employee, it is morally wrong.

A person who has lived on a farm knows something of the problems which face a man who is attempting to produce something to sell. Further, he understands property ownership in a way which the urban worker, who has never possessed his own means of production, cannot. To him organization among workmen to produce less than they are capable of doing is nothing short of criminal collusion.[15]

While the deviant worker refuses to conform to the production demands of the informal organization much out of sympathy, if not identification, with his employer, the same cannot be said of the deviant employee. Employee deviance is grounded in a basic distrust of management as well as an attempt to gain active mastery over the production process. Numerous studies have noted that employees feel compelled to restrict output for fear of the re-timing of jobs, rate cuts, and eventual unemployment.[16] Many social scientists view a restriction in output on the part of employees as symptomatic of a rebellion against increasing impersonal and sophisticated production techniques. Output restriction is thus viewed by some individuals as a means of unshackling themselves from the constant pace of the machine.

Even though the observations made in this section are admittedly based upon deviant behavior in the form of output restriction, there is little doubt of their applicability to other forms of deviance. Quite apart from its varied manifestations, worker deviance appears to stem largely from a concern over rendering unto the employer a "fair day's work." Employee deviance, however, seems grounded in anxiety and distrust with respect to being given a "fair day's pay."

ORGANIZATIONAL CONSEQUENCES OF BLUE-COLLAR DEVIANCE

Behavior adjudged to be deviant relative to one's co-workers (worker deviance) may or may not be in compliance with formal organizational demands. Actually, since informal or unofficial work norms may *supplement* as well as oppose those of the formal organization, certain forms of behavior may quite possibly violate *both* sets of work norms. An example of just such a situation

---

[15] Collins et al., op. cit., p. 12.

[16] See Roethlisberger and Dickson, op. cit.; and Roy, "Quota Restriction and Goldbricking," op. cit.

was shown to exist in connection with the output "chisler" described by Homans earlier, in that a severe restriction of output was found to have violated both informal and formal production norms. In short, only in those instances where the informal work norms and practices have been shown to conflict with those of the formal organization can worker deviance be viewed as engendering employee compliance, and vice versa.

Regardless of the degree of agreement or disagreement found to exist between informal and formal work norms, considerable caution must be taken in assessing the relative functions or dysfunctions stemming from both worker and employee deviance. For example, given the often-cited conflict between informal and formal production norms, it does not necessarily follow that worker deviance is functional, nor that employee deviance is dysfunctional. Dalton observed that worker deviants, while complying with formal work norms, generally created more trouble than they were worth in the form of friction and hostility among co-workers.[17] In so doing, the behavior of worker deviants was observed to have had dysfunctional rather than functional consequences for the work organization's overall goals of increased production, efficiency, profits. As pertains to the possible functional aspects of employee deviance, a case in point is found in a study done by Bensman and Gerver concerning the use of a "tap" (a tool used to insert a bolt through a wing section into a nut) by airplane workers.[18] Though officially outlawed as an illegal tool and its use considered to be deviant behavior, Bensman and Gerver nevertheless found the tap to expedite production considerably, thereby proving to be quite functional in terms of the organization's larger goals. A similar point was made by Merton when he observed that perhaps the most expedient way for employees to disrupt the organization in which they work is to follow its rules to the letter.[19] In short, employee deviance in the form of official work rule violations is quite likely to have definite functional consequences for the work organization. Only when such deviance is directed at the basic goals of the organization are dysfunctional consequences shown to occur.

ADDITIONAL REFERENCES

Bakke, E. Wight. *The Unemployed Worker.* New Haven, Conn.: Yale University Press, 1940.

[17] Melville Dalton, "The Industrial 'Rate-Buster': A Characterization," *Applied Anthropology* 7 (Winter 1948), pp. 5–18.

[18] Joseph Bensman and Israel Gerver, "Crime and Punishment in the Factory: The Function of Deviancy in Maintaining the Social System," *American Sociological Review* 28 (1963), pp. 588–98.

[19] Robert K. Merton, "Bureaucratic Structure and Personality," in *Social Theory and Social Structure* (Glencoe, Ill., Free Press, 1949).

Blau, Peter M. Patterns of Deviations in Work Groups." *Sociometry* 23 (September 1960) :245–61.

Brown, J. A. C. *The Social Psychology of Industry.* Baltimore: Penguin Books, 1954.

Dalton, Melville. "Worker Response and Social Background." *Journal of Political Economy* 55 (August 1947): 323–32.

Erikson, Kai T. "Notes on the Sociology of Deviance." *Social Problems* 9 (Spring 1962) :307–14.

Gross, Edward. "Some Functional Consequences of Primary Controls in Formal Work Organization." *American Sociological Review* 18 (1953): 368–73.

Kemper, Theodore D. "Representative Roles and the Legitimation of Deviance." *Social Problems* 13 (1966) :288–98.

Krupp, Sherman. *Pattern in Organization Analysis.* New York: Holt, Rinehart and Winston, 1961.

Ross, Arthur M. "The Natural History of the Strike," in Arthur Kornhauser, Robert Dubin, and Arthur M. Ross, eds., *Industrial Conflict.* New York: McGraw-Hill, 1954.

Swados, Harvey. "The Myth of the Happy Worker," in *A Radical's America.* Boston: Little, Brown, 1962.

Tausky, Curt. *Work Organizations.* Itasca, Ill.: F. E. Peacock, 1970.

4. Unethical Behavior: Professional Deviance

H. KIRK DANSEREAU

PROFESSION

At this point in the development of the sociology of work rehashing the plethora of discussions about efforts to define the term *profession* seems quite unnecessary. Although definitions and listings of criteria vary, consensus exists as to the principal characteristics that should be considered.

Following the lead of earlier writers, Krause mentions the skills and theory necessarily acquired, the nature of the relationship between the client and the practitioner, and the self-regulation within the practitioner group embodied in a code of ethics.[1] A decade earlier, Goode had written of a profession's autonomy, the existence of its own association, "prolonged specialized training in a body of abstract knowledge, and . . . a collectivity or service orientation."[2] Wilensky states:

> Any occupation wishing to exercise professional authority must find a technical base for it, assert an exclusive jurisdiction, link both skill and jurisdiction to standards of training, and convince the public that its services are uniquely trustworthy.[3]

He also points out that the differences between the professional and the lay public are: (1) The job of the professional is *technical*—based on systematic knowledge or doctrine acquired only through long prescribed training. (2) The professional man adheres to a set of *professional norms*.[4]

[1] Elliott A. Krause, *The Sociology of Occupations* (Boston, Little, Brown, 1971), pp. 75–76.
[2] William Goode, " 'Professions' and 'Non-Professions,' " in *Professionalization,* Howard M. Vollmer and Donald L. Mills (eds.) (Englewood Cliffs, N.J., Prentice-Hall, 1966), p. 36.
[3] Harold L. Wilensky, "The Professionalization of Everyone?" *The American Journal of Sociology,* Vol. 70, No. 2 (September 1964), p. 38.
[4] Ibid.

Using 18 occupations, he illustrates the process of professionalization in five steps, establishment of the work on a full-time basis, establishment of a training school, formation of an association, licensure, and formulation of a code of ethics. His findings indicate that the majority of the occupations studied followed the above order of development.[5]

ETHICS

Ethics is concerned with the determination of right and wrong in human relationships; a professional ethical code at least expresses a recognition of some of the behavioral standards endorsed by members of a profession. The fact that such codes exist is some evidence of their need; but, of course, their existence for the more recently arrived professions may well have been influenced at least minimally by an often-heard insistance that to be a profession an occupation must have its own code. MacIver speaks of professional codes as "the deliberate application of a generally accepted social standard to particular spheres of conduct."[6] He warns, however, "that group ethics will not by themselves suffice for the guidance of the group unless they are always related to the ethical standards of the community."[7]

Yet, are we professionals not honorable men? If answered affirmatively, is then such a code necessary? For reasons other than the potential unethical behavior of colleagues, two sociologists argued against a code of ethics for their own discipline. One contended that the proposed code was "equivocal or unenlighteningly vague in dealing with most of the problems distinct to social science" and encouraged his "colleagues to vote against the adoption of a code that obscures more than it illuminates, and to press instead for an officially sponsored symposium on the ethical problems of sociology." Another made the point, "A code of ethics, however, is at best an identification of issues, and it cannot fail to distort and oversimplify them."[8] He urged his *colleagues to vote against the adoption of any code of ethics by the Association.* Herein perhaps may lie a distinction between the thinking of members of a learned society in contrast to that of members of an association more directly servicing the ills of the public.

With reference to the latter type organization, Wood quite concisely promulgates reasons for a code's existence. He claims "an ethical code is a functional necessity to the very existence of a profession in contemporary

---

[5] Ibid., pp. 142–46.

[6] R. M. MacIver, "The Social Significance of Professional Ethics," *The Annals,* Benson Y. Landis (ed.), Vol. 297 (January 1955), p. 120.

[7] Ibid., p. 124.

[8] Howard S. Becker and Eliot Friedson, "Against the Code of Ethics," *American Sociological Review,* Vol. 29 (June 1964), pp. 409–10.

society." A second reason pertains to government-sanctioned monopoly status accorded the practitioners, preventing competition and "considerable self-regulation of recruitment and conduct standards." A third consideration is the "nonmaterial nature of professional service and often its confidential nature that lessens the effectiveness of a public or market evaluation of the 'product.' " Fourth, he posits "that so much may be at stake—is a matter that requires assurance of integrity among those who practice in these areas."[9]

Similarities in discussions of ethics are found almost without regard to the time of the writing. Different occupations may have been subject to current interest, but the basic moral themes that are stressed persist. Whether one draws upon the 1926 work of Tauesch or upon the *Annals* nearly three decades later, one sees, for example, that the professional practitioner is expected not to advertise, solicit, or accept kickbacks.[10] Influence peddling, undercover fee-splitting, and contingency fees are frowned upon; in some instances, however, the latter are permitted when limited to a percentage deemed reasonable by the profession. However, the guiding precept under which the specifics are subsumed is one of self-subordination; the interests of client, profession, and public are to supercede those of the professional himself. Infractions are expected to bring reprimand, threatened suspension, or expulsion from the association. In the most serious instances, colleagues may seek court action to have a violator's license revoked.

The blue-collar worker has considerable less opportunity than does the professional to engage in similar violations. As a hyperbolic illustration, the hod carrier does not have the lawyer's opportunity to mingle his funds with those of his employer. He can hardly split fees and is unlikely to be possessed of privileged information. Instead, the blue-collar worker can engage in some shoddy practices such as "borrowing" a few nails, boards, parts, or tools. He can occasionally get a fellow-worker to build something for him at the plant; or he may, given the capability, do it for himself. Somewhat more legally, he just goofs off, simply fails to produce.

The individual worker hardly has recourse to an action analogous to the professional's fee-raising. The counter argument that he does so in concert through his union is met with insouciance by the worker who has just won a raise. Workers, like professionals, view group solidarity and cooperation as essential to their survival even in situations in which there is an outcry that the public interest has been sabotaged. Further, workers, like professionals, often rationalize their seemingly untoward behavior in the name of

9 Arthur Lewis Wood, "Professional Ethics Among Criminal Lawyers," *Social Problems*, Vol. 7 (Summer 1959), p. 71.
10 Carl F. Taeusch, *Professional and Business Ethics* (New York, Holt and Company, 1926), passim; and *The Annals*, op. cit., passim.

their just due—apparent subordination by both of the precept of self-subordination.

BEHAVIOR IN SELECTED OCCUPATIONS

Somewhere between the blue-collar worker and the professional lies a considerable array of occupations, many of which see themselves as professionals in their own right or well on the way to acceptance as professionals. In a single issue of a nonmetropolitan daily there were stories dealing with several such lines of work: military and diplomatic personnel, business managers, and newscasters. One had to do with the credibility of reports pertaining to the escalation of American military activity.[11] Did administration accounts, passed on to friendly governments, jibe with the report held by the Pentagon; and was the person admittedly responsible for the "leak" that precipitated the question guilty of a breach of ethics or even illegal conduct?

A second story concerned the matter of excess profits of more than $65 million during a single federal fiscal year. It is the duty of the Renegotiation Board to eliminate overcharges in space and defense contracts; the above amount was based on 149 determinations.[12] Are those involved in the original negotiations not somehow culpable, at least at an ethical level; or were government negotiators "taken," and are those from the private sector to be excused in the name of sharp business dealings?

Another item pointed out the lack of knowledge that employees have about their fringe benefits. The condition is blamed both on worker apathy and on management's lack of enthusiasm and its failure to find a way to communicate "the intricate details of its plan." The article states that some "funds are invested solely in the company's own stock. In others, fraudulent loans are made; and many plans are not insured."[13] How ethical are these practices when one considers that approximately one-fourth of a pay-check is withheld for fringe benefits and an estimated $130 billion in assets is involved?

Finally, there was a wire service report about a congressional investigation of a television documentary. A House subcommittee minority report arguing against subpoena of the broadcasting company and its president stated:

[11] Arthur L. Gavshon, "Some U.S. Friends Are Conducting Credibility Tests," *Bowling Green–Park City Daily News,* An Associated Press Release (Sunday, July 11, 1971), p. 1.
[12] Jean Heller, "Report Excessive Contract Profits," *Bowling Green–Park City Daily News,* An Associated Press Release (Sunday, July 11, 1971), p. 1.
[13] John Cunniff, "People Know Surprisingly Little About Their Fringe Benefits," *Bowling Green–Park City Daily News,* An Associated Press Release (Sunday, July 11, 1971), p. 7.

The point is the subpoena is not narrowed to the specific allegations respecting "manipulative techniques," "rearrangement of the words of an individual," or making one appear to "deliver a statement which he did not in fact deliver."[14]

The minority report sought to protect against restraints on a newsman's judgment in formulating a story. Yet, is there here not some concern for ethics even in the absence of rigorous specification of complaint? Parenthetically, about the time this last item appeared in print, a congressman appearing on nonnetwork TV contended that four answers had been shifted in the editing of an interview conducted by a nationally known TV newscaster with a cabinet undersecretary. Whither the Television Code Seal of Good Practice?

Accountants may not accept contingency fees or split fees with a lay person. Architects may not compete with each other with regard to professional fees or participate in such profits from building enterprises as "would influence his professional integrity." Engineers may not sponsor or promote "commercial or other undertakings of a speculative character," nor may they seek a position held by another engineer. Teachers may not seek employment through "indiscriminate distribution of applications" or accept compensation from supply houses, having recommended purchases from them. Lawyers must set the fees they are to receive; one may not, without full knowledge of the client, accept any compensation "from other parties to the transactions in which he is employed, . . ." Doctors may not profit from the sale of appliances or medicines or accept compensation beyond that received for professional services rendered. Rabbis are not to engage in fee-splitting; priests may not engage in specified unbecoming occupational roles; Protestant ministers may not proselytize from another church or put themselves up for consideration for another pulpit that is already occupied.[15] It seems that, although the pastor may not increase his flock by "sheep stealing" or seek greener pastures, flocks are continually having their pastors purloined by raiders who sweeten the call with a financial incentive.

The bulk of all the codes is of other than financial canons, but the smell of green is strong; and in the mind of the public, violations related to money matters probably cause more stir than all other facets of professional behavior. The business of making a living is somehow expected to be segregated from the business of being a professional at least if one is seen as "doing a little too well."

[14] Peggy Simpson, "Minority Report Hits Probe of CBS," *Bowling Green–Park City Daily News,* An Associated Press Release (Sunday, July 11, 1971), p. 13.
[15] *The Annals,* op. cit., passim.

THE PHARMACIST

The occupation of the independent druggist is a familiar one in which the business and professional roles are thoroughly intermingled. As noted and hypothesized by Quinney:

> Structural strain is built into retail pharmacy. The pharmacist must, therefore, make some sort of a personal adjustment to the situation.
> It was hypothesized that retail pharmacists resolve the dilemma of choosing between different occupational roles—professional and business —by adapting to an *occupational role organization.*[16]

Having determined the orientations as professional, business, mixed, and indifferent, he learned that there were variations in the number of prescription violators. Most violators were found in the business-oriented category, followed by the indifferent and mixed classifications; no violators were found in the professional grouping.

An AP release relates the efforts of the University of Maryland's School of Pharmacy to "remake this image of the corner druggist," that is, that he is "an impersonal dispenser of pills."[17] The fifth year in school, eliminating the older practice of apprenticeship, is designed to give the student experience in approved community and hospital pharmacies. Referring to the school's dean, the article says:

> Kinnard believes the shift in emphasis has long been needed, citing the gap between the physician's knowledge of drugs and the high number of unfavorable drug reactions suffered by patients both in and outside the hospital.

Said one Baltimore pharmacist:

> I think the program is a good idea as far as theory goes, but I don't think doctors want to give up any of their powers. We're under the doctor's thumb and we're limited in what we can do.

Historically the pharmacist has been expected to recognize faulty prescriptions, in effect, to cover for a doctor's mistake. Moreover, he can beget further indebtedness by referral of patients and has a ready check on the prescription business as reciprocity.

[16] Earl Richard Quinney, "Occupational Structure and Criminal Behavior: Prescription Violation by Retail Pharmacists," *Social Problems,* Vol. 11, No. 202 (Fall 1963), p. 181.
[17] Sharon Joiner, "Hope to Remake Image of Corner Druggist," *Bowling Green— Park City Daily News,* An Associated Press Release (October 6, 1971), p. 21.

THE FUNERAL DIRECTOR

When it comes to being a professional, as laid out by Wilensky, the funeral director is classified as doubtful. True, he has gone through the steps; but by most people he is no doubt considered to be primarily a businessman, especially when one is reminded of the cost of the coffin. Still, during the past several years the works of Bowman and Mitford have created a somewhat sustained interest in this occupation which has undergone a metamorphosis of image from cabinet maker to undertaker to mortician to funeral director.

Throughout Bowman's book are found references to the costs of funerals. His studies reveal:

> ...the widespread feeling that costs are much higher than they need be; that undertakers do everything in their power to raise them to the highest possible level; and that the choice by the consumer of the less costly funerals is made difficult and disagreeable.[18]

Elsewhere he notes that it is the undertaker who assumes the right to decide what shall constitute the appropriate level of expenditure "according to the client's station in life and ultimate capacity to pay."[19] High prices have led to consumer efforts to form cooperatives, but in some instances Bowman indicates that "undertaker's lobbies create difficulties for the establishment of the nonprofit groups."[20] On nonfinancial matters, he contends that the limited time involved in the relationship between the funeral director and the bereaved family and the context within which it takes place are not conducive to the operation of professionalism. Put bluntly, "Funeral directing is not a profession."[21]

Mitford's best seller in its foreword dismisses:

> ... (misuse by undertakers of the coroner's office to secure business, bribery of hospital personnel to "steer" cases, the illegal re-use of coffins, fraudulent double charges in welfare cases) ...[as] "not typical of the trade as a whole."[22]

Like Bowman, she presents a case for lower costs reflected in the now defunct V. A. Contract Burial Program which provided a profit for a mere

[18] Leroy Bowman, *The American Funeral: A Way of Death* (New York, Paperback Library, 1959), p. 51.

[19] Ibid., p. 60.

[20] Ibid., p. 131.

[21] Ibid., pp. 85–86.

[22] Jessica Mitford, *The American Way of Death* (Greenwich, Conn., Fawcett Publications, 1963), p. 8.

$250.[23] She mentions a source of rift between mortician and florist in her chapter, "The Menace of P. O." Funeral flowers account for 65 to 70 percent of the floral trade, and although they are at tmes a trial for the mortician, notices to Please Omit Flowers are seen as a possible move toward omitting ministers, music, and "all but the plainest caskets." Morticians are not permitted kickbacks from flower sales and in some states may not own their own flower shops. Fearful too are they that the full floral blanket will advertise for the flowers at the expense of the coffin.[24] Chapter 16, "The Nosy Clergy," presents that profession as an especial nuisance to the director. Bishop Pike feels that the funeral should be a church service rather than one conducted in a funeral home, and a California rabbi, Sidney Akselrad, feels that simplicity should prevail and that one need not "go into debt over a funeral." Mitford refers to Fulton's study which found that "Catholic priests and Protestant ministers view the purposes of the American funeral differently."[25] The priests were concerned with the honoring of "the memory and the body of the deceased." "The ministers, on the other hand, viewed the funeral in terms of the peace and understanding it brings to the survivors."[26] Although priests saw little need for change, ministers stressed the need for less pagan display, less solemnity, and less expense.[27] Such suggestions, if adopted, could greatly affect the finances of funeral directing and concomitantly increase the business emphasis at the expense of professional development.

The funeral director may not consider droll the statement: "You can always trust your undertaker; he'll be the last one to let you down." If one can believe much of what he reads, friend, rest in peace in the knowledge that there are some who, monetarily and otherwise, have let down untold numbers before your turn.

THE LAWYER[28]

The lawyer's behavior is one of perennial concern, for he is seen as one who really knows the rules and therefore stands the best chance of being able to break them with impunity. It thus behooves him to demand of himself and

[23] Ibid., pp. 44–45.
[24] Ibid., Chapter Eight, passim.
[25] Ibid., pp. 196–97.
[26] Robert L. Fulton, "The Clergyman and the Funeral Director: A Study in Role Conflict," *Social Forces* 34 (May 1961) p. 318.
[27] Ibid., p. 319.
[28] The final two professions to be discussed, law and medicine, are treated more or less historically. Such treatment permits a view of the evolution of concern for some questionable practices within these professions throughout the last few decades. However, in fullest candor, it must be admitted that, in terms of sheer simplicity, the chronologic is eminently superior to the taxonomic.

his colleagues special consideration of "that which is expected of a reasonable and prudent man." The profession expects admission only of the qualified, avoidance of stirring up litigation, and representation even for those unable to pay.

In 1935, six lawyers were disbarred for professional misconduct. Commenting on their behavior the judges said:

> Such an agreement, to stand ready to defend future crimes, amounts to an agreement to encourage the agents to go on with conspiracy. It promises comfort to the criminal and makes his pathway as easy and safe as circumstances will permit.[29]

The practice was considered as having been "actual participation in the crime."

A particularly scathing attack on the profession was made by one lawyer who quit the profession "because he couldn't 'take' its ethics." He himself had become "adept in the juggling of facts to suit the pattern I desired." He stated:

> I found that the Canons of Ethics of the American Bar Association were glossy platitudes recited at annual conventions; to the profession at large, they were no more than fences to scale when the jumping was good.[30]

He spoke of the ambulance chaser and the bankruptcy specialist. Of accident litigation, he said, "the present slow shyster-ridden system continues solely because it is far more profitable to lawyers."[31] This criticism sounds much the same as in today's controversy over no-fault automobile insurance.

In frivolity, someone once said that abnormal psychology was a course taught by an abnormal psychologist. Wood's article on lawyers leads one to wonder whether criminal law is that practiced by criminal lawyers. Wood found little difference between criminal lawyers and civil lawyers regarding what matters constituted the basic unethical practices found in criminal law. Criminal lawyers, however, were somewhat more likely to have seen client pressure and uncertainty of fees as conditions contributing to unethical behavior. They also were more likely to have suggested that incompetent personnel and the conviction psychology of the D.A. were factors that contributed to unethical conduct in the criminal court. He also found that the better-educated lawyers were not only more indifferent to unethical practices

---

[29] "Philadelphia Lawyers Disbarred," *Current Notes* (May 1935), pp. 141–42.
[30] Weyland Cross, "Ex-Lawyer," *The American Mercury,* Vol. 52 (February 1941), p. 160.
[31] Ibid., p. 163.

but were no more active than others in joining professional organizations or in serving on grievance committees.[32]

A retired professor of criminal law discussed "the theory that an attorney must try to save *every* client is well established." He indicated that the crooked lawyer will frighten witnesses, bribe jurors, or resort to perjury. The goal of cross-examination was seen as that of destroying testimony, even the truth.[33] He blamed the criminal lawyer "as a protector of the guilty at the expense of truth" for a large part of the annual cost of crime.[34]

According to the work of Reichstein, ambulance chasing is rampant as a form of unethical solicitation. The chaser may be a single lawyer, a firm with an investigator-chaser, or an independent chase-entrepreneur with a network of informants.[35] One value of this practice, however, is to serve the function of ". . . equalizing the balance of power between injured parties and insurance companies by providing the former with legal representation which they might not get otherwise."[36]

Lawyers who are unfavorable toward solicitation cite unfair competition, association with fraud and client exploitation, and concern for "the public's image of the profession."[37] Some who favor solicitation rationalize the practice as a counter to the unfair practices of claim adjusters; some courts apparently concur.

Of considerable current interest is the backlog of cases jamming the courts. In many areas delays have occasioned comfortable and, in many instances, profitable waits for some lawyers. In Pittsburgh the courts have made a breakthrough in negligence cases by reducing continuances and initiating conciliation conferences before the trial date. Very few of these cases now get to the jury. Delays to build inventories of cases, to fit fees into more desirable tax years, and to impress juries have been virtually eliminated. Said Judge Ellenbogen: "Courts cannot be run just for the convenience of lawyers and judges."[38] Elsewhere the jam-up continues, sometimes for "professional reasons," meaning delay until the lawyer's fee has been guaranteed. Plea bargaining is one answer to the problem, but it may carry with it some ills, for example, giving away the defendant's rights, which may exceed the wrongs of delay.[39]

---

[32] Wood, op. cit., pp. 73, 75, 81, and 82.

[33] John Barker Waite, "How Ethical are These Lawyers?" *Readers Digest,* Vol. 71 (November 1957), pp. 57–58.

[34] Ibid., p. 59.

[35] Kenneth J. Reichstein, "Ambulance Chasing: A Case Study of Deviation and Control Within the Legal Profession," *Social Problems,* Vol. 13 (Summer 1965), p. 7.

[36] Ibid., p. 9.

[37] Ibid., pp. 11–12.

[38] Murray Teigh Bloom, "No More Law's Delay," *National Civic Review* (March 1969), passim, p. 106.

[39] Jack Star, "Jam-Up," *Look,* Vol. 35, No. 6 (March 23, 1971), pp. 34 and 39.

Another area of questionable legal behavior is that involving violation of customary rules of procedure. To cope with these actions it has been suggested that those who violate decorum in the courtroom be removed, that any lawyer who deliberately prevents the orderly procedure of the court be removed, that courtroom packing with adherents of defendants be controlled, that courts and bar associations act to suspend or disbar lawyers who engage in unseemly conduct, and that legislation make such conduct a felony.[40]

In this time of confrontation, demonstration, and intimidation, some young activist lawyers appear to be suffering harassment at the hands of some of their fellow professionals. A state bar association accused O.E.O. lawyers of soliciting clients, fomenting demonstrations, and preparing leaflets on consumer boycotts. An O.E.O. investigating team found the charges to be "without foundation."[41]

If the American Bar Association is perturbed about public attention to its members' affluence, its concern was not disclosed by its decision to have the second half of its 1971 annual convention in London. It was estimated that 15,000 American lawyers and their wives and children made the trek by plane and ship. Planned over a span of eight years, it was anticipated that the conventioneers would spend $2.5 million during their one-week stay.[42]

THE PHYSICIAN

The medical doctor, ever high on the prestige list, is, ironically, traditionally more likely than any other professional to be sued for malpractice, perhaps because his is felt to be an easy mark. He must be sensitive to public criticism of rising medical costs which have been an important contribution to the Cost of Living Index, noticeably since World War II. That this condition arouses mixed feelings among practitioners is illustrated in the following excerpt from an overheard conversation.

FIRST PHYSICIAN: Doctor, why don't you get rid of that old Plymouth and get a Cadillac like mine?

SECOND PHYSICIAN: I couldn't do that; my patients would call me an S.O.B.

FIRST PHYSICIAN: They already call you an S.O.B., so you may as well ride in comfort.

[40] Louis Nizer, "What To Do When the Judge is Put Up Against the Wall," *New York Times Magazine* (April 5, 1970), pp. 126 and 128.

[41] Lester Vellie, "The Angry Young Lawyers of OEO," *Reader's Digest* (May 1971), p. 196.

[42] Anthony Collings, "15,000 Americans to Invade London for ABA Convention," *Bowling Green–Park City Daily News,* An Associated Press Release (July 13, 1971), p. 3.

The mass media have played a lengthy role in portraying the image of the physician. In the old cowboy movies, even Ole Drunken Doc won the battle between bottle and professional duty. Today AMA technical consultants help perpetrate an image of competence and, it may be assumed, dedication. Despite the effort at image building (or maybe because of it) Montague reports the AMA opinion survey finding that "respondents had considerably higher regard for their own family doctors than they did for doctors as a group." Further, "people liked their doctors much better than they did the medical profession." In Montague's words, "The AMA has come to be thought of as an unnecessary drag on progress."[43]

Having read the works of Bowman and Mitford, one may momentarily question the credibility of Michelfelder's book *It's Cheaper to Die*. On second thought, however, most expect to die no more than once, but in a lifetime may be subject to repeated fee-splitting, fee-raising, charges for ghost surgery (nonexistent ghost surgery is nonexistent surgery, or minor surgery passed off as major surgery and billed accordingly), and the like. Michelfelder states:

> What anguishes organized medicine, however, is the "sensationalism" [meaning public exposure] accompanying bona fide and legally proved revelations of such things as workmen's compensation shakedowns, rebates, deals with smaller drug firms owned by misbehaving doctors, grand jury presentments on surgery abuses and private hospitals [usually owned by doctors], and unlawful arrangements with medical supply houses, opticians, and laboratories.[44]

In 1943 Seidman wrote of "the racketeers in white who traffic in human lives." He referred to fee-splitting and fee-padding, of abuses in the sale of oxygen and the rental of equipment, of defective apparatus, of referral fees, and of fraudulent bills.[45]

Time subsequently reported that within the year 1,000 of New York City's 16,000 physicians had been convicted of crooked dealing in compensation cases. Steerers, usually lawyers or insurance men, receive kickbacks from the doctor's padded bill.[46]

A 1953 interview with the Director of the American College of Surgeons brought out some ideas about fee-splitting, unnecessary operations, over-

---

[43] Joel B. Montague, Jr., "Medicine and the Concept of Professionalism," *Sociological Inquiry*, Vol. 33 (Winter 1963), pp. 48–50.

[44] William Michelfelder, *It's Cheaper to Die* (Derby, Conn., Monarch Books, 1961), p. 81.

[45] Harold Seidman, "Racketeers in White," *Survey Graphic*, Vol. 32 (August 1943), passim.

[46] "Racketeers, M.D.," *Time*, Vol. 44 (July 24, 1944), p. 54.

charging, and ghost surgery. Fee-splitting was reported as growing, in some cases being legalized to allow appropriate compensation of the family physician. Unnecessary operations were reported to result from "plain dishonest money making," with women as the principal patients. In the case of fees, to prevent overcharges, he suggested that the patient and the doctor reach agreement before the surgery. Ghost surgery, he stated, was largely performed in unethical hospitals, but "the great majority of the hospitals are as clean as a hound's tooth."[47] (What odds would a bacteriologist give on that?)

Through the mid-1950s the theme was pretty much the same: the kickback or referral fee, fee-splitting, the use of feeders, and unnecessary surgery. An article, "Patients for Sale," was well received by the surgeons themselves, or at least by their principal spokesman. A Pennsylvania doctor commented, "We have gilding on the dome and termites in the basement."[48]

In California a committee of physicians undertook to remedy some of the most common complaints. Among other steps, they set up local schedules of fair and reasonable fees; they established a telephone-answering service and an emergency doctor-dispatching program guaranteeing medical care regardless of ability to pay. Similar concern by physicians was reported in *Newsweek*.[49]

By 1958 the doctor-merchant had come under fire. Said *Newsweek* of efforts at self-policing: "Despite this self-surveillance, physicians have sometimes been attacked by their peers as well as their patients for practices labeled 'shady,' 'selfish,' and 'money grabbing.' " The same article commented that in New York there was a tie-up between 1,500 city doctors and a dozen laboratories. The result was estimated to be an added cost of $12 million to patients.[50]

By 1962 the Senate Antitrust and Monopoly Committee had taken more than a passing interest in the doctor-merchant. Its findings revealed 3,000 doctors who owned drugstores, 2,500 ophthalmologists who sold eye glasses, and 5,000 doctors who owned stock in 150 drug-repackaging firms. At least 10,500 of the nation's 2,000,000 doctors were selling products they had prescribed.[51]

---

[47] Paul R. Hawley, "Needless Surgery—Doctors, Good and Bad," *Reader's Digest*, Vol. 62 (May 1953), pp. 53, 54, 56.

[48] Steven M. Spencer, "Patients for Sale," *Saturday Evening Post*, Vol. 226 (January 16, 1954), p. 36.

[49] Milton Silverman, "The Doctors Who Crack Down on Doctors," *Saturday Evening Post*, Vol. 227 (February 12, 1955), pp. 32–33; see also "About Ethics," *Newsweek*, Vol. 52 (June 17, 1957), pp. 98–99.

[50] "Paying the Doctors," *Newsweek*, Vol. 51 (April 21, 1958), p. 106.

[51] "The Doctors Who Profit from Prescriptions," *Consumer Reports* (May 1966), p. 234.

Dr. S. J. Hadfield advised:

> ... a main object and function of a code of professional ethics is to protect the individual from the special advantages possessed by the professional as a result of his special knowledge and training.

"The Conscience of the Doctor" is tested says Dr. Hadfield in those "nontherapeutic situations where clear ethical guidance is not available." He mentions nontherapeutic abortion, contraceptive advice, and sterilization.[52] More and more new developments will repeat the test, for example, surgery before birth, germinal choice, and cloning.[53]

Dr. John Knowles intimated that within 10 more years doctors will be handed over to the government unless some of the AMA's present practices change. He said, "The price of freedom from federal control is responsibility for public interest." He continued:

> Are we asking the doctor to be beyond reproach more than the average citizen? Yes. It's my firm hope that we physicians will be in fact what society has assumed or wanted us to be since time began—above and beyond ordinary human frailties.[54]

Violations, though practiced by a minority, appear to be numerous. Young men who frown on unethical behavior have been known to have difficulty in establishing their practices; some of these same, however, have at least reduced the undesired activities in their localities. Until such time as unethical conduct is considerably reduced, the neologism, Hypocritic Oath, may in many instances supplant the venerated Oath of Hippocrates.

CONCLUSION

This paper is oriented toward occupational deviance and its contents should in no way be construed to imply that more than a minority in any profession are crooked at either the legal or ethical level. The sense of this statement holds as well for practitioners of callings of lesser prestige. However, these minorities are supplemented by a fringe of those who engage in "marginal ethicality." It may be appropriate to paraphrase and question whether the commandment can be interpreted as: Thou shalt not steal except maybe just a little bit.

[52] S. J. Hadfield, "The Conscience of the Doctor," *20th Century,* Vol. 177, No. 1041 (1969), pp. 14, 16.

[53] David M. Rorvik, "The Unborn," *Look,* Vol. 33, No. 22 (November 4, 1969), pp. 75, 83.

[54] John H. Knowles, "U.S. Health: Do We Face a Catastrophe?" *Look* (June 2, 1970), pp. 74, 78.

Harking back to the professions discussed herein, from the standpoint of ethics, what will be the balances sought, what designs rendered, what prescriptions proposed? What cryptic cases will plague those who would seek cures for professional ills?

Given present goals and means, current practices are likely to continue. Persistence of the competition between the business and the professional ethic will probably find mere mortals frequently succumbing to the temptation to serve Mammon. As long as professional attention is poorly balanced between cure and prevention and oriented more toward the dollar than toward service, a favorable climate for professional deviance exists. The presence of interprofessional conflicts and competitions for client loyalty are other potential contributors to that climate.

Clients seeking remedies are understandably sensitive to the treatment accorded them by the professional; had they not already felt some discomfort, they would not have sought help. To forestall any criticism, then, it is incumbent upon the professional to engage in conduct that is above reproach. More specifically, he must do what his code "guarantees": provide competent service at a fair price. Professionals must do their own internal policing or, surely, with loss of public trust, the much desired autonomy will be lost. With that will go the prestige and the professional authority that attracts much of the talent in which so many professionals take just pride.

II

OCCUPATIONAL CULTURE AND PATHOLOGICAL PATTERNS

Habituation, Addiction, and Abnormal Behavior

Many physical diseases are directly attributable to a mode of work such as the pneumoconiosis affecting coal miners; the "caisson disease" of "sandhogs" or tunnel builders; the various respiratory ailments, including lung cancer, often endemic to asbestos workers; and even the "blackjack dermatitis" or skin irritations caused by the green felt table covering which afflicts some gamblers and card dealers. Similarly, physical conditions such as "flat feet," "cauliflower ears," "dishpan hands," or "office pallor," are all obvious references to the dysfunctional residue of occupational specialty.

Practitioners of various occupational specialties often find themselves exposed to relatively unique hazards and subject to equally unique diseases and infirmities as a result of their work routines and requirements. Prostitutes, for example, are subject to "chronic pelvic congestion" as a result of seldom relieving "her pelvic turgescence by orgasm."[1] Prostitutes are also the frequent victims of venereal disease, and one Texas prostitute once sought (unsuccessfully) workmen's compensation payment claiming that "her breast had been bitten by a client."[2] More seriously, some prostitutes are beaten, mutilated, and even murdered by mentally disturbed clients. They simply accept it as an inevitable hazard of the job. One prostitute concluded that, "It's a chance one takes, you know, and if you're going to be afraid you might just as well give it up."[3]

Recently some Italian furniture-factory workers have complained of sex problems, including impotency and lack of sex drive, and blame their condition on the fact of having to work with machine tools that assemble furniture through high frequency electromagnetic shortwaves![4] Air traffic controllers are reported to be particularly more prone to peptic ulcer, diabetes, and hypertension than the general public because of their work stress.

The deleterious influence of work is not confined to physical impact. Military service and combat experiences may lead to "shell shock," or "com-

[1] Charles Winick and Paul M. Kinsie, *The Lively Commerce: Prostitutes in the United States* (New York, The New American Library, 1972), p. 69.
[2] Ibid.
[3] Ibid., p. 68.
[4] "Anti-Sex Machines," *Parade* (October 1972), p. 7.

bat psychosis," while the stressful routine and the frenzied demands of big business may lead to "executive stomach," neurotic disorders, or nervous breakdown. The dull monotony of industrial work has also been shown to be associated with a generalized mental *malaise.*

One's occupational specialty may not only be a significant contributive factor in regard to specific patterns of disease, injury, or addiction, but may also actually influence or even determine the circumstances and mode of one's demise. The person who drives a great deal in connection with his work may be more prone than average to a fatal accident. The naval captain may "go down with his ship," and the policeman may be gunned down by the criminal he seeks to apprehend. The coal miner may end his life entombed alive in a caved-in mine shaft, and the combat infantry soldier may meet his fate in an exploding land mine. The very routine of a man's work may condemn him to a particular form of death.

Work may affect its practitioners in other dysfunctional ways, too. The disaffective aspects and discomforts of certain kinds of work may drive individuals into pathological coping behavior and habituated practices that are physically and mentally erosive. Concomitantly, the subcultural behavioral demands of an occupational system may well engender degenerative addictive habits and perverted inclinations as normative patterns.

Alcohol, narcotics, even sexual perversion may be intimately related to, if not the direct causal result of, specific work specialty. Such pathological patterns may appropriately be viewed as arising from several characteristics attendant to particular occupational systems. Each work specialty has its own peculiar discontents which can be resolved or endured perhaps in an equally unique fashion. The options available to the individual in such a circumstance may be conveniently prescribed, even if only by the inherent informal structure, or offer an extremely limited array of coping techniques for individual exercise of choice, all of pathological flavor. Every work specialty houses a unique opportunity structure for pathological behavior, and both the formal and informal system may tend to motivate and facilitate the actualizing of this opportunity structure. Finally, the occupational subculture provides indoctrination and socialization as well as reinforcement and reward for such deviant patterns, rendering them seemingly relevant and functional as well as sanctioned.

Occupational specialty may, in some instances, also tend to drive one to self-inflicted death. Studies have shown a differential incidence of suicide among different occupations. For example, suicide is disproportionately high among attorneys, dentists, physicians, brokers, commission salesmen, and prostitutes.[5] Obviously, such a differential incidence of suicide suggests that

    [5] P. H. Blachly, H. T. Osternd, and R. Josslin, "Suicide in Professional Groups," *The New England Journal of Medicine,* Vol. 268, No. 23 (June 6, 1963), p. 1280.

a variety of occupational motivating and facilitating mechanisms are operant.

Much occupationally related suicide occurs, however, not out of a normative expectation associated with occupational role, but as the end result of some dysfunction or disaffection attendant to the occupational structure and routine. Some individuals, prostitutes for example, may pursue occupational specialties that are degrading or tend to erode the self-image of the practitioner.

Suicide is related to mental disorders. As one group of researchers put it, "We want to emphasize that investigations indicate that virtually all persons who commit suicide are psychiatrically ill. . . ."[6] Alcohol and narcotic usage are related to suicide as well. The same researchers point out: "It is well known that alcoholism is a factor in about 20 percent of suicides."[7] Occupational stresses and opportunity structure may precipitate alcoholism or narcotic addiction. The addicted behavior may be symptomatic of a depressed or disordered mental state, or the behavior may produce the psychiatric conditions. Suicide, as a subsequent development to alcoholism or narcotic addiction, would be an indirect outcome of occupational factors. Inasmuch as suicide represents a violation of social, religious, and legal norm, it must be considered deviant behavior.

WORK AND ALCOHOL

A limited few occupational specialties such as brewmeisters in breweries and whiskey "mixers" and "tasters" in distilleries may be required to imbibe as a constituent responsibility of their daily work routines. Similarly, the "B-girl" may have to drink (or pretend to drink) some form of diluted alcohol as an inducement to the bar patrons to purchase drinks.

Many individuals in other occupational specialties find that alcohol consumption is an unavoidable component of their daily work. For such occupational practitioners, drinking is only informally, but nevertheless inexorably, related to their jobs. Diplomats often discover, for example, that their duties include a seemingly never ending cycle of cocktail parties and alcoholic receptions at other embassies and at the homes of other diplomats. Everyone attending such functions is not absolutely required to drink, of course, but not to do so would be "undiplomatic." The beer salesman, as another example, when calling on a proprietor in his establishment, by custom may be impelled if not compelled to stand a round of his own product for the customers present and may have to quaff one himself to present a convincing image of the irresistibility of his company's beer.

[6] Ibid.
[7] Ibid., p. 1281.

College textbook salesmen must make the circuit of professional conventions at which they man the book stalls where their company's wares are on exhibit. As a collarary task, they frequently must be hosts at cocktail parties for their academic clientele, and at these gatherings the bookmen may have to participate in the imbibing to contribute to the sociability of the occasion. But book salesmen are by no means unique. Salesmen of all varieties often find that customers have to be "persuaded" and that for this purpose Ogden Nash was correct in his assertion that "candy's dandy, but liquor's quicker." Salesmen, sales managers, and sales executives often find that they have to drink with their customers. Some sales managers maintain well-stocked bars in their own offices for this purpose.

Work forces many individuals into routines and work patterns that are uncomfortable, demanding, or disaffective. The traveling salesman or agent must be "on the road," away from home, family, friends, and community for days on end. A motel room in a strange town is a lonely and monotonous place. In such a situation a salesman may drink to relieve the loneliness and boredom. Alternatively, however, he may seek companionship and conviviality in the motel bar. For some individuals who work under the demands of an exhaustive pace, alcohol may be necessary to relieve tension. Others may need the drink to "keep up the pace." Individuals who are forced to work early (and often cold) hours may need a "nip" to take the chill off. Some persons work in isolated and thus lonely settings and may also take a drink to alleviate their solitary discontent. Some work may be exciting, stimulating, even exhilerating and thus require alcohol as a mind sedative. Other work may be monotonous and stultifying and necessitate alcohol as a stimulant. Still other work may be so frightening or foreboding as to dictate alcohol in way of preparation. Historically, gin was issued to Dutch mercenary troops before battle to stiffen their combat resolve—hence the derogatory phrase "Dutch courage."

Many individuals who must face the public and perform find that they sometimes need alcohol to alleviate stage-fright or first-night jitters, or to simply "loosen" them up for their act and help them be more amusing or charming. Show business is reputed to possess an occupational subculture that includes alcohol as a major institutional component. The "beautiful people," it is said, interact over cocktails, celebrate over champagne, relax over beer, and reflect over brandy as part of the normative pattern. A number of movie, television, and broadway celebrities are notorious for their heavy drinking, and some well-known stars of the past and today such as Lillian Roth and Dana Andrews are admitted alcoholics. Some show business personalities have used alcohol to face "identity crises" in connection with their abrupt successes and similar problems with the fading of success and the decline of career.

The strains of work that contribute to heavy drinking would appear to be as varied as they are intense. A short time back it was reported that a police officer in San Francisco was granted a retirement with $1,161 per month disability pay because of alcoholism. His claim, supported by a psychiatrist, was that his alcoholism resulted from heavy drinking in which he indulged as a means of relieving emotional stresses he experienced because of "public hostility toward police."[8]

IMBIBING IN EXECUTIVE SUITE

It has been estimated that of the seven million alcoholic Americans, more than three million are "working" alcoholics, holding down a job.[9] These persons attempt faithfully to stand behind the machine or counter or sit behind the desk or wheel, even if in an alcoholic fog. The alcoholic worker may frequently miss work, be hungover and thus less efficient, and even on occasion be drunk on the job. His presence may be mildly disruptive, but not necessarily critical to a production schedule. His high visibility, moreover, makes it easy to identify and remove him. The alcoholic executive constitutes a proportionate, if not disproportionate, share of the alcoholic working force. While under the influence of alcohol, such an alcoholic may make a corporate decision that may have repercussions for months and even years and the financial ramifications of which may involve millions of dollars and the very economic success or failure of the company. Alcoholism among executives is quite expensive to his firm. The problem-drinker executive may be working at only 20 to 30 percent of his capacity. Frequently he is between 35 and 50 years of age—potentially his period of greatest value to the company. The executive works in a job where drinking is often a normative pattern. The three-martini lunch may, for example, be *de rigueur* for business discussions. The office bar may be a standard fixture, and an afternoon cocktail with a client or fellow-executive from another firm may simply be a routine demand of the job. Even as a leisure pattern, the executive moves in a social world of alcohol. For him the cocktail party, the champagne reception, drinks at the club, and weekend parties where alcohol is served are all simply part of his existence.

The first reading in this part, Paul M. Roman's "Settings For Successful Deviance: Drinking and Deviant Drinking Among Middle- and Upper-Level Employees" is an examination of excessive drinking among big business executives. As he points out, our stereotype of deviant drinking is often one of a lower-class activity and the deviant drinker is "driven to drink by forces

[8] See "Forum NewsFront," *Playboy,* Vol. 20, No. 1 (January 1973), p. 55.
[9] Susan Margetts, "The Staggering Cost of the Alcoholic Executive," *Dun's Review,* Vol. 9, No. 5 (May 1968), pp. 32–34.

beyond his control" and thus his excessive drinking is involuntary. In actuality, however, even heavy drinking is institutionalized for some segments of our population, especially the middle- and upper-middle classes. Cocktail parties, and weekend entertaining with alcohol provide a means of "unwinding" and, as Roman puts it, a "rewind" for the next week of work. Drinking may thus be pragmatically justified, and excessive drinking at the upper levels becomes essentially "successful deviance."

Roman advances the thesis that successful deviant drinking among executives may be explained by four factors that "have their base in occupational roles and the structure of work organizations": banks of conformity, occupationally adaptive drinking, cover-up opportunities, and exploitive relationships in work organizations. The so-called work-addicted executive in a sense "super-conforms" and thus generates "huge deposits" in his "bank of conformity." The executive with his freedom to overwork thus "earns" the right to "cut loose" occasionally in his drinking behavior. He can be "excused" for his deviant drinking behavior and can accordingly escape social sanctions.

The executive role is demanding and tends to generate tension with the attendant dysfunctional effects on job performance and energy expenditure. Heavy drinking as a tension release and relaxing activity may accordingly be functional to the executive and in effect take the place of a hobby.

Although the worker or lower-status employee may experience work tension in a manner similar to that of the executive, he does not possess the cover-up opportunities the executive does. Generally speaking, the higher up the bureaucratic hierarchy the executive climbs, the higher the degree of privacy and control of his own immediate circumstances he obtains. Even at home the executive enjoys privacy and insulation not often available to the person of lower occupational status. The business executive has the time, opportunity, and privacy to drink heavily without detection or sanction.

Finally, Roman suggests that in hierarchial work organizations one's success depends on climbing to the next level of the structure, thus most bureaucratic persons are particularly attentive to the behavior of their superiors. In the instance of the superior involved in a pattern of heavy drinking, the subordinate may move to "help" the superior by protecting him and assuming more of his work and responsibilities and thus making his superior more and more dependent on him. The executive, in a sense, becomes exploited by his subordinate, but because of dependence on alcohol cannot escape the "exchange" relationship with his subordinate. The subordinate, in turn, covers up for his boss because he stands to profit personally.

The problem drinker at work is by no means confined to either the worker or executive levels. Some studies have shown that perhaps one out of every 50 employees is a problem drinker.[10] Between the executive and the factory operative are a great variety of occupational specialties whose occupants have differential tendencies toward problem drinking and alcoholism. The so-called occupational "risk factors" Roman and Trice have suggested are related to the absence of supervision and low visibility of job performance.[11] Alcoholism or excessive alcohol use may then be partially a function of job structure and work routine.

HABITUATION BY THE NUMBERS: OLIVE DRAB DRUNKS

The American military establishment, with almost two and one-half million members, stands as perhaps one of the larger work systems in our society. It may also harbor one of the larger concentrations of work-related alcoholism and problem drinking. The Pentagon itself estimates that there are between 50,000 and 225,000 alcoholic servicemen in its ranks.[12] The actual number, of course, may be considerably higher inasmuch as the informal structure of the military, if not the formal structure of the military itself, tends to shelter alcoholism. The alcoholic military individual is often tolerated and "carried" by his peers and not infrequently by his superiors. If drinking reaches a level that is overtly dysfunctional to the military mission, however, punishment of the offending individual has traditionally been prescribed. Recently, a newer and more enlightened attitude on the part of military authorities prescribes treatment.[13]

In my article in this section, "Olive Drab Drunks and GI Junkies: Alcohol and Narcotic Addiction in the U.S. Military," I address the problem of pathological habituation patterns in the armed services. Military culture, in the U.S. as in most nations, is an occupational subculture where alcohol occupies a prominent normative position. Military authorities have often viewed alcohol as contributive to the accomplishment of their mission and developed elaborate mechanisms to insure the availability of alcohol to members of the service. Alcohol is usually available inexpensively and conveniently through formal channels. When not readily available through formal means, access is assumed through informally institutionalized clandestine means. Alcohol serves as a device for coping with the strains and anxieties of military life and also plays a significant ceremonial role in

[10] Harry Levinson, "Alcoholism in Industry," *The Meninger Quarterly*, Vol. XI, No. IIIA (1957), pp. 1–21.

[11] Paul M. Roman and Harrison M. Trice, "The Development of Deviant Drinking Behavior: Occupational Risk Factors," *Archives of Environmental Health*, Vol. 20 (March 1970), pp. 424–35.

[12] "Drydock for Sailors," *Time*, Vol. 100, No. 10 (September 4, 1972), p. 59.

[13] Ibid.

military life. Informally, the military subculture socializes the newcomer into patterns of heavy alcohol usage, reinforces, sanctions, and thus perpetuates such patterns. Patterns of extremely heavy drinking appear to be endemic to the military establishment and a signal illustration of pathological behavior arising out of the structural aspects of work.

WORK AND NARCOTICS

Although it is not generally well known, Sherlock Holmes was a junkie. Sir Arthur Conan Doyle saw fit to have his fictional super-sleuth hero be a sometimes narcotic addict. In one of the Holmes adventures, for instance, Doyle writes:

> Sherlock Holmes took his bottle from the mantelpiece and his hypodermic syringe from its neat morocco case. With his long, white, nervous fingers he adjusted the delicate needle, and rolled back his left shirtcuff. For some little time his eyes rested thoughtfully upon the sinewy forearm and wrist, all dotted and scarred with innumerable puncture-marks. Finally he thrust the sharp point home, pressed down the tiny piston, and sunk back into the velvet-lined armchair with a long sigh of satisfaction.[14]

Holmes, it appears, fluctuated back and forth between morphine and cocaine, and the account in question goes on to suggest that he was addicted at this time to the extent of requiring some three injections of a seven-percent cocaine solution each day. As a chemist, he would, of course, know of the physically deleterious effect of such drug usage and in fact, Doyle lets him admit this. He has Holmes state, for example:

> I suppose that its influence is physically a bad one. I find it [cocaine], however, so transcendently stimulating and clarifying to the mind that its secondary action is a matter of small moment.[15]

Holmes goes on to explain to Watson that his mind "rebels at stagnation." He must have mental stimulation and challenge at any cost. He seeks "mental exaltation." He apparently had not found full satisfaction of these needs in his chemistry work, for he points out to Watson that it is in fact because of the "dull routine" of his existence that he created for himself a unique "professional" specialty—that of "unofficial consulting detective."

[14] Sir Arthur Conan Doyle, "The Sign of the Four: Chapter 1, The Science of Deduction," *Famous Tales of Sherlock Holmes* (New York, Dodd, Mead & Company, 958), p. 171.
[15] Ibid., p. 172.

Unfortunately, his cases were more infrequent than his constitution could tolerate, and accordingly, he sought his "mental exaltation" via a hypodermic needle.

Many persons in the entertainment industry often live lives markedly different from others. The nature of their work requires that they travel frequently, spend only short periods of time at one booking, often work very late hours in comparison to other occupations, and are under considerable work tensions and intense anxieties for short periods of time, usually just before and during their performances. Because they are isolated socially they often become group isolates from the mainstream of community life and are thrown heavily upon their own group resources for support and approval. In many instances the entertainer is relatively immune to community control since except when he is performing he is effectively out of sight and thus out of reach. However, because he is thrown back largely on his own informal colleague group for primary response and approval, he finds himself subjected to relatively intense peer-group influence and control. In effect he becomes socialized into and exists in an occupational subculture of distinctive content and highly effective subcultural mechanisms of informal control.

Charles Winick, in an article published some years ago, suggests that certain kinds of persons in the entertainment field are especially prone to use narcotics.[16] Winick reports a relatively high incidence of narcotic usage among jazz musicians. A significant percentage of his jazz musicians reported some frequency of heroin usage, and more than one-half reported at least occasional use of marijuana (in today's more permissive times, an even larger percentage may smoke marijuana).

Various forms of narcotic addiction, as with alcoholism and other kinds of habituated and abnormal behavior, are apparently intimately related to occupational patterns and culture. Work with its inordinate influence on our routines, our perspectives, and our values not infrequently exerts pressure and effects motivation to indulge in behavior and practices that may relieve tensions and anxieties, moderate disaffections, and frustrations provide additional motivation and invigoration, afford escape and insulation, enhance and reinforce existing skills and capabilities, and contribute to a closer relationship with and sensitivity to colleagues and co-workers. Narcotic use and addiction is one such practice.

HABITUATION BY THE NUMBERS: GI JUNKIES

The military represents an occupational system with a long historical association with alcohol and narcotics. The waging of war and the duties of

[16] Charles Winick, "The Use of Drugs by Jazz Musicians," *Social Problems,* Vol. 7, No. 3 (Winter 1959–60); pp. 240–53.

the conqueror impose special pressures and mood requirements on those involved, and accordingly, alcohol and narcotics are used to insulate, moderate, or ameliorate the pressures or to effect mood or mental-state modification. Narcotics have also been used as a means of medical treatment for wounds and illnesses and to alleviate pain and fatigue. Alexander, Xerxes, and the Caesars all had medical personnel who marched with their legions, and presumably the medical troops had and administered narcotizing substances. However, truly effective narcotics were not widely used as anesthetic substances until the nineteenth century. In the wars of the 1800s medical treatment, which had advanced scientifically and technologically far beyond the previous century, nevertheless was still primitive by today's standards, and perhaps more importantly, was agonizingly slow in reaching the wounded soldier. A soldier might lie wounded on the battlefield for many hours if not days and then have to endure long painful journeys back to hospitals behind the lines and then have to wait for treatment at the hospital. The use of narcotic drugs relieved the agony of the wounded while they awaited treatment. In most instances treatment was minimal, inadequate, and largely ineffective. Many wounded soldiers had such residual health problems and discomfort after treatment that narcotics had to be continued for months and sometimes years. For many veterans of our earlier wars, such as the Civil War, narcotics became a way of life. As pointed out in the article "Olive Drab Drunks and GI Junkies," soldiers even today are often introduced to narcotics through military medical treatment for wounds and either never effectively dislodge the dependency or revert to drugs at some later date. Furthermore, the opportunity structure for narcotics in the military is unusual among occupational systems. In addition to the vast stores and varieties of narcotics to be found in the military medical services, an abundance of narcotics is often quite freely available in the regions where military personnel are stationed. Many servicemen were initially introduced to narcotics in one form or another as a result of their contact with the cultural patterns of the people in these foreign countries. Drug usage among servicemen may be viewed to some degree as a form of experimental cultural diffusion. Perhaps most important, however, is the fact that, just as alcohol use and subsequent dependence among military personnel in the past often grew out of a subculturally institutionalized pattern of drinking to relieve boredom, frustration, and fear, narcotic usage among servicemen has more recently become equally institutionalized and reinforced by the informal values operant in the subculture. Soldiers today smoke marijuana and in some instances use heroin because it is the informally accepted mechanism for tension release, the alleviation of boredom and anxiety. The military serviceman has occupationally generated motivation to indulge in drugs. He is exposed to and socialized in their use through his occupational experiences. The military occupational system affords him ample opportunity structure for his drug supply, and he obtains reinforcement and encouragement for his drug use from the informal values and practices of his occupational peer group.

HARASSED HEALERS AND CHEMICAL RESPITE

Drug addiction like most deviant behavior is not evenly distributed among the population. Specific deviant patterns are often more characteristic of particular age, sex, social-class, or occupational groups, to name a few variables. The physician is no exception to the factors that combine in some instances to precipitate and perpetuate specific forms of deviant behavior. In our society, with an opiate addiction rate of one in 3,000, government narcotic authorities estimate that perhaps one in every 100 physicians is an addict.[17] Furthermore, the addiction rate of physicians in other societies seems alarmingly high also. In England, for example, it has been reported that physicians account for "17 percent of that country's addicts."[18] Clearly the occupational structure of medicine and the subcultural millieu in which the physician works must be contributing factors to the high narcotic addictive rate reported among this occupational group. As Winick has put it:

> A substantial incidence of addiction among physicians has been reported from several other countries, suggesting that there may be something about the physician's role, independent of his nationality, which is related to his use of narcotics.[19]

Physicians, perhaps more so than in many other occupational specialties, endure particularly onerous stresses attendant to their routine and the nature of their work itself. These stresses begin in medical school and include lengthy, expensive, and difficult training and the deferment of a wide range of gratification. After beginning practice the physician still faces a grueling and emotionally demanding work schedule and a variety of personal and professional problems encountered in trying to play his occupational role.

Winick's study suggests that physicians use drugs as a means of coping with overwork, physical ailments, insomnia, marital problems, and to deal with depression and other kinds of job-related stresses.[20] Apparently medical

---

[17] Charles Winick, "Physician Narcotic Addicts," *Social Problems,* Vol. 9, No. 2 (Fall 1961), p. 174.
[18] Ibid., p. 175.
[19] Ibid.
[20] Ibid., p. 180.

students also turn to drugs, but more usually marijuana, in coping with some of their stresses.[21] Nurses also tend to use narcotic drugs in greater incidence than the general public.[22]

The physician then often has ample motivation for a "crutch" in the face of the stresses and conflicts with which he must cope, but alcohol is inappropriate because its use is usually obvious, and often its effect is debilitating. As one physician addict put it, "You can't walk into an operation reeking of liquor on your breath," and "alcohol makes you fumble."[23] Narcotics, however, are not so obvious and in many instances do not necessarily reduce the effectiveness of one's performance, at least at a nominal level. In some cases narcotics might even improve professional performance by alleviating fatigue or anxieties, bolstering self-confidence, or *at least appear to the individual to improve professional performance.*

One might assume that physicians, knowledgeable about drugs and their physiological and psychological effects, would accordingly be "too sophisticated" to indulge in narcotic usage regardless of the pressures and motivation; yet physicians often feel that their knowledge of drugs and physiology permits them to use drugs and stop when they wish. They could, in effect, "control" their use of drugs. According to one physician, "I thought I'd toy with it because I knew enough about it to inhibit its reaction and control its use."[24] Physicians are apparently selective in their choice of narcotics. They often tend to use meperidine, codeine, or morphine rather than heroin or cocaine as do the "street addicts." These are, of course, normal medical drugs and thus more readily accessible, but perhaps more importantly, such medical drugs are often deemed to be "less addictive and less toxic" than the conventional narcotics, and presumably this also helps maintain the self-image of not being an addict. Some doctors apparently prescribe medical narcotics for their own ailments and thus conceptualize the drugs as "treatment."

Some researchers have suggested that narcotic addiction is a function of knowledge about drugs and an obvious opportunity structure.[25]

Accessibility to drugs, while obviously a contributing factor in narcotic addiction is by no means the overriding condition. Pharmacists—who also

[21] Lawrence K. Altman, "Survey Finds Many Medical Students Use Marijuana," *The New York Times* (November 1, 1970), p. 80.

[22] See Edward R. Bloomquist, "The Doctor, The Nurse, and Narcotic Addiction," *GP*, Vol. 18 (November 1958), pp. 124–29; also Solomon Garb, "Narcotic Addiction Among Nurses and Doctors," *Nursing Outlook*, Vol. 13 (1965), pp. 30–34.

[23] Winick, "Physician Narcotic Addicts," op. cit., p. 181.

[24] Ibid., p. 180.

[25] See A. R. Lindesmith and John Gagnon, "Anomie and Drug Addiction," in Marshall Clinard (ed.), *Anomie and Deviant Behavior* (New York, Free Press, 1962), pp. 158–88.

have access to narcotics (perhaps more access) and can better cover up their illegal use since they control the dispensing records—demonstrate a far lower incidence of addiction than do physicians. One pair of researchers have addressed themselves to this discrepancy and have suggested that the professional training of the pharmacists perhaps makes them more sophisticated concerning drugs and the effect on the body than physicians but less knowledgeable in the area of intravenous injection techniques. The pharmacists are accordingly more likely to take an ingestable drug with narcotic properties than an injectable one.[26] The injectable drugs are more closely controlled and scrutinized and the pharmacists are better informed on the matter of control and drug law enforcement. They avoid detection by avoiding the injectable drugs, which are also more likely to be abused and to be addictive. According to these researchers, the assumption about low addictive rates among pharmacists may not necessarily be valid, but rather through a selective use of drugs they can better avoid detection and better control their drug use patterns.

Physicians are often detected by checks of prescription records, being reported by wives or nurses, or by close scrutiny of their treatment routines in a hospital by narcotic agents. When detected, unlike the "street addict," physicians may not be arrested or prosecuted. They may have to surrender their narcotic tax stamp, may have to submit to treatment or demonstrate abstinence for a period of time, or may have their medical license suspended or revoked. In many instances physicians are able to effect drug abstinence and return to practice, but they also encounter the same problems and stresses that originally precipitated their drug use and subsequent addiction.

The selection on occupationally related drug usage is Richard M. Hessler's "Junkies in White: Drug Addiction Among Physicians." Surveying the literature on narcotic usage among physicians, he points out that the addiction rate among doctors may be 100 times higher than among the general public. Compared to other addicts, physicians start their drug career later in life and tend to be addicted to drugs more pharmacologically dangerous than the conventional heroin or morphine. Physicians, it would seem, tend to have inadequate "awareness of the addiction hazard" of drugs such as meperidine. Hessler also suggests that the lack of judgment on the part of physicians may be related to the traditional "uncritical" acceptance of drugs in general long characteristic of the medical profession. Physicians usually have the economic resources to provide for their addiction (and get

[26] Paul R. Elmore and Larry Cohen, "Addiction Among Pharmacists and Physicians." Paper presented at the Pacific Sociological Association Annual Meetings, Anaheim, California, April 1970.

the reduced medical price for legal narcotics to boot), and if they can avoid detection, can usually continue to enjoy a lucrative medical practice.

In view of the envious social and economic position of the doctor and his intricate and accomplished medical skills, it is difficult to accept the idea of near-endemic narcotic addiction patterns in the profession. Given the almost incredible stresses and demands placed on the physicians in our society with its preoccupation with health and well being and its near worship of the practitioners who attend our health, it is perhaps not surprising to learn that even physicians also require brief respites from the burden of their work, even if the respite is of a chemical variety.

DEGENERATE PATRONS AND SYMPATHETIC FEMALES

Some occupational settings afford opportunities, tolerance, and seclusion for the exercise of other forms of deviant proclivities—deviant sexual practices and perversions—that are similar to those that enable military men, big business executives, and physicians, as examples, to indulge their deviancies. Some forms of sexual deviance are significantly related to occupational factors. Large-scale prostitution is especially associated with the military. As Winick and Kinsie have put it:

> The usual increase in prostitution during war is a reflection of many changes in social life. Lack of the restraints of living at home and a desire to emulate peers may lead many men in uniform into contact with prostitutes. Being thrown together with a number of other men in a situation that stresses manliness and a search for relaxation after the rigors of bivouac, combat, or a sea voyage, are among the factors related to servicemen's interest in prostitution.
>
> The imminent possibility of death seems to lead many participants in a war to feel that they ought to enjoy themselves while they can....[27]

Creative occupations such as show business, design, or literary activities might seem to attract, encourage, and support persons with a decided experimental bent in their sexual inclinations. Sex and even sexual perversion becomes something of a "tool" or mechanism of social and career mobility in some of the creative occupations. Many a starlet and aspiring actor have found that the career ladder may often be climbed faster via the "casting couch." Presumably the industry exploiters, those who effect the "sexual ripoff" of the aspirants, are not infrequently members of the same sex as their victims.

In two female occupations—prostitution and stripping—lesbianism is apparently not uncommon. Some researchers have suggested that lesbian

[27] Winick and Kinsie, op. cit., pp. 215–16.

activity among prostitutes is essentially a reaction to their basically degrading and unsatisfying relationships with their clientele. Winick and Kinsie have suggested, for example:

> Prostitutes may develop lesbian relationships because they distrust men and find it easier to develop affection for women. Lesbianism may be appealing to prostitutes who get tired of a continual round of men and turn to their colleagues for relaxation and a sentimental relationship after work. A woman with a strong personality and another who is submissive may develop a relationship based on their complementary needs. Men are ultimately paying the bills for such liaisons, adding a dimension that heightens the pleasure afforded by the relationship itself.[28]

Apparently lesbianism among prostitutes constituted a nuisance to brothel madames even at the turn of the century. One madame who retired in 1917 reflected:

> The girls make or break a house, and they need a solid hand. You had to watch out for Lesbians among them, and while I didn't mind the girls doing a bit of chumming and doubling up, if I found a dildoe, I knew it had gone too far. Girls that become libertines with each other don't satisfy the johns because they are involved with themselves.[29]

Much of the literature suggests that lesbian tendencies in a woman are relatively well fixed at least by the time of adulthood.[30] Such a line of reasoning would accordingly lead to the conclusion that if there is a relationship betwen lesbianism and occupational factors, it is the occupation attracting the lesbian rather than producing her. It is difficult to imagine, however, the confirmed lesbian being attracted into occupations like prostitution or stripping where the major emphasis is on serving men. Certainly there is little if any evidence to suggest that women become strippers or prostitutes "to get even with men," or to express hostility to men. In some instances they go into either occupational pursuit because of men, either to support a husband or boyfriend, because they like the attention of men, or because the

---

[28] Winick and Kinsie, op. cit.

[29] Stephen Longstreet, *Sportin' House* (Los Angeles, Sherbourne Press, 1965). Quoted in Charles A. McCaghy, James K. Skipper, Jr., and Mark Lefton, *In Their Own Behalf: Voices From the Margin* (New York, Appleton-Century-Crofts, 1968), p. 158.

[30] For overviews of lesbian behavior see William Simon and John H. Gagnon, "The Lesbians: A Preliminary Overview," in John H. Gagnon and William Simon (eds.), *Sexual Deviance* (New York, Harper & Row, 1967), pp. 247–82; also William Simon, "Femininity in the Lesbian Community," *Social Problems,* Vol. 15, No. 2 (Fall 1967), pp. 212–21; and Charlotte Wolff, *Love Between Women* (London, Gerald Duckworth and Co., 1971).

work seems "glamorous" and economically rewarding and may have residual benefits of attracting men. The disillusionment, it seems, comes later.

In the last article in this Part, McCaghy and Skipper argue that lesbianism can perhaps be viewed as arising out of facilitative and encouragement mechanisms inherent in occupational structure. In their "Lesbian Behavior as an Adaptation to the Occupation of Stripping," they examine the occupational structure of stripping and conclude that the "structural characteristics of the occupation contribute to the incidence of homosexual behavior." In their opinion homosexuality "is an important facet of the occupation," in spite of the fact that more than two-thirds of the individuals in their sample were or had been married.

Strippers become social isolates because of their hours and the places where they work, not to mention the social stigma attached to stripping. Furthermore, they operate with a female peer group, some of whom are lesbians, and thus they encounter cultural permissiveness toward and support, if not pressure, for lesbian practices. Strippers, like prostitutes, often become disillusioned with their male clientele and men in general. Strippers have sexual drives, but when faced with the prospect of exhausting and exploitive sexual liaisons with men, some strippers will instead seek the embraces of sympathetic females with whom, in the words of one of the respondents, "You can lay down on the floor, relax, watch TV, and let her do it."

5. Settings for Successful Deviance: Drinking and Deviant Drinking among Middle- and Upper-Level Employees

PAUL M. ROMAN

INTRODUCTION

Sociologists studying deviant behavior have concentrated their focus on acts of deviance committed by members of lower socioeconomic strata. The bases for this focus are three-fold. First, *official* rates of most types of deviance are highest for the lower socioeconomic classes,[1] often leading to the conclusion that this is the center of the deviant "action." Second, deviants with relatively low social power are much more accessible to the researcher; not only does the ecology of their life styles afford lesser degrees of privacy, but they often lack the sophistication to deny researchers access to their private lives. Third, the higher official rates of deviance and the lesser degree of social power of the lower class imply that social control agents will have greater proportions of lower-class deviants "captive" at any point of time. Many researchers have found it more convenient to conduct their studies of deviance among such easily accessible people instead of wheedling their way into the backstages of deviants' everyday lives. Thus most of what goes under the rubric of the sociology of deviant behavior is really the sociology of lower-class deviant behavior.

Sociologists also have been attracted to lower-class deviants because deviance-processing systems seem to smack of discrimination and social injustice.[2] Although sociology is ideally an objective science, many social researchers have the subtle as well as the not-so-subtle intent of exposing

[1] Aaron Cicourel, *The Social Organization of Juvenile Justice* (New York, Wiley, 1968).
[2] Howard S. Becker, "Whose Side Are We On," *Social Problems* 5 (1967), pp. 212–32.

situations and circumstances of social injustice, with the hope that such exposure will eventuate in social reform. However, the intent of expose can be a rationalization for the convenience and even the excitement of middle-class sociologists' research ventures to the lower-class "other side."[3]

Sociologists have been aware of the fact that high rates of deviance among the lower classes of society may not be truly reflective of the actual distribution of deviant acts within the social structure. Because of their low social power, lower-class people run a much higher risk of becoming labeled as deviants than those from the middle and upper classes. High rates of deviance seem to be consistent with the typical stereotype of lower-class life. In fact, our belief that such rates are "high" may in large part reflect middle-class bias.

Furthermore, being a lower-class person constitutes a deviant status in and of itself. Cherished American values are clearly descriptive of middle-class life. Achievement, success, cleanliness, sophistication in verbally manipulating others, and the possession of an accumulation of material objects constitute symbols of respectability in this society. By definition, those in the lower classes simply have not "made it," and by implication, the poor are defective human beings. Relatively high rates of deviance seem to be consistent with these projected defects. In any event, despite all the blatant clues about the unrepresentativeness of lower-class labeled deviants, the accumulation of data on deviant behavior in the lower classes continues, while data on the middle and upper classes remains relatively meager.

While accepting the fact that the probability of getting "caught" in deviant activity rises sharply as one descends the socioeconomic ladder, high rates of deviance in the lower classes may reflect even another bias in our research efforts. Simmons points out that while we typically view populations of labeled deviants as unrepresentative of the overall distribution of deviant behavior, we have neglected the dynamics of "getting caught."[4] The numerous activities involved in deviating from societal standards have norms of success and failure in much the same way that people succeed and fail at legitimate activities. In other words, the event of being caught and labeled as a deviant marks failure in deviating. Thus, as Simmons points out, treated deviants are not only unrepresentative of all deviants, in social-class terms, but also comprise the group of those who have failed in deviant pursuits. This raises the complex question of whether lower-class deviants are simply sloppier and less clever in their deviations than their middle- and upper-class counterparts. In any event, research limited to formally labeled populations may not only miss

<hr />

[3] Alvin Gouldner, "The Sociologist as Partisan," *American Sociologist* 3 (1968), pp. 103–16.

[4] Jerry L. Simmons, *Deviants* (Berkeley, Calif., Glendessary Press, 1969).

a considerable number of undetected deviants, but in doing so also totally neglects successful means of deviating.

The focus of this chapter is successful deviants, namely deviant actors from middle- and upper-status levels who may be regarded as relative successes in deviant activities of two types: excessive consumption of alcoholic beverages and regular use of alcohol in the work setting, behaviors that are generally prohibited in American society or which *are supposed to* generate negative sanctions when repeated on a regular basis. My focus is upon the social contexts of these types of deviant drinking behavior among those in the middle- and upper-status levels of work organizations. It is not unlike many other explorations of deviance at these status levels in that I lack systematic data on causes and consequences. However, a series of research activities in work organizations as well as consultations, participant observations, and analysis of one set of relevant survey data have provided me with a series of hypotheses about the prerequisites for "successful" performances of these deviant activities.

THE STEREOTYPE OF THE DEVIANT DRINKER

As background for our discussion, consider the social definitions of deviant drinking in American society to see how these definitions reflect American value orientations. For a variety of reasons, many Americans appear to associate chronic excessive drinking with the stereotype of the Skid-Row bum, the pathetic wino who has rejected society and has been rejected by society. He is pitied to a certain extent, but he is also viewed as bothersome, sometimes even as dangerous, and his habitat is regarded as a blight in most urban centers in America.

A range of efforts to educate Americans about the alleged epidemic proportions of their drinking problems have redefined alcohol abuse from a moral to a medical problem, while rejecting the validity of the Skid-Row stereotype. This has led to the introduction of a second image, the "sick" alcoholic. Probably because most people have encountered problem drinkers within their family or social circles, the reality of problem drinking beyond Skid Row appears to be widely accepted. Furthermore, the definition of the excessive drinking of our friends and relatives (or ourselves) as a "medical problem" presumably reduces the social distance between us and them, and increases our willingness to "do something" about them. But the stereotype of problem drinkers as "sick" may be as inaccurate as the notion that all alcohol addicts are Skid-Row types.[5]

---

[5] Samuel Wallace, *Skid Row as a Way of Life* (New York, Harper & Row, 1968).

The "sick" stereotype of deviant drinkers is supported by a variety of forces in American society; its assumptions obviously make the notion of "successful" deviant drinking difficult to comprehend. The medical definition that underlies this stereotype holds that the excessive drinker does not enjoy drinking, that he is caught up in an inevitable disease progresssion and driven to drink by forces beyond his control, and that if these forces could be controlled, he would cease drinking. This stereotype is supported by the overall negative image that generally characterizes alcohol, other drugs, and sources of "pleasure" in American society. The idea that the deviant drinker could want to engage in such behavior and find pleasure in doing so is totally inconsistent with this view. Nonetheless, while it is certainly true that many years of excessive drinking can produce physiological addiction and loss of control which make the drinker truly ill and truly miserable,[6] current evidence would indicate that chronic heavy drinking does not inevitably eventuate in alcohol addiction,[7] implying that many drinkers are not miserable or ill during lengthy periods of regular heavy drinking.

Regardless of this evidence, there is no doubt that the disease definition of problem drinking fits with and supports the anti-hedonism of American culture. At the same time, the disease definition serves to cover up numerous instances of successful deviant drinking. American emphases on personal achievement and self-control have always supported an intense anti-hedonism. Sex and alcohol stand alone as pleasures that have become institutionalized in American society, in the sense that opportunities for both are legitimately provided and negative sanctions for such activities are generally withheld until "intemperance" is evident. Despite institutionalization, sharp societal ambivalence remains. Our current multi-faceted obsession with sex reflects in part our concern that pleasure might be enjoyed without being earned. We appear to have adapted our Calvinistic heritage so that pleasure, much like salvation, is not a birthright but rather must be purchased via good works: occupational achievement, shoulder-to-the-wheelism, and acceptance of "costs"—marriage and children. Lewis and Brissett have pointed to another dimension in our management of pleasure, namely redefining it as work.[8] According to these writers, standards of performance and excellence have become to be associated with sex, converting it into a work-like activity involving scheduling, selection and placement, and performance appraisal. The magazine *Playboy* illustrates the purchase of pleasure, with its articles not-so-subtly emphasizing that the playboy's achievements, as reflected in his

[6] William McIlwain, *A Farewell to Alcohol* (New York, Random House, 1972).

[7] Don Cahalan and Robin Room, "Problem Drinking among American Men, 21–59," *American Journal of Public Health* 62 (1973), pp. 1473–82.

[8] Lionel Lewis and Dennis Brissett, "Sex as Work," *Social Problems* 15 (1967), pp. 8–18.

housing, clothes, and investment skills, are the symbolic gateway to payoffs implied in the centerfold. Current concerns over promiscuity among teen-agers may be another reflection of this accounting process. Although phys-ically able and equipped with contraceptives, adolescents have not earned the right to sexual pleasure. Consequently, while adolescent sexuality is con-demned on the basis of fears of venereal disease, illegitimacy, or moral con-fusion, a major basis for its rejection by adults may be a sense of distributive injustice: Adolescents are getting something for nothing.

Although alcohol use has been a part of American society since its found-ing, sharp ambivalences over the use of the substance remain,[9] reflecting anti-hedonism in a manner similar to sexual attitudes. The acceptable use of alcohol is usually attached to a "pragmatic justification." Thus, persons in American society "earn" their right to use alcohol. Evening cocktails and weekend drinking are seen as useful "unwinding" to reward the individual for work completed and "rewind" him for work ahead. Cocktail party drink-ing is usually accompanied by pragmatic justification. Hosting cocktail parties, as well as attending them, stand as symbolic elements for the enhance-ment of status and the maintenance of ongoing social exchange relationships. Many cocktail parties are deliberately arranged as pragmatic settings in that they provide occasions for new acquaintances and the enhancement of soli-darity within established acquaintances, both of which may set the stage for subsequent instrumental activities.

Obviously these pragmatic justifications are more widely available to persons in the middle and upper classes than to those in the lower classes. Such "justified deviance" can be seen as "successful deviance." Opportunities for such deviance likewise appear to increase with rising social-class level. Finally, the definition of excessive drinking as an illness allows for more effec-tive coverup of chronic excessive drinking in the middle and upper classes be-cause "impairment" is more ambiguous and difficult to define.

The coincidence of justifications, opportunities, and ambiguities set the stage for "successful" deviant drinking. Because most known problem drinkers are male and the cardinal status of most males is centered around work, it is appropriate to set our focus on occupational roles and the structure of work organizations. In this chapter we explore five work-based factors that form the basis for successful deviant drinking as well as successes at other types of deviant behavior: banks of conformity, occupationally adaptive drinking, coverup opportunities, exploitive relationships in work organizations, and ambiguity in the definition of impairment. Although our concern is primarily with the operation of these factors within the context of occupational and

---

[9] Seldon D. Bacon, "The Classic Temperance Movement of the U.S.A.," *British Journal of Addictions* 62 (1967), pp. 5–18.

organizational life, their effects may be generalized to the overall context of middle- and upper-class culture in American society.

BANKS OF CONFORMITY

A generally neglected fact in explanations of conforming and deviant behavior is the "bank of conformity," which may be drawn upon for idiosyncrasy credit."[10] Social status levels imply the existence of different "deposits" in banks of conformity. Furthermore, through their own behavior and independent of social class, individuals can increase or decrease the levels of deposits in their own "accounts."

Knowledge of a person's social class provides an observer with rough expectations regarding conforming or deviant behavior. Knowledge of lower social status is accompanied by greater expectations for deviance, an expectation that may decline as one moves up the social-class ladder. This "built-in" differential in expectations for deviance explains in part differential "basic deposits" in banks of conformity. Middle- and upper-status persons, by the very fact of their class placement, have conformed to the basic valued goals in Amerian society. Their status implies that they are hard-working, diligent, clean, generally thrifty, and generally prudent. The implications of lower-class status are somewhat the reverse; thus initial or basic deposits in banks of conformity are greater for middle- and upper- than for lower-status persons.

Furthermore, middle-class norms and mores dominate American society, one indication of the social power possessed by this class. Since the normative system is styled to accommodate the middle-class mode of life, opportunities for deposits in banks of conformity are greater for middle-class than lower-class people. Thus, the middle and upper classes are ascribed greater initial deposits in banks of conformity as well as greater opportunities for ongoing deposits.

Deviant behavior involves a "withdrawal" against existing "credit" in one's bank of conformity. The important part of this analogy is that the greater the size of the deposits, the greater the degree of permissible deviance. Thus persons who work hard, accumulate achievements, and generally conform to the everyday amenities of society are permitted to engage in deviant behavior on occasion without sanction. There are, of course, sharp limits on this tolerance, but the limits are definitely related to the size of the deposits. The important point is that deviance by middle- and upper-status persons

---

[10] Edwin Hollander, "Conformity, Status, and Idiosyncrasy Credit," in E. Hollander and R. Hunt (eds.), *Current Perspectives in Social Psychology* (New York, Oxford University Press, 1967), pp. 465–76.

may be tolerated because of their ascribed conformity to cherished American values and goals. This tolerance manifests itself particularly in regard to first-time occurrences of deviance. Whereas the lower-status individual may be immediately sanctioned for an initial act of deviance, middle- and upper-status persons are invariably given second chances. Looked at more bluntly, this differential in tolerance reflects the relative value of individual role performances in the eyes of the persons exercising social control. Recognition and labeling of deviance often requires social exclusion and isolation, either for "treatment" or punishment. Lower-class role performances are more often viewed as "expendable" than middle- and upper-class performances. This indicates that deposits in a bank of conformity are only a partial explanation for tolerated deviance; others' perception of the impact of the deviance on their welfare also plays a role.

Our research on deviant drinking in work organizations has revealed some extreme but illustrative instances of how banks of conformity may operate. Here it is obvious that deviant drinking is more apt to generate a sharp reaction if committed by a lower-class worker. Ordinary conformity to norms may yield an adequate "deposit" to prevent a middle-class individual from being sanctioned for an initial deviant act. Thus middle- and upper-class workers have an ascribed "edge" in terms of their chances of committing an act of deviance which is tolerated, and they have more chances for deviating before action is taken against them. But it is possible to overconform and even "super-conform" to cherished norms and values. Such behavior can produce huge deposits in banks of conformity, providing the individual with a range of opportunities for deviance as well as placing him at considerable risk for repeating the behavior to the point that he becomes a chronic deviant.

This phenomenon of super-conformity to output norms in work organizations may be described as "work addiction." The work addict not only works to excess in contrast to everyone else, but he takes on every additional responsibility that anyone can think to ask of him; he arrives at the office long before others and leaves long after everyone else; he takes home work nearly every evening; he works through weekends; and he refuses to take a vacation.

While the term *addiction* may be unfortunate, the concept is descriptive since this obsession with work clearly parallels the obsession with alcohol or heroin among these respective addicts. Some observers further the addiction analogy by arguing that such individuals will suffer "withdrawal" if forcibly removed from work—when excessive input into the job begins to take its toll in terms of physical health and the individual is either hospitalized or forced to take a rest. One widely quoted case describes a work addict who was forced to take a vacation for health reasons and subsequently committed suicide.[11] We emphasize, however, that the extent and consequences of work addiction remain a matter of speculation at present.

The constricting notion of addiction may be unnecessary when this behavior is considered from a role-set perspective. The status of the adult male in the middle- and upper-middle classes in American society carries a wide range of role expectations that are often in conflict with one another. Three basic areas of role responsibility may be delineated: work, family, and community participation. Attempts to perform all these roles adequately not only require a massive amount of time and energy, but the more one attempts to meet all demands, the greater the potential for conflict among expectations. Being a successful husband and father may lead to neglect of work responsibilities; full attention to work responsibilities may lead to neglect of home and family; meaningful participation in community affairs may likewise run into conflict with work and family-based expectations. The classic demonstration of these conflicts is the harried executive who comes home after a long day at the office to be faced with a long list of breakdowns of the physical and interactional equipment of the family and household. After trying to put out these brush-fires, he finds himself faced with coaching a Little League baseball team, attending a Kiwanis meeting, followed by a session of the Board of Deacons. The potential toll of such conflicting pressures is obvious.

Work addiction is a potential means for minimizing and sidestepping these conflicts. The individual who throws himself headlong into his job and whose job-based achievements rapidly accrue may find himself relieved of other responsibilities. Since the occupational role is central for the adult male in American society, attention to this single role is generally acceptable; by contrast, obsession with family or community responsibilities at the expense of work responsibilities may define one as a failure in the eyes of significant others.

The extent to which work addiction is accepted and even valued in American society is well illustrated by descriptions of various "cultural heroes" that regularly appear in the mass media, especially news magazines. An inspection of the descriptions of the daily activities of highly successful businessmen or government officials invariably describe them as working from 12 to 18 hours a day at their offices, bringing work home at night, sleeping five or six hours, and rarely, if ever, engaging in hobbies or other leisure activities. If the work addict does have leisure-time pursuits, they are typically carried out in an obsessive manner that bear close resemblance to his work patterns,

---

[11] Harry Levinson, "Who Killed Bob Lyons?" *Harvard Business Review* 41 (1963), pp. 127–43.

for example, he has a stamp collection valued in the millions, and he jogs ten miles per day. Although the published biographical descriptions generally include a listing of the individual's family, it can be inferred from the descriptions that the individual has little, if any, time to devote to them or to other nonwork activities. This inattention to the family is generally assumed to be a fair price for the prestige and monetary benefits accruing to family members living in the shadows of the great man's glory. If these descriptions can be regarded as indicative of society's standards for success, there is no question that obsession with work has become a highly valued and acceptable behavior.

How does work addiction relate to successful deviance? The work addict who continues to accrue achievements and whose activities become highly valuable to his work organization may inadvertently provide himself with opportunities for deviance, especially deviant drinking behavior. Those who are close to the work addict are clearly aware of the excessive energy that he puts into his job and the tensions that accumulate from these efforts. Thus, significant others, both at home and at work come to regard him as having earned the right to "cut loose." His excessively large deposits in the bank of conformity allow him to engage in excessive tension-release drinking without being socially sanctioned. Because of his overconformity to standards of achievement, others around him have little basis for intervention. He is clearly a success, and in most instances is much more successful than his significant others. Thus, his super-conformity produces opportunities for "excused" deviance. He himself may view these occasions of excessive drinking as totally justified earned rewards. Work addiction not only may generate tensions that make alcohol attractive but also can comprise a risk for the development of regularized patterns of sporadic excessive drinking or other deviance in which few if any outsiders feel that they have the legitimate right to intervene.

Work addiction is limited to executives, professionals, and independent workers. Low-status employees are actively prevented from working beyond the agreed-upon hours, unless unusual pressures require overtime. Furthermore, because of the nature of many work groups and the clear-cut output standards, the blue-collar work addict will often suffer sanctions as a "rate-buster." A lower-status person may become a work addict through setting up his own business or taking on a second job. Excessive deposits in banks of conformity may create justifications in the eyes of his family and subsequent opportunities for deviance that are similar to those described above, although the blue collarite cannot assume tolerance of his deviance among his supervisors or work associates.

Thus middle- and upper-middle-status persons are not only ascribed greater idiosyncrasy credit but generally have much greater opportunities to build up banks of conformity that subsequently allow for deviant behavior. This deviance may be inconsequential in the sense that it never gets out of control and destroys the individual's functioning. However, the use of banks of conformity in this manner clearly creates risks for developing regularized patterns for deviance; once deviance becomes routine, successful intervention may be extremely difficult.

OCCUPATIONALLY ADAPTIVE DRINKING

The observation that alcohol use can be functional and serve to maintain personal and social stability is a taboo topic. However, observations of drinking behavior among upper-status personnel of work organizations thoroughly illustrates some of these adaptive functions. In other words, the nature of middle- and upper-class work roles increases the likelihood of integrating deviant drinking with job performance that is judged by others to be adequate or even superior.

A study of members of Alcoholics Anonymous showed that a considerable number of them reported they had experienced upward mobility in their jobs during the middle stages of their becoming addicted to alcohol.[12] Subsequent observations indicated that the use of alcohol for tension release can definitely be functional in promoting occupational success. For example, the pattern of combined excessive drinking and work addiction may represent functional alcohol use as long as the use of alcohol does not significantly curb work performance.

Work life generates tension.[13] Tension accrues from role ambiguity, from competitive relationships, and from the simple overloading of high-level personnel with too many tasks. Such specifically job-related tensions are probably least prevalent among lower-class workers who usually show the least job involvement. The need for tension release is recognized in American culture, but the openly accepted avenues for obtaining such release generally do not include alcohol. "Social drinking" is permissible, but it is rarely defined as oriented toward altering one's mood or mind. Tense individuals are encouraged to obtain relief through leisure activities, which ironically often take on the trappings of a "second occupation." Thus Americans are encouraged and even required to "keep score" in their leisure activities in much the same way that they keep score of their occupational success. A successful camping enthusiast is one who can cover the greatest amount of territory in the shortest period of time. A successful golfer or tennis player is the one who wins. The

---

[12] H. M. Trice, "The Job Behavior of Problem Drinkers," in D. Pittman and C. Snyder (eds.), *Society, Culture, and Drinking Patterns* (New York, Wiley, 1962), pp. 218–34.

[13] Robert Kahn et al., *Organizational Stress* (New York, Wiley, 1964).

successful home gardener is the one who can grow enough to distribute fruits and vegetables to all his friends and relatives as well as filling his cellar and attic with enough canned goods to carry several hundred people through the winter.

The fact that tension release can be obtained through simply becoming "out of it" through the use of alcohol or drugs is privately recognized among Americans but never publicly acknowledged. Occasional and even regular events of heavy drinking can serve to reduce tensions and relax individuals, perhaps more efficiently than some occupation-like hobby. Because of the nature of work roles in the middle and upper classes, characterized by high deposits in banks of conformity and greater coverup opportunities, such tension release drinking will more likely be occupationally adaptive among upper-middle class and upper-class workers. In other words, while the lower class worker may obtain relief and escape through drinking, this behavior will much more likely have a visibly adverse effect on his work.

Such tension-releasing drinking can be either an individual or group activity. Drinking for tension release in private circumstances is probably much more prevalent than group drinking for the same purposes, but private drinking is risky if it becomes public knowledge: "He drinks alone!" Many Americans unwind and free themselves from the tensions, pressures, and depressions of the workday through systematically but partially removing themselves from reality on evenings and weekends ("climbing into my Martini"). Such drinking need not take the form of wild drunkenness and need not produce a hangover that leaves one bedridden. Persons in the middle and upper classes who are regular users of alcohol generally have knowledge (gained from experience) about their drinking limits in terms of the maximal effects that can be obtained without social disruption and without the creation of severe hangover (the degree of hangover that does not interfere with work performance is probably the lowest in the "working class").

Escape through drinking may be extremely functional when one is putting in a heavy energy investment in daily work activities. The expectation of rewarding escape at 5 o'clock allows one to endure stress. While alcohol has been stereotyped as a "demon" that can quickly gain control over its user, observation would tend to substantiate the fact that many persons who are driven toward occupational success can drink excessively but in a controlled fashion in such a way that they are able to obtain both occupational benefits and alcohol-generated relaxation that helps them "keep going." Surely many lose control of their drinking or decline in their ability to perform, beginning their drift toward the category of "unsuccessful" deviants. But not everyone ends up this way, although again the imagery created by the disease model would try to convince us that this is the case. Recent data from a national survey of drinking behavior among unlabeled individuals indicate that a substantial number of people drink heavily without significant interference with their role functioning.[14] Nonetheless, adaptive drinking where reliance is exclusively placed on self-control is risky.

Fewer risks obtain in circumstances where systematic tension-release drinking is carried out in group settings. This type of adaptive drinking is generated by shared work circumstances where the contingencies of loss of control over drinking are collectively recognized. My observations of graduate student drinking patterns clearly illustrated this phenomenon where work-based tension led to group-based tension-release drinking which had the ultimate effect of enhancing the achievements necessary for completion of degrees.[15] The anticipated "pay-off" of degree completion was a strong motivating factor that prevented the pleasures of alcohol from gaining control.

Certainly there are other work-based situations with similar degrees of tension and similarly high investments on the part of role incumbents wherein excessive drinking comes to serve adaptive functions. The greatest risk involved in such adaptive drinking occurs when such individuals subsequently experience occupational mobility. In other words, individuals who develop patterns of adaptive heavy drinking where they are relying upon social controls exerted by drinking groups risk personal loss of control should social controls be removed. For example, when the graduate student who drinks heavily to relieve tension completes his degree and enters a teaching position, he may find that the controls previously exerted over his drinking behavior by his peer group are now absent. College teachers usually have an excessive amount of freedom in setting their hours of work and a very low degree of direct supervision over occupational performance: role-based opportunities for relatively invisible deviant behavior. Most young college teachers are under intense pressure to establish reputations, to "prove" themselves and, in general, work very hard. When the social controls that previously held potential deviance in check disappear, definite risks emerge. The risks associated with this particular profession may be generalized to other work circumstances where mobility from one job to another involves a continuation of opportunities for deviance but a reduction in the built-in social controls often found in peer drinking groups.

For those who have been found to experience upward mobility in their occupations when they were doing some of their heaviest drinking, alcohol is an effective tension release during extremely stressful periods of the career. They work extremely hard during the day or throughout the week and then relieve their tensions through alcohol at night and on weekends. For a con-

---

[14] Don Cahalan, *Problem Drinkers* (San Francisco, Jossey-Bass, 1970).

[15] Paul M. Roman, "The Future Professor: Patterns of Drinking among Graduate Students," in G. Maddox (ed.), *The Domesticated Drug* (New Haven, Conn., College and University Press, 1970), pp. 204–18.

siderable time, this tension release is effective in "rewinding them" for more work activity, but for some loss of control over drinking occurs. Such loss of control appeared to occur when the stresses *declined* and the need for control was reduced, which was particularly highlighted in cases of occupational obsolescence.[16] The cases on which Trice's study was based were all members of Alcoholics Anonymous indicating that excessive drinking ended in "failure" as a deviant activity. All such adaptive drinking does not end in the disaster of alcohol addiction. Such adaptive drinking may illustrate "successful deviance" and that opportunities for such behavior are greater in the middle and upper classes because of the structure of occupational activity.

COVERUP OPPORTUNITIES

Stress is not the sole property of middle- and upper-status workers. Release from tension may be equally or more essential at lower-status levels, but adaptive drinking becomes problematic or even impossible in the absence of coverup opportunities.

As urbanization becomes a more omnipresent fact of modern life, the possession of "territory" and control over that territory has become closely correlated with socioeconomic status.[17] Privacy signifies prestige, which has reward value and many implications for lifestyle and behavioral opportunities.

One of the main differences in housing across socioeconomic strata is the amount of space in a given dwelling, which of course prescribes opportunities for privacy; numerous rooms, private entrances, protected yards, individually assigned garages and thick walls differentiate the expensive apartment or townhouse from the relatively cheap dwelling. Thus, in these terms alone, opportunities to engage in deviance without being caught are a function of the degree of space a particular individual can control. An individual living in a large house or apartment whose boisterous behavior cannot be heard or viewed by his neighbors is much less likely to be sanctioned for his deviance than the individual living in a crowded slum or cheap apartment house where sound travels easily.

Thus, the less space controlled by the given individual, the greater the probability that his deviant actions will disrupt the activities and the "peace" of others, leading them to initiate negative social sanctions. The variable of controlled space not only affects the degree to which one's deviance is disruptive to the activities of uninvolved "outsiders," but may also explain the

---

[16] H. M. Trice and James A. Belasco, "The Aging Collegeian: Drinking Pathologies among Executive and Professional Alumni," in Maddox, op. cit., pp. 218–34.

[17] Robert Sommer, *Personal Space* (Englewood Cliffs, N.J., Prentice-Hall, 1969).

degree to which an individual's deviance jeopardizes relationships within his own household. "Close" household living arrangements clearly set the stage for the classic family-based conflicts precipitated in the lower class when the head of the household comes home drunk, that is, he "beats up" the wife and children. Rather than attributing such events to unleashed latent hostility, the setting, which forces other family members into close interaction with the inebriate, may be a more appropriate explanation. The proximity to the deviant sharply increases chances of social friction. Such risks are considerably lower in the large house where the consequences of deviant activities need not affect all household members.

Privacy and control over a given territory are likewise directly associated with status levels in work organizations. Generally speaking, the higher the position in the organizational hierarchy, the lower the degree of direct supervision, and the greater the amount of territorial control. Common laborers typically work under the direct and steady eye of a foreman or supervisor. Middle-level clerical workers usually have unexpected visits by supervisory personnel at least once a day. In some situations, the on-the-job behaviors of lower-status employees are open even to the view of the general public.

Top executives, by contrast, may have an office suite comprising several rooms, sometimes including eating and sleeping facilities. Entrance into executive suites is typically closely controlled by a series of screening agents; one may have to pass through several reception rooms and "pass muster" by several guardians before actually encountering the executive himself. Thus the privacy involves not only the assignment of space but also controlled access to the space. A total outsider to a particular organization could probably deduce the organizational hierarchy by simply being provided with measurements of the office space accorded to different individuals. The privacy enjoyed by upper-status personnel clearly provides opportunities that are not available at lower levels in the system. The employee who can close or even lock his office door works in a much different structure of opportunities for deviance than the individual who is physically surrounded by his co-workers, supervisors, and the public.

Two additional physical features of upper-status positions may greatly increase cover-up opportunities. First is freedom of movement on the job. Most upper-status personnel can simply absent themselves from their offices without elaborate explanation on the pretense of visiting a field site, meeting clients, or other outside business. Because supervision is typically indirect in these positions, opportunities for physical mobility can be combined with drinking occasions and go undetected for a considerable period of time. Second is the freedom to set work hours. This may be particularly true in positions presumably involving some degree of creativity. Top management may not care when or where the individual does his work, just so long as the job is done. Freedom of scheduling clearly provides little or no opportunities for others to observe deviant drinking activities.

These opportunities may be summarily labeled *physical visibility*. Control over space and access to that space allows for considerable deviance. Not only does such privacy minimize the viewing of deviance and its consequences, but it also infers that such deviance has little chance of directly interfering with the ongoing activities of others. Such interference would probably be subtle and slow in coming to light, such as the delayed impact of impaired decision-making or deteriorating public relations directly caused by excessive job-related drinking.

SOCIAL VISIBILITY AND IDENTIFICATION OF IMPAIRMENT

A somewhat different type of opportunity-related visibility is found in performance appraisal, interdependence of job performances, and uniqueness of job requirements.

The ease with which job performance can be evaluated and job impairment detected is usually associated with status level: The higher the occupational level in the organization, the more ambiguous the criteria by which adequacy of performance can be judged. Middle- and upper-level executive roles are frequently centered around decision-making activities. An executive's performance cannot be evaluated by counting the number of people he sees in a given day, the number of letters he writes, or recording the length of his telephone conversations. If he is performing inadequately, the effects of deviance on work performance may not become visible for a considerable lapse of time. Herein we see the effects of varying *social visibility* on deviant drinking opportunities.

The degree of interdependence of job performances is another aspect of social visibility that varies across different jobs and may offer different opportunities for deviant drinking. In some work systems performance of one job is unequivocally contingent upon the completion of other jobs. The assembly line is the paradigm of total interdependence of job performances, although many white-collar "paper-processing" systems have nearly the same degree of interdependence. Executive positions vary in their degrees of interdependence, although it is generally much lower than that obtaining in lower-status positions. Interdependency of executives may however be unpredictable, viz. the circumstances where one executive suddenly needs marketing data or sales figures to deal with an unexpected problem with a client or when the sudden need for an evening meeting emerges. These unpredictable interdependencies can effectively expose deviant drinking activities if adequate precautions are not taken.

A related determinent of social visibility is that some jobs in an organization may involve such unique skills that no one in the organization is capable of evaluating a particular performance. This becomes particularly marked in organizations dependent upon complex technology. No one knows how long it *should* take to come up with a solution to a particular problem when they do not possess the problem-solving skills. While such one-of-a-kind positions can occur anywhere in an organization, unique *and* highly complex jobs will more likely be found in the upper echelons. To a considerable extent all executive positions have this one-of-a-kind quality, although the degree of performance feedback varies.

Persons in executive positions simply have greater opportunities for deviance because of factors that reduce social visibility. Our research has indicated that upper-status deviant drinkers are clearly conscious of these opportunities and aware of the possibility that they might get "caught." One of the distinguishing differences between upper- and lower-status deviant drinkers in work organizations lies in their absenteeism patterns.[18] Low-status deviant drinkers simply do not appear on the job when suffering from severe hangover or when under the direct influence of alcohol. Should they appear on the job, the facts of their deviance would become clear-cut, and the probability of negative sanctions may rise to 100 percent. Upper-status deviant drinkers tend to show up at work no matter what shape they are in, producing what we have labeled "on-the-job absenteeism." The privacy afforded them by their positions usually allows their deviance to go undetected. The pivotal point is that failure to appear at work might put the executive in jeopardy whereas physical presence (but psychological absence) may greatly slow down the possibility of detection of deviance; in fact, his continued presence may buffer the effects of other cues of inadequate performance since it represents accumulations in the bank of conformity. The variation in absenteeism draws attention to a major difference between job levels: Lower-status jobs typically require physical alertness which may be deleteriously and obviously affected by hangover or on-the-job drinking; upper-status jobs have more latitude for psychological lapses.

EXPLOITIVE RELATIONSHIPS IN WORK ORGANIZATIONS

A series of observations of executive and professional personnel who were excessive drinkers indicates that reward expectations of those around them

---

[18] H. M. Trice, "The Job Behavior of Problem Drinkers," op. cit.; H. M. Trice and Paul M. Roman, *Spirits and Demons at Work: Alcohol and Other Drugs on the Job* (Ithaca, N.Y., Cornell University, 1972).

may have borne a causal relationship to their excessive drinking. In other words, the deviance of X may have a payoff for Y, leading Y to encourage X's deviance. Such games have an unusual likelihood for development in the upper echelons of work organizations.

A basic fact of organizational life is a particular hierarchical structure of positions. Rewards, prestige, and power in a particular organization accrue as a function of one's success in climbing the organizational ladder. In most organizations persons pay particular attention to the behavior of those in the level immediately above them since this is often where a vacancy must occur if the lower-level person is to obtain a promotion. Thus a lower-level executive might be quite pleased to observe that several of those in the level above him are "go-getters" and that they are apparently hustling for promotion to the next status level, opening the promotion gate for the lower-level man. It may also be that lower-level executives obtain anticipatory satisfaction when they view clear-cut incompetence at levels above them, implying that such personnel will eventually be removed; the Peter Principle tells us, however, that such incompetence is not only likely, but that anticipation of the incompetent's removal is likewise in vain.

Being the replacement for either an over- or an underachiever may create work circumstances that are peculiarly undesirable. Replacing an overachiever involves meeting standards based on performance, which may require an extraordinary effort to carry out the "normal" requirements of the job. Replacing an underachiever may likewise call for an exceptionally high level of performance. Promotions under such circumstances usually emphasize the need for the new man to "straighten out" the series of problems generated by the previous incumbent's incompetence (who probably retired after having been tolerated for years).

Mobility aspirations may lead subordinates to encourage superiors' excessive drinking so that they may get their jobs. This relationship may involve less-than-subtle blackmail; it may involve a combination of cover-up and deliberately staged drinking opportunities, and it may require the subordinate to manifest aspects of the "Suffering Susan" role[19] so that the superior's eventual deterioration does not come as a total surprise to the powers-that-be when the game is over. The subordinate must cover his cover-up lest his true motives come to light and keep adequate control over the situation so that he does not end up with a dramatic "mess" for which he is ascribed partial responsibility. The overriding principle is that cover-up, rather than detection and whistle-blowing, may be the typical and more rewarding reaction to observed deviance among superiors.

[19] Joan Jackson, "Alcoholism and the Family," in Pittman and Snyder, op. cit., pp. 475–92.

The occurrence of visible excessive drinking by the top executive may create a somewhat different set of opportunities for subordinates. Observations by our research group clearly illustrated how the occurrence of excessive drinking by several company presidents set the stage for their exploitation by subordinates.[20] These observations indicated that knowledge of the top executives' repeated excessive drinking led to their becoming surrounded by a seemingly protective clique of subordinates. These subordinates made extraordinary efforts to "help" the executive carry out the responsibilities of his office as well as protecting and shielding his deviant behavior from others in the organization. Since he was one and they were several (as would be expected at the top of any organizational chart), outright efforts to displace him did not fit the situation; instead his continued incumbency was vital to the system that developed.

These company presidents had apparently developed an "adaptive" pattern of drinking concomitant with their upward mobility; drinking became out of control once full success was achieved and the need for compulsive activity reduced. They had become addicted to alcohol and thus had heavy emotional investments in maintaining their drinking behavior without interference. Subordinates saw the executive's impairment as an opportunity to broaden their own span of control, influence, latent power, and personal profit in the organization. They slowly eroded the executives' power. Although they never obtained the public prestige that would have accompanied a legitimate promotion, their relationship with the executive afforded them a range of opportunities for machinations and personal profit that set the stage for long-run success, perhaps in another organization where the internal knowledge they had obtained in this company could be put to good use.

While this appears to be a case of clear-cut unbridled exploitation, closer examination shows that what had developed between the executive and his subordinates was an exchange relationship. The executive was aware of the erosion of his power, but valued his drinking opportunities so heavily that this erosion was seen as a just price. The exchange became more "locked in" as time went on. The executive became increasingly unable to carry out routine functions; assistance and protection from subordinates became an absolute necessity. Thus, in a sense, both sides gained from the relationship over the short term, although the eventual total impairment of the executive and his forced removal dissolved the relationship, but not before the subordinates had the opportunity to consolidate their gains.

Such exploitive relationships can occur at other levels of the organization as well, but the success of such efforts is again tied to low visibility which is more likely in upper organizational levels. Keeping in mind the

[20] Trice and Belasco, op. cit.

primacy of climbing in organizational life, situations may develop at other levels where subordinates can advance through encouraging the impairment of their superiors. A protective subordinate may be able to maintain the myth of a superior's adequate performance for a considerable period until it is fortuitous to "spill the beans" and seek to replace the superior. Although this cynical formulation offers what appears to be a man-eating conception of intraorganizational relationships, such apparently pathological relationships are often built on a form of exchange where the individual who is finding excessive drinking very rewarding is willing to pay a price for the opportunity to continue his deviance in peace.

A SURVEY OF EXECUTIVES' DRINKING BEHAVIOR

Data from a national survey of 528 middle- and top-level executives in large-scale private companies which were collected early in 1972 provide some verification for notions discussed in this paper.[21] Since this survey was designed to assess attitudes toward company alcoholism policies, it does not allow for testing more than a few of the hypotheses advanced in this chapter.

When the executives are classified in the categories employed in the national drinking behavior of Cahalan et al.,[22] 18 percent of those executives with incomes in excess of $50,000 are "heavy drinkers" in contrast to 7 percent of those executives earning less than $25,000 and 12 percent of the general adult population in Cahalan's national sample survey. Furthermore, only 7 percent of the executives indicated that they were abstainers or infrequent drinkers in contrast to 47 percent of the national sample which fell in these categories. The bulk of the executives (48 percent) are concentrated in the "moderate" drinker category in contrast to 13 percent of the national sample. Thus the executives are much more likely to drink and to drink more than the general adult population. While this certainly does not label them as alcoholics, their environments tend to be more supportive and accepting of drinking than those of the general public. Finally, the data indicate a higher proportion of "heavy" drinkers in the highest income category.

Expression of worry about one's drinking behavior may be an index of both heavier drinking and of the absence of social controls over one's

[21] Paul M. Roman, "Executives and Problem Drinking Employees." Presented at the Third Annual Conference in Alcoholism of the National Institute of Alcohol Abuse and Alcoholism, Washington, D.C. These data were made available to me through the National Institute of Alcohol Abuse and Alcoholism, and I gratefully acknowledge the assistance of Donald F. Godwin. Analysis of the data was supported by National Institute of Mental Health Grant 5-R18-AA00494.

[22] Don Cahalan, Ira Cisin, and Helen Crossley, *American Drinking Practices* (New Brunswick, N.J., Rutgers Center of Alcohol Studies, 1969).

drinking: If one's drinking were regulated by others, personal worry would be less likely. If this reasoning is accurate, the data support the relative absence of social controls among the executives. Seventeen percent reported worry about their drinking in contrast to 9 percent of the national sample. The proportion of those reporting worry about drinking increases with increasing income, with 26 percent of those with incomes in excess of $50,000 reporting worry in contrast to 12 percent of those with incomes less than $25,000. The absence of social controls is further indicated when level of drinking is held constant: While 21 percent of the heavy drinkers in the general sample reported worry, this figure increases to 31 percent among the heavy-drinking executives.

The executives generally showed liberal attitudes toward work-related drinking, with 60 percent approving of drinking at a business lunch and 48 percent approving of drinking during a two-day sales conference. While no comparisons with the national sample are possible here, it would appear that these proportions of approval are much higher than would be found in the general population.

SUMMARY

Returning to Simmon's concept, successful deviant drinking is more likely as one's status in a work organization rises.[23] I quickly add that such successful deviance need not lead inevitably to alcohol addiction, given current evidence on the considerable proportion of problem drinkers who manifest "spontaneous remission" from this behavior pattern without medical or paramedical intervention.[24] Viewed in a different light, I am simply illustrating one more opportunity structure wherein the rich have more chances and more freedom than the poor.

[23] Simmons, op. cit.
[24] Cahalan and Room, op. cit.

6. Olive-Drab Drunks and G.I. Junkies: Alcohol and Narcotic Addiction in the U.S. Military

CLIFTON D. BRYANT

ALCOHOL AND THE MILITARY

Military men drink. They drink off duty and sometimes on duty. They drink often and in quantity and not infrequently do they drink to intoxication. It is interesting to note that a favorite colloquilism synonymous with extreme intoxication is "drunk as a Barbary Coast sailor on shore leave." Alcohol figures prominently in military subculture in our society and in others, now as well as historically. As Vath has put it: "Military customs and tradition make up a large part of military life. Heavy drinking is one such custom...." [1] In a similar vein, West and Swegan, in commenting on the role of alcohol in military culture, have observed:

> In the old days it was traditional for the military men to be a hard-drinking fellow. The lore of the military service is filled with stories about alcohol, its consumption in large quantities, its procurement and concealment, and the various adventures associated therewith. The role of alcoholic beverages in military society was generally accepted and many aspects of social status were influenced by the use of alcohol.[2]

Historically many nations have felt that alcohol was a desirable and necessary item of subsistence and morale and did (some still do) provide for

[1] Raymond Eugene Vath, *The Influence of Military Service on Rates of Alcoholism in the General Population*. A medical thesis presented to the University of Washington School of Medicine, Seattle, 1965, p. 1.

[2] Major Louis Jolyon West and Master Sergeant William H. Swegan, "An Approach to Alcoholism in the Military Service," *American Journal of Psychiatry*, Vol. 112 (1956), p. 1004.

a daily "ration" of some form of alcohol. The British Navy, for example, traditionally issued a daily rum ration to its sailors. Similarly, the United States Navy, at one time, also issued alcohol daily to each seaman in the form of "one gill of grog." A particularly vivid account of the practice of issuing alcohol rations on a man-of-war in the mid-nineteenth century is provided by Herman Melville:

> In the American Navy the law allows one gill of spirits per day to every seaman. In two portions, it is served out just previous to breakfast and dinner. At the roll of the drum, the sailors assemble around a large tub, or cask, filled with the liquid; and, as their names are called off by a midshipman, they step up and regale themselves from a little tin measure called a "tot." No high-liver helping himself to Tokay off a well-polished sideboard smacks his lips with more mighty satisfaction than the sailor does over his tot. To many of them, indeed, the thought of their daily tot forms a perpetual perspective of ravishing landscapes, indefinitely receding in the distance. It is their greatest "prospect in life." Take away their grog and life possesses no further charms for them.[3]

The alcohol ration was of such significance to the sailor that its curtailment could be used as a punishment for violation of naval rules. As Melville further comments:

> It is one of the most common punishments for very trivial offences in the Navy, to "stop" a seaman's grog for a day or a week. And as most seamen so cling to their grog, the loss of it is generally deemed by them as a very serious penalty. You will sometimes hear them say, "I would rather have my wind *stopped* than my grog!"[4]

Today it is against Navy regulations to drink or possess alcoholic beverages aboard ship.[5] Drinking then in theory occurs only on shore leave or liberty. For the armed services of some other countries, however, alcohol continues to be regular issue on and off duty.[6]

---

[3] Herman Melville, *White Jacket* (New York, Grove Press, n.d.), pp. 62–63.

[4] Ibid., p. 140.

[5] This rule is widely violated, especially by officers. Commander Bucher, for example, admitted that he had some whisky aboard the *Pueblo.* In the stage play and movie, *Mr. Roberts,* several of the ship's officers were constantly "manufacturing" whisky (even Scotch, using iodine for flavoring) from the ship's stores of medical alcohol.

[6] Wine is served with meals to some elements of the French Army, particularly the French Foreign Legion. Wine concentrates were airdropped to the beleaguered French troops during the siege of Dien Bien Phu so that the Legionnaires might continue to enjoy their *vin ordinaire* with their daily meals. Shnapps were also parachuted to the German Sixth Army surrounded at Stalingrad during World War II. Curiously enough, the Russian Navy permits its officers to drink in moderation on-

Usually alcohol is readily available to military personnel. If stationed overseas, there are normally copious supplies of indigenous beverages at close hand.[7] In the United States military posts sell alcoholic beverages by the drink or by the bottle at reduced prices because of tax reductions (this is an especially handy practice in "dry" areas). Drinks are dispensed in service clubs, N.C.O. clubs and officers' clubs. Prices are always reasonable, but frequent "happy hours" or "nickel beer hours" further reduce the cost of military personnel. In combat situations the military makes every effort to keep the troops supplied with their alcohol "rations." Even where cut off from normal alcohol channels, American military personnel have proved to be unusually resourceful at manufacturing their own with stills or more frequently concocting drinks from medical alcohol or "torpedo juice." With alcohol readily available and reasonably priced and with the subcultural traditions of alcohol consumption, it is perhaps not surprising that military personnel do drink and often heavily.

The use of alcohol apparently has several important functions that help account for its use (or misuse) by military personnel and the sanctioning of its use under certain circumstances by military authorities.

ALCOHOL AND BOREDOM

Military garrison duty is monotonous, often uncomfortable, sometimes unpleasant and frequently lonely. With nothing to do, nowhere to go, and often nobody (relatively speaking) with whom to do it, drinking becomes an institutionalized way of spending one's free time. "Fun" may have to be vicarious, and conviviality may have to be contrived. Alcohol facilitates these processes. From the standpoint of the authorities, alcohol serves to help solve

---

shore and even to drink white wine with meals while serving with the Black Sea Fleet. However, it absolutely forbids Soviet sailors to drink at all, at sea or on shore; see "Russia: Power Play on the Oceans," *Time,* Vol. 91, No. 8 (February 23, 1968), p. 27. The U.S. Armed Services, while not providing a formalized alcohol ration, do attempt to provide a periodic informal ration in combat situations in the form of cheer for the enlisted men and "Class VI" supplies for the officers. (In addition to the regulation five classes of supplies, officers' whisky is also designated informally as Class VI supplies.) Even informally, issuing alcohol to U.S. troops has often been controversial. During the Korean War, for example, beer "rations" were often flown into front-line units. The W.C.T.U. objected violently to this, however, because it was "corrupting the morals of our boys."

[7] The Arabic countries where alcoholic beverages are forbidden by Islamic law present something of a problem for both military and diplomatic personnel. With typical American ingenuity, however, the problem was solved in one major Middle Eastern country where a still was imported and set up in the American embassy. The Marine guard detachment had the responsibility of running it and the product was used for embassy social affairs and to supply diplomatic personnel and military officers attached to the embassy.

the problem of morale and boredom and helps prevent the buildup of potentially disruptive if not dangerous frustrations.[8]

ALCOHOL AND SEX

The large number of young single males concentrated in the typical military garrison makes it virtually a demographic impossibility for most of them to meet, date, or fornicate with young single females—or any females for that matter. Although many armies attempt to provide prostitutes (some even have prostitute units attached to military units), promote or encourage contiguous prostitution, or at least tacitly tolerate prostitution, this never provides an adequate range of sexual outlets for the troops. Alcohol serves the function of relieving the tension of or blunting sexual drives, acting as a kind of sexual anesthetic, as it were. It may either be a substitute for sex or at least tend to make prostituted sex more acceptable. Alcohol functions to maintain morale from the standpoint of the individual and as a control device from the standpoint of the authorities.

ALCOHOL AND THE TENSIONS AND ANXIETIES OF COMBAT

The horrors of combat are frightening and traumatic to many military men and difficult to live with both in terms of the personal dangers and the distasteful tasks of having to kill and maim, both before and after the fact of battle. Alcohol may prepare the soldier for the rigors of combat and let him deal with the unpleasant memories of combat later.[9]

---

[8] Kipling immortalized the soldier's preoccupation with alcohol while on garrison duty in the lines from his poem "Gunga Din":

You may talk o' gin and beer
When you're quartered safe out 'ere,
An' you're sent to penny-fights an' Aldershot it;

See Rudyard Kipling, "Gunga Din," *Kipling: A Selection of His Stories and Poems,* John Beecroft (ed.) (Garden City, N.Y., Doubleday, 1956), p. 420.

[9] This fact was alluded to by John Dryden in his classic poem "Alexander's Feast":

Bacchus' blessings are a treasure;
Drinking is the soldier's pleasure,
   Rich the treasure,
   Sweet the pleasure,
Sweet is pleasure after pain.

See John Dryden, "Alexander's Feast," *Selected Poetry and Prose,* Earl Miner (ed.) (New York, Modern Library College Editions, 1969), p. 484.

The term "Dutch courage" came from the practice of issuing gin to Dutch mercenaries before battle to give them the necessary "bravery." Vath refers to some military physicians encouraging the use of alcohol as a means of relieving the tensions and anxieties of combat. Vath, op. cit., p. 1.

ALCOHOL AND MILITARY CULTURE

Alcohol occupies a significant ceremonial niche in military culture. Many official military social functions may involve both alcohol and mandatory or pressurized attendance. Examples might be receptions, unit cocktail parties, formal messes, banquets and various military rites de passage such as promotions, retirements, or "prop blasts."[10]

ALCOHOL AND THE MASCULINE MYSTIQUE

The military role is a masculine role. In many cultures drinking may be a component of the male role. A "real" man can "hold his liquor." As Elkin points out: "Drinking in the Army, as in civilian life, was a symbol of virility and facilitated the forgetting of the self and the release of impulses of self-assertion and aggression."[11]

Thus the ability to drink large amounts of alcohol is something of a masculine test and in some ways a test of suitability for the demanding masculine military role. One of the respondents studied by Janowitz, for example, included alcoholic capacity as a requirement for success as a military officer. He states, "A man should be able to tell a good story but should not be a notorious braggart; a man should be able to *drink a lot,* but should not be an alcoholic. . . ."[12]

Military life dictates playing a masculine role and drinking is one of the ways in which the performance can be legitimized. Drinking bouts and sprees among military men may then become something of masculine *rites of intensification.*

An interesting account of the masculine military drinking mystique is found in a popular novel about the Korean War. Here some Marines are discussing Marine Corps heroes and their stories concerning the famous Lew Diamond (a genuine real-life Marine hero) are described as follows:

> Lew Diamond, in the Marine Corps, was a venerated legend; more so than Blackjack Pershing of the Army or two-time Medal of Honor winner in the corps, Dan Daly, who wound up as a guard in a bank.

[10] "Prop blasts" are initiation ceremonies that celebrate the acquisition of jump "wings" after airborne school. For a fuller description see Melford S. Weiss, "Rebirth in the Airborne," Trans*action,* Vol. 4, No. 6 (May 1967), pp. 23–26.

[11] Henry Elkin, "Aggressive and Erotic Tendencies in Army Life," *The American Journal of Sociology,* Vol. 51, No. 5 (March 1946), p. 410.

[12] See Morris Janowitz, *The Professional Soldier* (New York, The Free Press, 1960). This is cited by Vath, op. cit., p. 2. Vath also points out that the image of the soldier portrayed in many novels about the military such as Michener's *Tales of the South Pacific,* and James' *From Here to Eternity* is that of the hard-drinking soldier. Ibid., p. 2.

Lew Diamond, the Marine who was two thousand years old, a powerfully built man with a gray goatee and moustache who lived on slop-chute beer and never drank without his dog Piss Pot Pete right beside him every night of every year, both of them so drunk they had to be carried back to the barracks when the slop-chute closed.[13]

Diamond was a "tough" marine as his drinking "proved."

EFFECTS OF ALCOHOL

Although the heavy use of alcoholic beverages is sanctioned by military tradition and subculture and tacitly approved by military authorities, nevertheless excessive use of alcohol is officially discouraged as Vath describes it:

> Although military tradition favors heavy drinking, the official military policy is one of strong punitive action for drunkenness and alcoholism, especially when these conditions interfere with duty. This is made necessary by the seriousness of the military mission where drunken errors and impaired judgement cannot be tolerated. Compared with civilian law, military regulations prescribe harsh penalties for such behavior as being drunk on duty, being drunk and disorderly, and driving under the influence of alcohol. At times even moderate drinking is prohibited by regulation. SAC forbids drinking by aircrew members 48 hours prior to and during their being on alert. Navy ships are officially dry, and drinking on duty is a serious offense in all branches of the military.[14]

This disruption that alcohol contributes to good order, discipline, and performance is most important to the military. Alcohol abuse contributes to insubordination or disrespect for supervisors or the service and may impede or prevent the discharge of appropriate military role responsibilities. Inasmuch as the military operates in a much more socially and politically sensitive milieu today than in the past and this combined with the technological exigencies of the Cold War render alcohol abuse particularly threatening to today's military mission. As West and Swegan put it:

> The nature of the present peacetime military establishment requires a high level of alertness and a greater degree of individual responsibility than ever before. The irresponsibility that often comes with chronic alcoholism cannot be tolerated in an effective modern military organization. Thus punitive regulations have been evolved which place chronic alcoholism on a par with criminality and sexual perversion, subjecting the alcoholic to discharge without honor as unfit.[15]

[13] Jere Peacock, *Valhalla* (New York, Dell, 1962), p. 51.
[14] Vath, op. cit., p. 2.
[15] West and Swegan, op. cit., p. 1004.

In addition to excessive alcoholic consumption constituting violations of military regulations, heavy drinking patterns are often dysfunctional in other ways. While alcohol is supposed to relieve boredom and keep the men "occupied," in fact it frequently promotes aggressive acts by removing inhibitions and is thus often a factor in fights and brawls as well as the commission of various crimes against persons and property, including rapes and assaults, exhibitionism, thefts, and vandalism.[16]

Military patterns of heavy drinking may also lead to actual alcoholism. Although studies are inconclusive, the patterns of heavy drinking that are part of the culture of military life may be a contributory factor to alcoholism in a man after leaving the military life if not while still a member.[17] According to Vath, because alcoholism is a slowly progressive disease that may not reach the acute stage until late middle age, many potential alcoholics may have simply retired from military life before the onset of the disabling stage of the disease. Since the military exerts considerable control over the behavior of its members, the alcoholic behavior can be "controlled" to a degree while the individual is still in service. In addition, the structure of the military is such that alcoholic patterns can be concealed better than in other work settings. The military can, in effect, "carry" or shelter the alcoholic as long as he is in service.[18] In any event, Vath did find that military veterans have a higher rate of alcoholism than nonveterans on the basis of "their appearance in alcoholism treatment programs in greater numbers than expected from their distribution in the general population."[19] Other researchers have also suggested that military drinking may ultimately lead to alcoholism.[20]

Although military regulations expressly forbid drunkenness and alcoholism in spite of encouraging or at least facilitating heavy drinking patterns,

[16] While acting as Military Police duty officer in the Army some years ago, I had occasion to investigate or process a wide variety of offenses including those mentioned. In the majority of cases, the apprehended individuals were drunk or had been drinking heavily when they committed the offense. Many used the excuse that because of their drunken condition, they had more or less lost control of themselves. For studies of the relationship of drinking to offenses of military personnel, see A. C. Cornsweet and B. Locke, "Alcohol as a Factor in Naval Delinquencies," *Naval Medical Bulletin*, Vol. 46 (1949), pp. 1690–95; also N. Blackman, "The Problem of Military Delinquency: A Statistical Study of 2,142 General Prisoners," *Journal of Clinical Psychopathology*, Vol. 8 (1947), pp. 849–61.

[17] For a detailed study on this relationship, see Vath, op. cit.

[18] An excellent example was the "19-year" private in the recent movie *The Sergeant,* starring Rod Steiger. In the movie this character was an alcoholic "career" private with 19 years of service. His alcoholism had been covered up for years by his peers and superiors in order that he might be able to retire after 20 years and have a small income on which to live.

[19] Vath, op. cit., p. 21.

[20] The literature on military alcoholism is too extensive to list. See, for example, however, J. B. Wallinga, "Severe Alcoholism in Career Military Personal," *U.S. Armed Forces Medical Journal*, Vol. 7 (1956), pp. 551–61.

such behavior in the face of these regulations constitute criminal offenses. Heavy drinking may also in some instances lead to a variety of anti-social behavior that also may constitute legal violations.

NARCOTICS AND THE MILITARY

As with alcohol, there is a long historical association between narcotics and the military establishment. From ancient times until the present, military men, and especially those engaged in actual fighting, have turned to chemical substances to prepare them mentally for the ardors of battle and to sustain them in the monotony of garrison duty. In previous wars, however, narcotics usage by military personnel did not pose a significant problem in terms of extent, although the number of veterans who were addicted was relatively high. The Vietnamese War has produced a military drug problem of significant proportions. Some observers have reported that as many as three-fourths of the GIs there smoked marijuana, and even some official reports have indicated that thirty-five percent of troops used marijuana.[21] A staggering number of military personnel in Vietnam were also apparently "hooked" on or were at least heavy users of hard drugs such as heroin. The problem is not confined to Vietnam. Here in this country there is evidence of a considerable drug problem on our military bases. One Army authority at Fort Bragg estimated that 50 to 70 percent of the men at that base "use marijuana and about 800 to 1,000 are strung out on heroin and amphetamines."[22]

The military has traditionally been able to tolerate heavy alcohol use by its personnel. Alcohol consumption and the subsequent behavior of the drinker could be "controlled" to a degree in the sense of setting firm limits. Furthermore, the recovery from inebriation is relatively rapid. Drug abuse and its subsequent behavior is much more difficult to "control." It is almost impossible to set limits and enforce the limits in terms of narcotic behavior. The recovery from a narcotic state may be slow. For the regular user there

---

[21] Allen Geller and Maxwell Boas, *The Drug Beat* (New York, McGraw-Hill, 1969), p. 148. Interestingly enough, some authorities take issue with the assertions concerning both the extent and seriousness of the drug problem in Vietnam. Szasz, for example, suggests that military addicts are being used as "scapegoats," that the figures on heroin use among troops are being purposefully inflated in a kind of "pharmacological Gulf of Tonkin" manner, and that addicts may be able to function appropriately in many instances. For a fuller discussion of his view, see Thomas S. Szasz, "Scapegoating 'Military Addicts': The Helping Hand Strikes Again," *Transaction*, Vol. 9, No. 3 (January 1972), pp. 4 and 6.

[22] John Lengel, "Army Drug Problem Unique, Stoned Soldiers Do Dull and Dangerous," *Bowling Green–Park City Daily News.* An Associated Press release (Wednesday, April 7, 1971), p. 9.

may be no recovery from the narcotic state. In the last analysis, the military's prime concern is lower efficiency or the inability to perform adequately or to discharge military responsibilities satisfactorily. From the Army's standpoint, for example, the use of marijuana is incapacitating in terms of military duties. As viewed by the Army:

> ... "as a precautionary measure it is recommended that in general for administrative purposes persons may be considered voluntarily incapacitated for duty up to 12 to 36 hours after the use of marijuana, unless otherwise determined by medical or other appropriate authorities that a different time frame should be used in a particular case."[23]

Several years ago in Vietnam, the then Army Provost Marshall expressed his anxieties about GI marijuana smoking. "His biggest concern, though, was his conviction that the brain soaked in pot fumes would be dulled and unable to function in battle."[24]

If the ultimate mission of the military and particularly that of the infantry is indeed to close with the enemy and destroy them, anything that might hinder the attainment of this goal or erode the efficiency with which it is accomplished represents a form of deviance highly dysfunctional to the military system. The military is, however, largely, if indirectly, responsible for the drug abuse in terms of several factors that encourage, precipitate, or facilitate drug abuse among its personnel and are structured into the military system.

NARCOTICS IN MEDICAL TREATMENT

Because of the prevalence of wounds, injuries, and diseases encountered among military personnel, narcotics in various forms play a significant role in the attendant medical treatment. Narcotics are involved throughout the resultant treatment to a much greater degree than in civilian life. During World War II, infantrymen in combat situations often carried morphine syringes in their first aid kits. In Vietnam, the drug problem was such that morphine was not generally issued to the individual soldier. Narcotics will in all likelihood be administered to a wounded man for the pain since there may be a delay in reaching a medical facility. The principal medical strategy of the military is to "maintain" the wounded until they can be transported to a hospital facility with total medical resources. Although the military does maintain relatively complete hospitals, such as Mobile Army Surgical

---

[23] Ray Cromley, "Army Takes Practical and Humane Approach to Drugs," *Bowling Green–Park City Daily News.* A syndicated column in newspapers across the country (Tuesday, January 26, 1971).

[24] Geller and Boas, op. cit., p. 148.

Hospitals only a short distance from the combat area as well as hospital ships, the function of such facilities is to treat wounds of medium seriousness and perform preliminary surgical treatment on the wounded. Every attempt is made to transport the wounded serviceman to more sophisticated hospitals in the United States or in friendly countries. An elaborate system of transportation for the wounded has been developed by the military including helicopter and transport planes and hospital trains. Lengthy narcotic sedation is often necessary during transport of the wounded man and while he awaits intensive treatment. The nature of combat wounds with the attendant physical trauma and the often extensive surgical treatment is such that the individual may require narcotics for a considerable time period. Although every attempt is made to prevent the possibility of addiction, some wounded servicemen do develop a dependence on narcotics which they continue during extended convalescence, after discharge, or reestablish at some later date. After our earlier wars, the American Civil War, for example, when medical authorities were less sophisticated about narcotic addiction, the problem was apparently quite severe. It is interesting to note that in the period after the Civil War and up to the time of World War I and even later, the so-called "Soldier's Disease" referred to narcotic addiction among veterans. In fact, in recent years with the Vietnam returnees, the military hospitals themselves have often become centers of drug traffic. As columnist Jack Anderson has described the situation:

> Venerable Walter Reed Army Hospital where Douglas MacArthur and Dwight Eisenhower spent their final days has become a haven for narcotics users with patients briskly peddling a dizzying variety of drugs to fellow soldiers.
>
> Along the secluded walks of the famed rose garden, on the broad lawns and inside the buildings themselves, the bustling trade goes on even as a hospital spokesman denies vigorously that a drug problem exists.
>
> A reporter for this column, Sharon Basco, made two visits to the hospital in the nation's capital and learned from patients themselves that heroin, marijuana, LSD, mescaline, "speed," and demerol are all available for a price.[25]

From the standpoint of the pusher, the military and veterans hospitals make ideal locations for their commerce because they have available a "captive" group of consumers with a high concentration of addicts or users, or at

[25] Jack Anderson, "Veterans Do Bustling Business Pushing Dope at Reed Hospital," published in his syndicated column which appears in many newspapers across the country (August 13, 1970).

least individuals who may be familiar with marijuana and other narcotics as well as their effects.

THE PROPINQUITY OF NARCOTICS

The individual in the military finds narcotics more accessible than his counterpart in civilian life. In a combat situation, for example, various narcotics are widely available for treatment of the wounded and opportunities to steal narcotics are present. Fort comments, for example, "Some of them [addicts] had had opportunities to steal morphine while in service; a favorite method was to steal the morphine syrettes contained in parachute first aid kits."[26]

The sheer enormity of military supplies, including medical supplies, and the problem of distribution makes it difficult to impose controls as rigid as those usually encountered in civilian life and, accordingly, an addict can more easily maintain a supply of hard drugs through illegal channels and the marijuana user can more easily obtain hard drugs for initial experimentation. Other drugs such as "speed" (amphetamines) can often be obtained from Army medical channels in the line of duty "if the soldier says that he needs to stay awake or requires extra energy for a tough mission."[27]

Much military activity occurs in foreign countries. In such areas there may be more a cultural tradition to using various kinds of narcotics, and they may be relatively available in the indigenous open market or from the often sizable addiction population in the foreign country. As Fort further observed, "A few of them [addicts] had become addicted while in service, sometimes through association with foreign addicts (for instance, in Japan)."[28]

Some narcotics such as marijuana are relatively common in various tropical parts of the world and may be used by significant numbers of the indigenous population. Marijuana smoking may be a cultural pattern into which American servicemen may be socialized while stationed there. Such was apparently the case in the days of the "Banana Army." As Geller and Boas describe it:

> Back in 1925 the young American soldiers protecting the Panama Canal Zone were not much different from those scattered throughout the world today. It was a known fact that the men stationed in the Canal Zone had been smoking marijuana for some time, having picked up the habit from the local Panamanians. The military was aware of the prac-

[26] John P. Fort, Jr., "Heroin Addiction Among Young Men," in *Narcotic Addiction,* John A. O'Donnell and John C. Ball (eds.) (New York, Harper & Row, 1966), p. 77.
[27] Geller and Boas, op. cit., pp. 151–52.
[28] Ibid., p. 77.

tice, but they regarded it as a harmless diversion. However, the late twenties saw the emergence of the "marijuana menace" scare and, accordingly, pressure was placed upon the military to examine the drug's use in Panama.[29]

Furthermore, marijuana may simply grow wild in quantity and be readily available "for the picking" in some areas of the world. Such was apparently the case with some of the first contingents of occupation troops in Japan after World War II. Bowers reports, for example:

> The 11th Airborne Division was handed Yokohama until a few rapes and robberies and a couple of murders outside the New Grand Hotel (MacArthur's first temporary headquarters) caused another "point of occupation" to be opened, Sendai in the out-of-the-way north. There, some of the wiser paratroopers immediately spotted acres of wild marijuana, and the first year of the occupation also saw the first big dope bust.[30]

The situation in Vietnam was particularly serious. Southeastern Asia has traditionally been a center of opium and marijuana raising as well as drug production and distribution. There is also a long history of drug use among some of the indigenous peoples there. Oriental organized crime has found a lucrative market in the American servicemen stationed there. As one columnist reported:

> So far as can be gathered, the principal bankrollers—the men who furnish the funds and rake in the bulk of the profits after agents, officials, transporters, and sellers are paid off—are an interconnected group of Chinese financiers in Hong Kong, Singapore and Macao.
> These men are international, with business associates in Thailand, Laos, Malaysia, South Vietnam, Burma, and Communist China. In the main, however, the top men are themselves believed to be neither communist nor noncommunist.[31]

This columnist also reported that an estimated 1,000 tons of opium a year moves out of Thailand with most coming into South Vietnam. Furthermore, some of the highest quality marijuana—"Cambodian Red"—is grown in Vietnam near the Cambodian border and is available to the GIs from street vendors for a nominal price.[32] With marijuana and other narcotics

---

[29] Allen Geller and Maxwell Boas, "Pot and the GI: The Military Scene," *The Drug Beat* (New York, McGraw-Hill, 1969), p. 146.

[30] Faubian Bowers, "How Japan Won the War," *The New York Times Magazine* (August 30, 1970), p. 7.

[31] Ray Cromley, "Drugs-for-GIs Traffic Booms," *Bowling Green–Park City Daily News,* a syndicated column in newspapers across the country (July 11, 1971).

[32] Geller and Boas, op. cit., pp. 149–50.

freely available at low prices, a traditional background of narcotic usage in the region, a strong subcultural norm of marijuana smoking among the troops, and relatively lax enforcement of the regulations against drug use on the part of both South Vietnamese authorities as well as the U.S. military authorities, it is perhaps not surprising that between 35 and 75 percent of our troops in Vietnam (depending on whose estimate) smoked marijuana, and a significant percentage were hooked on hard drugs.[33]

NARCOTICS AND MILITARY STRESS AND DEMANDS

The military role is a difficult and demanding one. It is physically arduous and often mentally stressful and frustrating. It involves danger, fear, and depersonalization, sometimes dehumanization. The individual may be subjected to regimentation, humiliation, loneliness, privation, and pains. Obviously some are not "cut out to be a soldier (or sailor)." Others may only be able to successfully play the role with effort and difficulty. Few relish it. Marijuana and other narcotics, like alcohol, may serve as mechanisms to moderate the discomforts and stresses of the role. A marijuana user interviewed in World War II, for example, put it succinctly when he stated, "I ain't no soldier, and I ain't going to be one. When I want what I want, I got to have it. If I can't get any more reefers, I'm going A.W.O.L. again."[34]

The Army physician who interviewed this addict and others concluded that:

> The adjustment to military life was invariably very poor. In some cases this was due to a failure of adequate performance because of personal and character maladjustment. For example, many could not stand being reprimanded. Some could not endure being around other persons and liked to be off by themselves. Without his drug one claimed that he could not remember what he was supposed to do. Complaints of headaches and nervousness and inability to concentrate were exceedingly common and led to frequent visits to sick call and to the hospital. In fact, these symptoms were present in varying degrees in every addict whose case was studied in this series. In addition to inadequate perfor-

[33] Geller and Boas point out that: "Most MPs are taught to smell and otherwise establish the presence of marijuana. But since many of them turn on themselves, they tend to be casual about finding pot smokers except in cases where the violation is glaringly obvious." They also speak of "the link between the Vietnamese police and the pushers." Ibid., p. 151. A young captain of the artillery, recently returned from Vietnam, told us in an interview that he had confiscated a large quantity of marijuana from some GIs and attempted to turn them and the marijuana in at a Military Police station. The MPs refused to accept the soldiers claiming there was no case against them, but offered to "keep" the marijuana. The captain refused.

[34] Henry Myers, "The Marihuana Addict in the Army," *War Medicine,* Vol. 6 (December 1944), p. 389.

mance there waš difficulty in military adjustment expressed in the problem of discipline, especially as related to going A.W.O.L. and antisocial behavior toward fellow soldiers or superiors.[35]

If the regimentation, routine, and social demands of the military role in peacetime or garrison duty create adjustment and performance difficulties, the combat element of the military role in wartime poses special strains. Combat may involve suspense, intense fear, discomfort, or pain and personal revulsion beyond the limits tolerable to many persons. The soldier, of course, has no legal alternatives, and alcohol or drugs provide the only means by which he may moderate the stresses of combat and fullfill his military obligations. Alcohol may be unavailable or inconvenient to maintain in a combat situation. Marijuana, however, is light, convenient, and readily accessible to the troops. As a result, it is the preferred "escape" device. As Geller and Boas put it, "Marijuana found on dead and wounded GIs supplies ample evidence that smoking takes place under combat conditions."[36] They also point out that:

> Newsmen, interviewing GIs after the story broke, found that many a pointman or rifleman on patrol in enemy territory turns on not because he's looking for a different kind of kick, but simply to overcome a basic human and particularly marital emotion: fear. The boredom of war coupled with fighting an elusive enemy make the conflict in Vietnam one where the guard at the gate, the sentinel at the barbed-wire perimeter, and the radio operator monitoring suspicious sounds play key roles in the conduct of the war. Lighting up a joint doesn't make a task of drudgery easier to bear, according to many G.I.s.[37]

That any army today could train its men to feel comfortable in a combat situation is doubtful. While many tolerate it, for many others the only means of endurance is some form of chemical device for altering subjective reality.

MILITARY SOLUTIONS

In previous times the military more often overlooked occasional marijuana smoking as a trivial disciplinary problem or, in the instance of regular marijuana smoking or narcotic usage, viewed the practice as a detriment to the adequate performance of assigned military tasks and duties. Accordingly, such individuals were singled out for discharge under Section VIII of U.S. Army Regulations 615–368, which provides for release from active duty

[35] Ibid.
[36] Geller and Boas, op. cit., p. 152.
[37] Ibid., p. 148.

because of "inaptness or undesirable habits or traits of character," or courts-martial for breaches of discipline.[38] Such a disposition of the addict, however, serves only to hide the problem or transfer it to other responsibilities. It assuredly did not resolve the problem. As Marcovitz and Myers have commented:

> However, in our experience at least, most marijuana addicts avoid a general court-martial. At most, their breaches of discipline have led to special courts-martial, with sentences ranging up to six months in the guardhouse. The ones we have seen have never been led one step on the road to rehabilitation by such a procedure. On their release they immediately resume their use of marijuana and continue to be medical and disciplinary problems.
>
> Because they actually interfere with the efficiency of the Army and their potentialities for usefulness are slight, separation from the service under the provisions of Section VIII, AR 614–360 [later superseded by AR 615–368] eventually becomes necessary. However, it must be admitted that this merely released the addict to civilian life, where he continues to have his somatic and personality difficulties, with their expression in antisocial or criminal behavior, and he tends to foster the use of marijuana by others.[39]

More recently, the military has drastically altered its views on the problem and now considers the use of marijuana and other narcotics as essentially a medical problem calling for treatment and rehabilitation. On this subject Cromley, for example, has observed:

> The military services by now have perhaps more experience on a large scale with men affected by drug abuse—including marijuana—than any other institution in this country. . . .
>
> Whatever the regulations and whatever is said in policy statements, months of interviews convince that it is now U.S. Army policy at the highest levels to regard the use of marijuana (and other drugs) as a medical rather than as a legal problem.
>
> In Vietnam, Europe, and the United States, American GIs physically or emotionally "hooked" on drugs are being encouraged to report themselves in for treatment with no penalty.[40]

Unfortunately, however, the military's attempts at treatment and rehabilitation have been somewhat less than successful. In many instances, even where the addicts have been induced to undergo treatment under a

---

[38] See especially Captain Eli Marcovitz and Captain Henry J. Myers, "The Marihuana Addict in the Army," *War Medicine,* Vol. 6 (December 1944), pp. 382–91.

[39] Ibid., p. 390.

[40] Cromley, op. cit.

"no bust" amnesty policy, the men have often been uncooperative, violated military discipline, continued their drug usage and even engaged in a variety of other criminal activities. The following account illustrates this situation at one naval drug rehabilitation center:

> Many of the patients—among them are enlisted men who became addicted to heroin while in Vietnam—have refused to accept authority and discipline or to cooperate with psychologists and therapists seeking to inquire into the root causes of their addiction.
>
> Some have flaunted their special amnesty status before other Miramar [the name of the center] enlisted men who are subject to more rigid discipline. This has led to what a spokesman called "confrontations" and what other sources described as near riots on several occasions....
>
> As many as 20 of the center's 220 patients have been absent without leave at one time. Three were missing one day last week and another was in jail on suspicion of robbing a San Diego bank. Disciplinary action currently is being considered against 18 or 20 others suspected of smuggling drugs onto the base.
>
> ...An increase in barracks thefts and shoplifting at the Miramar Navy exchange has been attributed, at least in part, to the drug trafficking.[41]

Many servicemen addicts, especially blacks, remain suspicious of the amnesty program. Many of these men find that they can carry out their work even under the influence of drugs and without detection by authorities. In this sense the addicts are not taking advantage of the military's new enlightened attitudes toward drug usage.

As one battalion executive officer in Vietnam articulated it:

> "You talk about the Army's amnesty program—that's three days maybe, what the hell," he added. "But they (GI drug takers) don't trust the Green Machine—they're afraid if they turn themselves in they'll be documented by the Veterans Administration, or maybe exposed by the Army."[42]

Furthermore, where at one time the military made an effort to discharge its addicts and now even though rehabilitative treatment is available, many individuals in the service are using their addiction as a means of obtaining a discharge. A recent newspaper account, for example, states:

> American seamen appear now to be pleading drug usage rather than homosexuality as a quick way out of the service, Navy officials say.

---

[41] Everett R. Holles, "Navy Drug Center on Coast Is Vexed," *The New York Times* (Sunday, November 14, 1971).

[42] See "Navy Reports Rise in Drug Discharges," *The New York Times* (Sunday, October 10, 1971), p. 35.

A statistical study of administrative discharges shows that while in 1964 the Navy released 1,586 men for homosexuality, compared with 42 for drug use, last year it discharged 5,672 drug users and 479 homosexuals.[43]

Even in those instances where military personnel are confined as a result of disciplinary action, the authorities have been somewhat less than successful in cutting off their supply of drugs, as one account demonstrates:

> One of the biggest scandals to emerge out of the Army's marijuana investigations was the discovery that the same GIs confined for pot offenses to the Long Binh stockade, twenty-five miles north of Saigon, were blissfully whiling away their sentences with a supply of grass. How the contraband substance entered the stockade gates is a matter of conjecture. Despite a massive ring of security, an inordinate amount of military goods still manages to get stolen and the Viet Cong learn of classified secrets. Pot, like water, finds its level even in tightly guarded premises. Undoubtedly, it was smuggled in, either through Vietnamese civilians employed in the camp or by way of the guards.[44]

Although the military authorities have not enjoyed any great degree of success in their recent treatment and rehabilitation attempts, they have exhibited an enlightened attitude toward the problem. In the face of the fact that the use of marijuana and other narcotics by military personnel with the attendant illicit traffic in drugs often generates a significant crime problem in terms of thefts and antisocial actions, not to mention a morale and discipline problem, the military can ill afford not to continue exerting every effort to deal with the problem. Most important, narcotic usage adversely affects the performance of troops, and the lowered efficiency, particularly in a combat situation, can hardly be tolerated without affecting the outcome of the conflict. Hence, the military may be expected to turn even greater efforts and devote more resources toward finding a solution to the problem.

[43] Geller and Boas, op. cit., p. 149.
[44] Gloria Emerson, "A Major in Vietnam Gives All He's Got to the War on Heroin," *The New York Times* (Sunday, September 12, 1971), p. 2.

7. Junkies in White:
Drug Addiction among Physicians

RICHARD M. HESSLER

The widespread belief that physicians and other medical professionals are beyond the pale of something as ignoble, desultory, and perilous as drug addiction is as imaginary as the emperor's clothes. The facts are that, notwithstanding the anomaly of the most prestigious occupational group in our society[1] engaging in behavior traditionally associated with the "lower classes," drug addiction rates among physicians and to a lesser extent allied health professionals, are incredibly high relative to the problem of drug addiction generally. We must get used to seeing physicians as human, and accordingly we don the white coats of sociology and examine the dynamics of this fascinating albeit cheerless and wasteful phenomenon.

SOME STATISTICAL FINDINGS

National and international statistics exist on drug addiction among physicians. They give us a fairly credible picture of the high addiction rate among physicians who have had the misfortune or good fortune, depending on one's position relative to this issue, of falling into the hands of the law, or various public and private institutions of medical care. However, statistics on the extent of narcotic addiction among physicians inclusive of those who never get caught or treated for their drug problems are, practically speaking, non-existent. Consequently, what we know about the extent of the problem in the United States tends to come from extrapolations based on studies of the records of United States Public Health Service hospitals, federal narcotics hospitals, Bureaus of Narcotic Enforcement for State Departments of Justice,

I wish to thank David Griffard for his valuable insights and suggestions; Louise Enouch assisted with the literature review; and thanks are due Diana Attanasi for the typing of this manuscript.

[1] National Opinion Research Corporation, "Jobs and Occupations: A Popular Evaluation," *Opinion News,* Vol. 9 (September 1, 1947), pp. 3–13.

state boards of medical examiners (disciplinary boards for physicians), and records from large private psychiatric hospitals.

Studies of physician addiction have shown that the difference between addiction in the population at large and that among physicians is enormous. Quantitatively, doctors are much more likely to string themselves out on drugs than are people in general. Fox estimated that the narcotics addiction rate among the general population in 1957 was 1 in 10,000 whereas for physicians it was 1 in 100, a rate 100 times greater than the addiction rate for the public at large.[2] Hill and associates[3] and Jones[4] estimate the rate of addiction among physicians to be as high as 2.5 percent. If accurate, this means that the number of physician addicts each year would equal the graduating class of one large medical school. More recently, Garb has judged that it is conservative to estimate that there are twice as many physician addicts as are actually reported, and accordingly, the loss of physicians yearly to drugs is the equivalent of the graduating classes of three large medical schools.[5]

Looking at other societies, Quinn has noted that in England physicians and other medical personnel constitute less than one percent of the population, yet comprise 33 percent of all known addicts.[6] Jones has pointed out that the incidence of drug addiction among physicians is the same for the United States, England, Germany, Holland, and France, with 15 percent of the known drug addicts hailing from the ranks of physicians.[7] Ehrhardt's study of physician addicts in Germany turned up 12 to 14 percent physicians among the total number of known addicts.[8]

Of course, underlying these cold numbers are hundreds of instances of intense and at times horrific human degradation and suffering. The physician as junkie eventually shelves his family, profession, and friends in the course of devoting constant attention to his next "jolt" in order to hold a state of euphoria. For example, Quinn relates two cases where one physician junkie in delivering a baby, performed a routine episiotomy and

[2] J. D. Fox, "Narcotic Addiction among Physicians," *Journal of Michigan Medical Society,* Vol. 56 (February 1957), 214–17.

[3] Harris E. Hill, Charles A. Haertzen and Roy S. Yamahiro, "The Addict Physician: A Minnesota Multiphasic Personality Inventory Study of the Interaction of Personality Characteristics and Availability of Narcotics," *Research Publications of the Association for Research in Nervous and Mental Diseases,* Vol. 46 (1968), pp. 321–32.

[4] Charles H. Jones, "Narcotic Addiction of Physicians," *Journal of the Medical Association of the State of Alabama,* Vol. 37 (January 1968), pp. 816–27.

[5] Solomon Garb, "Drug Addiction in Physicians," *Anasthesia and Analgesia... Current Researches,* Vol. 48, No. 1 (January–February 1969), pp. 129–33.

[6] William F. Quinn, "Narcotic Addiction: Medical and Legal Problems with Physicians," *California Medicine,* Vol. 94, No. 4 (April 1961), pp. 214–17.

[7] Jones, op. cit., p. 817.

[8] H. Ehrhardt, "Drug Addiction in the Medical and Allied Professions in Germany," *Bulletin on Narcotics,* Vol. 11 (January–March 1959), pp. 18–26.

...nonchalantly cut through into the rectum, and with no sense of remorse whatever and no serious attempt to repair the damage, merely remarked that he must have been a little heavy with the knife.... Another one, in making a house call, took off his coat and gave himself a shot of Demerol in the vein in the presence of the patient and family, and stated, "Well now, I've solved my problem. What's yours?"[9]

Fox tells of a physician addict turned pusher who

...had been playing the races and lost heavily. In debt, he needed money quickly. A dope addict was tipped off to the doctor's plight. He stopped by the doctor's office, offered him $25 for a prescription for Demerol. This was not enough. The addict upped it to $100 and the doctor saw the answer to his indebtedness.

After he had written several $100 prescriptions, a dope peddler stopped in at his office to warn him that if he didn't write a "big" prescription for him he'd be turned in for treating the addict without notifying the authorities. The doctor was in a corner. He wrote the prescription for a large number of tablets and within hours was picked up by the T-men.

His narcotic license was immediately revoked, he was disgraced in his community by newspaper publicity and he had to leave town. His only comment to the T-men: "Oh, what a dope I was!"[10]

Finally, in an extremely rare personal account of his addiction, Dr. James DeWitt spares none of the grim details of his experiences as a wino and junkie on Boston's skid row. As he tells it:

I am a doctor. I am a drug addict.... I've been up to three grains of morphine every two hours around the clock...which is a tremendous dose. A quarter grain every four hours is a heavy dose for a big patient ...I did five voluntary admissions to Bridgewater just to stay alive during that time and had seven or eight arrests, all for drunkenness. Then I started the slow, hard comeback trail. And it is. If you go down far enough and you have a big enough history behind you, it's very hard to come back.[11]

PHYSICIAN JUNKIES AND OTHER JUNKIES

Social status and occupational prestige have a bearing on the style and content of deviance, including drug addiction. If one were to order deviant behavior along one continuum and occupational prestige or social standing

[9] Quinn, op. cit., pp. 215–16.
[10] Fox, op. cit., p. 217.
[11] John Currier, "A Doctor Tells What Drugs Do," *North Shore 1971* (January 30, 1971).

along another, he would find a strong association between them. If this is true, the special case of the physician junkie will show important differences from those junkies who do not belong to the most prestigious occupational group in existence. These important differences have to do with the origins of drug use, the types of drugs used, and the general style of drug addiction.

Physician junkies, unlike other addicts, start their dependence on drugs relatively late in life, after their careers in medicine have been established. Winick found that the average age at which the physicians in his study became addicts for the first time was 38.[12] Most street addicts get hooked much younger, usually by the late teens. While there is growing use of marijuana and amphetamines by medical students,[13] physician addicts generally start themselves off on drugs once their careers in medicine are going concerns.

Meperidine (demerol) is the drug used by most physician junkies, whereas heroin or cocaine tends to be the overwhelming choice of street addicts. Demerol produces a quick high and its effects are short ranged, making it an extremely dangerous drug. Garb cites research that demonstrates that it would be more desirable medically to be addicted to morphine than to demerol and furthermore that it is much easier to treat morphine addiction.[14]

This suggests that physicians make careless addicts who give little systematic thought to the choice of drugs. Garb states that "the awareness of the addiction hazard of meperidine among physicians seems grossly inadequate."[15] Winick argues that physician junkies use meperidine and erroneously claim that it is less toxic and easier to withdraw from than the other opiates.[16] Strangely, physician addicts seem to be quite similar to the typical Hell's Angel user who does not care about the dope he injects. Thompson reports on one Angel who took a massive dose of cortisone thinking it was aspirin. He discovered his mistake, went to bed and sweated out 10 days of boils and unmitigated pain. When he recovered, he concluded that he no longer had to worry about the kinds of pills he took since his recent experience had convinced him that his body could take anything he put into it.[17]

This fundamental lack of judgment on the part of physician junkies is not surprising when taken in the historical context of physicians and their relationship to drugs. Traditionally, physicians in this country have demon-

[12] Charles Winick, "Physician Narcotic Addicts," in Howard S. Becker (ed.), *The Other Side: Perspectives on Deviance* (Glencoe, Ill., Free Press, 1964), pp. 261–79.

[13] Stanley N. Smith and Paul H. Blachly, "Amphetamine Usage by Medical Students," *Journal of Medical Education,* Vol. 41 (February 1966).

[14] Garb, op. cit., p. 132.

[15] Ibid.

[16] Winick, op. cit., p. 264.

[17] Hunter S. Thompson, *Hell's Angels: A Strange and Terrible Saga* (New York, Random House, 1966).

strated uncritical acceptance of drugs generally. For example, the Public
Health Service has estimated that each year 1,368,000 nonfatal "therapeutic
misadventures" occur, all caused by doctors and most induced by the injudicious use of drugs. Historically, physicians in this country enthusiastically endorsed the widespread use of opium, first introduced to the United States in
1856, and the result was a flood of morphine-loaded household remedies
("soothing syrups") sold to consumers without prescriptions. By 1895 2 to 4
percent of the population of the United States was addicted to opium.[18]

In addition, there may be pragmatic reasons for physician addicts' heavy
use of meperidine. Rasor and Crecraft suggest that meperidine is more readily
available since hospitals take less precaution in safeguarding it than their
supplies of other narcotics, and consequently thefts of meperidine are easier
to conceal. Also, the stigma associated with the use of meperidine was felt to
be less severe than that attached to the use of other narcotics such as morphine, and as a result physician users may feel less anxious about the use of
meperidine.[19]

Physician junkies are usually in a much better position than others to
keep a pure supply of drugs steaming along.[20] Unlike other addicts, physicians who are hooked tend to maintain their careers for years while addicted,
and hence they have a steady and ample income. Physicians also have the
privilege of easy access to pure drugs. Nevertheless, as their habit grows, physician junkies seem to find the legal access to drugs insufficient, and they turn
to devious means to obtain fixes. In this respect the style of their addiction
tends to approximate other junkies', and one finds physician addicts performing decidedly unprofessional acts such as forging prescriptions, prescribing
massive doses for their patients and then withholding most of it for themselves, or simply stealing drugs from hospital pharmacies.

Street junkies tend to form loose groupings whereby they keep the company of other addicts, whereas the physician is a solitary junkie who seldom
if ever associates with other physician addicts.[21] Unlike the street addict,
physicians do not need other addicts for obtaining drugs or killing time and
consequently the physician junkie is a loner in his addiction.

Physician addicts are much more successful at avoiding legal authorities
than are street junkies. Their invulnerability stems partly from the prestige
and myths associated with the role of physician and partly from the physi-

[18] Marie Nyswarder, *The Drug Addict as Patient* (New York, Grune and Stratton, 1956), pp. 1–13.
[19] Robert W. Rasor and H. James Crecraft, "Addiction to Meperidine (Demerol) Hydrocholoride," *Journal of American Medical Association,* Vol. 157 (1955),
pp. 654–57.
[20] Winick, op. cit., p. 267.
[21] Ibid.

cian's unwillingness to seek help for his problem. Physicians find accepting their own illness and the status of patient extremely difficult,[22] and consequently they wait until "discovered" by the authorities or by a member of some helping hand society. Two factors peculiar to the profession seem to exacerbate the physician's unwillingness to seek help. One is that the general society of physicians is concomitantly extremely protective of its members and terribly harsh to those who violate the norms, thereby giving medicine a professional black eye. In many ways this sense of professional solidarity is fictive and has little or no bearing on the true nature of medical collegiality. Nevertheless, physician addicts perceive the push and pull of punishment and support of their colleagues and choose to remain protected,[23] perhaps thereby missing judicious opportunities to get the monkey off their backs. If one accepts Becker's definition of deviance as something created by society whereby "Social groups create deviance by making the rules whose infraction constitutes deviance and by applying those rules to particular people and labeling them as outsiders,"[24] the protectiveness of medical societies toward physician addicts can be understood as an attempt to avoid exercising the harsh prerogative of casting fellow physicians as outsiders.

The physician is trained to view himself as more powerful than others. Thus he slips easily into taking an unrealistic view of himself as somehow immune to addiction and omnipotent in dealing with his drug problem once he is hooked. The junkie in white is a prisoner of his profession, caught in a set of circumstances where all signals operate to keep him from recognizing and solving his addiction.

REASONS FOR ADDICTION

At the present time we do not have much of a clue as to why the drug addiction rate is so high for physicians. There is a dearth of prospective studies concerning personality factors of physician addicts, and where research has been done on the psychodynamics of physician junkies, it is confounded by the effect on personality that the addiction itself has. Thus, for example, Hill and associates compared addict physicians with nonaddict physicians and with unselected white hospitalized addicts on the Minnesota Multiphasic Personality Inventory (MMPI) and were unable to determine whether the con-

---

[22] John C. Duffy and Edward M. Litin, "Psychiatric Morbidity of Physicians," *Journal of American Medical Association,* Vol. 189, No. 13 (September 28, 1964), pp. 989–92; Herbert Bynder, "Physicians Choose Psychiatrists: Medical Social Structure and Patterns of Choice," *Journal of Health and Human Behavior,* Vol. 6, No. 2 (Summer 1965), pp. 83–90.

[23] Ehrhardt, op. cit., p. 25.

[24] Howard S. Becker, *Outsiders: Studies in the Sociology of Deviance* (Glencoe, Ill., Free Press, 1963), pp. 8–9.

siderable neuroticism and indications of maladjustment of physician addicts were the cause or the result of the addiction.[25]

Winick found four basic themes underlying the reasons physician addicts gave for their addiction.[26] Their self-reports included the manifestation of role strain whereby the physicians expressed highly negative attitudes toward their work, citing problems such as overwork, chronic fatigue, and physical pain. Apparently many of the addict physicians studied by Winick grew up in small towns within working-class families, were pushed into medicine by an ambitious parent, and found themselves practicing medicine in large urban areas. The physicians by and large internalized a drive to succeed and preoccupied themselves with thoughts of professional success, social status, income, and none of the physicians were person-oriented in their careers.[27] General overwork resulted, and Winick concluded that under these conditions the physicians became dissatisfied with their work and found the strain of their everyday life as doctors too much to bear. Associated with the role strain was the physician's feeling of omnipotence, but once he achieved successes in his career and demonstrated his omnipotence, as most addict physicians do, the victories seemed hollow to him, and his past achievements seemed foolish and meaningless. Thus he may be torn between giving up a profession that has lost its attraction or continuing his practice of medicine with its attendant stresses. In this context, meperidine could well become a temporary escape hatch. The third and fourth themes of physician drug addiction discussed by Winick are passive personalities found in the physician addicts and the simple fact that physicians took drugs because they liked the effect produced.

Another tenable reason for the high rate of physician addiction is the accessibility of drugs to the physician. This is certainly an appealing notion and one which holds a great deal of validity. Nevertheless, it leaves unanswered the issue of other health professionals such as pharmacists or dentists who have equal or better access to drugs than physicians, yet have a much lower addiction rate.[28] Thus access to drugs appears to be a necessary, albeit not sufficient, reason for physician addiction.

CONCLUSIONS

Physicians are generally an overstressed segment of the population. The nature of medicine as an occupation is such that it physically and psychologically breaks one down. The high physician drug addiction rate is one of a

---

[25] Hill et al., op. cit.
[26] Winick, op. cit., pp. 276–79.
[27] Oswald Hall, "Types of Medical Careers," *American Journal of Sociology*, Vol. 55 (November 1949), pp. 243–53.
[28] Rasor and Crecraft, op. cit., p. 657; Ehrhardt, op. cit., p. 18.

multiple series of responses to the considerable stress stemming from the work physicians perform.

It is intriguing that physicians, who represent the upper occupational levels of our society, tend to behave in ways typically thought to represent lower-class behavioral adaptations to stress. While physician addicts evidence a style and spirit of drug use different from other drug addicts, other aspects of physician addiction as well as the addiction to drugs itself is quite similar to a common form of adaptation to stress among many lower-class persons. What this might mean is that within our society, extremes of social stress fall on persons occupying the very top and very bottom of the occupational heirarchy. While the precise nature of the stress is different for an unemployed Mexican in Barrio Pascua, Tucson, Arizona, and a fully employed physician living in Concord, Massachusetts, the responses to the stress may be generally the same.

One may speak loosely of the occupational hazards of being a physician, but in looking closely at physician drug addiction, we might in fact be seeing an occupational anomaly syndrome. Physicians have a great deal working against them by way of stress associated with the structure and functions of their occupation. For example, physicians experience an extended period of deferred gratification during the course of their training, and ample opportunity exists for marital conflict. The incredible demands of the job with little or no control over one's own time keep the physician away from home and introduces a disruptive influence on the family interaction patterns. The social pressures of the necessity to maintain a socioeconomic image serves as a constant reminder to the physician that he cannot slow down the pace of his work. If such an occupational anomaly syndrome does exist, one would expect to find that drug addiction is just one of several negative responses by physicians to compensate for the occupational stress endemic to their calling. Other stress indicators such as alcoholism and suicide should be high as well,[29] and much research is needed before such a syndrome could be demonstrated.

Solutions to the problem of physician addiction lie in the reorganization of medical education and medical care delivery systems. Similar to the effort necessary to begin to solve the synonymous problems of his lower-class brothers, sweeping changes in the basic organization of medicine are necessary if drug addiction, alcoholism, and suicide among physicians is to be reduced. The biblical injunction to a physician to "heal thyself" is simply not enough.

---

[29] Alan G. Craig and Ferris N. Pitts, Jr., "Suicide by Physicians," *Diseases of the Nervous System,* Vol. 29 (November 1968), pp. 763–72; John C. Duffy, "Suicides by Physicians in Training," *Journal of Medical Education,* Vol. 43 (November 1968), p. 1196.

8. Lesbian Behavior as an Adaptation to the Occupation of Stripping

CHARLES H. McCAGHY

and

JAMES K. SKIPPER, JR.

In recent publications Simon and Gagnon (1967a and b) contend that too frequently students of deviant behavior are prepossessed with the significance of the behavior itself and with the "exotic" trappings which accompany it. One finds exhaustive accounts of the demographic characteristics of deviants, the variety of forms their behavior may take, and the characteristics of any subculture or "community," including its argot, which emerge as a direct consequence of a deviant status. Furthermore, Simon and Gagnon chide researchers for being locked into futile searches for ways in which inappropriate or inadequate socialization serves to explain their subjects' behavior.

Simon and Gagnon argue that these research emphases upon descriptions of deviant behavior patterns and their etiology provide an unbalanced and misleading approach to an understanding of deviants. Deviants do or, at least, attempt to accommodate themselves to the "conventional" world, and they play many roles which conform to society's expectations. Yet, for the most part, deviants' learning and playing of nondeviant or conventional roles are either ignored by researchers or interpreted strictly as being influenced by a dominant deviant role. The focus of most research obscures the fact that with few exceptions a deviant role occupies a minor portion of the individuals' behavior spectrums. What is not recognized is the influence which commitments and roles of a nondeviant nature have upon deviant commitments

From *Social Problems,* Volume 17, No. 2 (Fall 1969), pp. 262–70. Reprinted by permission of the *Society for the Study of Social Problems.*

This paper is a revised and expanded version of one presented before joint meetings of The Midwest and The Ohio Valley Sociological Societies in Indianapolis, May 1–3, 1969. We would like to express our appreciation to David Gray for his assistance during the data collection stage of this research.

and roles. To illustrate their contention, Simon and Gagnon discuss how homosexual behavior patterns are linked with the identical concerns and determinants which influence heterosexuals: aging problems, identity problems, making a living, management of sexual activity, etc. The authors argue convincingly for damping concern over ultimate causes of homosexuality and for concentrating on factors and contingencies shaping the homosexual role. In their words:

> Patterns of adult homosexuality are consequent upon the social structures and values that surround the homosexual after he becomes, or conceives himself as, homosexual rather than upon original and ultimate causes (Simon and Gagnon, 1967b:179).

Since past research on homosexuals has been dominated by an emphasis upon the sexual feature of their behavior and its consequences, it is fitting that Simon and Gagnon draw attention to linking deviant with nondeviant behaviors or roles. However, since in their scheme the choice of sexual object is taken as given, a complementary perspective is still needed to gain an understanding of the process by which individuals engage in homosexual behavior. We suggest a structural approach. Because sexual behavior, deviant or not, emerges out of the context of social situations, it would seem that the structure of certain situations might contribute to becoming involved in homosexual behavior and to the formation of a homosexual self-concept. We are not suggesting such structures as "ultimate" causes; rather, we are saying that different social structures may provide conditions, learning patterns, and justifications differentially favorable to the occurrence of homosexual contacts and self-concepts. This is not strictly a matter of etiology, then, but an epidemiological concern over differential incidences of deviance, regardless of how episodic or pervasive homosexual behavior may be for an individual case.

A pertinent, albeit extreme, example here is the incidence of homosexual behavior occurring among incarcerated populations. A large proportion of prisoners can be identified as "jail house turnouts": those whose homosexual behavior is limited to within an institutional setting (Sykes, 1965:72, 95–99; Ward and Kassebaum, 1965:76, 96). Evidence indicates that contingencies and opportunities inherent in the prison setting are related to the onset and possible continuation of homosexual behavior. There is no question that for some prisoners homosexual behavior emerges as an adaptation to the prison structure which not only curtails avenues of heterosexual release, but deprives inmates of meaningful affective relationships they would otherwise have (Gagnon and Simon, 1968b; Giallombardo, 1966:133–57).

We have little reliable information concerning the incidence of homosexuality among various populations outside the setting of total institutions.[1] Most researchers agree that homosexuals will be found across the entire socio-economic spectrum (Kinsey et al., 1948:639–55; Kinsey et al., 1953:459–60, 500; Gerassi, 1966: Leznoff and Westley, 1956). There is, however, continual speculation that relatively high proportions of male homosexuals are contained in certain occupational groups such as dancers, hair dressers, etc. Assuming this speculation to be correct, it is still unclear which is prior: occupational choice or commitment to homosexual behavior. The sociological literature is replete with examples of how occupation influences other aspects of social life; there is no apparent reason why choice of sexual objects should necessarily vary independently. This is not to say that occupations are as extreme as total institutions in their control over life situations regarding sexual behavior. We do suggest that *some* occupations, like the prison setting, may play a crucial role in providing pressures, rationales, and opportunities leading to involvement in, if not eventual commitment to, homosexual behavior.

In the course of conducting a study of the occupational culture of stripping, we found that homosexual behavior was an important aspect of the culture which apparently stemmed less from any predisposition of the participants than from contingencies of the occupation.

NATURE OF THE RESEARCH

The principal research site was a midwestern burlesque theater which employed a different group of four touring strippers each week. With the permission and support of the theater manager, two male researchers were allowed access to the backstage dressing room area during and after afternoon performances. The researchers were introduced to each new touring group by the female stage manager, a person whom the girls trusted. After the stage manager presented them as "professors from the university who are doing an anthology on burlesque," the researchers explained that they were interested in how persons became strippers and what these persons thought about stripping as an occupation. After this, the researchers bided their time with small talk, card playing, and general questions to the girls about their occupation.[2] The purposes of this tactic were to make the girls more comfortable and to allow the researchers to survey the field for respondents.

---

[1] Estimates of the proportion of males having homosexual contacts during imprisonment range between 30 and 45 percent, depending on the institution, characteristics of the population, and length of sentences (Gagnon and Simon, 1968b), p. 25. In one women's institution researchers estimated that 50 percent of the inmates had at least one sexual contact during their imprisonment (Ward and Kassebaum, 1965), p. 92.

[2] Data concerning stripteasers and the occupation of stripping may be found in a paper by Skipper and McCaghy (1969).

The primary data were gathered through in-depth interviews with 35 strippers.[3] Although there was no systematic method of selecting respondents from each touring group, an attempt was made to obtain a range of ages, years in the occupation, and salary levels. There were only four cases of out-right refusals to be interviewed, one coming after the girl had consulted with a boyfriend. In six cases no convenient time for the interview could be arranged because the potential subjects were "busy." It was impossible in these instances to determine whether the excuses really constituted refusals. In general, the researchers found the girls eager to cooperate and far more of them wanted to be interviewed than could be accommodated.

The interviews, lasting an average of an hour and a half, were conducted in bars, restaurants, and, on occasion, backstage. Although difficult at times, the interviewing took place in a manner in which it was not overheard by others. In all but one case, two researchers were present. Interviews were also conducted with others, both male and female, whose work brought them in contact with strippers: the theater manager, stage manager, union agent, and sales persons selling goods to strippers backstage. The interviews were semi-structured and designed to elicit information on background, the process of entering the occupation, and aspects of the occupational culture.

INCIDENCE OF HOMOSEXUALITY

Ideally, in order to posit a relationship between the occupation and homosexual contacts it would be necessary to establish that the incidence of such behavior is relatively higher among strippers than in other female occupations. However, statistics comparing rates of homosexuality among specific female occupational groups are simply not available. Ward and Kassebaum (1965:75, 148–49) did find as part of female prison lore that lesbianism is prominent among models and strippers. In our research the restricted sample and relatively brief contact with the subjects did not allow us to ascertain directly the extent of homosexual behavior among strippers. We were, however, able to gauge the salience of such behavior in the occupation by asking the subjects to estimate what proportion of strippers had homosexual contacts. Estimates ranged from 15 to 100 percent of the girls currently being at least bisexual in their contacts; most responses fell within the 50 to 75 percent

[3] The social characteristics of the interviewed sample of strippers are as follows: All were white and ranged in age from 19 to 45, with 60 percent between the ages of 20 and 30. On the Hollingshead (1957) two-factor index of social position, ten came from families in classes I and II, nine from class III, and 12 from classes IV and V. (Family background data were not obtained in four cases.) Their range of education was from seven to 16 years: 22 had graduated from high school, eight of whom had at least one year of college.

range. We also have evidence, mostly self-admissions, that nine of the thirty-five respondents (26 percent) themselves engaged in homosexual behavior while in the occupation, although in no case did we request such information or have prior evidence of the respondents' involvement. We did make some attempt to include subjects in the sample whom we suspected were maintaining relatively stable homosexual relationships. But these deliberate efforts were futile. In two cases strippers known to be traveling with unemployed and unrelated female companions refused to be interviewed, saying they were "too busy."

Despite our inability to fix an exact proportion of strippers who had engaged in homosexuality, it is clear from the subjects' estimates and their ensuing discussions that such behavior is an important facet of the occupation. The estimates of 50 to 75 percent are well above Kinsey's finding that 19 percent of his total female sample had physical sexual contact with other females by age 40 (1953:452–53). This difference is further heightened when we consider that a large majority of our sample (69 percent) were or had been married; Kinsey found that only three percent of married and nine percent of previously married females had homosexual contacts by age 40 (1953:453–54).

CONDITIONS CONTRIBUTING TO HOMOSEXUALITY

More relevant to the hypothesis of this paper, however, are the conditions of the occupation which our subjects claimed were related to the incidence of homosexual behavior, whatever its magnitude. It was evident from their discussions that a great part, if not most, of such behavior could be attributed to occupational conditions. Specifically, conditions supportive of homosexual behavior in the stripping occupation can be classified as follows: 1) isolation from affective social relationships; 2) unsatisfactory relationships with males; and 3) an opportunity structure allowing a wide range of sexual behavior.

ISOLATION FROM AFFECTIVE SOCIAL RELATIONSHIPS

Evidence from our research indicates that in general strippers have difficulty maintaining permanent affective social relationships, judging by their catalogues of marital difficulties and lack of persons whom they say they can trust. Aside from such basic inabilities, it is apparent that the demands of the occupation as a touring stripper make it exceedingly difficult for the girls to establish or maintain immediate affective relationships, even on a temporary basis. The best way to demonstrate this is to describe their working hours. Generally, strippers on tour spend only one week in each city and work all seven days from Friday through Thursday evening. They must be in the next city by late Friday morning for rehearsal. Their working day usually begins with a show about 1 P.M. and ends around 11 P.M., except on Saturday when there may be a midnight show. Although the girls' own acts may last only about 20 minutes in each of four daily shows, they also perform as foils in the comedians' skits. As a consequence, the girls usually are restricted to the theater every day from 1 to 11 P.M. except for a two-and-a-half hour dinner break. After the last show most either go to a nearby nightclub or to their hotel rooms to watch television. Many girls spend over 40 weeks a year on tour.

Such working conditions effectively curtail the range of social relationships these girls might otherwise have. It should not be surprising that a nearly universal complaint among strippers is the loneliness they encounter while on tour. One girl claimed: "When you are lonely enough you will try anything." By itself this loneliness is not necessarily conducive to homosexual activities since, aside from other girls in the troupe, there is isolation from females as well as from males. But strippers find that contacts with males are not only limited but often highly unsatisfactory in content, and homosexuality can become an increasingly attractive alternative.   .

UNSATISFACTORY RELATIONSHIPS WITH MALES

As stated above, women prisoners claim that lesbianism is very frequent among strippers. Data from our research tends to confirm this rumor. There is also some evidence that homosexual behavior is relatively frequent among prostitutes (Ward and Kassebaum, 1965:126–32). It is a curious paradox that two occupations dedicated to the sexual titillation of males would contain large numbers of persons who frequently obtain their own gratification from females. Tempting as it may be to turn to some exotic psychoanalytic explanations concerning latent homosexuality, the reasons may not be so covert. Ward and Kassebaum (1965:126–32) and others (Benjamin and Masters, 1964:245–46a) note that among prostitutes homosexual behavior may result less from inclination or predisposition than from continual experiences which engender hostility toward males in general.

A recurring theme in our interviews was strippers' disillusionment with the male of the species. This disillusionment often begins on stage when the neophyte first witnesses audience reactions which prove shocking even to girls who take off their clothes in public. Due to lighting conditions the stripper is unable to see beyond the second row of seats, but from these front rows she is often gratuitously treated to performances rivaling her own act: exhibitionism and masturbation. There is no question that strippers are very conscious of this phenomenon for they characterize a large proportion of their audience as "degenerates." This term, incidentally, occurred so often in the course of our interviews it could be considered part of the stripper argot. Strippers know that "respectable" people attend their performances, but they are usu-

ally out in the dark where they cannot be seen. Furthermore, a sizeable proportion of these "respectables" are perceived by strippers to be "couples,"
hence most of the unattached male audience is suspect.

There is no indication that strippers on tour have more off-stage contact
with their audience than does any other type of performer. But the precedent
set by the males in rows one and two persists for strippers even in their off-
stage contacts with men. They find that their stage identifications as sex
objects are all too frequently taken at face value. Initially, strippers may find
this identification flattering but many eventually become irritated by it. As
one subject put it:

> If a guy took me out to dinner and showed me a good time, I'd
> sleep with him. But most of them just call up and say "Let's fuck."

When checking into hotels while on tour most girls register under their
real rather than their stage name. Several girls pointed out to us that the
purpose of this practice was to eliminate being phoned by their admirers.
Furthermore, many of the girls avoid identifying themselves in public as
strippers, preferring to call themselves dancers, entertainers, and the like.
This enables them not only to steer clear of a pariah label but to minimize
unwelcome sexual reactions which they feel the name "stripper" engenders.

When strippers do form relatively prolonged liaisons with males during
the course of their stripping career, chances are good that they will result in
another embittering experience. In some cases the man will insist that the
girl abandon the occupation, something she may not be inclined to do; hence
a breakup occurs. But more frequently the girls find themselves entangled
with males who are interested only in a financial or sexual advantage. One of
our male informants closely connected with the stripping profession claimed,
"You know the kind of jerks these girls tie up with? They're pimps, leeches,
or weirdos." This of course is an oversimplification; yet the strippers themselves confirm that they seem to be involved with more than their share of
rough, unemployed males who are more than happy to enjoy their paycheck.

Strippers probably are not without fault themselves in their difficulties
with heterosexual relationships; in our sample of 35 we found that of the 24
who had ever been married, 20 had experienced at least one divorce. It is
evident, however, that their problems are compounded by the exploitive
males who gravitate toward them. Under these circumstances contacts with
lesbians are often seen as respites from importunate males. One subject
claimed that although she did not care to engage in homosexual activities she
would frequently go to a lesbian bar where she could "have a good time and
not be bothered." Another said that lesbians are the only ones who "treat you
like a person." As one reasoned:

Strippers go gay because they have little chance to meet nice guys. They come in contact with a lot of degenerate types. If they do meet a nice guy chances are he will ask them to stop stripping. If he doesn't he's likely to be a pimp. So the girls got to turn to a woman who understands them and their job. It is very easy for them to listen to the arguments of lesbians who will tell them basically that men are no good and women can give them better companionship.

Our argument should in no way be interpreted to mean that most strippers are anti-male or have completely severed all contacts with males. From our research it appears that the "career" homosexual is the exception among strippers. At best, the majority can be described as bisexual. The point is that experiences gained in the course of their occupation promote the homosexual aspect by generating caution and skepticism where relationships with males are concerned. Limited contacts with males plus the wariness which accompanies these contacts can be instrumental in severely curtailing the sexual activity of strippers outside of prostitution. Thus an opportunity for a warm, intimate relationship unaccompanied by masculine hazards becomes increasingly attractive. According to one of our subjects, when faced by the lesbian ploy, "Men are no good; I can do things for you they can't," many strippers find themselves persuaded, at least temporarily.

OPPORTUNITY STRUCTURE ALLOWING A WIDE RANGE OF SEXUAL BEHAVIOR

The final occupational condition contributing to the incidence of homosexual behavior among strippers involves the existence of both opportunities and tacit support for such behavior. As male researchers we found it difficult to fathom the opportunities available for female homosexual activities. Our respondents pointed out, however, that there is no want in this regard. Strippers on tour have easy access to information on the location of gay bars in any city they play; furthermore, the reception strippers receive in these bars is especially hospitable. More immediate opportunities are available, obviously, with the presence of homosexuals in the touring group itself. The group which, of necessity, spends most of the day together provides the novice stripper with at least an opportunity for sexual experimentation without the risks inherent in becoming involved with complete strangers.

There is some indication also that some strippers experienced in homosexual behavior are not particularly quiescent when obtaining partners. One subject informed us that she avoids touring with certain groups simply because homosexual contacts within the group are an expected mode of behavior and noncompliance is punished by ostracism. She claimed that being on tour was boring enough without having the other girls refusing to talk or associate with her. In this same vein, several of our subjects stated that certain older and established women in the occupation actively recruit partners with promises of career rewards. We were at first skeptical of such "casting couch" tactics among strippers, but the same stories and names recurred so often from such diverse sources that the possibility cannot be ignored.

We do not wish to overdramatize the pressures placed on the girls by others to engage in lesbian practices. No doubt such pressures do occur, but sporadically. More important is the fact that opportunities for homosexual contacts occur in an atmosphere of permissiveness toward sexual behavior which characterizes the workday philosophy of strippers. The strippers' principal salable product is sex; the music, dancing, and costumes are only accessories. The real product becomes, over time, effectively devoid of any exclusiveness and is treated with the same detachment as grocers eventually view their radishes. For some strippers sexual contacts are regarded not only with detachment but with a sense of indifference:

> I usually don't get kicks out of other women, not really, but there are times. Sometimes you come home and you are just too tired to work at it. Then it's nice to have a woman around. You can lay down on the floor, relax, watch TV and let her do it.

Add to this a sense of cynicism regarding sexual mores. Sexual behavior is generally not characterized by strippers as right or wrong by any universal standard but in terms of its presumed incidence in the general society; many of our respondents firmly expressed their view that lesbianism and prostitution are easily as common among women outside the occupation as among strippers. One respondent reasoned:

> Strippers are no different in morality than housewives, secretaries, waitresses, or anybody else. There is a certain amount of laxity of behavior which would occur in anybody, but with the occupational hazard of being lonely and moving from town to town, well, that's the reason.

The end effect of such attitudes is that no stigma is attached to either homosexual behavior or prostitution[4] among strippers as long as the participants are discreet, do not bother others, and do not allow their activities to interfere with the stability of the touring group. It appears, then, that strippers work in a situation where opportunities for homosexuality are not only available but where social pressures restricting sexual choice to males are minimal or non-existent.

---

[4] One perceptive respondent even questioned the rationality of the legal definition of prostitution: "There is a very hazy line between what people call prostitution and just going to bed with a man. What is the difference between taking $50 for it, or receiving flowers, going out to dinner, and then the theater, and then getting laid? One has preliminaries, otherwise there is no difference. There is a payment both ways."

SUMMARY

Previous research indicates that most homosexual careers, male or female, begun outside the total institutional setting involve enlistment rather than a system of recruitment through peer group or subcultural pressures (Gagnon and Simon, 1968a: 116, 118). As sociologists, however, we must not lose sight of the importance of situational conditions as explanatory variables for understanding rates of deviant behavior. We have attempted to demonstrate how sexual behavior may be an adaptation to social factors immediately impinging upon the actors; specifically we have argued that the stripping occupation may be analogous to the prison setting in that its structural characteristics contribute to the incidence of homosexual behavior.

REFERENCES

Benjamin, Harry, and R. E. L. Masters
1964   Prostitution and Morality. New York: Julian Press.
Gagnon, John H. and William Simon
1968a "Sexual deviance in contemporary America." The Annals of the Amer. Acad. of Political and Social Science 376 (March): 106–22.
1968b "The social meaning of prison homosexuality." Federal Probation 32 (March): 23–29.
Gerassi, John
1966   The Boys of Boise: Furor, Vice, and Folly in an American City. New York: Macmillan.
Giallombardo, Rose
1966   Society of Women: A Study of a Woman's Prison. New York: Wiley.
Hollingshead, August B.
1957   Two-Factor Index of Social Position. New Haven: Yale University (mimeographed).
Kinsey, Alfred C., Wardell B. Pomeroy, and Clyde E. Martin
1948   Sexual Behavior in the Human Male. Philadelphia: Saunders.
Kinsey, Alfred C., Wardell B. Pomeroy, Clyde E. Martin, and Paul H. Gebhard
1953   Sexual Behavior in the Human Female. Philadelphia: Saunders.
Leznoff, Maurice, and William A. Westley
1956   "The homosexual community." Social Problems 3 (April): 257–63.
Simon, William, and John H. Gagnon
1967a "Femininity in the lesbian community." Social Problems 15 (Fall): 212–21.

1967b "Homosexuality: The formulation of a sociological perspective." Journal of Health and Social Behavior 8 (September) : 177–85.

Skipper, James K., Jr., and Charles H. McCaghy
    1969   "Stripteasers and the anatomy of a deviant occupation." Paper read at American Sociological Association meetings in San Francisco (September, 1969).

Sykes, Gresham M.
    1965   The Society of Captives: A Study of a Maximum Security Prison. New York: Atheneum.

Ward, David A., and Gene G. Kassebaum
    1965   Women's Prison: Sex and Social Structure. Chicago: Aldine.

III

ILLEGAL ACTIVITIES
WITHIN A LEGAL
OCCUPATIONAL FRAMEWORK

Collar, Hat, and Coat Deviance
of Various Colors

Persistent patterns of deviant behavior in the form of varied, clandestine and often elaborate, illegal practices are found within the social organization of many legal occupational pursuits. Because of a unique opportunity structure and work-related subculture, these illegal activities are often endemic or distinctive to a specific occupational specialty and are therefore characteristic of given work systems. The relationship between work and a particular variety of deviant behavior is not always immediately apparent because the deviant behavioral configurations are frequently buried beneath the surface of occupational structure.

These illegal activities may constitute a concerted or at least combined effort on the part of the employer and employees to perpetrate fraud or theft on their clientele. They may represent a disguised form of theft residually employed by significant numbers of professional practitioners who, in disregard of ethical standards if not legal statutes, undertake to exploit the vulnerable position of client, patient, or customer. Illegal practices occurring within the framework of a conventional work structure may also be committed by employees against the employing firm. Entire work forces may be involved in such efforts. In some instances, the errant employee may even solicit the aid of client or customer in their misdeeds, sometimes as a collaborating accessory. In other cases, only single individuals or a small number of employees may undertake to commit the illegal acts, attempting to victimize employer, clientele, or both. Occasionally, groups of employees or individual practitioners undertake theft or sabotage against each other in a competitive fashion. The employer may also violate legal norms by victimizing his work force, individually or collectively. The combinations and permutations of principals involved in occupational crime of this variety are numerous and complex.

Some forms of occupational crime are so traditionally ingrained in popular stereotype that whole sets of folk humor have grown up around them— the butcher and his thumb on the scale, for example. Some kinds of occupational offenses are anticipated and largely tolerated—the B-girl who "be-

167

friends" a patron and orders an expensive drink at his expense but is served colored water, which maximizes her kickback, and the traveling employee who pads his expense account.

Occupational crime is difficult to prevent, is often not detected, is not infrequently tolerated; and when the culprit is apprehended, he is less likely than the conventional criminal to be indicted, prosecuted, found guilty, and punished. Occupational crime may far exceed conventional crime in the total amount of money stolen, extorted, or fraudulently acquired.

Deviant exploitative practices may occur at any status level of the occupational ladder, including the professions. In some instances a thin line is drawn between nonethical professional behavior and potentially illegal behavior. Professional ethics generally tend to address themselves primarily to relationships between colleagues and secondarily to relationships between practitioner and clientele. The essentially unknowledgeable clientele is relatively helpless and must place themselves unreservedly in the hands of the professional. The unscrupulous individual in the professions can readily exploit his client's ignorance and vulnerability to the point of outright fraud. Dentistry, for example, has been cynically termed by some as the "last bastion of American free enterprise," referring to the lucrative opportunities available to the dental practitioner who will disregard professional ethics and financially exploit his patients with low-quality but high-priced dental work, particularly "cosmetic" dentistry and replacement dentures. Recently one dentist, writing under a pseudonym, published an angry exposé of what he charges are unprofessional standards and exploitative practices in the dental profession.[1] He specifically mentions: fee-setting that encourages speedy but poor-quality dental work; overreliance on the more profitable, removable partial dentures than on hard-to-install fixed bridges; and the attempt to maintain the image of a painless dentist (thus attracting more business) by performing incomplete and ineffective work. While it may be argued that poor-quality work in most occupational pursuits is hardly a criminal offense, the fact remains that where any group of practitioners undertakes to maximize profits by deliberately providing substandard work while representing it as work of the highest quality, they are in theory, if not in fact, perpetrating an economic fraud and thus are in violation of legal statutes.

Other critics have painted equally indicting portraits of unethical, exploitative, and sometimes illegal practices and ploys among medical practitioners[2] and attorneys, to cite only a few of the professions involved. Last

---

[1] Paul Revere, D.D.S. (pseudonym), *Dentistry and Its Victims* (New York, St. Martin's Press, 1971).

[2] See H. M. Lewis, *The Medical Offenders* (New York, Simon & Schuster, 1970); see also Howard Whitman, "Why Some Doctors Should Be in Jail," *Collier's* 132 (October 30, 1953), pp. 23–27.

year, for example, in Manhattan and the Bronx complaints filed against lawyers rose 10 percent during a one-year time period.[3] While some of the complaints dealt with matters purely of an ethical nature, some concerned practices that might be in theoretical violation of legal statutes. Some professions have been accused of monopolistic practices that would not be tolerated if committed by corporate firms. Some professions have, in fact, been the recipients of governmental anti-trust actions. Many professions, nevertheless, do attempt to retain their monopolistic advantages and the attendant economic prerogatives. When the Price Commission of President Nixon's economic stabilization program required retailers, including drug store owners, to post price lists, the American Pharmaceutical Association rose up in arms, asserting that the dispensing of drugs is a professional service rather than a retail transaction, and prepared to go to court to protect their members from such a requirement.[4] Inasmuch as drug prices vary widely from store to store, posted prices would better permit a customer to "shop around" for the best savings. The druggists argued that price-posting puts "unreasonable emphasis on the cost of drugs while ignoring the value of the pharmacist's services." Consumer advocates, however, point out that "the lack of price competition tends to keep general price levels of prescriptions unreasonably high."

It has also been charged that druggists are sometimes guilty of other sorts of legal violations in the course of their work. Although there are many professional aspects of pharmacy operation, most of its occupational activities occur in a business establishment—the drugstore. Accordingly, the pharmacist often must attempt to play two occupational roles—a professional role and a business role. One researcher has hypothesized that such a role dilemma and its attendant strain are structural components of retail pharmacy and "that prescription violation may result, depending upon the individual mode of adaptation."[5] Using interview data from two groups of pharmacists, one consisting of known prescription violators and the other of nonviolators, the researcher concluded that prescription violators tended to have a business orientation, while nonviolators tended to have a professional or "professional-business" orientation. The business-oriented pharmacists stressed "the merchandising aspects of pharmacy" and were "primarily interested in monetary gains." They also felt less bound by professional norms. He concluded that prescription violation appeared to be related to the

<hr/>

[3] Lesley Oelsner, "Complaints Rise About Lawyers," *The New York Times* (Sunday, November 28, 1971).

[4] John D. Morris, "Druggists Battle Posting of Prices," *The New York Times* (Sunday, December 5, 1971).

[5] Richard Quinney, "Occupational Structure and Criminal Behavior," *Social Problems*, Vol. II, No. 2 (Fall 1963), pp. 180–85.

structure of the pharmacy occupation and was an "expression of that structure." It was his feeling that "the structure of the occupation and criminal behavior within the occupation can be better understood if they are considered together."

Even the hallowed halls of ivy are not free of occupational crime. A former college president and Undersecretary of Health, Education, and Welfare had a Ph.D. degree, granted in 1954 by the University of Texas, revoked because of charges of plagiarism. Plagiarism primarily raises ethical and moral questions, but when an individual goes on to accept positions that specifically require certain educational credentials, the possibility of legal violations arises. Plagiarism might be construed in some circumstances as fraud or misrepresentation. There have been instances of persons with falsified degrees or no degrees at all successfully misrepresenting themselves in order to obtain an occupational position. In the spring of 1972 a major educational scandal broke at the University of Wisconsin involving 600 students "suspected of submitting term papers they had bought from a commercial firm."[6] The papers had been purchased from a firm specializing in such products, which did a $2.2 million gross business in 1971. The Wisconsin Attorney General had subpoenaed the records of this and other firms and turned the records over to the university for investigation. In the marketplace today, one cannot only purchase term papers but can also buy "tailor-made" Ph.D. theses at prices ranging from $2.50 to $6.50 per page. In the Wisconsin case, some legal action, at least against the firms involved, is contemplated. In the tighter job market of the future, persons who misrepresent educational credentials or acquire such credentials through fraudulent or deceptive means may well be subject to legal sanctions.

Theft and pilferage by blue-collar employees is as endemic to industry as is economic exploitation and occupational crime in commerce and in the professions. In the late 1960s U.S. industry was estimated to be losing $2 billion per year in stolen property (and another $2 billion in pirated trade secrets).[7] At about this same time at one of Chrysler Corporation's main Dodge plants, so many compressed-air tools were stolen that "production almost stopped before police caught on."[8] Factories, stores, warehouses, and shipping terminals are naturally attractive targets for outside thieves, but not infrequently a firm's own employees may steal more company property than outside criminals. By the late 1950s and early 1960s department store sales in the United States were averaging $16 billion annually, but *shortages* of

---

[6] William B. Pollard, "Term-Paper Probe Blocks Some Degrees," *The Courier-Journal & Times* (Sunday, July 18, 1972), p. B8.

[7] "How to Steal $4 Billion," *Newsweek*, Vol. 69, No. 22 (May 1, 1967), p. 22.

[8] Ibid.

$200 million annually amounted to more than one-half the net profits.[9] Supermarkets were similarly losing $100 million per year as a result of employee thefts, which represented a significant proportion of profits on their gross sales of $5 billion.[10] Where an individual works around desirable goods and merchandise, there is motivation and opportunity to "take home samples." It is easy enough to take home an item or two from a grocery store, particularly if the can is dented or the label is soiled. One can rationalize that these items would not have sold anyway, that they represent little real value, and that the company is so large it will never miss the items. For the person working in a wholesale or manufacturing facility, the process of rationalization is even easier. There is so much or so many of the same thing that it becomes quite easy to convince oneself that a single item will never be missed. In fact, management has difficulty in determining that the items or materials are missing.

One researcher, Donald N. M. Horning, looked at "blue-collar theft" and its attendant attitudes and asserted that property in a plant is conceptually divided by the workers into the three categories: personal property, corporate property, and property of uncertain ownership.[11] Furthermore, he contends that within these categories there is a "continuum extending from a hard core of readily identifiable and nonmobile items to an outer fringe of uncertain, vacillatory items." The workers will establish "boundaries" between the category of company property and that of uncertain ownership. The work group will additionally develop norms concerning pilferage within the plant. The pilferage of personal or company property usually occurs without group sanction, especially if the firm has a strict policy against the pilferage of its property. Property of uncertain ownership such as scrap may be pilfered within the framework of group morality because such theft presumably has no victim. The appropriate circumstances and amount of such pilferage is also subject to group definition, and the overall values in this regard are "assimilated through precept and work group folklore."

Some blue-collar crime may well be the result of the frustrations and disaffections of the industrial worker who is caught in the economic squeeze of middle-class expectations but is also bound to the monotony and alienation of factory work.[12] If a worker sometimes strikes back at the depersonalization of the plant and his job by deliberately sabotaging his own product, he may

[9] Gibney, op. cit., p. 163.
[10] Ibid.
[11] Donald N. M. Horning, "Blue-Collar Theft: Conceptions of Property, Attitudes Toward Pilfering, and Work Group Norms in a Modern Industrial Plant," in Erwin O. Smigel and H. Laurence Ross (eds.), *Crimes Against Bureaucracy* (New York, Van Nostrand Reinhold, 1970), pp. 46–64.
[12] See especially Harvey Swados, "The Myth of the Happy Worker" in *A Radical's America* (Boston, Little, Brown, 1962), pp. 111–20.

accomplish something of the same goal by taking what he wants from an owner whom he perceives as having too much, anyway.

BUREAUCRATIC MISCREANTS

When Edwin H. Sutherland first articulated the concept of "white-collar" crime in 1939, he specifically referred to "crime committed by a person of respectability and high social status in the course of his occupation." The concept had particular reference for crimes committed by business *per se* such as conspiratorial practices involving price-fixing, anti-trust violations, misrepresentations, and the violation of various governmental standards and requirements concerning quality and labor practices. In recent years we have seen instances of "excessive rodent hair count" in candy manufacture, endemic efforts at price fixing and attempts to manipulate political leaders, and large-scale misrepresentation of product weights. In one instance a leading manufacturer of children's candy had been systematically showing a higher content weight for each candy bar than was actually the case. By shaving a minute weight from each piece of candy, the company was saving considerable sums in terms of its gross sales. The fact that in this instance the victimized consumers were children did not seem to deter the firm in the least. Only a few years ago a national scandal broke over a leading appliance manufacturer and its use of prostitutes to facilitate sales to wholesale buyers and distributors. During World War II the scarcity of many goods made black—and gray—marketeering especially profitable. Prices were controlled as an emergency procedure during the war, but many firms systematically violated the official "ceiling" prices established by the Office of Price Control.[13] Corporate tax evasion and fraudulent practices continue today from decades past, and hardly a month passes that some large firm is not found to be in deliberate violation of federal safety standards, fair labor practices, or anti-trust statutes.

Presumably, *white-collar crime* could also cover offenses committed between and among corporate entities. New and innovative types of intercorporate crime have grown in recent years. The battleground of such corporate conflict may on occasion take place within a giant computer. There have been recent cases of industrial espionage and sabotage involving theft of information from a computer by telephone.[14] A firm "breaks" the

[13] See Frank E. Hartung, "White Collar Offenses in the Wholesale Meat Industry in Detroit," *American Journal of Sociology,* Vol. 56, No. 1 (July 1950), pp. 25–34.

[14] See, for example, Edith M. Lederer, "Man Who Picked Brain of Computer by Telephone Accused of Theft," *Daily News,* Bowling Green, Kentucky (Thursday, April 1, 1971), p. 21.

computer code of another corporation and via telephone instructs the computer to "tell all," including company financial, personnel, sales, or engineering information. The old scenario of the individual disaffected with the impersonality of the computer who daydreams of punching additional holes in a data card and putting it into a computer to "disrupt" the computer's work may yet become a reality. Corporations may yet resort to computer sabotage by employing such tactics. But corporate espionage is very much alive and well and here now.[15] In some instances, one firm initiates the espionage against another company, while in other cases a corporation may simply be a willing customer of espionage information being sold by the defecting employee of another firm. Sometimes a company may reject such an offer and collaborate in the arrest and conviction of the spy, but this is not a hard and fast rule in American industry. A few years ago an overly greedy employee of Proctor & Gamble tried to sell the marketing plan for Crest Toothpaste to Colgate-Palmolive for $20,000.[16] Instead of buying the valuable information, Colgate-Palmolive notified and collaborated with the F.B.I. The culprit was apprehended and later at his trial pleaded guilty and received a suspended sentence because of his previously good record. (He could have been fined $10,000 and received a 10-year sentence.) Industrial espionage may take many forms. New dress designs by leading couturiers may be surreptitiously photographed at their premier showing and dispatched to garment "sweat" shops to be duplicated en masse for distribution to inexpensive dress store chains. Fierce competition among automobile makers engenders a significant amount of intercorporate spying activity, especially among the styling divisions. For example, the Dearborn Inn "has no trouble renting its terrace suites to General Motors men with field glasses in their luggage," because these suites overlook the Ford Motor Company proving grounds.[17]

Not only does intercorporate espionage involve the theft of ideas, it sometimes also involves materials and products. An interesting new variation of industrial espionage is music pirating. For years, of course, we have had book pirating where small "outlaw" publishers would copy and offset print expensive books without prior legal arrangement, thereby violating the copyright law. For some time, Taiwan was a leading center of such illegal trade. A cheap copy of an expensive medical or reference group could be ordered by mail for a fraction of its American list price. Finally, American

---

[15] For a detailed overview of such activity see John Perham, "The Great Game of Corporate Espionage," *Duns Review,* Vol. 96, No. 4 (October 1970), pp. 30–96.

[16] "Business Ethics: The Crestfallen Spy," *Time,* Vol. 85, No. 15 (April 9, 1965), pp. 97–98.

[17] Lawrence Stessin, " 'I Spy' Becomes Big Business," *New York Times Magazine* (November 28, 1965), pp. 105–06.

publishers put pressure on the U.S. Government, who cracked down on the Customs' inspections to effect seizure of such books as illegal contraband. With the boom in recorded music on record and tape, a highly profitable, albeit illegal, business has grown up around music piracy.[18] Music from a legitimate and copyrighted record or tape can readily be copied and mass produced. The practice can be quite lucrative because no royalties are paid. In some instances, even the labels can be forged or counterfeited. With the extremely large number of new and often small recording companies operating, plus the fact that tapes and records are sold practically everywhere, even at curb markets and truck stops, effectively halting record piracy has proven to be quite difficult.

White-collar crime may be nothing more serious than the career bureaucrat carrying home office supplies or a salesman diverting samples of his company's product to his own personal use or that of his friends. In some minor configurations the employee-perpetrator may even involve a client or customer as a kind of unintended accomplice in a small-scale criminal collusion system. An example might be the retail clerk who gives an unauthorized premium to the customer who makes a large purchase—a free shirt with a suit purchase, without the knowledge or consent of the store owner, in the hopes of attracting the customer back and thus increasing his future commissions. Such acts multiplied by the hundreds of thousands tend to magnify "minor" white-collar crime to its true enormity. Employee practices of this type have often seriously impaired corporate profits and have in some instances actually bankrupted some firms.

"Amateur" embezzlement is one of the popular and widespread forms of white-collar crime. This may be simply the routine procedure of "padding" an expense account. Many firms are aware of this practice on the part of their employees but tolerate it as a kind of "fringe benefit." Employees often prefer the privilege of claiming excessive expenses to a larger salary because expenses are not subject to income tax. The over-the-road truck driver who receives a discount at some stations because of the volume of gasoline purchased but who does not pass the saving on to his firm is a kind of amateur embezzler.

Embezzlement may take on more heroic proportions, however. In the late 1950s a New England attorney and ex-judge who dabbled in investments and embezzlement managed to steal more than $1,300,000 before he was discovered.[19] Since then, various political scandals have revealed em-

---

[18] Charles H. McCaghy and R. Serge Denisoff, "The Criminalization of Record Piracy: Analysis of an Economic and Political Conflict." Paper presented at the Interamerican Congress of the American Society of Criminology and the Interamerican Association of Criminology, Caracas, Venezuela, November 19–27, 1972.

[19] Frank Gibney, "Good Men Gone Wrong," *The Operators* (New York: Harper & Brothers, 1960), pp. 150–56.

bezzlements much larger, such as the Billy Sol Estes caper of a few years ago. Actually, one bank in every five sustains an embezzlement every few years.[20] Sometimes embezzlers are new employees who are dazzled by the opportunity for "easy money." Often, however, they are long-term, seemingly faithful employees who are usually "pillars of the community." An old-maid employee of a Norfolk, Virginia, bank who had 28 years of service went on trial in June 1956 for allegedly having embezzled $2,885,000.[21]

White-collar crime has become so endemic that an entire anti-business crime industry has grown up and flourished. Such firms provide information, security, and counterintelligence services in an effort to cut down on internal frauds and thefts, as well as help firms prevent the infiltration of the racketeer element.[22] Actually, some of the anti-business crime experts are quite cynical about employee white-collar crime. One such individual has estimated that in some firms from 75 to 95 percent of the employees have stolen from the employer.[23] Some measures of the pervasiveness of white-collar crime is demonstrated by the fact that a bibliography on white-collar crime compiled in 1967 was 85 pages long.[24]

There has been significant controversy among sociologists concerning the precise delineation of the phrase *white-collar crime,* with many writers contending that it should, much as Sutherland originally suggested, apply to a relatively narrow range of criminal offenses committed by persons of high occupational status within the course of their work.[25] I have taken a somewhat broader and more inclusive perspective, examining a wide range of work-related criminal activities. In the first article Donald J. Shoemaker and Donald R. South attempt to provide "a contemporary overview" of the topic. Taking a more traditionalist view, they focus on "occupationally relevant crimes (including embezzlement) committed by persons in 'upper' white-collar positions such as managerial, ownership, executive, and professional vocations." They point out the enormous financial extent of white-collar crime and suggest that it has import beyond the financial aspect. Identifying various social and economic trends relevant to white-collar crime, they speak of the growth of consumer fraud and the possibility of

[20] Ibid., p. 163.

[21] Ibid., p. 161.

[22] See Frank J. Prial, "Concern Fights Crime in Business," *The New York Times* (Sunday, July 26, 1970); see also Charles D. Hemphill, *Security for Business and Industry* (Homewood, Ill., Dow-Jones-Irwin, 1970).

[23] Herbert Brean, "Everybody Is Dishonest," *Life,* Vol. 45, No. 70 (November 24, 1958).

[24] Dorothy Campbell Tompkins, *White Collar Crime: A Bibliography* (Berkeley, Institute of Governmental Studies, University of California, 1967).

[25] For perhaps the most definitive collection of materials addressing themselves to the topic, including a number of essays that treat the definition and articulation of the phrase, see Gilbert Geis, *White Collar Criminal: The Offender in Business and the Professions* (New York, Atherton Press, 1968).

increasing use of computers and technology to perpetrate various kinds of offenses among other emergent developments. They predict that "its extent will, if anything, increase while its form will merely change with changing times." Employee loyalty to employing firms has tended to be eroded in recent years because of both the geographic and social mobility of our population. Inflation has tended to intensify the economic pressures of status striving which is encouraged by our advertising system and the mass media. The end of success all too often has become the justification of whatever the means. It has been charged that even the salesman perceives of his customer as "the enemy" and accordingly uses ruthless tactics to move his merchandise.[26] In the face of such a climate of business, there would seem to be little reason to believe that white-collar crime will subside or even diminish. Rather it may become increasingly sophisticated, omnipresent, and sinister as the complexity of modern mass society tends to obfuscate moral and legal distinctions in regard to work practices and procedures *vis-a-vis* clientele, government, employee, or employer.

In a society as populous and complex as our own, there must be formal impersonalized standards governing all aspects of the social enterprise. The enormity of economic intercourse in our social life renders impractical a reliance on personal experience and insight as a means of insuring a given level of quality and quantity. Similarly, we seldom rely on subjective measures of quality in regard to the various products we use and on which we depend. Instead we depend on agencies and institutions to develop and maintain objective procedures for grading, evaluating, and testing products and materials to ensure uniform and satisfactory standards of safety, purity, and quality for those products and materials. Where the externally imposed standards can be circumvented or subverted, however, there is obviously opportunity for maximizing profits.

Even the minute lowering of standards may provide the possibility of extremely lucrative increases in profit margins. Such an opportunity provides the motivation for many individuals to violate the regulations and statutes attendant to uniform quality standards. Standards laws and regulations are maintained and enforced, in some instances, by large and elaborate work systems involving individuals employed by government agencies, the producer, and occasionally by other entities. To circumvent or subvert the rules often means that numerous individuals must be involved in the criminal collusion efforts. This may require complex arrangements for bribery, fraud, kickbacks, and misrepresentation. Some such arrangements are widespread, pervasive, and institutionalized within some government settings and levels.

[26] "Confessions of an Appliance Salesman," *Consumer Reports,* Vol. 23 (October 1958), pp. 546–47.

The opportunities for quality inspection crime in our society are ample indeed in the face of our vast economy. Whether building bridges or bottling milk, there are often ways of cutting cost and thus increasing profit margin, if the appropriate inspector, grader, or functionary can be corrupted. With the lure of affluence and the attendant luxurious lifestyle to tantalize them many such individuals can be and are corrupted.

Quite recently a vivid example was brought to the attention of the American people in the form of an expose of criminal collusion involving government inspectors in the meat packing industry.[27] A number of inspectors who had worked in packing houses were indicted and charged with accepting bribes and favors for not enforcing some operant regulatory standards. Government regulations concerning meat are complex and numerous. The discretionary power of the meat inspector is considerable, and according to the author of the expose, "the inspector is not expected to enforce strictly every rule, but rather to decide which rules are worth enforcing at all." Such discretion does offer the opportunity for corruption, and in this instance the government decided to crack down—on the inspectors, although not on the packers who were also involved.

HOMBURG HAT CRIME: THE BETRAYAL OF PUBLIC TRUST

The very concept of the political entity assumes a social contract, as it were, between the individual member and the social collective. The individual gives up certain personal prerogatives and accepts some degree of control and regulation over his behavior and circumstances. In a sense, he subjugates his own desires and freedom for the common good. In return for these restrictions and sacrifices an individual receives the protection, support, and guidance of the social group. Because we are born into the group and thus inherit the social contract, it is not a voluntary covenant. One could, in some circumstances, abrogate the agreement and live apart from the group as a solitary human, but in actuality this is seldom practical and there are numerous impediments to the implementation of such a decision. The individual then, regardless of his preferences, finds himself subject to a variety of social controls and restraints as a result of the political organization of the society in which he lives. He may grow restive under the yoke of social control and undertake to violate some of the norms that serve to restrict or regulate his behavior. Violations of the existing norms, rules, and statutes are viewed as apparent threat and danger to the political state. Any criminal behavior then may be viewed as a kind of political offense. On a more

---

[27] Peter Shuck, "The Curious Case of the Indicted Meat Inspectors," *Harper's,* Vol. 245, No. 1468 (September 1972), pp. 81–88.

specific level, however, some violations of the norms are more directly aimed at disrupting the political equilibrium, seeking to subvert the effectiveness of the polity, inadequate, or faulty discharge of political responsibilities or undertaking to use inappropriate means of altering the political apparatus and processes. Such violations can properly be termed political crimes.

The "defector," who seeks to espouse the polity is a political criminal in the same sense as the "revolutionary" who attempts to overthrow the government by clandestine or violent means. Political leaders and functionaries may also commit political crimes, however, by their failure to properly discharge their responsibilities, through incompetence or malfeasance, by using their office to their own advantage, especially where this acts to the detriment of their followers or constituents, or by seeking self-aggrandizement in terms of power or fame.

In ancient and medieval times chiefs, commanders, and even kings were sometimes deposed, banished, or even executed when they were derelict in their executive duty. Some rulers undertook to commit suicide as a means of expunging their shame and guilt. In more recent times, especially in democratic countries, elaborate provisions have been made to permit the removal from office of those persons who violate the expectations of their position and betray the public trust. Presidents may be impeached, politicians may be recalled, and political functionaries may be dismissed in the event of malfeasance or gross incompetence. Although public officials who have been discovered and shamed in their misdeeds do on occasion still commit suicide, they may instead be more inclined to flee to Brazil or some other country that has no extradition treaty with the U.S. In spite of the fact that political office today carries with it many residual benefits, some individuals have sought to extend these benefits beyond the ethical and legal limits. Because "power corrupts and absolute power corrupts absolutely," the power, privilege, and prerogative of public office do, unfortunately, on occasion tempt the incumbent and motivate him to violate the expectations of his position and various legal statutes and accordingly be guilty of committing Homburg Hat Crime.

The nationally traumatic Watergate exposé and all of the attendant and ancillary disclosures of political misdeeds give ample and vivid testimony to the ubiquitousness and depth of Homburg Hat Crime in our society. The Watergate scandal hardly needs reiteration. There are other recent and equally disturbing illustrations. In 1972 Texas Congressman John Dowdy was convicted of bribery, conspiracy, and perjury in federal court.[28] His trial and conviction grew out of a case involving an alleged $25,000 bribe for "fixing" a federal case against a Baltimore contractor. Dowdy, facing a possible

[28] See "Congressman Convicted," *Time,* Vol. 99 (January 10, 1972), pp. 13–14.

maximum sentence of 40 years imprisonment and $40,000 in fines, refuses to resign his Congressional seat while his appeal is pending. *He became the 15th sitting member of Congress to be convicted of crimes in the twentieth century.* In 1971 a state court convicted Jersey City Mayor Thomas Whelan and several other Hudson County politicians of conspiracy and extortion.[29] The trial brought to light evidence of kickbacks, graft, and numbered bank accounts. In 1972 a Congressman from New Jersey was indicted in Federal Court on charges of conspiracy, perjury, and evasion of federal income tax;[30] and W. W. Barron, the ex-Governor of West Virginia, pleaded guilty to bribing a jury that had been trying him for another instance of bribery.[31] For his guilty plea, he was fined $50,000 and sentenced to two concurrent 12-year prison terms.

In Illinois a full-scale scandal broke involving special offers of race-track stocks to politicians and political favors in support of horse racing interests.[32] The racetrack inquiry is focused on a number of top politicians including a congressman, a top county official, a federal and a circuit judge, an ex-governor and an ex-state revenue director, all of whom may have been the recipients of funds that were, according to *Newsweek*, "impolitic." The federal investigation is continuing and a wealthy racetrack owner turned all of her books and records over to federal investigators, "in return for judicial immunity."

The role prescribed for political office holders is circumspect indeed and even extends back to their election activities. The Federal Corrupt Practices Act, passed in 1925, for example, establishes the maximum amounts that various candidates may expend in their election efforts.[33] It also contains various reporting and disclosure requirements. There are numerous loopholes, however, for evading the maximum expenditure stipulations, as well as means of disguising the amounts spent. Inasmuch as the actual cost of a successful campaign may be many times the maximum specified under the 1925 law, it has been charged that the "Corrupt Practices Act assures that the financial practices of practically everyone who attains national office will be corrupt."[34]

Politicians often begin their careers, even at the very lowest rungs of public life, with the problem of financing their election. To run a successful

[29] See "Weeding the Garden State," *Time*, Vol. 98 (July 19, 1971), pp. 12–13.
[30] See "Gallagher's Suitcase," *Newsweek*, Vol. 79 (April 24, 1972), p. 25.
[31] See "Ex-Official of W. Virginia Faces Trial," *Roanoke Times* (Monday, September 18, 1972), p. 1.
[32] "Illinois Off To The Races," *Newsweek*, Vol. 78 (October 11, 1971), p. 28.
[33] See "Annals of Politics: A Fundamental Hoax," *The New Yorker*, Vol. 47 (August 7, 1971), pp. 37–38.
[34] Ibid.

campaign they may exceed the legally established expenditure limits. Unless they are personally wealthy, they have to depend on contributions, ideally many small ones. More realistically, however, contributions will likely come in the form of a relatively few large contributions, not infrequently from persons, groups, and organizations with vested interests who may seek political favors. The politician goes into office "indebted" to his campaign contributors. Once in office, the public official may discover that his income is barely adequate to maintain a lifestyle appropriate to his position. Because of his strategic occupational location and his participation in political decision-making, he may well be opportuned from time to time to exercise bias in his political efforts. Requests for help, information, and political favors may all involve personal profit or benefit, mutual aid and favors, and opportunity for maximizing power and influence. The public official is often also privy to information and opportunity structure that affords him special prerogatives and privilege in terms of profit-making and of political favor performance. A politician may, for example, know in advance of the general public about the building of a public facility or road, and this information may well permit him to acquire potentially valuable real estate nearby at a price that will allow ample profit. Inasmuch as politicians move in and out of public life subject to the vicissitudes of the democratic process, many public officials move into the public sector of the economy after one or more terms of office and in some instances move back into government at a later date in another administration.[35] In some cases, this public-private job shuffle would seem to suggest the possibility of conflict of interests.

A political leader may be in office only a short time. He may have few prospects and little security upon leaving office. This lack of future security may motivate him to maximize his income or wealth while in office; preparing for a "rainy day" so to speak. Political crime can often be readily covered up, and there is a tendency of other politicians to be tolerant of each other's misdeeds. The public is often uninformed and the complexity of contemporary government is such that graft and conflict of interest may be difficult to discover and prove.

In our society, as in some others, we have experienced a long history of political crime, some blatantly flagrant. Cynical politicians see crime and graft among politicians as something of a way of life. In Chapter 10 James Boyd articulates the "rules" for "The Ritual of Wiggle: From Ruin to Reelection." Detailing a list of 13 cynical but nevertheless seemingly valid guides for avoiding and evading discovery, recrimination, or indictment and legal and political sanction, if involved in political scandal and crime.

[35] Michael C. Jensen, "Public-Private Job Shuffle Booming in Washington," *The Roanoke Times* (Sunday, November 12, 1972), p. D–2.

THE TARNISHED SHIELD

The law enforcer is one of society's representatives of social control. He is entrusted with special powers and prerogatives to enforce the norms of society. He is, by definition, a minion of the law; he is, in theory, above reproach in his own observance and conformity to the law. Unfortunately law enforcement personnel are all too human and not infrequently violate the law themselves, in spirit if not in letter, in the course of their work.

Police work deviance may take a number of sinister forms. Some law enforcement officers *overcomply* with the requirements of their job and in their zealousness to uphold the law and apprehend the lawless, sometimes resort to illegal means. The classic "third degree," while perhaps an effective interrogation method, is in violation of police regulations, criminal and civil statutes, and the constitutional rights of the individual being interrogated. In spite of efforts to prevent or control excessive violence on the part of policemen in apprehending and interrogating persons suspected of committing crimes, such treatment is endemic in many police forces. William A. Westley, in his classic study of police violence, pointed out that the use of violent means by policemen is "a consequence of their occupational experience and that the policemen's colleague group sanctions such usage."[36] The policeman is under pressure to arrest and make a case against the felon. Through arrest and the development of a convincing and convicting case against the offenders, the police can justify themselves to the community. Furthermore, "The police are responsible for the enforcement of laws regulating sexual conduct." Sexual offenses are often difficult to solve and when suspects are found, they are difficult to convict because of the reluctance of victims to cooperate or testify. The use of violence then, for some policemen, seems particularly appropriate in the instance of sex crimes. They also feel that the public is particularly sensitive to sex crimes and wish to see the perpetrator punished regardless of the legal subtleties involved. The policemen may take the matter into their own hands and use brutality as a means of "punishing" the offender. They often react similarly if the suspect is abusive or disrespectful to the arresting policemen. In instances of these sorts, Westley found, violent behavior is approved and supported by the police informal group.

Although some court decisions of recent years have clearly pointed out that deliberate brutality is unconstitutional and may be grounds for acquittal or reversal of conviction, the practice continues. Albert J. Reiss found in 1968 in a study of police behavior on the job that patrolmen did resort to unnecessary beatings and brutality in making arrest and in questioning

[36] William A. Westley, "Violence and The Police," *The American Journal of Sociology*, Vol. LIX (July 1953), pp. 34–41.

suspects.[37] His data suggest that "one officer in 10 in high-crime areas uses force unnecessarily, at least occasionally." Although it had previously been charged that officers were more likely to use brutality in arresting blacks than whites, Reiss found that "the rate of beatings of whites was higher." Inasmuch as "negro suspects make up a larger proportion of the total criminal population than whites," however, "the negro's chances of improper treatment are closer to the white's chances."[38] In some instances, courts have ruled than some kinds of violent methods are permissable as long as they are "not unreasonable or brutal." In the case in point, a judge ruled that a police officer may use a "sleeper hold" to render a drunk-driving suspect unconscious so that a blood sample may be taken.[39]

While there is perhaps a certain public toleration of police brutality as a kind of practical and expedient necessity, police corruption is somewhat less palatable. Whether police corruption is getting worse or more of it is simply coming to light is difficult to say, but according to the commander of the New York Police Department's anti-corruption unit, the number of public complaints about police corruption increased threefold during 1971 alone.[40]

In his study of police activities in three northern cities, Reiss found that 27 percent of the policemen in the study were involved in misconduct, including "such things as shaking down traffic violators and accepting payoffs to alter sworn testimony."[41]

When in 1970 the press reported police graft in New York City to be a million-dollar business, Mayor John V. Lindsay appointed a blue-ribbon citizen's commission to investigate police corruption in New York, the largest police force in the United States.[42] It was reported that Mayor Lindsay established the commission "to winnow out the few individual rotten apples and thereby restore the New York police force's reputation as a whole." After the commission had explored the parameters of corruption in the department, Knapp reported that "the whole barrel is so rotten that corruption has become the rule rather than the exception." The Knapp Commission turned up an almost unbelievable amount of graft, kickbacks, and corruption. As the testimony was gathered before the commission, it began to appear that

[37] Jerry M. Flint, "Most Police Unbiased, Study Shows," *The Louisville* (Ky.) *Courier-Journal & Times* (Sunday, July 7, 1968), p. A 16.

[38] Ibid.

[39] "Judge Rules Police Can Use 'Sleeper Hold,' " *The Louisville* (Ky.) *Courier-Journal & Times* (Sunday, July 7, 1968), p. 2 and 16.

[40] David Burnham, "Public Complaints of Police Corruption Are Reported to Have Tripled in a Year," *The New York Times* (Sunday, November 14, 1971), p. 53.

[41] David Burnham, "27 Percent of Policemen in Study Involved in Misconduct," *The Louisville* (Ky.) *Courier-Journal* (Sunday, July 7, 1968), p. A 16.

[42] New York's Rotten Apples," *Newsweek,* Vol. 78, No. 2 (July 12, 1971), p. 78.

few had not been touched by the corruption. One New York City patrolman, for example, testified that "all but two of the 70 to 75 policemen he worked with in the Bedford-Stuyvesant section of Brooklyn regularly took small bribes from gamblers, tow-truck operators, check cashers, and supermarket operators."[43] Another patrolman testified that "gamblers were paying bribes to the police in every division in the city" and that "during his 14 years in the department he had never known a policeman in a gambling enforcement unit for more than two months who did not take graft and that he had never found a construction site foreman who did not pay the precinct police."[44] The Knapp Commission had articulated two kinds of crooked cops—the "grasseaters" who took minor bribes and the "meateaters" who went for big graft. There appeared to be a significant number of "meateaters."

Police deviance may assume less ominous but still obnoxious forms in some instances. An example is the deviant practice known as "cooping," or sleeping on duty, which is according to a police informant, a "traditional and widely accepted practice within the Police Department."[45] It has been suggested that sleeping on duty is particularly endemic among policemen who attempt to hold down second full-time or heavy part-time jobs. They may try to catch up on sleep in patrol cars at night while on duty. Pulling into an alley, a patrolman sleeps while his partner maintains the illusion of patroling by continuing radio contact with the station. The policemen are derelict in their duty, thus violating regulations and defrauding the taxpayer.

At times policemen may, under pressure from an arrest quota system, be inclined to make arrests or issue citations when they are not strictly called for. A traffic patrolman may, for example, elect to violate the informal norm for citations listed and instead try to give extra citations by apprehending "hummers"—improper arrests or citations that should not have been made because they are borderline cases.[46]

In Chapter 11 Ellwyn R. Stoddard details "The Informal 'Code' of Police Deviancy." Looking at "blue-coat" crime, Stoddard examines a variety of illicit activities in which policemen engage including "shopping" (larceny), extortion, bribery, and shakedowns, as well as unethical practices

---

[43] David Burnham, "Patrolman Says 'All but 2' of Colleagues Got Bribes," *The New York Times* (Saturday, October 23, 1971), p. 1.

[44] David Burnham, "Gambling Bribes to Police Alleged in Every Division," *The New York Times* (Wednesday, October 20, 1971), p. 1.

[45] David Burnham, "Paper On Cooping Gets a High Grade," *The New York Times* (Sunday, August 3, 1969), p. 68.

[46] David M. Petersen, "Informal Norms and Police Practice: The Case of the Quota System," *Sociology and Social Research,* Vol. 55, No. 3 (April 1971), pp. 354–62.

such as mooching, chiseling, and practicing favoritism. The police recruits are socialized into these illegal or unethical practices which are sanctioned by the "informal code." These deviant patterns are encouraged and maintained by various groups processes. According to Stoddard, deviance of this variety found in a police department "is a reflection of values which are habitually practiced and accepted within that community."

CRIME IN THE REAR RANKS

Major General Benedict Arnold was a military criminal because of his treasonous attempt to betray the fortification plans of West Point to the British during the American Revolution. In the same war Nathan Hale was also considered to be a military criminal, in this instance by his British enemy. Inasmuch as he was on an information and intelligence gathering mission, wearing as a disguise the civilian clothing of a schoolmaster when captured, the British considered him to be in violation of the "rules" of war and thus a spy. As an enemy spy and accordingly as a military criminal by their standards, the British hanged him. The defendants at the Nuremberg trials, after World War II, were considered to be and were tried as "war criminals" by their enemies who presumably represented "humanity" in exacting justice. The 95 American soldiers who were executed by the army in Europe during World War II for murder and/or rape of unarmed civilians were military criminals. So too was Private Eddie D. Slovik who was executed by a firing squad in January of 1945 for cowardice and desertion before the enemy.[47] Private Slovik was the only American serviceman to have been executed for such an offense since 1864. Mutiny, being insubordinate to an officer, being A.W.O.L., pretending to be sick to avoid work or battle, violating uniform regulations or misappropriating military property for personal use are all forms of military crimes and are punishable as such.

Some forms of military crime are as old as the pyramids and the campaigns of Alexander. Others are recent as yesterday's news. It was only in the Vietnamese conflict that the public heard of United States soldiers "fragging" officers (although of course there have been attempts by military personnel to assault and murder their officers as long as there have been military organizations). Theft in armed service PXs presumably occurred even in World War II, but it was the summer of 1972 before the fact was called to our attention that recent investigations had shown that even Army generals and military chaplains were committing such offenses. Perhaps most timely, however, were the recent reports of inappropriate economic activities with the intention of exploitative profit-taking on the part of our astronauts.

[47] For a detailed chronicle of this incident see William Bradford Huie, *The Execution of Private Slovik* (New York, The New American Library, 1954).

The military represents a large socal entity of distinctive characteristics and unique circumstances. Often the normative system of social control of the society of which the military is a part may be inappropriate or inadequate to the military itself. The military may, of necessity, have operated physically apart from its parent society and this separation may dictate a separate system of social control. The nature of the military's task is so unique from other work systems and the circumstances within which it may have to operate are so extraordinary that a social control system additional and supplemental to the conventional operative civilian system may be necessary. For these and other reasons, military entities are normally subject to special systems of military justice, in the place of, or in addition to regular systems of legal constraints. The ancient Greek and Roman armies relied to s〈 me degree on separate systems of military justice. The Crusaders from Europe, however, developed the first "formal Military code."[48] By the time of the American Revolution, the Continental Congress developed the first national code of military justice in the form of its own Articles of War.[49] The Articles of War went through a number of revisions over the years, and in 1950 the comprehensive Uniform Code of Military Justice was adopted and made effective the following year.

A separate and often more stringent system of justice is necessary for the military for a number of reasons. The military is normally made up of a population on which social control is inherently more difficult to impose than on the civilian population. The military population consists largely of males in their younger and middle adult years. The majority of the enlisted personnel in the United States Army tends to be minimally educated (frequently high school or less) and often of lower and lower-middle socioeconomic status. In general, they are least likely to have internalized the upper- and upper-middle-class values of order and propriety. They are prone to operate more on an emotional level than persons of more education. Being less articulate, they are more likely to resort to overt hostility or violence when frustrated. They are less equipped for self-discipline, logical examination, or for rational concerted action—in the absence of external control. For these reasons and others military discipline is necessarily imposed. The less sophisticated are the troops in the military, the more stringent and authoritarian will be the system of military justice.

Military discipline is also necessary because of the nature of the military mission. Not every individual is sufficiently imbued with either the warrior spirit or the patriotic zeal necessary to motivate him to risk death or terrible

---

[48] Richard D. Knudten, Chapter 19, "The System of Military Justice," *Crime in a Complex Society: An Introduction to Criminology* (Homewood, Ill., Dorsey, 1970), p. 472.
[49] Ibid.

infirmity in battle or to kill and maim. Military discipline removes from the individual the necessity of making a choice in the matter. If conscripted and ordered into combat, the individual has no recourse but to follow legitimate orders even if they mean death. Failure to do so constitutes a violation of military regulation and is appropriately punished. As a case in point, Private Eddie Slovik, who deserted from his unit in World War II as means of avoiding combat duty and was captured and court-martialed for violating Article of War 50 1/2, was found guilty and subsequently "shot to death with musketry."[50] Many military authorities, including one of the legal officers who reviewed the court-martial record, contended that Slovik was shot "not as a punitive measure nor as retribution, but to maintain that discipline upon which alone an army can succeed against the enemy."[51] Close-order drill is traditionally retained in military systems not so much for the purpose of preparing for orderly movement from place to place or for aesthetically satisfying parade ground performance, but to instill in the troops a reflexive obedience to orders that will carry over into combat orders, ensuring an immediate and complete obedience to command regardless of the circumstances.

The vast amounts of rations, supplies, and equipment in the military must be appropriately allocated and utilized if the military mission is to be accomplished. The traditional reflection about the battle being lost for the want of a horseshoe nail has considerable validity in military fact. The ubiquitous abundance of material in the military means that its control and maintenance of security is difficult to effect. For this reason, a significant proportion of military regulations concerned themselves with offenses against government property and in this regard military justice is often severe. To maintain proper equipment allocation, considerable effort is expended by military systems to ensure appropriate equipment accountability in terms of both units and individuals. In spite of the elaborate configurations of supply controls and regulations, the fact remains that military existence is often an existence of deprivation, at least relatively speaking. Military personnel frequently resort to misappropriation of government property for their own personal or group use, either directly or indirectly, with the intention of improving their comfort, effectiveness, and chance of survival. Military activities frequently occur in areas and circumstances of extreme material deprivation, economically depressed countries, or countries destroyed by war, and accordingly military supplies and equipment take on an inordinately high economic and social value to the indigenous populations. American GIs who initially occupied Germany in World War II discovered that government rations and cigarettes would buy almost anything from sex to art treasures. The temptation was too much for many American military servicemen,

[50] Huie, op. cit.
[51] Ibid., pp. 10–11.

who undertook to acquire lucrative incomes from black-market activities and advantageous currency exchanges.

Military operations do not occur within a social vacuum. Rather, they often involve both enemy and allied armed forces and civilian populations. To be most effective, armed forces often find that they must "fight by the rules," so to speak. As a result of international treaties and historical tradition, not to mention formal and informal diplomatic understandings, laws, regulations, and protocols concerning the "rules" of war and the treatment of captured personnel are established. To "not take prisoners" sometimes becomes expedient, however, and there is often great individual motivation, especially to take "souvenirs" of personal property from a P.O.W. Such behavior represents violation of military norms.

No military organization can operate with any degree of effectiveness that does not maintain internal discipline to the extent that all act in harmonious concert to effect the mission. Any disruption to the teamwork capability and internal discipline is usually severely sanctioned. Fights and assaults between peers or subordinates and superiors are examples of such disruption. In recent years the increasing number of black servicemen in the U.S. military, coupled with the growing militancy of some blacks and their impatience with residues of racial prejudice and discrimination, has tended to create a climate conducive to interracial fights and disturbances within the ranks of the military. In 1972 the U.S. aircraft carrier Constellation had to interrupt maneuvers at sea to put 237 crewmen ashore. The men had staged a protest on the ship "to complain about what they called 'calculated racism' on the part of the ship's officers in administering discipline and work assignments."[52] The same year a bloody riot between white and black sailors took place aboard the carrier Kitty Hawk and lasted more than five hours. In it 46 crewmen were injured, and 21 black sailors were arrested and held for court-martial or discipline. Now the Navy has taken steps to ensure that any remaining forms of racial prejudice or discrimination in the service are eliminated and to promote racial equality. Similarly, however, the Navy has also cracked down on racial militancy, specifically prohibiting such manifestations as the "black power" clenched fist salute or the "dap" (an involved handshake currently popular with black-power militants). The Army has also had its share of racial disturbances both among its troops in Vietnam and those stationed in Germany. Such disturbances are costly and deleterious to the prompt and efficient discharge of its mission, however, and the military will probably employ its most severe sanctions to minimize or eliminate such disruptive breakdowns of discipline.

The mission of the military is usually considered critical to the survival

[52] "Navy Schedules Hearings on Bias Charges," *The Roanoke Times* (Sunday, November 12, 1972).

of a society. Discipline is clearly essential to the operation of the military, and the appropriate discharge of individual duties and responsibilities is therefore considered to be a mandatory requisite of overall success. Accordingly, crimes against performance are considered to be especially serious from the standpoint of the military, and a significant proportion of the various articles of war concern themselves with such offenses. Military regulations dictate extremely circumspect demeanor and comportment in regard to fulfilling the appropriate role obligations, responsibilities, and expectations. A member of the military is expected to keep himself ready and fit to perform his duty, to behave in an exemplary manner when in civilian public, and to refrain from any behavior that would tend to bring discredit to the military or his country. Most important, however, is his performance before the enemy. According to military prescription, the serviceman should be tolerant of hardships and deprivation, he should be aggressive and obedient in combat, even to death, and if captured, he should be stoic in endurance and resolute in conviction.

There is a considerable gulf between the real and the ideal, however, and an individual may deviate from the officially expected and thus become a violator of military law and regulation. Chapter 12 is an examination of the normative system of the military and the contribution and facilitation of military training itself to the process of "Socialization for Khaki-Collar Crime."

9. White-Collar Crime

DONALD J. SHOEMAKER

and

DONALD R. SOUTH

BACKGROUND AND CURRENT STATUS

The concept of white-collar crime was introduced by Edwin Sutherland in 1939 in the presidential address to the joint annual meetings of the American Sociological Society (now Association) and the American Economic Society. Sutherland attempted to convince his audience that crime was not a lower-class phenomenon.[1] Indeed, many offenses, both patently criminal and morally reprehensible, are committed by persons of high socioeconomic status in business and the professions. Although Sutherland gave no exact figures, he estimated that white-collar crime "is probably several times as great as the financial cost of all the crimes which are customarily regarded as the 'crime problem.' "[2] Sutherland then proceeded to list specific examples of white-collar offenses, each running into hundreds of thousands of dollars.

A decade later Sutherland published a book entitled *White Collar Crime* in which he backed up more adequately the statements and contentions he made in the presidential address of 1939. He defined white-collar crime as "a crime committed by a person of respectability and high social status in the course of his occupation."[3] Using this definition, Sutherland studied (without prior knowledge of the degree of law-breaking) the life histories of 70 of the nation's largest nonfinancial corporations. He found that each of the corporations had at least one decision against it during its history (one corporation had 50).[4] The decisions concerned such things as "restraint of trade; misrep-

[1] Edwin H. Sutherland, "White-Collar Criminality," *American Sociological Review*, Vol. 5 (February 1940), p. 2.

[2] Ibid., pp. 4–5.

[3] Edwin H. Sutherland, *White Collar Crime* (New York, Dryden, 1949), p. 9.

[4] Ibid., p. 20. According to Sutherland, a "decision" referred to formal findings of wrongdoing by courts or administrative commissions, stipulations agreed to by courts or commissions, confiscations by permission of law, and findings that the defendant had committed wrongdoings in the past even though condoned by a court.

resentation in advertising; infringement of patents, trademarks, and copy-rights; 'unfair labor practices' as defined by the National Labor Relations Law ... ; rebates; financial fraud and violation of trust; violations of war regulations; and some miscellaneous offenses."[5] In all, 980 decisions were rendered, 158 in criminal courts (16 percent). However, the 158 criminal court decisions covered 60 percent of the corporations with an average of four convictions each.[6] In addition, Sutherland noted that 779 of the 980 decisions were decisions that a crime had been committed (that is, a law had been violated) and that many of the decisions could have been tried in crim-inal court under such patently criminal laws as the Sherman Antitrust Law, a violation of which in itself is a misdemeanor. Most of the decisions, how-ever, consisted of cease and desist orders (violations of which sometimes con-stitute contempt), stipulations that the corporation would not be "bad" again, and treble damage suits (where the violator was ordered to pay dam-ages equal in amount to three times the cost of "injury" suffered), or other civil suits. Even in civil suit awards, the corporations were given advantages by being allowed to plead *nolo contendere* to the charges, thus negating the decision as evidence in civil suits.[7] All of this demonstrated that white-collar crimes did exist, although most of the acts were not violations of criminal law, and that the violators were merely "slapped on the wrist."

A few years later, Clinard studied the violations of the Office of Price Administration's (OPA) wartime (World War II) price regulations of civil-ian products, military supplies, rents, and the rationing of such commodities as "gasoline, tires, meat, coffee, and sugar."[8] Clinard chose to call violations of these regulations "black-market" activities, of which several types existed. Between February 1942 and June 1947, the OPA had instigated almost 260,000 sanctions, including more than 19,000 criminal sanctions. Of these numbers, 170,708 proceedings had been closed, 4,553 local criminal prosecu-tions had been won, and more than 11,000 federal prosecutions had ended with imprisonment, fine, probation, or suspended sentence. As with Suther-land's study, Clinard found most of the sanctions to be light, consisting of cease and desist orders, damage suits, and suspensions of licenses and trans-action rights. Sentences for federal criminal convictions were mostly on the misdemeanant level, with most criminal violators receiving sentences of six months or less. Those receiving stronger sentences (say, over one year) were involved in dealings with other than black-market activities. While one might question the propriety of studying black-market activities as white-collar crimes, Clinard demonstrated time and again that these activities involved

[5] Ibid., p. 18.
[6] Ibid., pp. 22–25.
[7] Ibid., pp. 33–40.
[8] Marshall B. Clinard, *The Sociology of Deviant Behavior* (New York, Holt, Rinehart and Winston, 1952), p. 9.

numerous men of high socioeconomic status and respectability acting during the course of their occupations.

Hartung investigated the black-market activities during World War II involving the wholesale meat industry in Detroit.[9] His findings were similar to Clinard's. From December 1942 to July 1946 233 sanctions were imposed involving 83 firms, 132 persons, and 195 offenses. The sanctions were much the same as those found by Clinard—the range of prison terms was three months to one year; damages involved a low of $40 and a high of $6,000; and fines went from $100 to $15,000.

These studies and the concept around which they focused did not go unchallenged. Tappan,[10] Burgess,[11] Geis,[12] and Caldwell,[13] among others, have all criticized the legitimacy of the concept of white-collar crime as it involves noncriminal laws; the absence of strict criminal proceedings for assessing guilt (including the matter of criminal intent) ; and the verification of corporations, businesses, and the like.[14] Others, such as Quinney[15] and Clinard and Quinney,[16] have argued for adoption of the term *occupational crime* to emphasize the phenomenon of crimes committed on the job or in conjunction with occupational pursuits. Along this line, concepts such as blue-coat crime (see Chapter 11 in this volume) and blue-collar crime[17] have been used to emphasize crimes committed on the job in various occupations and occupational structures.

The concept of white-collar crime, however, has remained the subject

[9] Frank E. Hartung, "White-Collar Offenders in the Wholesale Meat Industry in Detroit," *American Journal of Sociology,* Vol. 56 (July 1950), pp. 25–34.

[10] Paul W. Tappan, "Who Is the Criminal?" *American Sociological Review,* Vol. 12 (February 1947), pp. 96–103.

[11] Ernest W. Burgess, "Comment," *American Journal of Sociology,* Vol. 56 (July 1950), pp. 32–34.

[12] Gilbert Geis, "Toward a Delineation of White-Collar Offenses," *Sociological Inquiry,* Vol. 32 (Spring 1962), pp. 160–71.

[13] Robert G. Caldwell, *Criminology,* 2nd ed. (New York, Ronald Press, 1965), pp. 139–48.

[14] Sutherland dealt at length with the argument that a consideration of white-collar criminality could further the discipline of criminology. Edwin H. Sutherland, "Is 'White-Collar Crime' Crime?" *American Sociological Review,* Vol. 10 (April 1945), pp. 132–39; *White Collar Crime,* op. cit., Ch. III. Newman presents an excellent defense for the acceptability of considering white-collar crimes from a legislative viewpoint. Donald J. Newman, "White-Collar Crime," *Law and Contemporary Problems,* Vol. 23 (Autumn 1958), pp. 735–53.

[15] Richard Quinney, "Occupational Structure and Criminal Behavior: Prescription Violation by Retail Pharmacists," *Social Problems,* Vol. 11 (Fall 1963), pp. 179–85; "The Study of White-Collar Crime Toward a Reorientation in Theory and Research," *Journal of Criminal Law, Criminology, and Police Science,* Vol. 55 (June 1964), pp. 208–14.

[16] Marshall B. Clinard and Richard Quinney (eds.), *Criminal Behavior Systems: A Typology* (New York, Holt, Rinehart and Winston, 1967), Ch. 4.

[17] Alvin L. Bertrand, *Basic Sociology* (New York, Appleton-Century-Crofts, 1967), pp. 252–53.

of a large amount of scholarly, legislative, and popular concern.[18] Shortly after Sutherland's book on corporate violations was published, numerous studies appeared in an apparent attempt to clarify the extent and nature of white-collar crime. Reports appeared concerning the working conditions of domestic help in Norway,[19] embezzlement,[20] labor-law violations,[21] prescription violation by retail pharmacists,[22] income tax evasion,[23] and the unethical and in some states outright illegal medical practice of "fee-splitting."[24] Fee-splitting, a practice specifically noted by Sutherland,[25] refers to the sharing of a patient's fees between a physician and a specialist or surgeon to whom the physician sent the patient. The practice sometimes results in a patient being referred to a specialist not for his expertise, but rather for the amount of kickback the referring physician will receive. In addition, a survey conducted by *Reader's Digest* (actually before Sutherland's major work) concerning consumer fraud in the repair industry (sometimes an example of blue-collar crime) illustrated convincingly the existence of cheating among automobile, radio, and watch repair establishments.[26] Indeed, as the author of a recent and extensive bibliography on white-collar crime states:

> Since 1939, the term *white collar crime* has come to mean a vast array of illegal and illicit enterprises by individuals or corporate bodies. The term is often used to embrace restraint of trade, monopoly practices, pilfering of office supplies, income tax evasion, fraudulent advertising, and even sharp practices.[27]

The focus on white-collar crime in this chapter, however, is not so broad as the material just cited; indeed, we feel that it is the inclusion of such a

[18] Dorothy Campbell Tompkins, *White Collar Crime: A Bibliography* (Berkeley, Institute of Governmental Studies, University of California, 1967).

[19] Vilhelm Aubert, "White-Collar Crime and Social Structure," *American Journal of Sociology,* Vol. 58 (November 1952), pp. 263–71.

[20] Donald R. Cressey, *Other People's Money: A Study in the Social Psychology of Embezzlement* (New York, Free Press, 1953); Norman Jaspan and Hillel Black, *The Thief in the White Collar* (Philadelphia, Lippincott, 1960).

[21] Robert F. Kennedy, *The Enemy Within* (New York, Harper & Row, 1960).

[22] Quinney, "Occupational Structure," op. cit.

[23] Phillip M. Stern, *The Great Treasury Raid* (New York, Random House, 1964).

[24] Howard Whitman, "Why Some Doctors Should Be in Jail," *Collier's,* Vol. 132 (October 30, 1953), pp. 23–27; Paul B. Horton and Gerald R. Leslie, *The Sociology of Social Problems,* 3rd ed. (New York, Appleton-Century-Crofts, 1965), pp. 596–97; Herbert A. Block and Gilbert Geis, *Man, Crime, and Society,* 2nd ed. (New York, Random House, 1970), pp. 307–09.

[25] Sutherland, "White-Collar Criminality," op. cit., p. 3.

[26] Roger Riis and John Patric, *Repairmen Will Get You If You Don't Watch Out* (Garden City, N.Y., Doubleday, 1942).

[27] Tompkins, op. cit., p. 2.

wide range of activities that has confused the issue of just what white-collar crime is.[28] Tempting as it may be to discuss "illicit" and otherwise shrewd and unethical business and professional practices, these activities are not the concern of this discussion. The discussion of white-collar crime in this chapter is congruent with Sutherland's original formulations—outside of his inclination to include almost any type of trust violation within the rubric of white-collar crime. That is, "white-collar crime" refers to violations of criminal laws as well as administrative regulations.

In addition, we focus on Sutherland's original formulation concerning the occupational characteristics of white-collar offenders. Some of the confusion in this respect focuses on what occupations should be accorded high social status.[29] Aside from the philosophical question of being forced to conclude that *no* person who commits a crime should be thought of as having high social status, this problem appears to be directed at occupational *rankings*. While clerical and sales positions are considered to be "white-collar" jobs in most western societies, these positions are often spoken of as lower white-collar occupations, and the prestige (not to mention income) associated with them is very close to many skilled, blue-collar jobs.[30] While lower white-collar employee theft and embezzlement is responsible for losses (to employers and indirectly to customers) of billions of dollars a year,[31] inclusion of these activities is felt to be getting too far away from Sutherland's original concern. Rather, the focus in this paper is upon occupationally relevant crimes (including embezzlement) committed by persons in upper white-collar positions such as managerial, ownership, executive, and professional vocations, as well as those committed by corporations (through administrative personnel). Sutherland's original intentions are not clear on this point. Although Sutherland concentrated on corporate crime, his definition of white-collar crime certainly implies criminality at the individual level. Furthermore, crimes committed by individuals in respectable positions may well be as costly to their victims as are corporate crimes. Nor are examples of corporate crime necessarily more indicative of wide-spread disrespect for laws than are individual crimes, especially if these individual crimes are collectively numerous.

Since the previously mentioned initial surge of publications on white-

---

[28] Ibid., p. 3.

[29] Bloch and Geis, op. cit., p. 319.

[30] Robert W. Hodge et al., "Occupational Prestige in the United States: 1923–63," in Reinhard Bendix and Seymour Martin Lipset (eds.), *Class, Status, and Power: Social Stratification in Comparative Perspective,* 2nd ed. (New York, Free Press, 1966).

[31] "Why Employees Steal," *Reader's Digest,* Vol. 99 (September 1971), pp. 83–86; Jaspan and Black, op. cit.; Gerald David Robin, *Employees as Offenders: A Sociological Analysis of Occupational Crime.* Ph.D. Dissertation (University of Pennsylvania, Philadelphia, 1965), Ch. 1.

collar criminality, systematic scholarly interest in the subject began to wane. Indeed, much of the current academic concern with white-collar crime is expressed in criminology textbooks and readers.[32] However, the topic of white-collar crime is still popular, as is attested by the heavy emphasis given to such activity in popular and trade magazines and legislative commission reports.

Sutherland gave no exact figures on the monetary extent of white-collar crime in the U.S. This condition remained relatively unchanged until 1967 when the President's Commission on Law Enforcement and the Administration of Justice estimated the economic impact of crime to American society at that time. The total figure in 1967 amounted to about $21 billion, with embezzlement and fraud, tax fraud included, amounting to over $1.5 billion. The figure for tradtional FBI-index property crimes—robbery, burglary, larceny ($50 and up), and auto theft—was $600 million.[33] Crimes of fraud and embezzlement by no means represent all white-collar crime, and much of white-collar criminality will never end up in the FBI *Uniform Crime Reports* or any other official source of crime. In 1971 the economic unit of *U.S. News and World Report* estimated the total cost of crime in the U.S. to be slightly over $51 billion, or 5 percent of the Gross National Product.[34] The estimated economic impact of kickbacks was $5 billion, and the impact of fraud and embezzlement (some of which is not white-collar crime) was $1.5 billion, whereas the impact of robbery, burglary, and theft was $2 billion.

A good example of huge losses to the public resulting from white-collar crimes is the famous "incredible electric conspiracy" which came to "light" in 1961.[35] Forty-five executives of 29 of the nation's leading heavy electrical equipment companies, including General Electric and Westinghouse, were convicted of (pleaded *nolo contendere*) conspiracy to set bid prices for electrical equipment in violation of the Sherman Antitrust Law. Testimony brought out during investigative proceedings clearly indicated that the execu-

[32] An excellent review of the literature on white-collar crime may be found in a bibliography compiled for the President's Commission on Law Enforcement and the Administration of Justice, Tompkins, op. cit. A comprehensive reader covering various aspects of white-collar crime is Gilbert Geis (ed.), *White-Collar Criminal: The Offender in Business and the Professions* (New York, Atherton, 1968). One of the best reviews of white-collar crime in general may be found in Bloch and Geis, op. cit., Ch. 12.

[33] President's Commission on Law Enforcement and the Administration of Justice, *Task Force Report—Crime and Its Impact: An Assessment* (Washington, D.C., U.S. Government Printing Office, 1967), p. 44.

[34] "Crime Expenses Now Up To $51 Billion a Year," *U.S. News and World Report*, Vol. 69 (October 26, 1971), pp. 30–34.

[35] Richard Austin Smith, "The Incredible Electrical Conspiracy, in Donald R. Cressey and David A. Ward (eds.), *Delinquency, Crime, and Social Process* (New York, Harper & Row, 1969), pp. 884–912; John Herling, *The Great Price Conspiracy* (Washington, D.C., Luce, 1962); Gilbert Geis, "The Heavy Electrical Equipment Antitrust Cases of 1961," in Clinard and Quinney, op. cit., pp. 139–51.

tives knew that what they were doing was illegal. What these executives were "doing" was colluding and conspiring to fix bid prices for providing electrical equipment to public and private contractors. The price-fixing, in turn, virtually reduced competition in the field and enabled the companies to show small but steady profits year after year. The price-fixing involved such things as switch-gear equipment (like circuit breakers), insulators, and turbine generators. The meetings occurred in hotel rooms during or after conventions or fabricated business trips (at company expense), country clubs, private parties, and so on. The price-fixing group was also well organized with different levels of conspirators (one concerned with making contacts, another with juggling books, etc.), with division of labor by time cycles and with separation of price-fixes among companies according to type of equipment (dividing up the market). While no exact figures were given concerning the direct economic loss to victims (including, ultimately, consumers), the value of the "fixed" equipment was around $1.75 billion annually for a period of about eight years.[36]

Large economic losses from white-collar crime, however, do not have to come from corporate conspiracies, such as the one just mentioned. Popular accounts of the exploits of Billie Sol Estes and Bobby Baker are cases in point. More recent examples include the activities of Frank Sharp, Houston real estate dealer,[37] although Sharp was not alone in his dealings (indeed, W. R. Wilson, Chief of the Criminal Division of the Justice Department, was implicated in Sharp's dealings and recently resigned). Specifically, Sharp pleaded guilty to swindling a Jesuit preparatory school of $6 million, forcing into receivership two insurance companies and forcing a greater Houston bank to close.[38] For his efforts, Sharp was fined $5,000 and placed on three years' probation.[39] The forcing of banks to close might even be the coming "thing" in white-collar crime. Recently, for example, the president of the Eatonton, New Jersey, National Bank "misapplied" $5 million of the bank's funds, forcing it to close.[40] One can imagine the immediate repercussions this had on the small town of Eatonton. For example, stores in a shopping center where the only branch was located were disrupted, stockholders were hurt financially, and a security problem arose from the transfer of cash from nearby banks.

Embezzling, whether on a large or small-scale, is not peculiar to the

[36] Smith, op. cit., p. 884.
[37] "The I.O.U.'s of Texas Are Upon Us," Editorial, *America*, Vol. 124 (February 13, 1971), p. 139; Donald Jackson, "The Promoter and the Crime Buster," *Life*, Vol. 71 (September 24, 1971), pp. 59–62; "Enforcer Steps Down: Financial Wheeling and Dealing of Fraud," *Time*, Vol. 98 (October 25, 1971), pp. 16–19.
[38] *Time*, ibid., p. 19.
[39] Jackson, op. cit., p. 62.
[40] "The $5-Millions that Disappeared," *Business Week* (August 15, 1970), pp. 17–19.

United States. The red bean industry in Japan, for example, is felt to be in-directly "responsible" for a series of embezzlements amounting to millions of dollars.[41] Since the market value of red beans is unstable, a large amount of speculation occurs concerning red bean investments. Often these speculations lead to economic disasters, eventuating in embezzlement. Embezzlements in Japan are estimated to have increased from 84 in 1969 to more than 100 in the first half of 1970, during which time red bean prices fluctuated. A recent report indicates that a veteran of the French Foreign Legion became in-censed over France's abandonment of Algeria. In retaliation, the veteran be-came a business executive and proceeded to steal the equivalent of approxi-mately $2 million from his company in eight years.[42]

White-collar crime, however, often has consequences other than financial ones; personal health and safety are often at stake. The quality of materials used in the manufacture of children's toys, for example, has recently become a topic of concern. Many toys can be truly harmful to unsuspecting children. In 1969 Congress passed the Child Protection and Toy Safety Act, admin-istered by the Food and Drug Administration (FDA) of Health, Education and Welfare. The enforcement of the act, however, has been slow and appar-ently has not affected the toy industry much at all. Not only is the act legally "loose," but also many toys become obsolete so fast that they are no longer being marketed by the time the FDA can effectively deal with them.[43]

Another area of white-collar criminality involves the medical and phar-maceutical professions. In the early to mid-1960s Congress and several states took an active interest in restraining medical trade. The primary activity with which these legislative bodies were concerned was physician ownership of pharmacies in violation of antitrust laws. A net result of legislative hearings and committee reports was the passage of laws prohibiting physician owner-ship of pharmacies.[44] The "cost" of such ownership to the public is really two-fold. Not only may a patient be led or practically forced to buy pre-scribed drugs at the physicians' pharmacy where he may pay higher prices, but he may also be given a prescription more for its economic impact on the attending physician than its medicinal impact on the patient. In addition, doctors, dentists, and druggists file false claims on Medicaid (medical care to the poor) policies.[45]

The biggest area of white-collar crime today is consumer fraud. This

---

[41] "A Hill of Beans Leads to a Scandal," *Business Week* (October 31, 1970), p. 29.

[42] "$2,000,000 Grudge," *Time* Vol. 96 (October 5, 1970), p. 30.

[43] "Danger in Toyland," *Time* Vol. 96 (November 30, 1970), p. 78.

[44] Tompkins, op. cit., pp. 34–35.

[45] Albert Q. Maisel, "Profiteers Are Wrecking Medicaid," *Reader's Digest,* Vol. 95 (October 1969), pp. 151–56.

type of white-collar criminality is reflective not only of the predominance of mass communication and advertising techniques, such as mail and television, but also of emergent social and economic trends. One of these trends is an apparently increasing fascination in America with the occult.[46] A recent account of fraudulent activity involving the occult indicated that astrology is about a $200-million-a-year business involving more than 40 million people. The chances are "right" for fraud in this kind of situation, and indeed, fraud has occurred.[47] Closely related to astrology and the occult is the practice of faith healing. Here, too, white-collar crime continues. In 1968, for example, a Gulfport, Mississippi, minister with a nationwide audience was fined $2,000 and sentenced to one year in prison for using the mail to defraud. His faith-healing programs had helped him to take in more than $10 million (over a 20-year period) as payment for promised financing of religious and mission-ary activities. Around the same time, a Los Angeles physician was convicted and sentenced to 10 years for defrauding the public of around $2 million through a clinic "where God and medical services joined hands."[48]

The subject of consumer fraud has received so much national and state legislative attention in recent years[49] that we may now be said to be operat-ing under the assumption of *caveat vendor* as opposed to *caveat emptor* (especially with the passage of the Consumer Protection Act in 1971). Part of this concern for consumer protection has no doubt been the result of an increasing awareness of the poor's vulnerability to market and housing con-ditions so poignantly analyzed by Caplovitz.[50] Another source of consumer protection interest, however, is the increasing aged population of the country. Between 1950 and 1970, for example, the number of people aged 65 and over in the United States increased from 12,295,000 to 20,050,000—an increase from about 8 percent of the population to about 10 percent of the popula-tion. When one includes the population aged 55 and over, the 1970 percent-age of the total population becomes nearly 20 percent, or about 40,000,000 people.[51] Many of these people are good subjects for consumer fraud, and they are relatively powerless to do much about it. Examples of fraudulent activities aimed directly or primarily at the aged include: (1) requiring pre-

---

[46] "The Occult: A Substitute Faith," *Time* Vol. 99 (June 19, 1972), pp. 62–68.

[47] F. Glen Loyd and Theodore Irwin, "How Quackery Thrives on the Occult," *Today's Health,* Vol. 48 (November 1970), pp. 21–23.

[48] O. K. Armstrong, "Beware the Commercialized Faith Healers," *Reader's Digest,* Vol. 98 (June 1971), pp. 179–86.

[49] Tompkins, op. cit., pp. 61–75; Sidney Margolius, *The Innocent Consumer vs. the Exploiters* (New York, Simon and Schuster, Pocket Books, 1968).

[50] David Caplovitz, *The Poor Pay More: Consumer Practices of Low-Income Families* (New York, Free Press, 1963).

[51] U.S. Bureau of the Census, *Pocket Data Book, U.S.A., 1971* (Washington, D.C., U.S. Government Printing Office, 1971).

payment funeral service fees without putting them into trust funds as part of the burial contract, including fraudulent mail-order burial plans;[52] (2) fraudulent mail-order or otherwise "sight unseen" land sales;[53] and (3) "stop-gap" health insurance plans that promise to fill in the uncovered portions of clients' existing health insurance policies (including Medicaid provisions) but do more emptying of pocketbooks than filling of insurance deficits.[54]

Fraudulent advertising on television has been the subject of much Congressional concern at least since the late 1950s. Recently the Federal Trade Commission (FTC) has taken action to control television advertising in the areas of unsubstantiated claims, retractions or corrections of previous false advertisement in subsequent ads, and advertisements aimed primarily at children.[55] In addition, the FTC is taking aim at faulty testing procedures in gasoline advertisements concerned with "antipollution" devices (which themselves are primarily the result of the current "ecology scare" in the U.S.).[56]

TRENDS FOR THE FUTURE

White-collar crimes today still include such traditional examples as fraud and embezzlement. Most of the studies, reports, or comments involving white-collar crime, however, are purely descriptive, providing little if any theoretical framework.[57] At this time, one may conclude that there exists no "theory" of white-collar crime as such. Nonetheless, Sutherland did imply in a theoretical vein that white-collar crime was reflective of social, economic, and technological conditions or changes.[58] Consistently, many of the "modern" examples of white-collar crime discussed in this paper seem to be linked to changes in the social structure of American society, such as an emphasis on new "gimmicks" in children's toys (perhaps a product of increasing concern for providing more and more stimulants to children) ; an increasing proportion of aged population with no consequent national programs to provide for their needs; and an increasing demand that goodness, beauty, and youth all come together, especially for the American female. This theme may be ex-

[52] Tompkins, op. cit., pp. 35–37.

[53] Ibid., pp. 39–41.

[54] Margolius, op. cit., pp. 193–97; "Health Trap," *Newsweek* Vol. 78 (August 2, 1971), pp. 62–64; "Health Care: Supply, Demand, and Politics," *Time* Vol. 97 (June 7, 1971), pp. 86–88 ff.

[55] "The FTC Zooms in on the 'Better' Buys," *Business Week* (February 20, 1971), pp. 20–21.

[56] Ibid.; see also Susan Berman, "Chevron's Pollution Solution, the F-310 and Scott Carpenter," *Commonweal*, Vol. 93 (March 5, 1971), pp. 48–58.

[57] Exceptions include Cressey, op. cit.; Hartung, op. cit.; Quinney, op. cit.; and Geis, "Deliniation of White-Collar Offenses," op. cit.

[58] Sutherland, *White Collar Crime,* op. cit., Ch. 3; Aubert, op. cit.

panded in an attempt to predict future examples of white-collar crime as they pertain to emerging social, economic, and technological trends. The rest of this discussion is focused on some of these changes in the United States.

With increasing attention being given to environmental pollution and the sources of pollution, such as large factories, one would expect white-collar crimes to increase in this area. With the passage of the Environmental Control Act of 1970, enforced by the Environmental Protection Agency (EPA) (a familiar refrain with white-collar crimes), such an occurence has already happened. In November of 1971, 16 factories in Birmingham, Alabama, were sanctioned by the EPA for not adhering to its standards and were enjoined from further production until such standards were met.

A second trend in American society that will probably lead to new white-collar crime is increasing federal control over the nation's economy. In August of 1971 President Nixon placed a three-month wage and price freeze on most of the economy—Phase I. Then in Phase II restrictions were placed on price and wage increases according to the Pay Board and Price Commission with enforcement help from the Internal Revenue Service. A rather safe prediction from these events would be a re-occurrence of wage and price violations similar to the ones uncovered during World War II by Clinard and Hartung.

Another trend in America concerns the increasing use of computers and technology. In light of developing duplicating and audio-visual surveillance techniques, new possibilities will emerge not only for the invasion of privacy,[59] but also for illegal monetary gains. The case of novelist Clifford Irving and his accomplices (including his wife) offers an example. Irving and associates were given prison terms for stealing documents about the life of Howard Hughes and selling them to a publisher for hundreds of thousands of dollars as an autobiography. The practices used by Irving could just as well be used for other private (monetary) and government espionage purposes. An example of such government activity is the Watergate scandal. The implications of this event, however, tend to support the contention that white-collar crime involving surveillance techniques will begin to appear in the political arena.

White-collar crime in politics could also arise from yet another trend in America: concern for excessive expenses in political campaigns. Legislative acts for dealing with this situation are now being proposed. If these proposals are enacted into law, another source of white-collar crime will have been created—this time involving aspirants to political office rather than businessmen or professionals as such.

[59] Arthur R. Miller, *The Assault on Privacy: Computers, Data Banks, and Dossiers* (Ann Arbor, University of Michigan Press, 1971).

Each of these trends was related to future white-collar criminality through legislative enactments. Actually any future condition concerning potential economic (or political) loss or gain to high-status people but regulated by law could be considered a future source of white-collar crime. White-collar crime is likely to be with us as long as we literally reward achievement of economic and political success over and above any pretentious regulation of means of achieving that success. Whenever a profit is to be made but a regulation is attached to the making of the profit, white-collar crime will likely occur through what Mills has termed "structured immorality."[60] In short, the general prediction of the future of white-collar criminality is that its extent will, if anything, increase while its form will merely change with changing times.

[60] C. Wright Mills, *White Collar: The American Middle Classes* (New York, Galaxy, 1956).

10.   The Ritual of Wiggle:
from Ruin to Reelection

JAMES BOYD

This is the era of the impeached Congressman. As of this writing, one member is in jail, two are under indictment, a former member was just convicted in Trenton, one has been censured, one expelled, four defeated after ruinous press exposés, and several are being held in protective custody by the Attorney General. And if the ratio of detected to undetected offenders is as low within Congress as without, there lurks a battalion of nervous legislators, each of whom feels a premonitory twinge every time he reaches for the morning newspaper.

Among the intelligentsia, an impugned legislator is as much ridiculed as the streetwalker was until Dostoyevsky explored her whys and found a saint. Perhaps we dote too much on the shady politician's final bequest to us—the poisoned meat or the polluted water or the tax hike or the sandy cement that causes our neighborhood school to cave in—to properly savor the brighter scenes of his act. Recall Adam Clayton Powell on Bimini, hiding out from the law with Miss Ohio; or Hugh Addonizio lamenting to the judge that being on trial for extortion all day was impeding his reelection campaign by limiting him to nighttime rallies; or Senator Dodd daring God to strike him dead if he were lying, while colleagues inched out of range; or the great Dirksen, at Governor Stratton's trial, telling the jurors that it was perfectly proper for Stratton to pocket the campaign funds and not pay taxes, because if the first lady were to appear regularly in public, didn't she need lots of corsets and stepins and frillies? So even when you consider the poisoned meat, the act is still funny. Besides, we're going to get the crash landing anyway, so why not enjoy the sleight-of-hand and the feats of levitation while we're airborne?

And what we enjoy we study. We go to the circus and laugh at the

Reprinted by permission from James Boyd, "The Ritual of Wiggle: From Ruin to Reelection," *The Washington Monthly,* Vol. 2, No. 7 (September 1970), pp. 28–43.

clowns; if we are of an inquiring bent we begin to notice that what at first appeared as madcap foolery is in fact the unfolding of a painstaking art, and our mirth becomes tinged with understanding, respect, admiration. So it is with our apprehension of the indicted solon. Old Porky up there on the platform amid the red, white and blue bunting—weeping his heart out after avowing his innocence before God, while the wife and kids embrace him and the crowd cheers—is not the slob he seems. Off the stand he is quite sensitive and stoic. Study him from month to month as he fends off conviction and wiggles toward reelection: you will see that what at first seemed spontaneous idiocies, the desperate acts of an inferior man at bay, are instead integrated parts of a ritual as exacting and delicate as the hand fluttering and eye rolling of the Balinese dancer.

When Congressman James Michael Curley, a cultivated man who read Shakespeare aloud in the evening, chose upon his release from prison not to slip quietly home but rather to be met by five brass bands, it was not that he was uncouth. He was grappling with the enigma of modern politics: how to be at once both a defendant and a candidate. The politician cannot run for office and at the same time plead insanity or take the Fifth or turn state's evidence. As defendant, he must hide from snoopers and process servers; as candidate, he must be everywhere accessible and seem to confront all accusers boldly. As defendant, he must be secretive, devious, sullen; as candidate, open, forthright, gregarious. As defendant, he must measure his every word; as candidate, perjury is a way of life. Even as he enters into stipulations with the prosecution, he must shout his innocence. He teeters through the minefield with one eye on the jury and one on the public, and so to the undiscriminating it looks like an elephant's ballet. But there is logic and precision to it all.

The moment which launches all the bawdy gaucheries to come is always a solemn, interior one. Usually it begins on the telephone. Senator X phones his office one morning and young Foster tells him in a squelched voice that Jack Anderson has exploded a stinkbomb in his 600 newspapers—the slush fund, the Swiss bank account, the works. The Senator's strength drains out in a puddle. He slumps in a flaccid heap and stares glassily at the accusing phone; the knowing place in the pit of the stomach sinks into infinity. Helpless tears come and hysteria ferments. It is the moment of maximum hazard to a political career; a too-defiant denial, a tell-tale dodge, an injudicious admission can in a flash proliferate into a major investigation and undo 30 years of patient conniving. The Senator's glazed eyes conjure up newspaper headlines, the dock, the recall of Congressional credit cards, the cell door clanking shut. But it need not be so. Of all the colleagues to drink from his cup in the past 10 years, only one, Representative Tom Johnson, actually did a stretch. Most escape with nothing lost save honor. They laugh again, prosper, and get reelected. And those who don't, if you study it, have invariably botched up their defense by straying from the rules and precedents carefully developed by the elders.

Rule 1. *Admit nothing until you know the worst; if it looks like a one-shot affair, hide till it blows over.*

The redeeming facet of a scandal is that people soon forget. Yesterday's tax evader, Robert E. Tehan, is today's federal judge in Milwaukee. Who remembers now that in 1964 Senators Sparkman and Smathers went through their secular Gethsemanes when their peculiar banking and investment ventures were headlined during the Bobby Baker hearings? No one, except the keeper of newspaper morgues, because they did not rush forward to testify and clear their names. They played possum, there was no follow-up of any consequence, and today they remain esteemed public figures. When Congressman John Dent was shown by *The Wall Street Journal* to have violated the Corrupt Practices Act, he yawned, remained incommunicado for a spell, and his seniority still accumulates. Senator Dirksen was for years hounded by reporters for the details of his fabulous law practice in Peoria, which somehow commanded fat retainers from many of our greatest corporations; but he'd always shush-shush the reporters with his mock curlicued wrath and he took those details to the grave. Now they are planning statues in his honor.

One of the more effective nondefenses was made by Julian G. Sourwine, chief counsel of the Senate Internal Security subcommittee. It was shown at a Senate hearing in 1967 that Sourwine had knowingly passed a check for $2,500 that bounced in a Las Vegas bank. Moreover, he had duped a Senator into endorsing the check, and the Senator eventually had to make it good. This was a rather delicate matter, for Sourwine was and is the chief Senate watchdog against security risks in government, people who, for instance, get in such desperate financial straits that they write bad checks in four figures. Had the matter received a second day of publicity it might have been farewell for Sourwine, but the foxy old Red-fighter just shut off the phone switchboard and hid for a while; and the charge faded, uncontradicted but forgotten.

Sometimes, of course, circumstances just won't permit waiting out the squall. Sometimes reporters have the answers instead of just the questions, or the blow may fall in the middle of a campaign, or it may be so explosive that one has to respond. For such occasions, study the following rules.

Rule 2. *If you must speak out—confess to what is known, evade what is unknown, and cry.*

The ritual of the bogus public confession of the no-longer-hidable has been popular ever since Grover Cleveland publicly confessed to bastardy. On that day, Cleveland, who theretofore had been known mainly for drinking beer in the back rooms of Buffalo saloons, became "Mr. Integrity." No one remembers the President Cleveland who sent troops into Chicago to help the railroads beat up starving strikers; all that remains is the sturdy image of the benign old walrus who owned up and made his support payments.

Senator Richard M. Nixon's 1952 Checkers performance is perhaps the classic in this genre. Up on slush fund charges, he confessed frankly to having received a puppy for his infant daughters and to having kept his wife in a cloth coat; his slush fund disappeared in a flood of congratulatory telegrams, never to reappear. On a tawdrier but nonetheless effective level, Thaddeus Dulski, chairman of the House Post Office and Civil Service Committee, just broke down and bawled when it was revealed in 1967 that he had accepted an $11,000 purse from the postal unions and the third-class mailers while he was authorizing legislation to raise postal salaries and cut third-class rates. His tears washed away the suspect $11,000, and nothing more has ever been heard of it.

Rule 3. *If at all possible, give the money back—or at least give it to someone.*

According to his defense counsel, Senator Thomas Dodd was in jeopardy of a long prison term if the Senate convicted him, as was recommended unanimously by its Ethics Committee, of having fraudulently charged the government for travel expenses actually paid by others. So Dodd gave back the $1,767 to the Senate disbursing office, and the Senate dropped the charge by a vote of 51 to 45. Emboldened, Dodd offered to refund any of the $116,000 in campaign contributions he had diverted to his personal use, if the donors asked. "Even if I have to sell my shirt," he said. But that one didn't wash and the Senate censured him 92 to 5. Apparently, the offer wasn't imaginative enough. He should have consulted John Byrnes or Seymour Halpern of the House. Congressman Byrnes was shown in 1964 to have helped obtain a favorable tax ruling for the Mortgage Guaranty Insurance Corporation and to have then bought restricted stock on advantageous terms not available to ordinary citizens. Five days after exposure, Byrnes announced that he was giving the stock to Scholarship, Inc., for aid to deserving youths. Case closed. In 1969, Seymour Halpern, ranking Republican on the House Banking Committee, was revealed by reporter Jerry Landauer to have put himself $100,000 in hock, mostly in unsecured loans to banks which were virtually interested in matters before Halpern's committee. The documentation was so airtight it made even reporters feel sorry for Halpern, an amiable man with a beautiful young wife and a flair for high living. But the Congressman rose to the challenge with a virtuoso application of Rule 3. He announced that he would pay back the loans by auctioning off his prize collection of famous signatures, the passion of his life which he had been devotedly gathering from early childhood. What more could be said?

Rule 4. *If partial confession and restitution fail to stem the headlines, arrange a quickie exoneration from a semirespected source.*

The traditional sources are (a) the House Speaker, (b) the respective chairmen of the Senate and House Ethics Committees, or (c) the Attorney General. Milton Friedman has observed that all regulatory agencies soon become fronts for the malefactors they are supposed to regulate; certainly this is true in the Congress. There are so many precedents here that the difficulty is to sort them out for the model most appropriate to the occasion.

Less than 24 hours after Representative Dulski was accused, Speaker McCormack summarily cleared him without a look at the documents. Career saved.

When it was disclosed that Senator George Murphy was one of the politicians being subsidized by California tycoon Patrick Frawley—Frawley gave Murphy unrestricted credit cards, paid half his rent, and threw in $20,000 a year; Murphy in turn watched movies for Frawley on a special screen Frawley had installed in Murphy's apartment—the Senator immediately produced a statement from Senate ethics watchdog John Stennis that there was nothing improper about this arrangement. Before that, Chairman Stennis turned in the same verdict for Senator Edward Long of Missouri. *Life* had revealed that for years Long had been receiving a $2,000 check each month from M. A. Shenker, attorney for imprisoned Teamster boss James Hoffa. Long contended this was "shared fees" for several cases he was helping Shenker with, but no proof was ever published that this was so—nor was any explanation given why the "shared fees" always amounted to $2,000 a month. It was messy, but after a private probe Chairman Stennis declared "not guilty."

Before Stennis, the ethics watchdog was Senator Everett Jordan of North Carolina, who presided over the Senate investigation into Senate aide-in-chief Bobby Baker. In that inquiry, it turned out that so many Senators were tangled up with Baker's finances that it was almost impossible to investigate Baker without probing them, too. Almost but not quite. First, Senator George Smathers was discovered to be mixed up with Baker in a real estate deal that reportedly returned $75,000 to Smathers on a $9,000 investment. Jordan heard Smathers out in chambers and found "nothing improper." He certainly wasn't going to investigate Smathers, he said. The next day he summarily exculpated former Senator Lyndon B. Johnson. But this piecemeal approach was making the committee look ridiculous and the Senate nervous, so Jordan issued a blanket amnesty for all Senators who had been or might ever be involved with Baker. "This committee," he said, "is not investigating Senators."

The House Ethics Committee is even more reliable in time of need. In its five-year suzerainty over 435 Congressmen, it has yet to find one needful of investigation. Its staff director is an ex-lobbyist who is not even an attorney.

Apparently, all ethics committees are destined for this fatuous role. When the labor movement had its flirtation with probity, wise old John L. Lewis guffawed from the start; and on the first anniversary of the A.F.L.-C.I.O.'s Committee on Ethical Practices, Lewis wired an inquiry, "Have you found any ethical practices?"

Unfortunately, clearances so routinely obtained begin to lose public credence. Attorney General John Mitchell has rushed in to fill the void.

Does the U.S. Attorney for New Jersey announce he is probing alleged ties between the underworld and Senate candidate Nelson Gross? Mitchell quickly announces that there is no such investigation and what's more there won't be one.

Does the U.S. Attorney for Maryland ask for an indictment of a contractor who a grand jury found had entered into bribery negotiations with several prominent Congressmen? Mitchell says nothing doing and sees to it that the grand jury presentment is suppressed.

Are 21 G.O.P. finance chairmen in open violation of the Corrupt Practices Act for failing to report where they got their money? Not interested, says Mitchell.

Does the Internal Revenue Service, after a two-year investigation, recommend that Senator Dodd be indicted for criminal income tax evasion? Mitchell gives Dodd a letter of exoneration to read at his campaign rallies.

Are a dozen corporations, from Delaware to California, indicted for making illegal contributions to Members of Congress? It is so arranged that the corporations may plead *nolo contendere* without the identity of the Members being revealed.

We touch here upon the greatest boon in our legal system—the blocked indictment. There is no appeal from the prosecutor who refuses to prosecute or the investigating committee which refuses to investigate. However grisly the facts, they are harmless in locked vaults; of course, come the close roll call, one may feel an inclination to vote with the side that holds the keys.

Rule 5. *If the unpleasantness persists, use the "stranger in paradise" routine: You can't help it if goodhearted friends have an urge to shower you with gifts or if lucky fate strews your path with roses.*

People accept the fact that politicians, like movie actors, live in a world where fantastic things happen. When John Doe contracts for house renovations, the bill is usually twice what the work is worth, not half. Yet, he'll believe House Whip Hale Boggs' story that the construction company with the House Office Building garage contract just happened to charge him $21,000 for $45,000 worth of home improvements—because Congressmen live in a world where those things happen. Whenever John Doe buys stock it goes down; but he is not so jaundiced by that as to discredit the explanation of Representative Multer that his windfalls in banking investments were just lucky breaks that had nothing to do with his being a member of the House Banking Committee.

The favorite "stranger in paradise" device is the "very close friend" who is always doing wonderful things for you and expecting nothing in return. Take the wife's vacation syndrome: when ex-Congressman Addonizio was confronted with checks signed by other people for his wife's vacations he was unperturbed. "Just a very close friend," he shrugged. If John Doe had a friend who offered to pay for *his* wife's vacation, he'd start to worry about it; but for a Congressman's or a mayor's he accepts it. Representative Giaimo of Connecticut collected $32,000 in 1966 as a tax-free gift from a group of friends who wanted to pay tribute to his public service. Now John Doe never had anyone pay him a cash tribute, let alone tax-free. But he is not intolerant of Giaimo's explanation; the Congressman was renominated without difficulty and is a favorite for reelection. "Just a close friend" is a phrase which echoes through Congressional history: Senator Birch Bayh's Florida vacations, Dodd's Oldsmobiles, the turnpike bonds of Congressmen Herlong and Watts, Happy Chandler's swimming pool, the dozens of testimonial purses raised in Washington each year from friends who happen to be lobbyists. It's a warming phrase when you're caught with something that muckrakers outside the charmed circle say you shouldn't have.

Rule 6. *Insist that you would have done the same favor for any constituent.*

There's a problem here, admittedly. The gift of stock or the home renovation job was just explained by Senator X as the generous, disinterested act of a very close friend. Now it is asked why Senator X officially intervened to get that friend a pardon or a tax loophole. Special favors for friends? No. With as much aplomb as possible it must be argued that any constituent, had he but asked, would have received the same favor.

Jim Curley was in trouble once for violating the Civil Service Act by taking a classification test under an assumed name. When hecklers would taunt Curley with it, he was not in the least defensive. "A man came to my door seeking help," he would intone, jutting his jaw toward the crowd. "He needed a job. His children were hungry. But he couldn't pass the examination because he had no education. So I took that test for him and he got that job. And thereafter he held his head up among men and his family was nourished. And I want every citizen of Massachusetts to know that I would do the same for you and *you* and You and YOU" until the crowd would explode in a frenzy of adulation.

The giants of the past are departed; yet in small ways they can be emulated. When headlines proclaimed that Congressman Giaimo had set up a Caribbean vacation cruise at government expense for a man who turned out to be a racketeer, he calmed the flap overnight. There was nothing unusual, Giaimo explained; he would gladly arrange the same cruise for any of his 461,086 constituents. There's a logical flaw in this, as in the old campaign promise to give every American boy and girl a Harvard education. But the history of these things is that people don't look that closely.

The only caveat here is: don't carry the definition of "constituent" too far. At the recent trial of Martin Sweig, aide to Speaker McCormack of Boston, Congressman Leggett of California was called by the defense to bolster up Sweig's contention that it was an accepted practice to give New York lobbyists the run of one's offices, phones, and secretaries. Leggett testified that he regarded the whole United States as his constituency and had no hesitancy about letting any constituent use his office or telephone on behalf of commercial clients. This seemed a bit much to the jury. One of the jurors later confided to *The New York Times,* "After hearing him, it is my opinion they should investigate *all* the Members of Congress."

Rule 7. *At the moment of deepest personal disgrace, announce for re-election.*

In other lands, the exposed statesman commits hari-kari or resigns; here he declares his candidacy. Nixon turned his 1952 slush fund explanation into an election rally; Powell always reannounced after each brush with the law; on the day of his Senate censure, Dodd declared for a third term; John McCormack's first public response to the Voloshen-Sweig indictment was to re-up for the Speakership.

There are three reasons. One, even the rumor of a possible vacancy 10 years ahead of schedule excites the animals in the party hierarchy back home; a quick announcement keeps them in line. Two, as long as one is in office and seems likely to stay there, he has the Indian sign on the prosecution; no one believes, for instance, that Senator Daniel Brewster would ever have been indicted for bribery had he been reelected instead of defeated in 1968. Three, the thought of one's constituency as a jury of last resort sitting above the real jury, even above the Supreme Court, is a comforting one. So as the indictments come down, the far-sighted politician will keep reiterating that the real verdict won't come in until the people vote several years from now. After all, that's a jury he's always fooled in the past.

Rule 8. *Set up a series of endorsements by prominent churchmen.*

The predilection of the American church for mountebanks has been known to discriminating politicians since at least 1858, the year of the Lincoln-Douglas Senate campaign. Both candidates were citizens of Springfield, Illinois, where they were personally known to all the clergy. Douglas was a braggart, a boozer, a man facile with truth and money; Lincoln was humble, a teetotaler, a man of almost fanatical veracity, the fellow who walked all those miles to return the penny. The issue was the most important moral question ever before the nation—the extension of human slavery. Douglas was for it, for reasons of political expediency; Lincoln was against it and stated his opposition in the most exalted spiritual terms ever heard in partisan debate. It was inevitable, therefore, that 21 of the 23 Protestant pastors of Springfield endorsed Douglas over Lincoln and that the Catholics of Illinois voted almost unanimously for Douglas—the winner.

Since then, the politician in trouble has intuitively turned to the church, knowing that whatever the accusation, a cardinal can be found to pose with, a Protestant pulpit is open for a guest sermon, a denominational college is ready with an honorary degree, a Communion breakfast is in need of a speaker. All this lends a patina of innocence.

When Truman aide Matt Connelly was convicted, a great dinner was held in his honor, presided over by the Archbishop of Boston. Such gambits paled a bit in the latter days of the Truman Administration, when too many indicted officials told juries that they were Papal Knights of Malta with credentials from Pope Pius XII. But it quickly revived.

The case of Senator Robert Byrd of West Virginia, now the Senate's third ranking Democrat, is illustrative. In the midst of an early campaign for Congress, Byrd's puritanical, idealistic, patriotic image, which had made him the odds-on favorite, suddenly was drenched with a pail of garbage. It was revealed that in happier days he had been a wine-biber, a Ku Kluxer, and a draft dodger. But Byrd, dressed in clerical black and with the face of an accolyte, had been a preacher of the gospel, had conducted a noted radio Bible school that reached half of rural West Virginia, and regularly elevated his rallies with poetry readings of "The Touch of the Master's Hand." The parsons rose as one to his defense. His conversion to temperance, brotherhood, and war was certified as genuine and the unpleasantness blew over.

But Members in trouble need not assume that proof of reform or even contrition is at all necessary to gain ecclesiastical endorsements. Adam Powell was once the most conspicuous sinner in America. He had kicked out his wife and confiscated her income. He had been proved a forger who regularly traveled to vacation spots under an alias, with lady friends under aliases, all at government expense. He had been found guilty of lying about an old woman in Harlem and had refused to pay damages. He was perpetually in contempt of court. He was a fugitive from justice, and his every entry into New York to preach his Sunday sermon was accompanied by national speculation as to whether or not he would get out by sundown or be arrested. He had abandoned his Congressional duties and openly reveled in his beach-comber's tryst with Miss Corinne Huff. And he was impenitent; worse even, he flaunted his sins as religious acts. "Keep the faith, Baby," he would say, raising his glass.

By January, 1967, when the House of Representatives had to formally question Powell's credentials, who was left to defend him? The Church, of course. The Greater New York Baptist Ministers Conference, the New York City Presbytery, the National Council of Churches, announced resolutions of support for Powell. The Reverend Walter Fauntroy demanded a national work stoppage in his behalf. Powell, they all said, had been a great chairman, an inspiring symbol to blacks. And besides, his morals were no worse than the other Congressmen's.

Rule 9. *It's time to pick a scapegoat.*

The scapegoat, or decoy, is the *sine qua non* of all major political scandals. It's undignified but essential.

The routine decoy is the opposition political party. You are being persecuted by political enemies who want to discredit you and take away your seat. This was, in essence, the response of Senator Vance Hartke to press reports that he was under federal investigation for accepting a bribe.

But blaming "politics" is too flabby a scapegoat to really win the public. Better results are obtained by crying "yellow journalism" and charging a frame by the "power hungry media." The late Drew Pearson made a marvelous decoy because so many Congressmen had been burned by him that the latest third-degree casualty to be wheeled onto the Floor always had a majority on his side. The following attacks on Pearson illustrate the statistical and the oratorical methods. Senator George Smathers: "I join two Presidents, 27 Senators, and 83 Congressmen in describing Drew Pearson as an unmitigated liar." The late Senator Kenneth McKellar: "Pearson is an ignorant liar, a pusillanimous liar, a peewee liar . . . a revolting, constitutional, unmitigated, infamous liar!"

Better even than being the hapless victim of the press is to be a martyr, for then you are being tortured not for your indiscretions, but for your virtues. A young Congressman with larceny on his mind should get into the field of anti-Communism. Congressman J. Parnell Thomas, jailed for taking salary kickbacks, remained a martyr to the end to those who were sure he was framed by the Communist conspiracy he fought so energetically. To millions, Senator Joe McCarthy, too, was censured for his anti-Communism, not for evading committee inquiries into his finances. Roy Cohn uses his Red-hunting kudos at all his fraud trials. Dodd, who was the victim not only of the Reds but of a sex ring that infiltrated his office, still draws applause in New Haven when he says, "I may well be the only honest man in Congress. . . . I am the most maligned figure in human history."

Once the case reaches the hearing room or the courtroom, a personal scapegoat must be arraigned—the chief witness for the state. It was *he* who did what he says *you* did. This is the inviolable rule of Senator Russell Long, defender of impeached Senators. Long on witness Michael O'Hare: "That crook, that thief, that liar, that scoundrel, that bandit . . . that murderer!" Long on witness John Sullivan: "Danny Brewster never took that money. These charges were made by a former employee who is trying to divert attention from his own conduct."

Rule 10. *If newsmen persist, bolder moves are advisable: issue a statement requesting an official investigation.*

Rule 11. *Threaten a multi-million dollar libel suit against your accusers but don't file it; if you must file it for tactical reasons, withdraw it before it gets to trial.*

These rules are closely related and should be discussed together. "X" has been accused. If he is innocent, he can just open his books to the public, answer all questions from the press, and use the vast media resources at his disposal to propagate his vindication. If not innocent, the mock investigation and libel suit enable "X" to seem to be doing the same thing, while actually doing nothing of the sort. As soon as "X" has announced these moves, he can with virtuous air refuse to answer all further questions from the press.

Suggested release: "I have placed the matter before the proper authorities. I have brought suit to clear my name. Under the American system of jurisprudence, it would be contumacious for me to discuss this litigation in the press, so I am forced to withhold all further comment, no matter how much it pains me, until proceedings before the proper tribunal commence."

This statement will get you through an entire campaign; after a few days, the reporters will even stop asking.

The three most suitable agencies to demand investigation from are, depending on the locus of your clout, the F.B.I., the House Ethics Committee, and your local grand jury. All three can proceed only in secret. None can investigate without a nod from the higher-ups, and even then the findings can't be published. Even if on the level, the typical political investigation takes years to complete; all that time you can pose as a maligned innocent awaiting justice. If once in a hundred times a runaway grand jury, an oddball U.S. attorney, or an overwrought committee counsel gets out of hand, the Attorney General or the chairman has the last word and can keep the lid on.

As for the libel suit, a mere threat of it may achieve the objective. Timing is the key element. The *Life* exposé on Governor James Rhodes of Ohio, a 1970 Senate candidate, came in May, 1969. Rhodes made the standard move and said he'd sue. But if he had sued then, the case might have been called up for trial or preliminary deposition before the Senate campaign was over and he'd have to either take the stand and answer questions or back out ingloriously. So he waited almost a year to file suit. That way, the case couldn't possibly come up until after the election. In the meantime, he was ostensibly confronting his accusers.

Senator Dodd's libel strategy is instructive for the victim of a protracted imbroglio. With tremendous fanfare, Dodd filed a $5 million, 14-count suit in 1966 against Pearson and Anderson—truly a man defending his reputation! But at each critical stage of the litigation he would quietly withdraw various of the counts; thus Pearson's attorneys could not depose Dodd under oath concerning them. Dodd could not win anything this way, of course; his case was disappearing like a tube of baloney in a meat slicer, but a political libel suit is brought for pretense, not money. Eventually, all 14 counts were withdrawn. But Dodd's ingenuity persisted. Abandoning the charge that he was the victim of lies, he now pleaded that others had invaded his privacy and taken information with which he could have made money himself. All told, the courts were tied up for three years without one public cross-examination. Dodd eventually lost out on all counts, but in the meantime he appeared to his followers to be stoutly defending his honor while in fact he was dismantling piece by piece the suit he himself had brought.

Artful dodgers have filled the records with precedents, but the most brilliant evasive tour de force in American annals was the 1968 finesse by Congressman Cornelius E. Gallagher of Bayonne, New Jersey. He was in the midst of his reelection campaign when the Time-Life empire boffed him. Gallagher was a collaborator with the Mafia, *Life* said, was a partner in business ventures with underworld boss Joe Zicarelli, had used his Congressional office to further the business and personal interests of Zicarelli, had used political muscle to squash a gambling probe in Bayonne, and had been linked to the underworld in the tapped phone conversations of gangland figures. As if this wasn't enough, *Life* also alleged that a paid murderer and convicted extortionist with the macabre name of Kayo Konigsberg had, under Mafia orders, removed from Gallagher's cellar the body of one Barney O'Brien, a small-time hood. *The New York Times* reported that these revelations stunned even Members of Congress. So grotesque were they, in fact, that the Hudson County Democratic organization, which regularly ingests scandal without belch, panicked and demanded the death penalty— that Gallagher resign "within three days" both as its candidate for Congress and as delegate to the upcoming Democratic National Convention.

But Gallagher did not panic. Who among the captains of history can claim such perfection under fire as the embattled Gallagher now displayed? Immediately, he invoked Rules 2, 4, 5, 6, 7, 8, 9, 10, and 11. He redeclared his candidacy. With no cardinal available on short notice, he sought an endorsement from Governor Richard J. Hughes. He then requested a grand jury investigation and a House Ethics Committee probe. He announced plans for a libel suit against *Life*. He confessed to certain harmless business ventures with close friends and said that whatever he had done for Zicarelli he would do for any constituent. He described *Life* as "a modern court of inquisition." A House colleague, Congressman Charles Joelson, roughed up Attorney General Ramsey Clark over the disclosed wiretaps.

Within 72 hours, though not a fact had changed, the contretemps was resolved. Governor Hughes declared Gallagher to be "a very great man, a wonderful man." The Hudson County Democratic organization reversed itself and announced united support for Gallagher; Boss John V. Kenney, alias "The Little Guy," declared that by asking for a grand jury probe and announcing a libel suit Gallagher had shown the organization he would prove his innocence. Attorney General Clark said he knew nothing about any references to Gallagher in any Mafia wiretaps. On the campaign trail, Gallagher was cheered as never before; petitions were circulated to dissuade him from resigning; he was overwhelmingly reelected. What does it matter today that Gallagher never filed the libel suit that caused "The Little Guy" to revoke excommunication? Or that the grand jury probe never began and never could have begun because, as Hudson County prosecutor Tumulty announced, "the statute of limitations had already expired" on all charges made by *Life*. Or that the House Ethics Committee investigation never materialized? Or that Ramsey Clark was wrong and the Justice Department did have Mafia tapes and they did mention Gallagher? What counts is that in the moment of maximum danger, Gallagher was ready with his precedents.

Rule 12. *When judicial proceedings become inevitable, claim constitutional immunity.*

A scandal that survives to Rule 12 must be recognized as truly dangerous. The grand strategy has failed; now one must try to worm out on technicalities.

The Constitution provides that Members of Congress cannot be interfered with by anyone on their way to Washington nor held accountable for anything they say on the Floor. These safeguards were intended to banish fear and thus protect the integrity of Congress, but they have been gradually converted into protections against prosecution for theft, fraud, bribery, extortion, felonious assault, and lascivious carriage.

The modern phrase began when two New York cops surprised Senator Warren G. Harding of Ohio in a hotel room with nubile Nan Britton, who was later to write a book about her illegitimate child entitled *The President's Daughter*. Threatened with arrest for fornication, carnal knowledge, and drunk driving, Harding awed the local police by charging contempt for the U.S. Constitution. He was released and journeyed on undisturbed, his peccadillos remaining undisclosed until he was our martyred President. In recent years, new constitutional theory has been proclaimed by Congressmen Powell, Johnson, and Dowdy.

Powell established the doctrine that no person elected to Congress can be excluded for any reason other than failure to meet the requirements of age, residence, and citizenship. Johnson got a Supreme Court reversal of his conviction for conspiracy to defraud on the grounds that part of his defrauding was done on the Floor of the Congress where he was immune (but he was retried and convicted for off-the-Floor activities). John Dowdy of Texas is today the chief constitutionalist in the Congress. Indicted early this year for bribery and perjury, Dowdy asked dismissal on the grounds that any briberies and perjuries committed by him in the performance of his duties were ipso facto beyond the reach of the policeman's knout; he also asked for change of venue, from Baltimore to Texas, where he may be tried not only by his peers but by his constituents. At this writing, Dowdy has lost the early rounds, but the appeals process has scarcely begun and will consume many years.

Rule 13. *During trial or impeachment proceedings, observe all the traditional formalities listed below:*

(a) From now on, never appear in public without your wife. Be sure your entire family, including pre-school children, attend every court session. The spectacle of your wife and children being subjected to all the evidence of your wrongdoing day after day will distress the jury and incline them toward pity for you. Although the experience may cause emotional damage to younger children, psychiatry can repair that later. Right now, it's go for broke.

(b) Feign illness and a sort of stunned vacuity, as if the indignity of it all is too much for your sensitive nature; this glazed mien is a must as groundwork for a convincing loss of memory when you take the stand. Loss of weight, a sickly pallor, a cane, the general look of a man about to break are mandatory if one is to create the "hasn't he already suffered enough" atmosphere.

(c) When questioned by the press in the hallways, emphasize how you welcome the chance to clear your name, how you asked for this trial, how the only thing that bothers you is the suffering it's inflicting on your family, how you'd still go after the Reds if you had it all to do over, how glad you'll be when the verdict is in and you can get back to your duties.

(d) Employ the "partial expert"—the hired C.P.A. to give a tidied statement of your net worth, the paid handwriting expert to testify that it was *not* your signature after all, the tax consultant (retired) who will swear he told you not to list those testimonial purses.

(e) If convicted, abandon all dignity and beg for mercy. Congressman Johnson petitioned the court not to send him to prison on the grounds that the resultant indignity would so affront his honor as to cause him to commit suicide.

(f) If, despite this plea, you are sentenced to prison anyway, follow Johnson's example and announce you are getting the warden to assign you to the V.I.P. hospital. That way, you will be constantly attended by doctors, and subsequently remembered not as a jailbird but as a patient.

(g) Don't despair. Remember that Congressman Tom Lane won re-election after he was convicted. So did Jim Curley and Adam Powell. Besides, there is always the probability of a presidential pardon. It has been the custom for the President to let all convicted politicians out of jail every year at Christmastime, when the public is preoccupied and forgiveness is in the air. Late in the Administration of President Johnson, yuletide pardons were so numerous that the custom began to get a bad name and was suspended temporarily. But Attorney General Mitchell has persuaded President Nixon to reinstitute it.

The foregoing has been set down not as a how-to-do-it tract for charlatans, nor as a guide for detecting the falsehoods of guilty men, though I suppose perverted minds could misuse the information for both purposes— just as a chemistry book could be misused to construct a bomb or an illustrated text on gynecology exploited for erotic pleasure. My purpose is scientific and philosophic.

I set out in the beginning to show that from an exposed Congressman's first laryngitis attack to his Christmas eve release from jail and subsequent strategy meeting to plan the next campaign, he acts out of folk wisdom known only to politicians. The ritual, partly glimpsed here, is preserved by Congressional elders, and all Members in trouble master it by rote. To prove this point, I shall cite the travail of a man as different from an ordinary

Congressman as a swan is from a hippopotamus. My object is to show that even in this case the ritual was followed without deviation down to the most banal detail. I refer to the misfortune of Senator Edward Kennedy. Recall the steps by which a patrician gentleman with the most spohisticated advisers in the West defended himself exactly as would the commonest Boston pol:

After the private moment of despair—the panic and hiding in the Shire-town Inn; the cryptic statement to the police; the precipitate smuggling out of the body, before autopsy, to a jurisdiction beyond reach of subpoena; the long period incommunicado at Hyannisport while the Kennedy proconsuls hammered together a plausible story; the appearance at the Kopechne funeral wearing a neck brace and the vague reports about a brain concussion; the rumors from the Compound about a stunned listlessness; the clandestine negotiation with friendly authorities to set up a traffic violation as the charge; the guilty plea to that charge which cut off all public proceedings; the suspended jail sentence; the television broadcast in which what was publicly known was confessed and the rest glossed over; the announcement for reelection with the added refinement of a plebiscite by mail; the public welcoming of an investigation when it finally became unstoppable; the assurances that all the facts would be aired at the proper time while stealthily maneuvering to block any public airing; the involved constitutional gimmickry which added up to the Senator's claim to personal immunity; the "reluctant" refusal to answer reporters' questions on the grounds of protecting the dignity of the court; the hiring of "partial experts"—this time air bubble experts; the public concern for "getting this over so I can get back to my Senate duties" while privately employing every possible instrument of delay; the loss of memory and the lying under oath (in the opinion of Judge Boyle) ; the brilliant series of technicalities on which the serious charges which might have been brought were one by one eliminated. And now the careful period of rehabilitation, the press build-up that the Senator has become serious, cut down on drinking, is dieting and exercising, and no longer is activated by pretty girls. Not a pirouette missed in the elephant's ballet.

Examined individually, how gross, ignominious, and transparently fraudulent these maneuvers are; but in the aggregate, how efficacious! How many times did you chortle as Teddy numbered preposterously with his subterfuge? But look at the results: the Senate Majority Whip post retained, reelection assured, credibility damaged but salvageable, presidential prospects rising, a climate irresistibly building in which it begins to seem unsportsmanlike to bring up Chappaquiddick. In another year or two the whole affair will dissolve into the morning mists off Martha's Vineyard.

The basic premise behind a ritual so manifestly successful ought to tell us something important about our society. In my opinion, it is this: in American public life there is no sense of honor, no concept of it, no expectation of it, no reward for it. Wherever honor exists it is an unrequired discipline a man imposes on himself for private reasons. This is the reverse side of the blessing of popular democracy, and may yet turn that blessing into a curse.

We are a country of Falstaffs and the shrewder politicians all know it. Many civilized nations have soldiers who will shoot down unarmed civilians; in America they are lionized in their home towns, praised by Congressmen, and favored by a clear majority in the Gallup Poll. Many nations have cops who bludgeon unarmed adolescents and fire machine guns into the windows of the girls' dormitory; here they are extolled by their governor and have fan clubs organized and bumper stickers printed in their honor. Many nations have district attorneys who stage an occasional massacre and then dramatize the scene on television as self-defense; here, when such a creature is exposed as a calculated liar, he not only keeps his job but begins to dream of the governorship. Many nations have legislators who are shown to lie, cheat and steal; here church synods, panels of distinguished citizens, and ideological movements pass resolutions praising them. Such egalitarian buffooneries are the key to our political process. Once the politician masters this, he will face his indictments with equanimity.

The difficulty in catching on to this reality has unfairly retarded the political progress of our more recent arrivals, particularly those of ethnic strains which retain a hereditary respect for "face" and personal dignity. Signs abound that this handicap is passing. Having learned the rules, Greeks, Jews, Poles, and Japanese are regularly winning reelection to Congress; and recently 100,000 Italian-Americans held a mass rally in New York to protest police repression of the Mafia.

11.   The Informal "Code" of Police Deviancy: A Group Approach to "Blue-Coat" Crime

ELLWYN STODDARD

It has been asserted by various writers of criminology, deviant behavior, and police science that unlawful activity by a policeman is a manifestation of personal moral weakness, a symptom of personality defects, or the recruitment of individuals unqualified for police work. In contrast to the traditional orientation, this paper is a sociological examination of "blue-coat crime"[1] as a functioning informal social system whose norms and practices are at variance with legal statutes. Within the police group itself, this pattern of illicit behavior is referred to as the "code."

Following an examination of these contrasting viewpoints, this case study will provide data to ascertain the existence of the "code," its limitations and range of deviancy, and the processes through which it is maintained and sanctioned within the group. The guiding hypothesis of this study is that illegal practices of police personnel are socially prescribed and patterned through the informal "code" rather than being a function of individual aberration or personal inadequacies of the policeman himself.

Reprinted by special permission of the *Journal of Criminal Law, Criminology and Police Science,* Copyright © 1968 by Northwestern University School of Law. Volume 59, No. 62.

Revision of a paper presented at the Rocky Mountain Social Science Association, Air Force Academy, April 1967. It was supported in part by a grant from the University Research Institute, University of Texas at El Paso.

[1] This concept is a restricted modification of Sutherland's term "White Collar Crime." Edwin H. Sutherland, "White Collar Criminality," *American Sociological Review* 5 (1940), pp. 1–12. However, the stress of Sutherland's thesis is the lowering of social morale *of the larger society* by the violation of trust by those holding these social positions. The present emphasis is upon the group participating in those violations and *their* reactions, morale and behavior, rather than the consequences accruing the larger society as a result of these illegal actions. The same violation of trust might produce a degree of disorganization and lowering of morale among nonparticipants, while producing a heightened morale and cohesion among all of those in the norm-violating clique.

THE INDIVIDUALISTIC APPROACH

Three decades ago August Vollmer emphasized that the individual being suited to police work was the factor responsible for subsequent deviancy among officers. This approach implicitly assumes inherent personality characteristics to be the determinant which makes a police recruit into a good officer or a bad one.[2] A current text of police personnel management by German reaffirms the individualistic orientation of Vollmer, and suggests that the quality of police service is ultimately dependent upon the individual police officer. There is no evidence of an awareness of group pressures within his analysis.[3]

A modified version of this individualistic approach is the view that perhaps the individual chosen had already become "contaminated" prior to being hired as a member of the force, and when presented with chances for bribery or favoritism, the "hard core guy, the one who is a thief already, steps in."[4]

A third factor, stressed by Tappan,[5] is the poor screening method at the recruitment stage. Such an officer might have had inadequate training, insufficient supervision, and poor pay and is ripe for any opportunity to participate in lucrative illict enterprises. This author then goes into great detail to show the low intelligence and educational level of police officers. Another author adds that improved selection and personality evaluation have improved the quality of the police considerably over the past 20 years,[6] thereby attacking this problem directly. One recent author wrote that low salaries make more difficult the attraction of applicants with the moral strength to withstand temptations of "handouts" and eventual corruption.[7] Sutherland and Cressey, although aware that graft is a characteristic of the entire police system[8] rather than of an isolated patrolman, stress the unqualified appointments of police officials by corrupt politicians as the source of police deviancy. They state:

---

[2] August Vollmer, *The Police and Modern Society* (1936), pp. 3–4.

[3] A. C. German, *Police Personnel Management* (1958), pp. 3–4.

[4] Mort Stern, "What Makes a Policeman Go Wrong? An Ex-Member of the Force Traces the Steps on Way from Law Enforcement to Violating," by a former Denver police officer as told to Mort Stern, *Denver Post,* October 1, 1961. Reprinted in *Journal of Criminal Law, Criminology, and Police Science* 53 (1962), pp. 97–101.

A similar reaction is given by James F. Johnson, a former state trooper, Secret Service Agent, security officer and private investigator in *World Telegram and Sun,* March 10, 1953, quoted in Tappan, *Crime, Justice and Correction* (1960), p. 290.

[5] Tappan, ibid., p. 309 ff.

[6] Wilson, "Progress in Police Administration," *Journal of Criminal Law, Criminology, and Police Science* 42 (1951), p. 141.

[7] Johnson, *Crime, Correction and Society* (1964), p. 452.

[8] The Lexow Committee in New York (1894–95), and the Seabury Committee a generation later found the same situation of *departmental* corruption quoted in Sutherland and Cressey, *Principles of Criminology,* 6th ed. (1960), p. 338.

Another consequence of the fact that police departments often are organized for the welfare of corrupt politicians, rather than of society, is inefficient and unqualified personnel. This is unquestionably linked with police dishonesty, since only police officers who are "right" can be employed by those in political control. Persons of low intelligence and with criminal records sometimes are employed.[9]

THE GROUP APPROACH

In contrast to the individualistic approach of these foregoing authors, the emphasis on the social context in which police deviancy flourishes has preoccupied the sociological criminologists. The present case study would clearly reflect this latter orientation.

Barnes and Teeters mention police deviancy in conjunction with organized syndicated crime.[10] Korn and McCorkle,[11] Cloward,[12] and Merton[13] see political and police corruption as a natural consequence of societal demands for illegal services. When these desired services are not provided through legal structures, they are attained through illegal means. However, documentation in support of these theoretical explanations is sketchy and limited in scope. Bell suggests that "crime is an American way of life." In the American temper there exists a feeling that "somewhere, somebody is pulling all the complicated strings to which this jumbled world dances." Stereotypes of big crime syndicates project the feeling that laws are just for "the little guys." Consequently, while "Americans have made such things as gambling illegal, they don't really in their hearts think of it as wicked."[14] Likewise, the routine discovery of an average citizen in overt unlawful activity rarely inflames the public conscience to the degree that it does when this same deviant behavior is exhibited by a police officer. Thus, the societal double standard demands that those in positions of trust must exhibit an artificially high standard of morality which is not required of the average citizen.

A measure of role ambivalence is an inevitable part of the policeman occupation in a democratic society. While he is responsible to protect the members of his society from those who would do them harm, the correspond-

---

[9] Sutherland and Cressey, ibid.

[10] Barnes and Treeters, *New Horizons in Criminology*, 2nd ed. (1958), pp. 245–47.

[11] Korn and McCorkle, *Criminology and Penology* (1959), pp. 85–86 and 125–36.

[12] Richard A. Cloward, "Illegitimate Means, Anomie, and Deviant Behavior," *American Sociological Review* 24 (1959), p. 167.

[13] Merton, *Social Theory and Social Structure*, revised and enlarged ed. (1958), Chs. 1, 4, and 5.

[14] Bell, "Crime as an American Way of Life," *Antioch Review* 13 (1953), pp. 140–44.

ing powers for carrying out this mandate are not delegated.[15] To perform his designated duties, the conscientious policeman often must violate the very laws he is trying to enforce. This poses a serious dilemma for the police officer since his attempt to effectively discourage violation of the law among the general public is often hinged to extra-legal short-cut techniques[16] which are in common practice by his law enforcement cohorts. For example, the use of "illegal" violence by policemen is justified by them as a necessary means to locate and harrass the most vicious criminals and the Organized Syndicates.[17] These procedures are reinforced through coordinated group action.

> The officer needs the support of his fellow officers in dangerous situations and when he resorts to practices of questionable legality. Therefore, the rookie must pass the test of loyalty to the code of secrecy. Sometimes this loyalty of colleagues has the effect of protecting the law-violating, unethical officer.[18]

Such illegal practices which are traditionally used to carry out a policeman's assigned tasks might well be readily converted to the aims of personal gain.

In these tight informal cliques within the larger police force, certain "exploratory gestures"[19] involving the acceptance of small bribes and favors can occur. This is a hazy boundary between grateful citizens paying their respects to a proud profession, and "good" citizens involved in corruption wishing to buy future favors. Once begun, however, these practices can become "norms" or informal standards of cliques of policemen. A new recruit can be socialized into accepting these illegal practices by mild, informal negative sanctions such as the withholding of group acceptance. If these unlawful practices are embraced, the recruits membership group—the police force—and his reference group—the clique involved in illegal behavior—are no longer one and

[15] Sutherland and Cressey, op. cit., p. 331.

[16] This dilemma is presently being compounded by recent Supreme Court decisions involving police powers and personal civil rights. The fear of an emergent police state (which may or may not be valid) leads the present Justices to feel that freedom of the individual will result when police powers no longer encroach upon individual rights. The paradox is that the police are required to fulfill their traditional protection duties in spite of these new formal procedures designed to limit their investigative activities. To fulfill the social expectations of "catching criminals, dope peddlers, etc.," the policeman must adopt certain extra-legal procedures strictly on an informal basis, while appearing on the surface to be adhering to the formal limitations imposed upon him. See Arthur Niederhoffer's recent monograph *Behind the Shield: The Police in Urban Society* (1967).

[17] Westley, "Violence and the Police," *American Journal of Sociology* 59 (1953), pp. 34–41.

[18] Westley, "Secrecy and the Police," *Social Forces* 34 (1956), pp. 254–57.

[19] This concept was taken from Cohen, *Delinquent Boys: The Culture of the Gang* (1955), p. 60.

the same. In such circumstances the norms of the reterence group (the illegal-oriented clique) would clearly take precedence over either the formal requisites of the membership group (police department regulations) or the formalized norms (legal statutes) of the larger society.[20] When such conflicts are apparent a person can

> (1) conform to one, take the consequences of non-conformity to the other. (2) He can seek a compromise position by which he attempts to conform in part, though not wholly, to one or more sets of role expectations, in the hope that sanctions applied will be minimal.[21]

If these reference group norms involving illegal activity become routinized with use they become an identifiable informal "code" such as that found in the present study. Such codes are not unique to the police profession. A fully documented case study of training at a military academy[22] in which an informal pattern of behavior was assimilated along with the formal standards clearly outlined the function of the informal norms, their dominance when in conflict with formal regulations, and the secretive nature of their existence to facilitate their effectiveness and subsequent preservation. The revelation of their existence to those outside the cadet group would destroy their integrative force and neutralize their utility.

This same secrecy would be demanded of a police "code" to ensure its preservation. Although within the clique the code must be well defined, the ignorance of the lay public to even its existence would be a requisite to its continuous and effective use.[23] Through participation in activity regimented by the "code" an increased group identity and cohesion among "code" practitioners would emerge.

> Group identity requires winning of acceptance as a member of the inner group and, thereby, gaining access to the secrets of the occupation which are acquired through informal contacts with colleagues.[24]

Lack of this acceptance not only bars the neophyte from the inner secrets of the profession, but may isolate him socially and professionally from his

---

[20] Sherif and Sherif, *An Outline of Social Psychology*, pp. 630–31 and 638. For a sophisticated treatment of reference group theory see Chs. 4, 16, and 18. Revised ed. (1956).

[21] Stouffer, "An Analysis of Conflicting Social Norms," *American Sociological Review* 14 (1949), p. 707.

[22] Dornbush, "The Military Academy as an Assimilating Institution," *Social Forces* 33 (1955), pp. 316–21.

[23] Moore and Tumin, "Some Social Functions of Ignorance," *American Sociological Review* 14 (1949), p. 791.

[24] Johnson, op. cit., pp. 445–46.

colleagues and even his superiors. There is the added fear that, in some circumstances in which he would need their support, they would avoid becoming involved, forcing him to face personal danger or public ridicule alone.

The social structure in which law enforcement is maintained has a definite bearing on what is considered normal and what is deviant behavior. The pattern of "Blue-Coat Crime" (i.e., the "code") seems far more deviant when compared to the dominant middle-class norms of our society as when compared to lower class values. Whyte maintains that in the Italian Slum of Cornerville, the primary function of the police department is not the enforcement of the law, but the regulation of illegal activities

> ... an outbreak of violence arouses the "good people" to make demands for law enforcement ... even when they disturb police racketeer relations. Therefore, it is in the interest of the departments to help maintain a peaceful racket organization ... By regulating the racket and keeping peace, the officer can satisfy the demands for law enforcement with a number of token arrests and be free to make his adjustment to the local situation.[25]

Since an adjustment to the local situation might well involve adopting some of the "code" practices, the successful police rookie is he who can delicately temper three sets of uncomplementary standards: (1) the "code" practices adopted for group acceptance, (2) the societal standards regulating the duties and responsibilities of the police profession and (3) his own system of morality gained from prior socialization in family, religious, educational and peer-group interaction.

METHODOLOGICAL CONSIDERATIONS

The difficulties connected with any intensive investigation into the "code" are self-evident. The binding secrecy which provides the source of its power would be disrupted if the "code" were revealed to an "outsider." Thus, standard sociological research methods were ineffective in this type of investigation. The traditional ethnographic technique of using an informant familiar with the "code" and its related practices made available the empirical data within this study. Obviously, data from a single informant do not begin to meet the stringent scientific criteria of reliability for the purpose of apply-

---

[25] Whyte, *Street Corner Society*, enlarged ed. (1955), pp. 138–39.

Another author conceptualized this problem by delineating it as two separate police functions. "Law enforcement" has specific formal legal procedures whereas "keeping the peace" is vague and without a clear-cut mandate. This study updates by three decades the classic work of Whyte. See Egon Bittner, "The Police on Skid-Row: A Study of Peace Keeping," *American Sociological Review* 32 (1967), pp. 699–715.

ing the conclusions from this case to police agencies in general. It is assumed that subsequent research will establish whether this is a unique episode or more of a universal phenomenon. However, the decision to enrich the literature with this present study in spite of its methodological deficiencies was felt to be justified inasmuch as an intensive search through the professional literature revealed no empirical accounts dealing directly with deviant policemen.[26]

Because of the explosive nature of such materials on the social, political and economic life of the persons involved, the use of pseudonyms to maintain complete anonymity is a precaution not without precedent, and was a guarantee given by the director of this study in return for complete cooperation of the informant.[27] The informant was a police officer for 3½ years before he was implicated in charges of Robbery and Grand Larceny. He was subsequently tried and convicted, serving the better part of a year in prison. At the time of these interviews, he had been released from prison about three years.

The initial design of this study attempted to correlate these empirical data with two journalistic accounts[28] but the subjective handling of those stories neutralized any advantage gained from an increased number of informants. The present design is based exclusively on the single informant.

THE CODE AND ITS PRACTICES

Some of these terms used to describe police deviancy are widely used, but because of possible variations in meaning they are defined below.[29] These practices are ordered so that those listed first would generally elicit the least

[26] Many authors have written of police deviancy as tangential to their central theme. However, persistent search failed to reveal recent empirical studies focusing directly on the deviant policeman himself. Most applicable were Westley's *Violence and the Police,* op. cit., and *Secrecy and the Police,* op. cit., although even here the data were gained from policemen still "in favor," who might well have reservations about revealing the full extent to which the "Code" was practiced.

[27] A graduate assistant from the Department of Sociology, Mr. Ivy L. Gilbert approached ex-officer "Smith" as a friend, and under guidance of the present author was able to gain "Smith's" cooperation for a scientific study. Taped interviews over a period of several months were recorded and transcribed by Gilbert. Many of these materials were used in Gilbert's Master's Thesis, *A Case Study of Police Scandal: An Investigation into Illegitimate Norms of a Legitimate Enforcement Agency* (June 1965).

[28] One article is a composite of personal experience as a police reporter, David G. Wittles, "Why Cops Turn Crooked," *Saturday Evening Post,* April 23, 1949, p. 26 ff; the other is an account of a former Denver policeman as retold by a news editor, Mort Stern, op. cit. supra note 4.

[29] The majority of those terms and definitions are modified from those listed by Gilbert, op. cit., pp. 3–4, and discussed by German, op. cit., supra note 3 at p. 173.

fear of legal prosecution and those listed last would invoke major legal sanctions for their perpetration.

Mooching—An act of receiving free coffee, cigarettes, meals, liquor, groceries, or other items either as a consequence of being in an underpaid, undercompensated profession *or* for the possible future acts of favoritism which might be received by the donor.

Chiseling—An activity involving police demands for free admission to entertainment whether connected to police duty or not, price discounts, etc.

Favoritism—The practice of using license tabs, window stickers or courtesy cards to gain immunity from traffic arrest or citation (sometimes extended to wives, families and friends of recipient).

Prejudice—Situations in which minority groups receive less than impartial, neutral, objective attention, especially those who are less likely to have "influence" in City Hall to cause the arresting officer trouble.

Shopping—The practice of picking up small items such as candy bars, gum, or cigarettes at a store where the door has been accidentally unlocked after business hours.

Extortion—The demands made for advertisements in police magazines or purchase of tickets to police functions, or the "street courts" where minor traffic tickets can be avoided by the payment of cash bail to the arresting officer with no receipt required.

Bribery—The payments of cash or "gifts" for past or future assistance to avoid prosecution; such reciprocity might be made in terms of being unable to make a positive identification of a criminal, or being in the wrong place at a given time when a crime is to occur, both of which might be excused as carelessness but no proof as to deliberate miscarriage of justice. Differs from mooching in the higher value of a gift and in the mutual *understanding* regarding services to be performed upon the acceptance of the gift.

Shakedown—The practice of appropriating expensive items for personal use and attributing it to criminal activity when investigating a break in, burglary, or an unlocked door. Differs from shopping in the cost of the items and the ease by which former ownership of items can be determined if the officer is "caught" in the act of procurement.

Perjury—The sanction of the "code" which demands that fellow officers lie to provide an alibi for fellow officers apprehended in unlawful activity covered by the "code."

Premeditated Theft—Planned burglary, involving the use of tools, keys, etc. to gain forced entry or a prearranged plan of unlawful acquisition of property which cannot be explained as a "spur of the moment" theft. Differs from shakedown only in the previous arrangements surrounding the theft, not in the value of the items taken.

Mooching, chiseling, favoritism and *prejudice* do not have rigid interpretations in the "code." Their presence appears to be accepted by the general public as a real fact of life. Since the employment of one of these practices can be done while in the normal routine of one's duties, such practices are often ignored as being "deviant" in any way. Ex-Officer Smith sees it in this light:

> ... the policeman having a free cup of coffee? I have never thought of this as being corrupt or illegal because this thing is just a courtesy thing. A cup of coffee or the old one—the cop on the beat grabbing the apple off the cart—these things I don't think shock too many people because they know that they're pretty well accepted.

But when asked about the practice of *mooching* by name, it assumed a different character of increased importance to Smith!

> I think mooching is accepted by the police and the public is aware of it. My opinion now, as an ex-policeman, is that mooching is one of the underlying factors in the larger problems that come ... it is one of the most basic things. It's the easiest thing to accept and to take in stride because it's so petty. I think that it is the turning point a lot of times.

The "Sunday Comics" stereotype of a policeman initiating mooching, bribery and favoritism is incorrect according to Smith's experience:

> Generally, the policeman doesn't have to ask for things, he just finds out about them. Take for example the theaters. I know the Roxy theaters would let the policeman in on his badge, just about anytime. It's good business because it puts the owner in a closer relationship with the policeman, and the policeman is obligated to him. If they had a break-in, a fire, or a little favor such as double parking out front to unload something, they'd expect special consideration from the policeman.
>
> When I walked the east side beat the normal thing was for bartenders to greet me and offer me a pack of cigarettes or a drink. When I walked the beat I was pretty straight laced, there were a few bartenders that I felt were just trying to get along with me, and I loosened up a little with those people. One bartender gave me cigars when he found out that I didn't smoke cigarettes. I always accepted them; he always pointed out there wasn't any obligation. Some of the beat men accepted cigarettes, some cigars, some took cash, and these men know when they're dealing with bootleggers, and why they're being paid. Different businessmen in the loop area give policemen Christmas presents every year.

Shopping and *shakedown, extortion* and *bribery* are all clearly unlawful, but in these practices the manner in which they are carried out contains a measure of safety to the policeman should his presence or behavior be questioned. A policeman's investigative powers allows him entry into an open building in which a "suspected robbery" has occurred, and various types of articles such as cigarettes and the like cannot be traced to any given retail outlet. Hence, his presence on such occasions is not *suspected;* rather, it is *expected!* Also, should a clumsy job of *shopping* or *shakedown* result in witnesses reporting these unlawful practices, the "code" requires that participating officers must commit *perjury* to furnish an alibi for those colleagues observed in illegal activities. This is both for the protection of the deviant officer and to preclude public disclosure of the widespread involvement of fellow officers in "code" practices. How extensive is *shopping* and *shakedown* as practiced by a department?

> As far as the Mid-City department is concerned I would say that 10 percent of the department would go along with anything, including deliberate forced entries or felonies. But about 50 percent of them would openly go along with just about anything. If they found a place open or of there had been a break-in or if they found anything they could use and it was laying there, they'd help themselves to it.
> Whenever there's an open door or window, they call for all the cars and they shake the whole building down—loot it!

Would those policemen involved in shopping and shakedown participate in something more serious? According to ex-officer Smith, they would.

> Most of the policemen who shop or go along with shopping would go along with major theft, if it just happened. I think where you've got to draw the line is when you get into premeditated, deliberate thefts. I think this is where the big division comes.
> In shopping, the theft just happens. Premeditated theft is a cold, deliberate, planned thing.

Here Smith points out the limits of the "code" which, through condoning any level of theft that "just happens," cannot fully support *premeditated theft.*

> I think in premeditated theft that the general police attitude is against it, if for no other reason just for the matter of self-preservation, and survival. When you get to a premeditated, deliberate thing, then I think your police backing becomes pretty thin.

At the time when Smith was engaged in the practice of *premeditated theft* in Mid-City, it looked somewhat differently to him than it did later.

When he took an objective look, he was aware of just how little this extreme deviancy *actually was practiced*.

> When I was involved in it, it seemed like all the people around me were involved in it, and participating in it. It looked more to me like the generally accepted thing then, than it does now, because actually the clique that I was in that did this sort of thing was a small one. I'm not discounting the fact that there may have been a lot of other small çliques just like this.

Looking at his behavior as an outsider, after his expulsion, Smith saw it in this light:

> After taking a long, hard look at my case and being real honest about it, I'd have to say that this [premeditated theft like mine] is the exception. The longer I'm away from this thing the more it looks like this.

In Mid-City, *extortion* was not generally practiced and the "code" prescribed "street courts" (i.e., bribery for minor traffic offenses) as outside the acceptable pattern.

> [Extortion is] something that I would classify as completely outside the law [here in Mid-City], something that in certain areas has been accepted well on the side of both the public and the police. There's a long standing practice that in Chicago if you are stopped for a traffic violation if you had a five dollar bill slipped in your plastic holder, or your billfold, the patrolman then asks for your license, and if that's in there you'll very rarely be issued a summons. Now this thing was something that was well known by truck drivers and people who travel through that area.

Smith maintains that the "code" is widespread, although from the above analysis of extortion it can be clearly seen that specific practices have been traditionally practiced and accepted in certain areas, yet not found acceptable in another community. Would this mean that the bulk of these "code" practices occur in police departments other than the one in which Smith served his "apprenticeship" in "Blue-Coat Crime"? Our informant says "yes" and offers the following to substantiate his answer:

> I think generally the Mid-City police department is like every police department in the world. I think the exceptions are probably in small towns or in a few cities that have never been touched by corrupt politics, if there are any. But I think that generally they are the same

everywhere,[30] because I have talked to policemen from other cities. I know policemen in other cities that I've had contact with that were in those things. I've discussed open things, or out and out felonies, with policemen from Kansas City on. And I know that at least in that city that it happens, and it's a matter of record that it happens in Denver and Chicago. And I think that this happens in all cities.

From a scientific point of view, other than the incidence of police scandals from time to time, there is no evidence to confirm or deny this one ex-officer's opinion regarding the universal existence of the "code."

THE RECRUIT'S INITIATION INTO THE "CODE" CLIQUE

Bucher describes a profession as a relatively homogeneous community whose members share identity, values, definitions of role, and interest. Socialization of recruits consists of inducting them into the "common code."[31] This occurs on two levels: the formal, or membership group, and the informal, or the reference group.

In the Mid-City police department the failure to socialize most of the new recruits into the "code" would constitute a threat to those who presently practice it. Thus, all "code" practitioners have the responsibility of screening new recruits at various times to determine whether they are "alright guys," and to teach by example and mutual involvement the limitations of "code" practices. If the recruit accepts such training, he is welcomed into the group and given the rights and privileges commensurate with his new status. If he does not, he is classified as a "goof" and avoided by the rest.

In a journalistic account of police deviancy, it was argued that if corruption exists in the political structures controlling police department appointments, this "socialization" into deviancy begins at the point of paying for the privilege of making an application or of buying an appointment.[32] Although Smith did not "buy" his appointment, he cited the existence of factions hav-

---

[30] Smith's evaluations are heavily influenced by his experience. He was a patrolman in a police department totaling about 250 personnel, serving a metropolitan area of a quarter of a million persons.

However, other sources have suggested that when a community gets larger than 80,000 people, political corruption and graft are inevitable. Wittels, op. cit., p. 26.

[31] Rue Bucher and Anselm Strauss, "Professions in Progress," *American Journal of Sociology* 64 (1961), pp. 325–26.

[32] One Policeman reported having paid $300.00 to take the police examination. He also was required to pledge his family's vote to the "right" party. After some wait, he took a "special exam," then more waiting lists, and a final $300.00 to the party fund was required before he was hired. Then he had to purchase his own uniform on contract at the "right" store. Before this man became a member of the department, by his participation in the recruitment process, he was an involved member practicing the "code." Wittels, op. cit., pp. 105–07 and 111.

ing influence in recruit appointments, even within the structure of a Civil Service Commission.

> There are four different requirements to the whole thing. One is your written test, one is your agility, one is your physical examination, and the fourth is the oral examination which is given by the civil service commission. I really crammed before I took the test. When I took the test it was a natural for me, it was a snap. I scored a 94 on my test for the police department. With my soldiers preference, which gives you 5 points, I scored a 99.[33] I passed my agility test and my physical. I could have had a 100 score, I could have been a gymnast, gone through the agility test and made everyone else look silly and still I could have failed in the oral exam. And this is the kicker where politics comes in.
>
> There are three old men that are aligned with different factions, different people on and off the department, different businessmen that have power, different groups, different lodges and organizations and all thse things influence those men, these three people that make up the civil service board.

The existence of the "code" had hurt the level of morale generally in the Mid-City department. In fact, the breakdown of each new recruit's morale is an important step in gaining his acceptance of the "code."[34]

> The thing that hurt the morale was the fact that a large percentage of the people on the department were involved in illegal practices to some degree. And actually you take a man that has just joined the department, has good intentions[35] and is basically honest, and in this, to a man that's never been dishonest and hasn't stepped over the line, there aren't degrees. It's all either black or white. And the illegal activity I know shocks a lot of these young men ... because it was the thing to do. It's a way to be accepted by the other people. It's a terrible thing the way one policeman will talk about another. Say an old timer will have a new man working with him and he'll tell you, "You've got to watch him, because *he's honest!*"

[33] In spite of Smith's remarkable test level, he was left off a list of highest 10 eligible applicants, and some three months later was put on the list through the influence of his father, a respected member of the police department with many years of unblemished service. Otherwise, he may never have been placed on the appointment list.

[34] This is not unlike the planned removal of old civilian standards and values when a new soldier recruit is given basic training. The formal regulations are presented to him, but in company with "old Salts" he learns how the system can be worked and what a person must do to participate in it.

[35] One writer corroborates this by stating that young recruits who show traits of being ambitious, as well as those with family responsibilities, are the most susceptible to graft. The pressures toward success and achievement are clearly indicated by either or both of these factors. Wittels, op. cit., p. 27.

For a recruit to be accepted in the Mid-City police department he must accept the informal practices occurring in the department. Illegal activity is pursued within the police force as the dominant "norm" or standard.

To illustrate the group pressure on each policeman who dares to enforce the law as prescribed in the legal statutes, the following account is typical.

> We'll take a classic example—Mr. Sam Paisano. Now when I was on the force I knew that whenever I worked in the downtown area, I could go into Sam's restaurant and order my meal and never have to pay a dime. I think that just about every patrolman on the force knew that. If I had run across Sam doing anything short of murder, I think I would have treaded very lightly. Even if I hadn't accepted his free meals. Say I had turned it down; still, if I stopped this man for a minor traffic violation, say I caught him dead to rights, I'd be very reluctant to write this man a ticket because I'd suffer the wrath of the other men on the force. I'd be goofing up their meal ticket. Now he in turn knows this. The rest of the officers wouldn't waste any words about it, they'd tell you right off, "You sure fouled up our meal ticket." The old timers would give you a cold shoulder. If it came to the attention of the gold braid, your immediate superiors, they'd make sure you had a little extra duty or something. In most cases if you did this just to be honest, just to be right, it would go badly for you.
>
> This special treatment of Mr. Paisano wasn't something that you concealed, or that you were ashamed of because it was the normal accepted thing to do. I'd have been more ashamed, and I'd have kept it quiet if I'd stopped such a man as this, because I'd have felt like some kind of an oddball. I would have been bucking the tide, I'd been out of step.

Yet, such general practices must be converted to individual participation at some point, and to be effective this involvement must be on a primary group relationship basis. Smith's account of his introduction to the "code" follows the first steps of the assimilating process.

> The first thing that I can recall seeing done [which was illegal] was on the night shift when I first went on patrol. The old timers were shaking buildings down and helping themselves to whatever was in the building. The first time I saw it happen I remember filing through the checkout counter at a supermarket, seeing all the officers grabbing their cigarettes or candy bars, or whatever they wanted and I passed through without anything.
>
> I got in the car and this old timer had, of all the petty things, two of these 25 or 30 cent candy bars and he sat them down in the seat and told me to have some. I told him I really didn't want any. And he asked me if "that shook me up" or something. And I told him, "Well, it sort of surprised me." He said that everybody did it and that I should get used to that.

And as it went on it progressed more. Well, in fact, he justified it at the time by telling me he had seen the same market one time, when there had been a legitimate break-in and one particular detective had been so busy loading the back seat of his car full of hams and big pieces of beef that he was stumbling and falling down back and from the cooler to the alley, and he didn't even know who was around him he was so busy carrying things out. And he named this officer and I don't doubt it because I've seen the same officer do things in that same nature.

And this was the first direct contact I had with anything like this.

The old timers would test the new recruits with activities which could be laughed off if they were reported, such as the 30 cent candy bar taken from the supermarket in the above account.

The old timers would nose around 'til they found out whether a young guy was going to work with them and "be right" as far as they were concerned, or whether he was going to resist it and be straight as far as the rest of the world was concerned.

If the recruit cooperated, the practices were extended and the rookie became involved. Once he was involved there was no "squealing" on fellow policemen breaking the law. Then he could have some personal choice as to how far he personally wished to go. However, those who were straight-laced and wanted to stay honest had their problems too. Social isolation appears to be a powerful sanction as can be seen from Smith's information.

There are a few policemen that are straight-laced all the way. I can remember one policeman who might have made an issue of another policeman taking something. He had that attitude for the first six months that he was on the force but by that time, he had been brow beaten so bad, he saw the writing on the wall. He knew better than to tell anything. In addition to brow beating, this man in very short order was put in a position where they had him on the information desk, or kicked around from one department to another, 'cause nobody wanted to work with him. This kind of a man they called "wormy," because anything that would happen he'd run to the braid.

This fellow, I knew, wanted to be one of the boys, but he wanted to be honest, too. As it turned out, this guy was finally dismissed from the force for having an affair with a woman in his squad car. Just a couple of years before that he would have had a fit if he thought that somebody was going to take a drink on duty, or fool around with a woman, or steal anything. For this reason this man spent a lot of time on the information desk, working inside, and by himself in the squad car.

Negative sanctions were applied against "goofs" who advocated following the legitimate police ethic. Group acceptance by senior officers was the reward to a recruit accepting the "code," and the "code" was presented to the recruit as the police way of life having precedence over legal responsibilities.

> This small fraction that ... are honest and would report illegal activity, are ostracized. Nobody will work with them. They look at them like they're a freak, talk about them like they're a freak, and they are a freak.
>
> The goofs that would talk about doing things the way they should be done, they had to be ignored or put down. There were older policemen that as they found out I would go along with certain things, pressed to see how much further I would go. And showed me that they went farther, whether I cared to or not. So naturally I went along quite a ways with some of them. And I don't really remember how we first became aware of how far the other person would go. I think this is just a gradual thing.

The existence of a social system of an informal nature working quietly under the facade of the formal police department regulations has been clearly demonstrated in Mid-City. One further note in explaining the motivations of policemen toward illegal activities involves the condition of low salaries. Smith's department pay scale and working conditions would suggest that economic pressures were a factor in condoning or rationalizing "code" practices.

> The pay wasn't good. I went on the department and earned $292 a month. The morale of the force was as low as that of any group that I've ever been around. There was constant complaining from all them about everything.
>
> The training programs were set up so that you would have to come in on your own time and weren't compensated for it. . . . They dictated to you how you lived your whole life, not only what you did during the eight hours you were a policeman but how you'd live your whole life. This as much as anything hurt the morale.

But when Smith was asked directly, "With the policeman's low salary, do illegal activities become necessary to keep up financially?" he discounted it as a major factor.[36]

> I don't think this is the case. I don't think there are very many policemen that I knew, and I knew all of them, that were social climbers or that tried to keep up with the Jones, by illegal activities anyway.

---

[36] To evaluate Smith's statement on economic pressures, an additional personal datum is relevant. Smith used most of his money from *premeditated theft* for his "habit"—a racing car. He later declared he probably wouldn't have participated in this crime *so much* had it not been for the "habit." His responses did not seem to indicate that he *began* theft for racing money, but that he *continued* it to counter the economic drain created by owning and driving the racing machine.

Actually most of the police officers think that they are even above those people that have money, because they have power. Those people with money are pretty well forced to cater to a policeman. And you'll find that very few people ever tell a policeman what they think of him, whether they like him or not. They know that a policeman will do him harm. The businessmen, especially the bigger businessmen, pamper the policemen. They will treat them with respect when they face them.

SANCTIONS FOR PRESERVATION OF THE "CODE"

Normally, practitioners of the "code" would consist of a united group working to protect all fellow patrolmen from prosecution. However, Smith had exceeded the "code" limits[37] by committing *premeditated theft,* and in order to protect the "code" from being exposed during the scandal involving Smith and two accomplices, the "clique" socially and spatially isolated themselves from the three accused policemen.

Everybody ran for cover, when the thing hit the front page of the newspapers. I've never seen panic like there was at that time. These people were all ready to sell out their mother to save their own butts. They knew there was no holding back, that it was a tidal wave. They were grabbing just anything to hang on. The other policemen were ordered to stay away from us, myself and the other men involved. They were ordered to stay away from the trials. They were told to keep their noses out of this thing, that it would be handled.

There were a few policemen who came around during this time. Strangely the ones who came around were the ones who didn't go in for any of the illegal activity. They didn't have anything to worry about. Everybody else ran and hid.

During a time like this, group consensus is required to preserve the "code." A certain amount of rationalization is necessary to mollify past illicit activity in light of present public exposure. Smith continues:

I think if they had really gone by the book during the police scandal, that 25 percent of the policemen would have lost their jobs. I've talked to some of them since, and the worst violators all now have themselves convinced that they weren't guilty of a thing.

[37] One officer reports that he wondered why he was not promoted—perhaps they thought he was lazy. He was tagging cars of all violators, and even reported a broken sidewalk belonging to an "organization" man. He couldn't get ahead. He made a couple of outstanding arrests and was made a detective. Later, he ran a "vice" raid against a "protected" place, and was back as a rookie on a beat in "Siberia." He finally took some payoffs and cooperated and eventually became a Police Captain, but exceeding the "Code" limits, was caught and prosecuted. Either not accepting the "code," or exceeding its limits, had negative effects. Wittels, op. cit., pp. 111–22.

I've never referred to myself as this before, but I was their goat, their scapegoat. The others stuck together and had support. I got what I deserved, but if I compare myself with the others, I got a real raw deal.

Preservation of the "code" occurs when policemen work with another person who has similar intentions and begin to "trust" one another in illegal activities without fear of the authorities being informed. A suggestion of rotating young officers from shift to shift to weaken the "code" had been given public discussion. To this, Smith reacted thus:

> I think that the practice of rotating young officers will serve a purpose. It will eliminate a lot of things because you just can't take a chance with somebody that you don't know. If you don't know but what the next person they throw you with might be a CID...short for Criminal Investigation Department. They're spies! Say there are just 10 percent of the men on the department that wouldn't go along with anything, and they are switching around with the new system, you don't know when you're going to catch one of them, and if you do you're a cooked goose. The old system you were 90 percent sure of the people you were with.

This same process used to preserve the illegal "code" as a group phenomenon is also the same process used to develop and promote the acceptable professional ethics of the police. A situation in which it is "normal" for a policeman to "squeal on his fellow patrolmen," would undermine professional ethics. Personal insecurity would mount with the constant fear of just being accused with or without supporting evidence. Such an anarchical system lends itself to intrigue, suspicion and an increased possibility of each officer being "framed." Thus, these same procedures which would effectively reduce the continuation of the "code" would also prove dysfunctional to the maintenance of the ethics which are the core of the police profession itself. These concurrent processes reflect the dual standards extant in society at large.

DIFFICULTIES INVOLVED IN BREAKING THE "CODE"

If a "code" does exist in a law enforcement agency, one of the major factors which protects it from attack is secrecy. This factor is compounded by public acceptance of the traditional view of illegal behavior as only an individualistic, moral problem.

Another shield of the "code" from attack is the apathy resulting from the myriad of complex demands and responsibilities placed upon the average citizen. So many things touch him with which he *must* become involved that he does not pursue problems which do not directly concern him. Inextricably connected with this is the realistic fear of retaliation, either through direct harassment by the police or indirectly through informal censures.[38]

Smith says that only a real big issue will provoke an apathetic public to action.

> Everybody's looking out for number one. And the policeman can do you harm. It's such a complex thing, there are so many ways, so many different people are affected by the police—Most people will back off. Most people are afraid to do anything, if it looks like it's going to affect them adversely.

If the police have carefully practiced *prejudice,* in their day-to-day operations, the chances are slim that the persons against whom these illegal practices were committed possess either the social or political power to break the "code" before the system could retaliate. Knowing this fact keeps most of the persons with any knowledge of the "code's" operation silent indeed.

The rigid procedures of obtaining legal evidence and the dangers of committing a *false arrest* are gigantic deterrents to bringing accusations against any suspicious person, especially a policeman. Ex-Officer Smith discusses the realistic problems involved in attempting to enforce legal statutes against *shopping* or other aspects of the "code":

> I think that any law against *shopping* would be hard to enforce against a police officer. You'd really have to have the evidence against him and really make it public, cause it would be soft pedalled all the way otherwise. Let's say you see a police officer in a restaurant taking a pack of cigarettes or let's say it's something other than a pack of cigarettes, something you can prove came from the restaurant. And along comes a radio news unit and you stop the unit and say you just saw a policeman steal a pack of cigarettes or something bigger. When other police arrive on the scene the newsman would probably pull the other policemen off to the side and tell them that their buddy just took a pack of cigarettes and that goofball [the informer] wants to make trouble about it. You insist that they shake down the policeman and they find the item. Here you're in pretty good shape. In this case you'd have a policeman in a little bit of trouble. I don't think he'd lose his job or do any time over it, but I'd say there would be some scandal about it. Unless you were real hard headed they'd soft pedal it.
> Let's back up a little and say the policeman threw the item back into the restaurant, and then you made your accusation. Then you're in trouble, 'cause when they shake him down he doesn't have a thing.

[38] The campaigning attack on the "untouchable" image of J. Edgar Hoover and the FBI has made political news. The very act of exposing methods used by Hoover's organization, which though admittedly effective were clearly unlawful, caused the political downfall of an otherwise popular politician in the November 1966 Nevada election.

Now you're a marked man, because every policeman in town will know that you tried to foul up one of their boys. Even the honest policemen aren't going to like what you did. In other words, they are tightly knit, and they police this city by fear to a certain extent.

In Mid-City only those who are involved in practicing the "code" are equipped with the necessary information to expose its operations. Whether one *can* inform on his fellow officers is directly connected with the degree of his illegal involvement prior to the situation involving the unlawful event.

It all depends upon how deeply you are involved. If you've been a guy who has gone along with a free cup of coffee, the gratuities, the real petty things and you'd happen to drive up on a major theft, drive up on another policeman with his shoulder against the door, then you might take action. However, if you had gone a little farther, say you'd done some shopping, then you're forced to look the other way. It's like a spider spinning a web, you're drawn in toward the center.

It appears obvious that those who are involved in the "code" will be the least useful instruments for alleviating the problem. Only the professionally naive would expect a "code" practitioner to disclose the "code's" existence, much less reveal its method of operation, since his own position is so vulnerable.

SUMMARY OF FINDINGS

From data furnished by a participant informant, an informal "code" of illegal activities within one police department was documented. The group processes which encouraged and maintained the "code" were identified. It was found that the new recruits were socialized into "code" participation by "old timers" and group acceptance was withheld from those who attempted to remain completely honest and not be implicated. When formal police regulations were in conflict with "code" demands among its practitioners, the latter took precedence. Since the "code" operates under conditions of secrecy, only those who participate in it have access to evidence enough to reveal its method of operation. By their very participation they are implicated and this binds them to secrecy as well. In this study the public indignation of a police scandal temporarily suspended the "code" but it flourished again when public apathy returned.

Although some individual factors must be considered in explaining police deviancy, in the present study the sanction of group acceptance was paramount. This study clearly demonstrates the social genesis of the "code," the breeding ground for individual unlawful behavior. From evidence contained herein, an individualistic orientation to police deviancy may discover the "spoiled fruit" but only when the "code" is rooted out can the "seedbed" of deviancy be destroyed.

From related research in group deviancy, it can be stated that the social organization of a given community (including its respectable citizens) is the milieu in which a "code" flourishes. Thus, a police department is an integral element of that complex community structure, and deviancy found in an enforcement agency is a reflection of values which are habitually practiced and accepted within that community. This was found to be true in the present study.

The findings of this case study should not be interpreted as applicable to all police departments nor should it be a rationalization for the existence of an illicit "code" anywhere. Rather, it is a very limited effort to probe the very sensitive area of "Blue-Coat Crime" and describe its operation and method of perpetuation in one enforcement agency.

12. Socialization for Khaki-Collar Crime: Military Training as Criminalization Process

CLIFTON D. BRYANT

Sociologists have long demonstrated interest in deviance, but curiously, they have tended to ignore the unique patterns of crime and deviance associated with one of the largest work systems in the world: the United States military establishment.

The military is an occupational and social system embracing upwards of three and one-half million men and women in the various armed services (and to some degree, their families as well). It represents a formidable population with the attendant need for appropriate mechanisms of social control.

As citizens of the United States, members of the military are subject to the full range of civilian legal regulations and constraints, including conventional civilian sociolegal codes at federal, state, and local levels. They are also subject to the additional social control imposed by military law and are accountable under supplemental sets of legal constraints governing their occupational behavior, including the U.S. Uniform Code of Military Justice and various international treaties. Such constraints are normally enforced and severely sanctioned by the U.S. military establishment. In the event of violation of these prescribed rules of conduct, the offender is subject to military justice and its attendant punishments.

The armed forces postulates three reasons for effecting its own system of law.[1] These include the fact that the military often operates in foreign countries as well as in other situations in which civilian courts are not readily available. The military must, in effect, transport its own legal system in its

An earlier version of this article was read as a paper at the Interamerican Congress of the American Society of Criminology and the Interamerican Association of Criminology in Caracas, Venezuela, November 19–25, 1972. A similar version of this paper also appeared in Terence P. Thornberry and Edward Sagarin (eds.) *Images of Crime: Offenders and Victims* (New York, Praeger, 1974).

[1] Headquarters, Department of the Army, *Military Law and Boards of Office,* ROTCM 148–85 (Washington, D.C., U.S. Government Printing Office, 1963), p. 4.

operations. Also, the military has found necessary "additional rules of conduct not normal to civilian life ... in the training and operation of a disciplined army." Finally in some foreign countries where "Status of Forces" treaties are in effect, military personnel are usually immune to local civilian justice and, generally, U.S. civilian courts as well: "thus there must be some method of trying the individual concerned for civilian type crimes committed."[2]

In spite of the complex normative system and severe sanctions, violations do routinely occur. Military life is the scene of a wide variety of deviant behavior ranging from excessive use of alcohol and narcotic addiction, to sex crimes, theft, and even mass murder. Much of this behavior may perhaps be attributed to the opportunity structure of the military system and the sociocultural and geographical settings in which the military normally operates, the informal pressures and strains inherent in military culture, as well as the structured subversion of organizational goals frequently component to the military enterprise.

Crime and deviance in the military must be viewed against the backdrop of the generalized mission of the military, the attitudes and values defining and supporting this mission, the process of occupational selection, the thrust of subcultural socialization, and the posture of the operant formal normative system. The resultant subcultural perspective, linked with the composition of its labor force, combine to produce a unique military pattern of deviance that may perhaps be appropriately labeled "khaki-collar crime," and which has been discussed in conceptual detail elsewhere.[3] As suggested by this previous conceptual overview, khaki-collar crime may be horizontally articulated into three broad categories including: (1) crimes against property; (2) crimes against person; and (3) crimes against performance. It can be further vertically divided into five loci of occurrence, dependent on the systemic context of its commission: (1) intraoccupational; (2) extraoccupational—American civilian, foreign friendly civilian, and enemy civilian; and (3) interoccupational.

INTRAOCCUPATIONAL MILITARY CRIME

Much of the deviant behavior committed by members of the armed forces is internal to the U.S. military system itself. Such deviance is directed against the military and may involve theft or misuse of government property, interpersonal violence, and inappropriate military behavior.

---

[2] Ibid.

[3] Clifton D. Bryant, *Khaki-Collar Crime: A Neglected Form of Occupational Deviance.* Paper delivered at annual meetings of Southern Sociological Society, New Orleans, La. (April 1972).

CRIMES AGAINST PROPERTY

The protection of and appropriate allocation of supplies and equipment is especially important to the efficient implementation of the military mission. Servicemen, however, may seek to supply themselves or their units with government-issued property not normally authorized or available as a means of enhancing their comfort and contributing to their survival—with the result there is widespread theft and misappropriation of government property often involving elaborate illicit barter[4] and "scrounging" systems, or theft simply redefined as "moonlight requisitioning."

CRIMES AGAINST PERSON

The social organization of the military rests on an elaborate set of formalized status relationships involving highly specific and circumspect subordinate–superordinate roles. Interaction between superordinate and subordinate should not involve physical coercion or violence. The imposition of authoritarian discipline can be onerous, however, and the behavior demanded may be distasteful or excessively dangerous. Subordinates, in their pique and frustration, may rebel and assault their superiors. In Vietnam, for example, it was reported that "fragging" (throwing a fragmentation grenade at disliked officers) was endemic in many units.[5] Similarly, some officers may define physical abuse as necessary or desirable in their interaction with their subordinates.

CRIMES AGAINST PERFORMANCE

The specificity of expected military performance is such that a variety of deviations from the extensive statutory norms concerning the obligations and duties of the individual member constitute criminal offenses. These norms are frequently violated, however, even though violations often are punishable by prison sentences, fines, loss of rank, or dishonorable discharge. Military personnel on occasion desert, go A.W.O.L., malinger, and incapacitate themselves with liquor or drugs. Other crimes against performance include misbehavior of a guard or sentinel, dereliction of duty, bringing discredit to the armed forces, conduct unbecoming an officer and a gentleman, insubordination, and—most serious of all—mutiny.

EXTRAOCCUPATIONAL MILITARY CRIME

Military personnel, while members of a separate social system, are also frequently involved with civilian society both here and abroad. In the course of

[4] Louis A. Zurcher, Jr., "The Sailor Aboard Ship: A Study of Role Behavior in a Total Institution," *Social Forces,* Vol. 43 (March 1956), pp. 389–400.
[5] Eugene Linden, "Fragging and Other Withdrawal Symptoms: The Demoralization of an Army," *Saturday Review,* Vol. LV (January 8, 1972), pp. 12–17.

their interaction with civilian society, American, allied, or enemy military personnel sometimes commit crimes involving abuse of the civilians by directing acts of theft and violence against them.

CRIMES AGAINST PROPERTY

Where property crimes against American and friendly foreign civilians committed by servicemen occur, they are perhaps most liable to include damage to property as a residual effect of brawling or disorderly conduct. Property crimes involving the violation of financial trust such as defaulting on debts and cashing checks on insufficient bank funds are, however, not rare. In wartime among foreign civilians, property crime in the form of "looting" is quite common among combat troops. Malcolm McCallum, for example, reported that in World War II, 80 percent of the men in his company were looters.[6]

CRIMES AGAINST PERSON

Because the military constitutes a separate and "alien" social system adversity, if not antagonism, is natural between servicemen and civilians, whether American, foreign friendly, or enemy, which sometimes results in altercations and violence. Sex crimes involving American military personnel and civilians also occur with some frequency and create significant problems for military authorities. In Vietnam, perhaps more than any of our wars in the past with the exception of the Indian campaigns, atrocities involving civilian victims, such as the so-called massacres at My Lai and Son My, were flagrantly committed.

CRIMES AGAINST PERFORMANCE

Members of the armed forces do on occasion create public disturbances or act inappropriately in violation of civilian law, thereby bringing discredit to the military. In foreign settings military personnel sometimes are involved in currency manipulation and black-market activities as well as violating regulations concerning fraternization and transactions with enemy civilians.

INTEROCCUPATIONAL MILITARY CRIME

The treatment of enemy military personnel and the disposition of their equipment is rigidly specified by U.S. military regulations and international treaties such as the articles of the Geneva and Hague Conventions. The exigencies of war and the predilection of individual members of the military, however,

---

[6] Malcolm McCallum, "The Study of the Delinquent in the Army," *American Journal of Sociology,* Vol. 51 (March 1946), pp. 479–82.

often engender deviant behavior directed against members of the enemy military system.

CRIMES AGAINST PROPERTY

Just as looting from friendly or enemy civilian populations is forbidden by military regulations so too is the appropriation of enemy military property by the individual soldier. In actual practice American servicemen have often been quick to dispossess the captured enemy troops of "souvenir" material. In some instances this has been confined to the retention of various personal items such as watches, medals, or hand guns from individual P.O.W.s by American servicemen. In other instances "souvenir" collecting has taken on more the aspects of large-scale systematic plundering and theft of items of significant economic worth.

CRIMES AGAINST PERSON

In the interest of "military expediency" the proprieties of regularized warfare cannot aways be observed. Killing prisoners of war, systematically mistreating or depriving them of the essentials of life, or torturing them to obtain intelligence information have sometimes been considered necessary and efficacious. (It was reported that in Vietnam occasionally a captured Viet Cong prisoner will be dropped to his death from a helicopter in order to "loosen the tongues" of other prisoners who observed his treatment. The mutilation and beating of Viet Cong prisoners by American troops was reported to be common practice.) In addition some military personnel persist in using weapons outlawed by treaty, such as expanding "dum dum" bullets or shotguns, or in attacking forbidden targets, such as hospitals.

CRIMES AGAINST PERFORMANCE

The military is most specific concerning military behavior *vis-a-vis* the enemy. Cowardice, desertion, or dereliction of duty in a combat situation represent some of the most serious of all military crimes and call for the most severe sanctions. Similarly, the Code of Conduct constrains American P.O.W.s from collaborating with the enemy, giving "confessions" of American war crimes, or acting to the detriment of other American P.O.W.s

SOCIALIZATION FOR MILITARY DEVIANCY

CANDIDATES FOR MILITARY TRAINING

The population of the military, by virtue of its unique demographic and social composition, may have a predisposition toward deviance in spite of the rigid social control imposed by the formal structure. The military is disproportionately made up of young single males who are in the process of rejecting parental control and substituting peer control. At this juncture in their lives, when they are between spheres of social control (family and career work organization, for example), they are perhaps more prone to antisocial behavior and particularly behavior that is hostile toward authority. Interestingly enough, the presumably sham *Report From Iron Mountain on the Possibility and Desirability of Peace* suggests that the military serves society, as a custodial institution for potentially antisocial youth. The *Report* states: "The younger, and more dangerous, of these hostile social groupings [youth] have been kept under control by the Selective Service System."[7]

The military also has a large number of lower- and lower-middle-class individuals who, lacking college deferments, were more likely to be drafted or to elect enlistment as one of a limited number of occupational alternatives. Such youths may be lacking in the emphasis on control and channelization more characteristic of the upper and upper-middle-class, particularly in regard to aggressive behavior.

Additionally, the armed services are not infrequently used by judicial mechanisms as correctional "dumping groups" for adjudicated delinquents and deviants or as an alternative to jail for young men facing trial.

The general picture that emerges is a population of young men who in terms of socioeconomic characteristics and sociocultural predisposition are prime candidates for subculturally determined deviant activity. At the same time, they are particularly susceptible to intensive socialization into an authoritarian social system such as the military.

In addition to a unique demographic base that is prone to certain kinds of deviance and an informal subculture that tends to promote it, the formal training strategy and specific objectives of the U.S. military may contain latent dysfunctional elements that tend to facilitate and encourage the violation of formal military regulations.

MILITARY TRAINING

The military may often operate in a noncombative context and may also frequently undertake responsibilities of a peaceful nature, but basically it stands as a work system whose unique function is to implement political decisions by force of arms or threat of force of arms. Its mission, therefore, of necessity must include the development of an effective capability to wage war. This is accomplished through concerted training efforts. As the United States Army officially states its training mission:

---

[7] Special Study Group, *Report from Iron Mountain on the Possibility and Desirability of Peace* (New York, Dell, 1967), p. 42.

To attain and maintain the Army at a state of operational effectiveness which will assure the capability of closing with and destruction of the enemy through prompt and sustained combat operations on land, along or jointly with the Navy, Air Force, or both, and to conduct effective counterinsurgency operations including the support of friendly or allied counterinsurgency operations.[8]

To effect this training mission and "its supporting tasks," the U.S. Army further articulates five basic objectives.[9] These objectives include military discipline, health, strength, and endurance, technical proficiency, teamwork and tactical proficiency. These particular objectives, while patently functional to the attainment of the stated training mission and subsequently to military performance and especially combat performance, would also seem to be dysfunctional in the sense of contribution to the commission of "khaki-collar" crime. As indicated in Table 12.1, their contribution to "khaki-

Table 12.1   *Structural Subversion of Military Training*

United States Army Basic Training Objectives	Residual Dysfunctional Training Elements Facilitative to Military Deviancy
Military Discipline	Authoritarian indoctrination, reflexive discipline and unhesitating obedience, while desirable for military purposes, may also lead to a dilution of personal responsibility and misinterpretation of goals.
Health, Strength, and Endurance	The attainment of fitness and confidence may result in "toughness." This may in turn breed insensitivity and brutality. Regard with health often leads to overconcern with comfort and luxury, even if illicitly obtained.
Technical Proficiency	Overemphasis on mechanical expertise and efficiency, particularly with weaponry and in combat skills, leads to "overkill," and adroitness in the violation of regulations.
Teamwork	Overreliance on informal structure, both for accomplishing formal expectations as well as for personal support, leads to excessive influence of informal groups in determining norms and effecting sanctions.
Tactical Proficiency	The attainment of military goals and military activities in general is conceptualized as a "game." The violation of formal norms also becomes a "game."

[8] Headquarters, Department of the Army, *Military Training Management: Department of the Army Field Manual FM 21–5* (Washington, D.C., U.S. Government Printing Office, 1967), p. 2.

[9] Charles J. Levy, "ARVN as Faggots: Inverted Warfare in Vietnam," *Transaction*, Vol. 8 (October 1971), p. 18.

collar" crime may well grow out of a subverted interpretation and relevancy and the process of operationalizing them in an exigent nontraining situation.

Military discipline. The military is an authoritarian social system that undertakes in its training a near total readjustment of values and frame of reference from civilian to military perspective. Military indoctrination and socialization revolve around absolute discipline and mental and physical control of the individual. The extent of physical control is such that marine recruits, for example, are "not permitted a bowel movement for the first week of boot camp."[10] The product of successful training will, according to military design, "recognize and respect authority and give unhesitating obedience to that authority." Such reflexive-like discipline tends to permit the individual to transfer to his superior the responsibility and, thus, the guilt for any action ordered even if in violation of social, if not military, norm. A disciplined social system is essentially an unreasoning social system. Crimes such as theft of equipment from other units or even the murder of prisoners may be committed by an individual when ordered or even if he *thinks such action is desired by his superior*. Lt. Calley, for example, is alleged to have said to a subordinate, "You *know* [italics ours] what I want you to do with them [My Lai civilians]. . . ."[11]

Health, strength, and endurance. Requisite to the obvious military need for boldness and endurance on the part of individual servicemen is fitness, strength, and confidence (including determination and aggressiveness), and to this end a significant proportion of military training is devoted to developing stamina and confidence. Many of the physical fitness "obstacle" courses are labeled "confidence" courses. The bayonet course, also called a "confidence" course, involves much yelling and grimacing which is supposed to develop determination and aggressiveness.

Fitness and confidence, however, often militarily defined as "toughness," may breed insensitivity and antisocial aggressiveness. "Elite" combat troops, such as paratroops, rangers, and marines, famed for their "toughness" are also notorious for their fighting and brawling with civilians and other troops, both American and friendly foreign, as well as their savage combat ability. "Tough" units take what they want from civilians and other units, and frequently "do not take prisoners."

Ancillary to the emphasis on confidence and aggressiveness is the training concern with health, and thus collaterally, hygiene, food, shelter, medical treatment, and recreation. A significant proportion of training is devoted to these topics. Such concern may tend to underscore the American

10 Ibid.

11 Seymour M. Hersch, "My Lai 4: A Report on the Massacre and Its Aftermath," *Harper's,* Vol. 240 (May 1970), p. 65.

preoccupation with creature comforts and physical condition. American troops are conditioned to anticipate a high level of logistical luxury. Unlike Oriental armies, which may fight poorly clothed and meagerly fed and with little else but a weapon, the American armed forces anticipate and demand being superbly equipped regardless of where they go or fight. When the formal bureaucratic channels will not provide the appropriate items of equipment and supplies for individual or unit comfort and survival, informal, clandestine, unauthorized, or illegal means of obtaining these materials will be employed including elaborate systems of "scrounging" and barter and various means of theft, misappropriation, and black marketeering. Similarly, American troops, in their preoccupation with material affluence, may also illegally confiscate, acquire, or misappropriate foreign friendly or enemy property, or captured enemy equipment.

Technical proficiency. The military man, no different from his civilian counterpart, derives intrinsic satisfaction and personal pride from expertise in his occupational skill. The bombardier may take justifiable pride in the accuracy of his bomb drop, and quartermaster officer may derive occupational satisfaction from the knowledge that his equipment accounting records are above reproach. The military places considerable emphasis on the acquisition and maintenance of expertise in occupational skill. In the Navy appropriate occupational skills may justify a *rating*. It is significant to note that the annual evaluation reports on U.S. Army officers are known as *efficiency* reports, and commendations of various kinds are frequently awarded for jobs performed well. Purely military skills are particularly emphasized and excellence in skill is recognized. The M.O.S. (Military Occupational Specialty) is *awarded* after demonstration of proficiency in the given specialty. Proficiency in weaponry is recognized by awarding appropriate Marksman, Sharpshooter, or Expert badges after demonstration of a specific level of competence and firing ability with particular firearms.

The ultimate aim of military skills, however, is effectiveness in combat, and effectiveness in combat implies destructiveness. Historically, the military man has taken pride in his destructive ability. John Hersey, for example, in his novel *The War Lover*, has his protagonist, Buzz, the B-17 pilot in World War II, proudly proclaim: "I like to fly," he said. "I like the work we're doing. . . . " "Listen," he said, with flashing eyes, "Bowman (his co-pilot) and I belong to the most destructive group of men in the history of the world. That's our work."[12]

Such an orientation is, of course, the ultimate aim of military training, for the ultimate combat soldier is the most efficient killer. In his detailed analysis of violence as a military process, Joseph A. Blake has pointed out that

[12] John Hersey, *The War Lover* (New York, Knopf, 1947), p. 144.

military socialization involves equipping the soldier to be such an efficient combat killer. As he put it:

> The opening phase of the socialization process begins shortly after recruitment and entails the attempted destruction of previously held roles and the preliminary fitting of the actor to the role of organizational killer. This latter entails two analytically distinct processes; first, instilling the military rationale into the actor and second, giving him the technical training required to make him a proficient killer.[13]

Proficiency in destruction acquired in training is frequently reinforced in a combat situation. It was reported, for example, that in Vietnam "one brigade commander ran a contest to celebrate the unit's 10,000th enemy kill."[14] Such a practice was common in many units. With competitive zeal, the troops were not always particular about identification of the enemy. In Vietnam there was a saying, "anything that's dead and isn't white is a VC."[15] Technical proficiency, even in killing apparently provides some measure of intrinsic satisfaction. In referring to the incident at My Lai, Hersh reports that, "Some GIs were shouting and yelling during the massacre, Carter [a participant] recalled: 'The boys enjoyed it. When someone laughs and jokes about what they're doing they have to be enjoying it.' "[16] He also relates the story of an American battallion commander who listed his "kills" of Vietnamese by stenciling rows of conical hats on the fuselage of his helicopter, which he named the "Gookmobile."[17]

Interestingly enough, as war has progressed technologically, the actual contact between fighting man and enemy has become more mechanical and depersonalized, and the enemy has become essentially dehumanized. Blake points out that those troops who are most technologically removed from the enemy and who thus are more prone to think of the enemy in dehumanized terms are the ones who require the least socialization as killers.[18] The bombardier never sees his victims, and his targets have no human characteristics; therefore he need not acquire the "killer" spirit to the same degree as, say, the marine who may have to meet the enemy bayonet to bayonet. Philip Slater, in his *The Pursuit of Loneliness,* speaks of "extermination at a distance" and comments, "Flying in a plane far above an impersonally

---

[13] Joseph A. Blake, "The Organization as Instrument of Violence: The Military Case," *Sociological Quarterly,* Vol. 11 (Summer 1970), p. 338.

[14] Hersh, op. cit., p. 55.

[15] Ibid., p. 56.

[16] Ibid., p. 67.

[17] Ibid., p. 55.

[18] Blake, op. cit., p. 339.

defined target and pressing some buttons to turn fifty square miles into a sea of flame is less traumatic to the average middle-class American boy than inflicting a superficial bayonet wound on a single soldier."[19]

In Vietnam members of the Armed Forces could sometimes see the enemy, but often only from the vantage point of a "Huey" gunship (a helicopter equipped with machine guns, rocket launchers, and sophisticated aiming devices) where people are reduced to ant proportions. The pilots who strafe enemy troops and sometimes civilians believed to be "guerillas," speak of "rabbit shoots," "barbecuing" peasants, and "hosing" a suspect with machine gun fire until he "blows up like a toy balloon."[20] Being a good shot in a "Huey" is perhaps not unlike being expert at skeet shooting. The line between effective combat proficiency and war atrocities is a thin one.

So, too, is the line between shrewd quartermaster administration and the misappropriation of government equipment. Embezzlers in civilian life are frequently highly skilled accountants who become "overly proficient" at their trade. Their skill affords them an opportunity structure not often available to the less skilled plus an attitude of impunity. Some confidence men are so good at their criminal specialty that they literally cannot resist the chance to "con" someone, even if only for a few dollars. The expert is tempted to exceed the limits imposed on him for the sake of perfection or continual demonstration of his expertise. The master craftsman, even a military craftsman looks for new work worlds to conquer; he seeks to experiment even at the risk of violating the rules. Some of the most able surgeons in America, for example, have been accused of undertaking operations that had no hope of success simply because they were "challenging." They were, in effect, using patients unethically as surgical guinea pigs to demonstrate their technical expertise. The expert is often overzealous to a fault. He may violate the norms of propriety in his enthusiasm for efficiency. As Hersey reflected "Genius in flying, as in the performance of music, lies not in precision, not in being exactly on pitch and in time, but rather in the ability to perform with absolute accuracy and then to *break the rules by inspiration for the sake of a higher perfection*" [italics ours].[21]

The individuals who are most adept at breaking the rules are the "old timers" and the ones most steeped in military know-how. Familiarity with technical routine, in a sense, breeds boredom with, if not contempt of, the normative structure.

Teamwork. Warfare historically has been essentially a collective enterprise. Military activities, even at the most elementary level, involve concerted

---

[19] Philip Slater, *The Pursuit of Loneliness: American Culture at the Breaking Point* (Boston, Beacon, 1970), p. 4.

[20] Ibid., pp. 38–39.

[21] Hersey, op. cit., p. 55.

effort and coordinated behavior. From the Macedonian Phalanx to the "crew-served" weapons of recent wars to today's sophisticated electronic weapons systems, the military apparatus is a man and machine *system*. It is, therefore, not surprising that the military emphasizes teamwork in its training and operations.

The development of strong teamwork linkages in the formal organization also tends to engender equally strong symbiotic relationships at an informal level. The reliance on the informal structure is intensified by the fact that the military, as a bureaucratic enterprise, is sometimes ponderous and rigid. Not infrequently, as Zurcher suggests, the informal organization employs "patterned evasions"—regularized ways of getting around the demands of the formal organization, usually with the result of accomplishing the formal expectations in a quicker and more efficient way. The formal organization tolerates and overlooks, if not accepts, these patterned evasions in the interest of efficiency and end results. Zurcher has pointed out, for example, that on board ship there are numerous informal behaviors or "secondary adjustments" employed by members of the crew to subvert the regulations and official procedures and obtain favored treatment or living conditions for themselves.[22] Over time the illicit procedures employed at an informal level became ritualized as part of the informal culture. Dornbusch, for instance, has pointed out that in the U.S. Coast Guard Academy, a first classman might dispatch a "swab" on an illicit errand. If caught, the swab would receive demerits. The first classman, to compensate the "swab" however, would informally tell his classmate to withhold the same number of demerits from the "swab" for other offenses.[23] The informal culture of the military becomes in many instances a deviant culture with an elaborate value system that defines ways of violating formal military and civilian norms as well as the rationalization and support for such violations.

The informal structure serves as a particularly potent reference group for another reason. Initial training in the military attempts and often succeeds in separating the neophyte from his former identity and ties. Military discipline is demanding and often oppressive, and military life not infrequently stressful. Enduring and coping with military discipline and life is made easier by the presence of a strong supportive informal structure.

Tactical proficiency. War, unlike most other forms of human hostile behavior and certainly unlike other varieties of work (if war is, in fact, work), has been most often analogously compared to a game. As late as the Crimean War (and to a limited extent during the American Civil War),

[22] Zurcher, op. cit., p. 393.
[23] Sanford M. Dornbusch, "The Military Academy as an Assimilating Institution," *Social Forces,* Vol. 33 (May 1955), p. 317.

some civilians went to witness specific battles and even carried picnic lunches and refreshments. War was a sort of spectator sport or game. Military maneuvers are often referred to as war games, and practically all armies periodically have their senior level officers engage in map exercises or map games. Much formal military training is structured in a game format, and similarly, informal training often takes on the characteristics of a game. Not infrequently, some of this informal training actually involves the violation of various military regulations. Thus, "moonlight requisitioning" may on occasion be used as a means of instilling aggressiveness and resourcefulness in recruits. Initiative, resourcefulness, aggressiveness, and decisiveness—all characteristics developed by stealing equipment from other units—are also traits that contribute to tactical proficiency and thus the effective soldier. Coincidentally, these characteristics, helpful to the soldier in his military tactics and patently contributory to combat effectiveness, appear to make for an equally effective criminal. A thief stealing an automobile may employ tactics similar to an infantryman on combat patrol. Werner J. Einstadter, in his study of armed robbery, concluded, "Military experience of a certain variety, for example, lends itself readily to robbery."[24]

Armed with the game orientation acquired from the emphasis on tactical proficiency in military training, some individuals make a game of many of their military activities including looting enemy property, wheeling and dealing on the black market, escaping from the military police after a raid on a brothel, outwitting a superior officer or skillfully misappropriating military property for personal use. In all instances it is essentially a game where the object is to violate the rules and not get caught. It is interesting that this has been a reoccurring theme on several of our popular television shows such as McHale's Navy and the Sergeant Bilko Show. In such programs the sly servicemen constantly outmaneuver their superiors in a "game" of wits. For many individuals, military life itself becomes a game one plays using various kinds and degrees of subterfuge. The good tactician can maneuver just as well in breaking the rules as in combat.

[24] Werner J. Einstadter, "The Social Organization of Armed Robbery," *Social Problems,* Vol. 17 (Summer 1969), p. 77.

IV

MARGINALLY ILLEGAL OCCUPATIONS AND WORK SYSTEMS

The Deviant Fringe

Within the vast continuum of work specialties reside occupational pursuits of varying degrees of legality and conformity to the norms of propriety and respectability. At one end of the scale are many occupations of exemplary piousness, circumspect comportment, and unimpeachable respectability, which represent the very quintessence of honesty and legality with the attendant community approval. At the other end of the continuum lie those occupational specialties that stand clearly outside the boundaries of societal legality and community acceptance. Such occupations, deemed deviant by the standards of respectability and normative tolerance, are considered to be largely without redeeming social worth and therefore reprehensible and despicable. The hired assassin, the narcotic "pusher," the kidnapper, and thief all exist outside the pale of normality, approval, or even sufferance, and they pursue occupational goals alien to the collective purpose.

Somewhere in between on this occupational continuum, however, lie a significant number of work specialties and systems that may be classified as marginally illegal—a kind of occupational "twilight zone" or deviant fringe. While such work pursuits may not constitute an ongoing and flagrant violation of social norm and legal statute, they may at times transgress the boundaries of legality and regulatory correctness. In effect, they violate the spirit, if not the letter, of the law. At times, however, depending on condition and circumstances, they may violate not only the letter of the law but the whole sentence. Such illegality, however, is usually ephemeral and erratic. The practitioners of such trades may wear a thin veneer of orthodoxy and respectability and may on occasion operate with all the external trappings of honesty and legality. Their basic aim is, however, profit without regard for the quality or worth of goods or services rendered. Their orientation is basically exploitative. Frequently they operate openly and attempt to merchandise their goods and services as articles of genuine value and function. Unfortunately, the goods and services rendered are often unnecessary, ununutilitarian, misrepresented, undependable, or even dysfunctional to the clientele.

Fraud and deception are relative, not absolute, processes, and the occupation does not exist that does not employ some degree of misrepresentation and deceit, regardless of how minor, in attempting to manipulate the client. The dentist may, for example, minimize the pain and discomfort, not to mention the cost, of expensive dental "restoration" when discussing the need for this work with his patient. Some writers have also pointed out that the funeral director may on occasion utilize the psychologically disabled condition of the bereaved family to his advantage in "merchandising" funeral services and appurtenances beyond the financial means of the family. As Leroy Bowman has described it:

> Grief on the part of the family is recognized by undertakers as a disabling factor, but the number of cases in which it leads them to moderation in recommendations for elaborate funerals seems to be very small. For the majority of them the vulnerability of the family due to grief is an advantage in the bargaining situation not to be neglected. Further, through their process of rationalization, the very grief of the family comes to be a reason for more expensive and elaborate funerals, on the assumption that the larger the expenditure the greater the solace for the grieving.[1]

Real estate salesmen may neglect to mention that the back of the lot they are attempting to sell stands a foot deep in water after a heavy rain because of inadequate drainage. The stereotype of "Honest John," the used car dealer, who "loses on every sale, but makes it up on volume" is brutal in its indictment of the high pressure sales tactics employed in selling used automobiles. In a similar vein, appliance salesmen admit to a wide array of questionable sales techniques including such hoary standbys as "PM" or "spiff" (push or extra bonus money), "burning" and "switching" (changing the customer's brand preference to a product more profitable to the dealer), and disguising high interest rates by quoting only the amount of monthly payment.[2]

Even in the instances of these less-than-honest occupational practices, however, the practitioners in question are still pursuing a respectable or at least acceptable occupational specialty and are producing or rendering a basically sound good or service of significant worth.

The marginally illegal occupational practitioners (like some totally illegal pursuits), however, operate to serve certain existing, even if clandestine, social needs but as such do not necessarily enjoy the total and enthusiastic approbation of the community. In the process of rendering the services requirement, practitioners may operate within a wider latitude of deviant variation than conventionally afforded and tolerated by the normative sys-

---

[1] Leroy Bowman, *The American Funeral* (New York, Paperback Library, 1964), p. 40.
[2] For an elaborate discussion of such sales tactics, see "Confessions of an Appliance Salesman," *Consumer Reports,* Vol. 23 (October 1958), pp. 546–47.

tem. Some individual requirements and wants may themselves, because of their baseness or idiosyncratic bent, lie beyond the pale of normality, convention, or even legality. Such needs are met in the marketplace, for where there is demand there will be supply. The occupational deviant fringe exists to serve this demand and does so usually within a fragile and ephemeral context of legality. Such a work specialty requires considerable dexterity in walking the razor-thin edge of conformity and community tolerance.

Since violation of community moral standards and legalistic requirements do occur, marginally illegal occupational practitioners are frequently physically mobile, for mobility permits utilizing the time lag of community and legal tolerance as a device of evasion. The practitioner may simply be able to deviate from normative expectations for that length of time before the discovery of norm violation and the subsequent application of social or legal sanctions. Even when faced with exposure and punishment, physical mobility may offer a mechanism for escape from social control. When customers begin to complain about the quality of Dr. Wonder's Marvelous Medicine for Maladies, Dr. Wonder may elect to "pack his tent and silently steal away." Almost all of the occupational specialties treated in this Part demonstrate a considerable capability for rapid physical mobility and minimal ties to the community. Some of the work systems described have physical mobility as a constituent characteristic—the carnival and the traveling evangelist show, for example. Other occupations discussed, such as the gypsy fortune-teller, may operate out of a trailer or even a suitcase. Even occupational specialties, such as strippers and "hustlers" of various kinds, are by their very nature transient, often following the season and the "action," if not avoiding the pressure of law enforcement.

In some instances occupational practitioners may subvert the rendering of some legitimate and respected service. Evangelism, as a case in point, has proved to be a prosperous "industry" in our nation and has, accordingly, attracted its share of exploitative con men and charlatans, along with the sincerely motivated. Taking advantage of the fears and anxieties of the less culturally sophisticated, such "self-ordained" religious hucksters have frequently offered to "heal" the ailing and the infirm. William C. Martin, in his description of the "God-Hucksters of Radio," has pointed out:

> The "healers and blessers," who dominate the radio evangelism scene, address themselves to the whole range of human problems: physical, emotional, social, financial, and spiritual. Like their colleagues in the nonmiraculous healing arts, some evangelists develop areas of special competence, such as the cure of cancer or paralysis. Brother Al is something of a foot specialist—"God can take corns, bunions, and tired feet, and massage them with his holy love and make them well." A. A. Allen tells of disciples who have received silver fillings in their teeth during his

meetings and asks, sensibly enough, "Why not let God be your dentist?" But most are general practitioners.[3]

Spreading the word with the help of paraphernalia such as holy oil or water, amulets and pins, "prosperity billfolds," and prayer cloths, they have given spiritual assurances to the troubled and the tormented and afforded emotional release for the frustrated—as long as they continue to hear the clink and rustle of money being dropped into the everpassing collection plate or to receive the fan letters containing "love" donations. The fast-buck evangelist subverts faith and attempts to separate the faithful from their money, with their own brand of commercialized religion, frequently however, only staying two jumps ahead of the district attorney and the grand jury.

Our society, with its elaborate culture and attendant complex division of labor, has produced an enormously rich array of goods and services available to be consumed by the members of society. Our society has afforded to its members an unusually high level of material resources with which to indulge their heterogeneous and elaborate tastes and wants. Not surprisingly, whole categories of predatory and exploitative occupations have arisen that supply exotic demands ranging from the erotic or prurient to the idiosyncratic and fantasiful. Among the frustrated, the anxious, and the greedy, the deviant occupational fringe practices business as usual.

"PROFESSIONAL" OVERSKILL AND DECEPTIVE COMPETITION

America is a competitive society, perhaps pathologically so. This emphasis on competition derives from several sources. Our form of capitalism, for example, provides the mechanism for economic competition, and the Protestant ethic provides the impetus. Ours is a society that values success (and thus social mobility) and also places considerable importance on material goods and comforts and emphasizes aggressive (and thus competitive) behavior. This penchant manifests itself in many ways including our very language, which concentrates on things and quantities and purposive and energetic action. Houses are described in terms of number of floors and rooms, and cars in terms of number of cylinders and doors. Politicians "run" for office; we "dig into" our food and "push ahead" in our studies.

To compete aggressively is not enough; there must be a pay-off—for the spectator as well as the participant. Some of our professional athletes are among the highest paid individuals in society. In addition, their prestige is so

[3] William C. Martin, "The God-Hucksters of Radio: Keep Those Cards and Letters Coming In," *The Atlantic,* Vol. 255, No. 6 (June 1970), p. 52.

great athletes can amass small fortunes simply by providing endorsements for products. Many competitive sports and activities involve institutionalized types of gambling such as the pari-mutuel betting arrangements at most race-horse and dog tracks and Jai-lai courts, and spectators may profit from the outcome of the competition. Even where not legalized, means of gambling on competitive events such as the so-called "grid-pick" football gambling cards, the office pool on the world series baseball game, and the sizable betting associated with cockfights are still often institutionalized.

Americans love to gamble; they love to compete, even if with the "system" or the machine. Bingo in carnivals and at church bazaars, for example, is a national pastime. Individuals will play slot machines until their arm wearies, and some are addicted to the pinball machine in their local cafe or bar, even though the economic gain is only symbolic in the form of free games. The carnival represents a whole work system built around several basic themes. One of these is the opportunity to compete in a variety of games of chance and "skill." If you succeed, you "win," even if only a plastic doll worth five cents (such prizes are called "slum" in the carnival industry).

Much of the attraction of gambling unquestionably lies in the remote but possible opportunity of getting rich quick or getting something for nothing (relatively speaking). As a result, millions of Americans gamble on a regular basis (some compulsively). This gambling ranges from modest bets of 50 cents on "numbers" to thousands of dollars bet on racehorses. Gambling has other attractions, however, as evidenced by the fact that many extremely wealthy individuals are inveterate gamblers also. The sheer fact of "winning" may likely be the most satisfying element of gambling.

Many persons cannot compete aggressively at a physical or even verbal level. Instead they may have to rely on vicarious competition by supporting "their" team or by the use of surrogate competitors as in the case of cock-fighting where the roosters fight, and die or win for the glory of the owner.[4]

Many Americans who are not adequately equipped for the more physically demanding sports may take up other games, such as pool, golf, or bowling, or leisure pursuits like card playing. Such persons may gamble in connection with these games and activities and enjoy some degree of economic success as a result of proficiency. These individuals are likely prey, however, for professional "hustlers."

A hustler is a person who develops inordinate skill in a given activity and utilizes that skill (plus other insights and devices) to win money from less skilled but overconfident opponents. The hustler takes advantage of his

---

[4] For a detailed discussion of this kind of surrogate competition, see Clifton D. Bryant, "Feathers, Spurs and Blood: Cockfighting as a Deviant Leisure Activity." Paper read at the Southern Sociological Society Meeting held in Miami, Florida (May 7, 1971).

gambling competitors in a largely one-sided contest. As Louis Mahigel and Gregory Stone describe him:

> To say of a gambler that he is a hustler says little about how he plays cards except that he probably plays very well. It certainly doesn't mean that he cheats, either all of the time or only when he can. Cheaters are hustlers who use illegitimate techniques. But not all hustlers are cheaters, even though they are thoroughly familiar with most, if not all, the cheaters' techniques.
>
> There is another useful connotation of the word hustler. It points to a conscious manipulation of people and things in the field of play—football, sex, survival, advertising, or gambling—to the end of winning.[5]

The hustler uses the overconfidence of his opponent to his own advantage. He permits the opponent to try and "hustle" him. Armed with his own skill, considerable experience, knowledge of the "tricks of the trade," and other advantages, he maneuvers the "mark" or "sucker" into a gambling contest and then proceeds to win the game and the bet.

Because of our national preoccupation with competition there are many individuals to be hustled and plenteous opportunities to do so. Accordingly, hustling has become an occupational specialty existing to prey on the less skilled and brash, but it is deviant to the mainstream of American work life. A hustler is not a "sportsman." He uses guile and deception and takes unfair advantage of his opponents. The fact of his overskill alone makes the contest both unfair and unwelcome. In our sports we go to such great lengths to even the competition, by handicapping the abler participants, that any attempt to bias the outcome, especially with underhanded and nefarious methods, strikes a note of discord in the public's sense of fair play and propriety. Furthermore, the hustler is a gambler and thus a law violator in many instances. The fact that he unfairly deprives his opponents of their money makes him a depraved person in the public's mind. Finally, he leads an unconventionalized work routine and lifestyle, often consorting with an unsavory element of society, the "sporting" population. In discussing the pool hustler, Ned Polsky, for example points out:

> The hustler's offense in the eyes of many is not that he breaks misdemeanor laws against gambling (perhaps most Americans have done so at one time or another), but that he does so daily. Also—and again as a necessary and regular part of his daily work—he violates American norms concerning (a) what is morally correct behavior toward one's fellow man and (b) what is a proper and fitting occupation. For one or another of these related reasons the hustler is stigmatized by respectable

---

[5] E. Louis Mahigel and Gregory P. Stone, "How Card Hustlers Make the Game," *Transaction*, Vol. 8, No. 3, Whole No. 64 (January 1971), pp. 40–45.

outsiders. The most knowledgeable of such outsiders see the hustler not merely as a gambler but as one who violates an ethic of fair dealing; they regard him as a criminal or quasi-criminal not because he gambles but because he systematically "victimizes" people. Somewhat less knowledgeable outsiders put down the hustler simply because gambling is his trade. Still less knowledgeable outsiders (perhaps the majority) regard hustlers as persons who, whatever they may actually do, certainly do not hold down visibly respectable jobs; therefore this group also stigmatizes hustlers—"poolroom bums" is the classic phrase—and believes that society would be better off without them. Hustling, to the degree that it is known to the larger society at all, is classed with that large group of social problems composed of morally deviant occupations.[6]

Charles Gillespie takes up a very unique form of hustling in Chapter 13. He describes the activities of the shuffleboard hustler. In this instance the shuffleboard refers to the small shuffleboard machines found in taverns, cafes, and bars. Patrons of such establishments play table shuffleboard to pass the time and to have a basis for gambling. Some develop real expertise at the game and become local "champions." When Glenn Young, the hustler, appears, however, the local "champion" looks like an amateur in comparison after the bet is made. Glenn Young, master shuffleboard hustler, is "overskilled" to the point that he is near perfect at the game and apparently retains much of his expertise even when playing shuffleboard blindfolded or left-handed. He invariably leaves his opponents dazed, poorer, sadder, but wiser.

CONTRIVED CLAIRVOYANCE AND "FUTURE" CHICANERY

America is a nation sustained by the accomplishments linked to science and technological progress. Our great universities with their splendorous edifices and elaborate facilities are little more than temples of science. Our children's toys are scientific toys, and many of our national heroes are heroes of science or technology. We would appear to be a people rooted in rational thought and dedicated to logic and empirical truth. Curiously, however, Americans also appear to have an inordinate bent in terms of their predilection for superstitions, the mystical, the irrational, and the occult. The United States abounds with bizarre clubs, clans, cults, and esoteric religious movements that espouse causes that operate outside the pale of normality, if not rationality.[7] They range from the more benign food fadists groups to the seemingly patho-

[6] Ned Polsky, *Hustlers, Beats, and Others* (Garden City, N.Y., Doubleday and Company, Anchor Books Edition, 1969), p. 32.

[7] For a detailed inventory of esoteric religious movements, see Arthur Ormont, *Love Cults and Faith Healers* (New York, Ballantine Books, 1961).

logical activities of covens of "witches" who actively attempt to conjure up the devil. Some of the members of such exotic followings can be genuinely labeled as the "lunatic fringe." In other instances, seemingly rational persons of impeccable credentials are at the very core of the activities.

Generally speaking, such followings can be broadly divided into four categories based on the principal concern or focus of the cult: a concern with extraordinary physical or mental states or conditions, a concern with the supernatural, a concern with the extraterrestrial, and a concern with the future.[8]

The first category includes food fadism, especially "health foods" or "organic" diets, yoga or other body developing and "mind expanding" exercises and meditations, as well as the whole continuum of psychochemical use that alters perception and awareness, especially when an element of mysticism or the sacred is involved.[9] Interest in the survival of bodily death[10] and unorthodox methods of healing[11] may also be included in this category.

The second category includes religion and religious-type activities regardless of the nature. Our culture has spawned a whole host of unconventional and unusual religious preoccupations ranging from store-front fundamentalism to Bahai. Perhaps none have been more bizarre than the recent interest in witchcraft and devil worship that has surfaced. A belief in the occult, of course, is by no means new in this country, but the contemporary fad is impressive in both its extent and intensity. The so-called "church of Satan" which is headed by Anton Szandor La Vey, "America's black pope," claims 10,000 members.[12] There are reported to be some 300 covens of witches and warlocks operating in the United States.[13] Voodoo has been prominent among rural blacks in the South for years and is appearing with

[8] Marcello Truzzi, "The Occult Revival as Popular Culture: Some Random Observations on the Old and the Nouveau Witch." Paper presented at the Annual Meeting of the Ohio Valley Sociological Society in Akron, Ohio, May 1, 1970. Truzzi discusses this phenomenon but articulates a somewhat different set of categories.

[9] For an interesting treatment, see William Keoman, "Banality of the New Evil," *Esquire,* Vol. LXXIII, No. 3, Whole No. 436 (March 1970), pp. 115–16 and 182–84.

[10] In recent years a sizable number of individuals have become personally interested in the phenomena of cryonics, the practice of freezing persons after death with the intent of thawing them out at some distant time in the future and, based on the assumption of marvelous scientific breakthroughs, resurrecting them from the dead. The persons with this interest have conventions, publish a journal devoted to the subject, and in some instances actually help freeze deceased enthusiasts.

[11] Among such healing methods might be included acupuncture, faith healing, and naturopathy.

[12] See Brian Vachon, "Witches are Rising," *Look,* Vol. 35, No. 17 (August 24, 1971), pp. 40–44.

[13] See Truzzi, op. cit., p. 38.

increasing frequency around the country.[14] There are occult study groups, and even groups of white-collar suburban couples are solemnly sitting around pentagrams in the nude on full-mooned nights attempting to summon up demons and cast spells. Needless to say, such activities have generated an elaborate set of deviant (although not necessarily illegal) occupational specialists, including witch coven high priests and priestesses, writers and publishers of occult literature, and functionaries and fund raisers in the various demoniac religious systems.[15]

Another category of irrational preoccupation is the national concern with extraterrestrial life. Americans have been intensely interested in outer space for decades. They have followed the space program with its lunar achievements with great pride and enthusiasm. Science fiction has traditionally been a favorite form of literature and radio and TV entertainment. The Orson Welles so-called "Invasion from Mars" program in 1938 created such an impact because the American people could and did believe that life on another planet was both possible and probable. The excitement and concern with which the nation responded during the height of the flying saucer or unidentified flying object craze is therefore not surprising. Millions of Americans were convinced that they had seen space ships of assorted sizes and shapes zooming about and even landing on occasion. The most popular shape was, of course, the saucer, and sightings of such space ships were extremely common. A significant number of persons began writing and publishing their accounts of the space ship sightings, and at least one woman claimed to have been kidnapped by the occupants of such a flying saucer. She was spirited away to the planet Venus and became emotionally involved with one of its citizens before being returned to earth. Later she published the torrid account of her amorous activities under the title of *My Vesuvian Lover*. At the height of the craze there were even conventions of flying-saucer enthusiasts. One such gathering held at Highfields, New Jersey, attracted a large crowd of the faithful. Many exchanged stories about their own experiences and listened to the main speakers such as the woman with the Vesuvian lover. One delegate came armed with an "instrument" designed to measure the wingspread of invisible delegates. Those more monetarily inclined set up booths to sell flying saucer and outer space books, toys, and souvenirs. A few of the more enterprising were selling LP albums of Martian and Vesuvian "music." During

[14] See Vachon, op. cit., pp. 41–42. Some years ago we heard of a black voodoo practitioner in a Southern rural town who charged a fee to put a spell or hex on someone. It turned out that he had "an arrangement" with another voodoo practitioner a short distance away who removed curses and spells for a price from those persons who had been hexed by the first practitioner.

[15] Vachon, op. cit.

this same period various associations and "bureaus" were formed for the purpose of acting as clearinghouses for information on space ships and extraterrestrial life. Such organizations provided vocational opportunities for a number of individuals who also went on speaking tours as outer space "experts" and often issued newsletters and bulletins to the true believers for a price.

The final category of superstitional preoccupation is concerned with the future and the manipulation of future events. With their scientific and technological prowess, Americans have actually been able to influence the future and their destiny. This has apparently not been sufficient or satisfactory, and some Americans desperately seek further insight into the future. Where there is demand, there will be supply. Some persons, because of supposed clairvoyance or special ability, have become unusually accurate in their future predictions. A few such as Edgar Cayce, Criswell, and Jean Dixon have become national celebrities, and some appear on the late-night TV talk shows with predictable regularity. These professional soothsayers also often publish prediction books that enjoy impressive sales.

Astrology is almost a national disease and has generated a number of occupations. Leading newspapers and periodicals carry regular columns dealing with horoscopes and an incalculable number of persons profit from the astrology fad by working for industries, such as publishing, that supply the astrology market. Perhaps as many as 40,000,000 Americans are involved in astrology.[16] Approximately 10,000 full-time and 175,000 part-time astrologers practice in this country. Some astrologers have a clientele of national and international fame and command fees that are astronomical, if not astrological. In a sense even children are socialized to believe in future telling, so to speak, in that a favorite toy for youngsters (and adults) is the ouija board, which in its "comeback" in 1967 outsold Monopoly with sales of over two million boards.[17]

The spiritualist or medium assists persons in communicating with a deceased relative or friend, but a frequent intent of such communication is, however, to gain insight and direction concerning the future. For sheer yeoman duty in providing visions of the future, however, the fortuneteller is the most venerable and traditional. Fortunetelling dates back into antiquity and the basic form of this service has not drastically changed. The fortuneteller with her "gifted" clairvoyance shares her vision of the future with the individual concerned—for a price. The fortuneteller may employ cards, tea leaves, crystal balls, or other devices, but they are basically theatrical props rather than aids, for the fortuneteller has the "insight" or "future" sight.

[16] Truzzi, op. cit., p. 7.
[17] Ibid.

Fortunetelling is illegal in some areas and only barely tolerated by the law in others. Through a variety of guises, such as "counseling" and "advice giving," the fortuneteller is able to practice her trade, albeit often at the high cost of "licenses" or payoffs to local politicians or law enforcement officials. Some fortunetelling is carried on as a kind of entertaining, such as in night club acts, but the great bulk of it takes place to provide reassurance and emotional support for the anxious and the uncertain. Some seek out a fortuneteller for amusement, but many others go in search of help, advice, knowledge, and solace, not to mention a peek into the future, particularly concerning romance, health, or economic problems. Some patrons may seek a "blessing" for their infirmity or for an undertaking. In any event, the fortuneteller provides comforts, assuages concern, and allays curiosity for those who can afford it.

In a substantial number of instances, fortunetellers are gypsy women, and fortunetelling is for them a traditional occupation and if proficient and economically successful, the source of much subcultural social approval. The fortunetelling concession or "mitt camp" is an often encountered element in the traveling carnival.[18] Not infrequently, such concessions are staffed by gypsies who perform the *dukkerin* (fortunetelling) within a framework of palmistry, and thus the term *mitt camp*. However, increasing numbers of *gorgio* (nongypsies) fortunetellers are found today. Fortunetelling may run the gamut from the "rag heads" operating in the slum areas to the society "white readers" who cater to a more affluent clientele.

During depressions many people feel insecure about their future as they do when moving into an urban area where they may not be able to cope with their new environments successfully. In such instances the services of a fortuneteller may be particularly sought. The rising educational level of the population and the trend toward more secular and cosmopolitan philosophies of life in the future may all portend ill fortune for fortunetelling. But for the time being, however, if there are those who seek glimpses of the future, there will be readers who will provide it, if only their palm is crossed with silver.

PROFITABLE PANACEAS AND NEFARIOUS NOSTRUMS

Americans are notorious hypochondriacs. They are, however, merely the victims of their culture. The economy, including the mass media, caters to

[18] For a relatively elaborate account of gypsy fortunetellers practicing their trade with traveling carnivals, see William Lindsay Gresham, *Monster Midway* (New York, Rinehart, 1953), especially Chapter 7, "The Romany Trade," pp. 113–36; see also Dan Mannix, *Step Right Up!* (New York, Harper & Brothers, 1951), especially Chapter 11, pp. 211–22.

the health consciousness and hypochondriasis of the public in the form of industry producing a vast array of goods and services designed to improve health and alleviate infirmity and then enthusiastically merchandising these goods and services. The sponsors of our television programs parade a constant stream of headache, stomachache, backache, hemorrhoid ache remedies, antihistamines, and antiappetite nostrums. Many such drug advertisers deliberately demonstrate their products with models that simulate the "innards" of the human body (albeit in a simplistic and mechanistic fashion) because hypochondriacs are morbidly fascinated by the internal workings of the human body and can thus more easily identify with such products. We have special TV documentaries on various kinds of illnesses and conditions, and some of our most popular movies and television programs concern physicians and hospitals. Our periodicals are filled with articles and regular columns about disease and infirmity. Typical articles reveal self-administered tests to determine the presence of everything from mental illness to leprosy, and some articles even attempt to animate or glorify various organs of the body such as "I am Sam's Gizzard" or the "The Marvelous Spleen: Miracle Organ of the Body." There are even regularly published magazines that concern nothing but health, disease, and the body. Several years back a noted English physician remarked that it was amazing that all Americans were not hypochondriacs in the face of their cultural concern with illness and disease and their almost constant exposure to the mass media presentations concerning illness and disease.

In some ways our culture is also the victim of our population. The hypochondriasis of our public has shaped and molded our culture with its present health and bodily preoccupation. It has been said that if several Frenchmen get together they will talk about food, politics, and women, but if three Americans get together they will elect to talk about baseball, high prices, and their last operation or illness. Concern with health and well being perhaps stems from several sources. Americans, moving more and more from the sacred toward the secular, are less assured of an afterlife and are consequently more concerned with hanging on to this life because of their fear of death. Americans are also far from stoic and with their hedonistic bent are usually not content to endure any discomfort, especially from disease if medical treatment will alleviate it. America is a youth-oriented society. Disease and infirmity ravage the body and erode the image of youth and beauty. Cultural concern with health and treatment of disease is an outgrowth of fear of death, fear of pain and discomfort, and fear of aging and ugliness.

Americans are also prone to the lax and neglectful in actually caring for their health. They permit themselves to grow fat and slovenly; they overindulge themselves in alcohol, tobacco, and food; they often neglect early symptoms of illness; and their diets are not infrequently unnutritious, if not harmful. They have a tendency to seek the easy way or the "short cut" to health. They sometimes avoid competent medical treatment because of the cost, and on occasions will not follow their doctor's orders because they dislike the medication, are fearful of the treatment procedures, or find the treatment regimen odious. They want health, beauty, and vitality, but with as little effort, cost, and discomfort as possible.

Such a situation provides ample opportunity for economic exploitation, and a vast number of deviant occupational specialties have arisen to exploit people and tap the "health" market. Probably no other society in the world has such a colorful history of "quackery," medical fraud, and thievery in the name of health. Among this array of health hucksters have been misguided idealists (albeit with some exotic ideals), super salesmen with more sales enthusiasm than ethics, genuine visitors from the lunatic fringe, professional practitioners with extreme economic motivations, and confidence men who skirt and often cross the thin edge of legality.

Many of them have enjoyed a national, if brief, following. Bernarr Macfadden, for example, was something of a national celebrity and amassed a fortune publishing health magazines and books.[19] Some years before World War II one enterprising quack attempted to promote the idea of grafting goat's testicles onto aging men as a means of rejuvenating them and restoring their virility. "Goat Gland Brinkley," as the press labeled him, even aspired to be governor of Kansas before he was forced to flee to Mexico to avoid prosecution. Some of the drugs, treatments, and devices have included all sorts of allegedly nutritional substances such as "royal jelly" (as eaten by queen bees), seaweed and kelp, alfalfa and watercress, apricot pits, and garlic pills. Devices such as rebuilt electric blankets called "arthropacifiers" have been sold in the Ozarks and elsewhere as cures for rheumatics who cannot be cured by regular doctors. One ingenious device sold to cure cancer, dandruff, and cataracts was the "radon bell" which attached to water faucets and "treated" the water that ran through it. A classic example of such a treatment device was the "dynamizer" which at the turn of the century was purported by its inventor, Albert Abrams, as a machine that could diagnose an illness by placing in it one drop of the patient's blood. Other imaginative Rube Goldberg machines and devices include "radiumators" which retail for $10,000 and "cure" heart and kidney ailments, the "oscilloclast," and the "sonus-film-o-sonic"—a device that transmits controlled audible energy and music to cure the patient; "Holiday for Strings" allegedly cured arteriosclerosis and "Smoke Gets in Your Eyes" did the same for cancer.

---

[19] For an interesting account of Macfadden's career, see Ronald M. Deutsch, "The Bare Torso King" and "The Bare Torso King Rampant," *The Nuts Among the Berries* (New York, Ballantine Books, 1961), pp. 112–30.

Over the years a whole host of cult-like approaches to disease treatment have sprung up, often made fortunes for their progenitors, fleeced thousands of hopeful patients, and faded into obscurity (if their practitioners were not prosecuted and imprisoned). Examples of such approaches or "therapies" include "sine-wave therapy," calonic irrigation therapy (enemas), "spectrochrome therapy," "zone therapy," depolarays, Z-rays, and iridiagnosis (the diagnosis of ills from the appearance of the iris of the eye), and other such exotic approaches to the treatment of disease.[20] Some of the legal but still medically unorthodox treatment disciplines or cults such as homeopathy, naturopathy, acupuncture, osteopathy,[21] and chiropractic[22] continue to be the center of heated medical and legal controversy.

The "quack" fringe of medicine and health has provided a fertile opportunity structure for the nefarious schemes of the medical and health "quacks." In 1970 persons in the United States suffering from arthritis are estimated to have spent more than $138,000,000 seeking relief for their condition. Much of this did not go for reputable medical treatment but rather went to buy a colorful assortment of worthless "quack cures" peddled by "doorbell doctors" such as pouches of "moon dust" at $100 and copper bracelets.[23] (There were 500,000,000 copper bracelets sold that year, many presumably for the alleviation of arthritic symptoms.) It is said that the annual quack bill runs far in excess of $100,000,000.

Drugs themselves have traditionally been the mainstay of the marginal medical field. The earliest quacks were the so-called "snake oil doctors" with their traveling "medicine shows." Such individuals traveled the rural and frontier areas staging free performances to attract a crowd and then selling the assembling throng on the virtues of their medicinal products, good for all

[20] For some detailed elaborations on quackery from which much of our discussion here derives, see Ralph Lee Smith, *The Health Hucksters* (New York, Thomas Y. Crowell, 1960); Maurice Beam, *It's a Racket* (New York, MacFadden, 1962), especially Chapter 4, "Quacks," pp. 126–36; Frank Gibney, "Pills, Pride, Profits," *The Operators* (New York, Harper & Brothers, 1960), pp. 55–88; Walter Wagner, "The Quacks: Snake Oil Scientists," *The Golden Fleecers* (New York, Doubleday, 1966), pp. 99–121; and Martin Gardner, "Medical Cults," and "Medical Quacks," *Fads and Fallacies in the Name of Science* (New York, Ballantine Books, 1952), pp. 98–154.

[21] Osteopathy has managed to generate some degree of legitimacy as a medical discipline in recent years. In many states osteopaths can administer drugs, give injections, and perform surgery. The army drafts them for medical service like conventional M.D.s.

[22] See, for example, Ralph Lee Smith, *At Your Own Risk: The Case Against Chiropractic* (New York, Trident Press, 1969); and Harry Schwartz, "Chiropractic: Is the Name of the Game 'Flimflam?' " *The New York Times* (Sunday, July 18, 1971), p. 7.

[23] A Guest Editorial, "Quackery Still a Problem," *The Clarion-Ledger* (Jackson, Mississippi), (Tuesday, August 3, 1971).

ailments (many were heavily spiked with alcohol and/or morphine. They might cure no illness, but at least you would feel minimal discomfort while ill). Today, the so-called "patent" or over-the-counter drugs involve 150,000 to 500,000 products and a $2.7 billion-a-year business.[24] Many of these drugs are effective and useful, some are harmless and superfluous, while others are questionable if not downright dangerous. Many are misrepresented in the claims made for their effectiveness. Many household remedies are family standbys, and many have made fortunes for their inventors and manufactors. Some of the more famous are Lydia E. Pinkham's vegetable compound for which its makers had to modify its curative advertising claims in the face of pressure from the Federal Drug Administration and Dudly J. LeBlanc's Hadicol which also was forced to modify its advertising claims. Some controversial drugs have had the support of prominent professionals and have created a national furor among medical circles. A case in point is the drug "Krebiozen" reputedly a cure for cancer, which was championed by a distinguished research physician who participated in the sale and distribution of this drug and was ultimately indicted by the Federal Government (he was acquitted but was forced to drop out of the AMA). In other instances controversial drugs have been promoted and merchandized by persons who have few if any credentials that would legitimate their advocacy of the drug in question.

In Chapter 15 Julian B. Roebuck and Robert B. Hunter present an overview of medical quackery as deviant behavior and elaborate on a variety of deviant practices in this area. They point out that "quackery" is concerned with three forms of medical deviancy: spurious nostrums, spurious devices, and spurious treatments. Designating health-care quackery as a kind of "folk crime," they articulate "five formal, rule-making, labeling, and sanctioning bodies within the broad area of medical quackery."

Although health care quackery, like other folk crimes, is often characterized by "light sanctions and social stigma—and by large numbers of offenders," it is a detestable type of deviance because it preys on man's rawest emotions: fear and desperation. It victimizes those who are least prepared to defend themselves, those of modest economic means and the unsophisticated. As Roebuck and Hunter have pointed out elsewhere, however, "We suggest that recent advances in medical science may have gone beyond common knowledge of what is efficacious or deleterious in the area of health care. The general public and the rule and lawmaking bodies may therefore be faced with a quandary in this amorphous field."[25]

[24] See Earl Ubell, "F.D.A.: A Hard Look at Over-the-Counter Drugs," *The New York Times* (Sunday, January 9, 1972), p. 6.
[25] Julian B. Roebuck and Bruce Hunter, "The Awareness of Health-Care Quackery as Deviant Behavior," *Journal of Health & Social Behavior,* Vol. 13, No. 2 (June 1972), pp. 162–66.

EPIDERMAL EXPOSURE AND ECDYSIASTIC EROTICISM

Americans have, for some time, demonstrated a remarkable appetite for the erotic. Recent years have, however, seen a significant whetting and enlargement of this appetite. The coy naive film comedies of the 1930s and 1940s have given way to a plethora of R- and X-rated movies that play neighborhood theaters weekly. More exotic fare may be viewed at the so-called "adult" movie houses which now offer films from the "underground" studios.[26] Respectable books have become, erotically speaking, what forbidden books were some years ago. The average best seller today often contains explicit passages describing fornication, fellatio, and cunnilingus and plots detailing adultery, incest, homosexuality, and sado-masochism. Recent Broadway hits provide equally explicit portrayals of sex and perversion replete with total nudity. Song lyrics have often moved beyond the *double entente* stage and now tend to "tell it like it is." "Swinging" for fun and therapy has allegedly become a national pastime among young sophisticated suburbanites, according to many authorities; on our college campuses, say the experts, courtship is accompanied by the pill, and sex is viewed simply as a more casual but profound way of "relating" to the opposite sex. Although the so-called erotic "revolution" is presumably only a few decades old, there is reason to believe that even in previous centuries Americans, and particularly those on the frontier, enjoyed a ribald existence. The Victorian ethic may have been rampant among the middle and upper classes in the eastern cities and towns, but the lower classes and denizens of the frontier were presumably more lusty and earthy in their recreational pastimes. At the very core of Victorian morality and proprietous comportment was the tabu placed on viewing the nude female body. As Skipper and McCaghy describe it:

> Traditionally, in American Society, the human body has been considered relatively private and sacred. This has been especially true of females. Generally an adult woman is not expected to expose her nudity to any male not her spouse, with the exception of a physician and then only under highly structured circumstances involving health reasons. Over the past 20 years the amount of female skin which may be uncovered in the presence of males and the situations where it may be properly displayed have rapidly become more liberal.[27]

---

[26] Some of these adult movies obviously cater to those with "exotic," if not depraved, taste. One shown to capacity audiences in San Francisco a year or so back was titled "Animal Lovers" and portrayed various types of beasts engaged in coitus.

[27] James K. Skipper, Jr. and Charles H. McCaghy, "Stripteasers: The Anatomy and Career Contingencies of a Deviant Occupation," *Social Problems*, Vol. 17, No. 3 (Winter 1970), pp. 391–405.

The nude female body has traditionally been a principal object of wide-spread erotic interest, and many of our erotic art forms developed around this interest. Subsequently our cultural penchant for commercialization led to the economic capitalization and exploitation of interest in the nude female body. Perhaps the oldest and most durable means of nudity exploitation, however, is the nude and/or erotic dance. It is particularly popular in its character-istically American form of striptease dancing: the gradual disrobement of the performer down to the minimal covering of the genital area while keeping time or step to some musical accompaniment. It is designed to provide enter-tainment and sexual stimulation through vicarious identification. Presumably, it originated in America, but now is quite fashionable in much of the west-ernized world.

Because stripping is an institutionalized erotic "art form," there is a relatively constant demand for such performances, and accordingly, it pro-vides occupational specialization and employment for some 7,000 women in our society.[28] Because it offers full-time employment and career experiences and involves the usual work processes of recruitment, socialization, and con-trol, it may be considered a regular occupation, although one that is largely considered deviant.

Stripping, or at least some form of it, is theoretically legal in many parts of the country, but it is outlawed, directly or indirectly, in some states and municipalities. Even where legal, however, there are often limits of propriety and taste imposed; where the performance becomes too suggestive or obscene or if the stripper removes more clothing than the statute specifies, she may be in violation of the law. The strictness of interpretation of laws governing stripping is subject to the whims of law enforcement officials and in some instances the contribution of tourist revenue to the local economy. Thus, the law may call for relatively circumspect performances, but the local police may tolerate obscene performances and "flashing" (lowering a G-string from time to time) if this is popular with the tourists and conventioners who spend considerable money in the community. The law or ordinance may even specifically prohibit striptease and allow only exotic dancing, but the local officials may be quite lax or permissive in enforcing the law, and stripping may occur in the face of a law prohibiting it. Hence, the stripper is essentially a marginally illegal occupational specialty. A new district attorney may come along, however, and undertake to "clean up" the town including the acts of the local strippers.

Inasmuch as the citizenry of a community may be less pragmatic than the local chamber of commerce, they may be less cognizant of the tourists'

[28] *Ibid.*, p. 393.

dollars and more critical of the presence of striptease and especially if the act is "strong" (involves flashing and especially suggestive gestures).

As an illegal (even if marginally) occupational practitioner, the stripper is a deviant, and she may be considered a deviant for other reasons. By exhibiting her body and performing in an obscene manner she is in violation of community standards of proprietous comportment and "good taste." As Marilyn Salutin puts it, "Strippers are viewed as 'bad,' then, because they strip away all social decorum with their clothes. They taunt the public with their own mores by teasing them and turning them on."[29] The stripper is, in effect, exploiting her body and her sexuality and is, accordingly, a prostitute of sorts. Skipper and McCaghy found that college students held a negative image of strippers and tended to think of them as "immorals" or "prostitutes."[30] The students also spoke of strippers as "oversexed" and "hard women." Because their occupational specialty involves the selling of sexuality and thus caters to a clientele seeking sexual stimulation (even if vicarious), theirs is thought to be basically a depraved occupation serving a depraved clientele. This idea may include an element of truth. While many patrons of the striptease show or burlesque are simply tourists or young people seeking entertainment and a little "spice," a substantial number of other patrons may have mental or emotional problems or at least have some difficulty in controlling or suppressing the sexual stimulation they derive from the striptease performances. Ann Terry D'Andre, for example, pointed out that many strippers complain of the "degenerates" in the audience who publicly masturbate during their performances.[31] These masturbating patrons are commonly referred to as "the gentlemen of the press" according to D'Andre. She also mentions strippers commenting about fan letters with obscene statements which they sometimes receive from their patrons. Arthur H. Lewis relates the incident of a middle-aged prominent Philadelphia obstetrician who returned night after night to see the striptease performance and always stood in the first row with his elbows on the platform. One night the stripper was squatting at the edge of the stage as part of her act when this individual suddenly leaped up and bit the stripper on her vagina; the wound required several stitches.[32] Carnival strippers in "strong shows" work extremely close to the patrons, even in some instances permitting the patrons to touch them. Such occasions are called "audience participation nights." A physical hazard is

[29] Marilyn Salutin, "Stripper Morality," *Transaction: Social Science and Modern Society*, Vol. 8, No. 8, Whole No. 68 (June 1971), p. 13.

[30] Skipper and McCaghy, op. cit., p. 392.

[31] Ann Terry D'Andre, "An Occupational Study of the Strip-Dancer Career." Paper delivered to the Pacific Sociological Association annual meeting held in Salt Lake City, Utah (April 22–24, 1965).

[32] Arthur H. Lewis, *Carnival* (New York, Trident Press, 1970), p. 225.

involved, and an experienced stripper will move back away from the patrons if they gather in too closely while watching. As one stripper put it, "If you don't do that, you'd lose control of the crowd and they could be dangerous."[33]

Strippers are also viewed as deviant as a result of the social milieu in which they must work and the people with whom they are thrown into contact—the B-girls and hustlers, the narcotic addicts and alcoholics, and all of the other regular habitués of bars and strip joints. Often there is a kind of guilt by association.

Some strippers are able to throw off the public image of deviant and a few, like Gypsy Rose Lee, have even become national celebrities. For most however, the deviant public image lingers on and affects their own self-image. Strippers are sensitive to the negative image of them held by the public, and they use several devices for the maintenance of their own self-image. They rationalize that what they do is basically no different from what other women do. All women, even wives, are really exhibitionists and prostitutes, but just charge a different kind of price such as a dinner or marriage. They often attempt to redefine stripping as good and socially redeeming. They also try and promote the idea that they are talented and creative "show" people. In addition, they attempt to conceal information about their private lives and especially their sexual behavior that might compound their negative public image as deviant. Since stripping provides them with economic reward, seemingly glamorous excitement and personal recognition, they can justify their occupational specialty, at least to themselves.[34] As Salutin put it: "Strippers like stripping because it makes them feel important, especially when the audience claps and cheers. They feel exhilarated. They also like the money."[35]

Chapter 16, Jacqueline Boles and A. P. Garbin's "Stripping For a Living: An Occupational Study of the Night Club Stripper" represents a recent and hitherto unpublished sociological study of stripteasing as an occupational study. The authors point out that many girls became strippers through a relatively casual or unintentional route. Some had been in other phases of the entertainment business such as B-girls, or go-go dancers. Some girls were led into the occupation by boyfriends or husbands; others drifted into it accidentally; and others took it up following a "crisis situation" such as a divorce or losing a job. They did not appear to enter the field as a result of long-range planning and effort as with other occupations. Stripping involves a

[33] Ibid.

[34] These ideas are discussed at length in Salutin, op. cit.; Skipper and McCaghy, op. cit.; D'Andre, op. cit.; and James K. Skipper, Jr. and Charles H. McCaghy, "Stripteasing: A Sex Oriented Occupation," in James Hensilin (ed.), *The Sociology of Sex* (New York, Appleton-Century-Crofts, 1970).

[35] Salutin, op. cit., p. 18.

socialization period and entails learning the technical skills of dancing and artistic disrobement as well as the necessary social skills, such as the occupational "code of ethics"; how to handle hecklers and overly enthusiastic patrons; and how to relate to other strippers, managers, and club owners. According to Boles and Garbin, stripping affords both extrinsic rewards, such as money, and job security, as well as intrinsic rewards such as creativity and ego satisfaction.

SAWDUST SHENANIGANS AND THE EXPLOITATION OF FUN

Life might be unendurable if man could not enjoy brief respites from his burdens. These respites have taken the form of leisure, holidays, recreation, avocation, sports, festivals, and ceremonies, which have afforded diversion, stimulation, and "fun" for the individual and have tended to transport him temporarily away from the mundane and often monotonous nature of everyday life.

The traveling carnival has figured prominently in providing such a respite and escape. Some evidence of the carnival's impact on the American recreational scene is the fact that in many states the occasion of a state or county fair often is declared a local holiday so the population, and especially school children, may take in the carnival. Chartered school buses may bring children from more than 100 miles away. The county or state fair is often one of the more significant events in the annual calendar, and families in some regions save their money for some weeks prior to the fair in order to be able to have ample funds to spend.

The carnival provides "fun." The fun takes the form of excitement, thrills, suspense, erotic stimulation, competition, symbolic achievement, as well as visual, audio, and olfactory stimulation. The carnival permits one to be almost totally immersed in lights, color, music, smells, and sound. It affords a cacophony of stimuli, a total sensory and emotional experience, in a sense providing a "trip." It also provides more earthy or pedestrian opportunities such as the opportunity to gamble and to look at girls taking their clothes off, for a significant attraction of the carnival is that it offers many pleasures forbidden at other times.[36]

An essential component of most carnivals is the "girlie" show, often appearing in the guise of a "musical review." Girlie shows are striptease shows,

[36] For a detailed discussion of the carnival, see Clifton D. Bryant, "Sawdust in Their Shoes: The Carnival as a Neglected Complex Organization and Work Culture," in Clifton D. Bryant (ed.), *The Social Dimensions of Work* (Englewood Cliffs, N.J., Prentice-Hall, 1972), pp. 181–82.

or "kootch" shows as they are known in the carnival business. Carnivals often play small towns and rural areas where striptease acts are usually illegal and certainly violate community standards of propriety and comportment. Lewis reports that in some regions of the country (where the nude or semi-nude female body may be particularly "forbidden" by religious tradition and community custom) the girlie shows enjoy an especially brisk trade.

> Carnivals that hit the rural South or the Pennsylvania Dutch Country—Kutztown, Dallastown, and Red Lion, Hummelstown—they have to carry as many as three girl shows to handle customers who spend the whole night going from one to the other and returning to the first and starting it all over again.[37]

While some carnivals claim the label of "Sunday School Shows" (shows where the girls don't take everything off), other carnivals boast strip shows that are considerably "stronger" than the acts normally encountered in the average tourist night club strip act. In such acts the performers are more likely to "flash" or rely on the use of a "snorting pole." (The strippers pretend the pole which extends from the top of the carnival tent to the floor, is a man and simulate coitus with it). They may conclude their act by squatting on the edge of the stage and thereby better exposing their genital area. (They sometimes emphasize this by inserting their fingers into their vagina and spreading it open for more detailed inspection. In this connection, this type of activity often occurs during the "blowoff," or show after the regular performance. Sometimes this squatting is done in the dark and the spectators are permitted to use flashlights and examine the stripper's genital area in clinical detail). In a few carnivals "audience participation" is permitted or encouraged, and the spectators may touch or handle the genital area of the girl performers.[38] Where "audience participation" is permitted there appears to be a real professional concern for the clientele or patrons—a "show biz" craftsmanship as it were. Lewis reported that one star stripper whom he interviewed complained of her problem of keeping her girls (the lesser strippers in the act) clean. As the articulated it:

> When a guy touches them and his hands smell, he's got every right to complain. That's what I keep tellin' em. The girls we got workin' here now are all right but some others! They never even knew what a douche was.[39]

[37] Lewis, op. cit., p. 19.
[38] For a detailed discussion of all these practices, see ibid., especially pp. 223–27 and 262–76.
[39] Ibid., p. 277.

Although many of the offerings of the carnival are authentic, many attractions and exhibits are spurious and misrepresented. The "bally" banners out in front of the tent may proclaim that the largest snake, rat, or turkey in the world resides within, but to the zoologically knowledgeable the animals displayed are only a boa constrictor of modest length, a Capybara (a common South American large rodent), or an Australian Cassowary. The animals or reptiles are never so large or ferocious in real life as portrayed.

Many exhibits are based on "illusions" and are clearly deceptive and thus border on the fraudulent. "Frozen monsters" (wax figures in ice), "headless girls," and girls who turn into gorillas are but a few examples. The girl without a head was a classic illusion in the carnival industry. "Olga the Headless Teuton" was supposedly a girl who, having lost her head in a train wreck, was kept alive by a set of tubes that circulated blood and other fluids into the girl's neck. It was done with mirrors and fooled most people who saw it. Some fainted, others couldn't bear to watch, and one individual was moved to want to marry the hapless girl.[40] The girl into gorilla act is also done with mirrors, and each act usually empties the tent by sending the spectators out running in fear before the great ape.[41]

Some persons find the exhibition of "freaks" and human oddities disgusting to attend and degrading to those on display, and from time to time there has been considerable public opposition to what they consider to be an exploitative and deviant practice. The public, however, continues to pay its money to see those deformed specimens of mankind who "deviate" so pitifully from the normal. Some communities have statutes that prohibit some carnival acts such as the geek chicken-eating act.[42]

Although some carnival "games of chance" called "hanky panks" permit the patron to "win" every time, all he may "win" is some type of cheap prize called "slum" which costs considerably less than the cost of playing the game. Some games of chance like bingo may be normally illegal by local community standards. Still other games may be "gaffed" or rigged so that the customer has little if any statistical opportunity to win. The worst such offenders are the so-called "alibis" and "flat stores" where the aim is clearly to separate the "mark" from his money, sometimes in amounts running into the hundreds and occasionally even thousands.[43]

---

[40] Ibid., pp. 66–71.
[41] Ibid., pp. 256–61.
[42] Bryant, op. cit., p. 203.
[43] See Lewis, op. cit., pp. 279–84. See also Marcello Truzzi and Patrick Easto, "Carnivals, Road Shows, and Freaks," *Transaction: Social Science and Modern Society*, Vol. 9, No. 5 (March 1972), p. 30; and Patrick C. Easto and Marcello Truzzi, "Towards an Ethnography of the Carnival Social System," in John M. Roberts and Marcello Truzzi (eds.), *Anthropology on American Social Life* (Englewood Cliffs, N.J., Prentice-Hall, 1971).

One may be lured into the "fun house" by prerecorded or canned laughter, and the rides may appear to be more appealing and thrilling because the screams of the riders are sometimes amplified. A skilled "jam" auctioneer, using guile and skillful psychological persuasion, may be able to convince his "tip" or audience to bid exorbitant prices for merchandise of questionable quality and value.[44] Cotton candy at 50 cents' a serving is not called "sweetened air" for nothing, and many a patron of the carnival has discovered that his "fun" at the fair is an expensive and perishable commodity.

The carnival can manage to violate local community statutes and regulations as well as community standards of ethics, morality, propriety, and honesty by virtue of the fact that it is temporary and mobile. It is here and gone before the full import of its deviant offerings are recognized or realized. Because it comes only once a year, it is tolerated as an escape mechanism or device of patterned evasion of the norm. Since many of the forbidden offerings are popular with segments of the population, the local norms may be difficult and even undesirable to enforce. Carnivals often subvert local law enforcement and governmental officials to their own deviant purposes through payoffs and graft. The carnival attorney is appropriately named the "patch" or "fixer." Being involved in the deviant, even to the extent of being victimized, is tolerated and offset by the fact that the forbidden is enjoyable, even if expensive, and "fun" is requisite to endurance of monotonous day-to-day life.

The final selection in this Part is Patrick Easto's and Marcello Truzzi's conceptualization of the carnival as a marginally legal work activity. They provide an overview of the carnival and articulate some of the exploitative, deceptive, and unconventional practices and activities that have helped earn the deviant label for carnivals.

The carnival is not, as the authors put it, a "conforming work system;" rather as they see it, it is a "mixture of conforming and deviant work activities in relation to both legal and community norms."

---

[44] Lewis, op. cit., pp. 243–55.

13.   The Open Road for Boys:
Meet Glenn Young, Master Shuffleboard Hustler

CHARLES GILLESPIE

Occasionally Glenn Young, age 36, accepts employment. He is alert, intelligent, and a pleasant man to be around, quite capable of success in businesses like Success Unlimited, where he recently worked as an associate of his younger brother.

His employment is always short lived, however, because in his heart and life Glenn Young is a shuffleboard hustler, the best shuffleboard player in the world in his own professional estimation. Unlike many hustlers who have devoted their lives to a specialty, Young has already done many things well and someday soon he plans to do something else better than anybody. Lindbergh, after all, flew the Atlantic only once.

The shuffleboard Young hustles is not the shipboard game played on a deck with platter-sized discs and long-handled sticks, though that game no doubt attracts its own brand of sophisticated hustler. Young competes on a narrow table, 23 feet long, generally located in the rear of the sort of bars, lounges, and taverns which do not have topless dancing, untrained singers, or any other entertainment that cannot be connected by electrical plug.

The shuffleboard table is glazed over with a powder, according to taste or local custom. The object of the game is to place a set of palm-sized weights in scoring position at the far end of the table. Failing that, the secondary objective is to keep the opponent from scoring by knocking his weights off the table. This, of course, is like explaining that the object of baseball is to score runs. It is the nuances, the strategies, the psychology, and the big bankroll that make shuffleboard fascinating and profitable for Glenn Young and his contemporaries.

Propelling a metal puck along a polished table does not sound like the

Reprinted, with additions, by permission from Charles Gillespie, *Aloft,* Vol. 3, No. 3 (Summer 1971), pp. 11–13.

most dramatic game in the country but more than casual skill is required to bump another puck off the table and then spin into the high-scoring corner— extra points for dangling over the edge. A version of the game, played on a smaller table and requiring banked shots off a felt bumper is also popular, but the game and the ground rules are different in the way Baltusrol is different from the Wee Willie Winkie Miniature Links Lighted.

Insofar as pure skill with the weights is concerned, Glenn Young can place his pucks precisely where he wants them. So can most of the other 200 shuffleboard hustlers in constant march across the continent, earning their daily bread.

Allowing for occasional liberties of definition, the hustler seems to have crept among us throughout the centuries. Along with idols and iconoclasts, some have been more successful than others, the most successful being those whose names you have never heard. Although recent films and literature have usually arranged the term as synonym for pool shark, hustlers thrive in every arena of competitive endeavor, unnatural heroes who pursue success to unlikely extremes.

The hustler as athlete admires a solid gold medal only in the sense that it may be transformed into legal tender; praise in the sports columns is a preliminary obituary notice. His reward is easily calculated and quite portable: snapping neatly into one of those hand-crafted money clips so often displayed in the miniature street bazaars of Mexican border towns.

The hustler, by necessity, remains an individual playing an individual's game. He cannot hustle a team effort—a football game, a polo match, a tug of war—although on occasion he will enlist the aid of a lackey, a lesser hustler to pique the curiosity of the crowd. Unlike a 20-game winner or a champion prize fighter his ideal opponent is not a man with easily-calculated weaknesses but is a man who can play well, believes he can play better than anyone, who reacts at every intimated challenge with an instinctive plunge into his wallet. The hustler as con man preys on the professional on the professional's home grounds. He searches out the club champion, not the man who carries his putting problems over his heart.

Aside from the satisfaction that accrues from financial independence the hustler's rewards are pale trophies visible only to himself. To remain effective he cultivates anonymity. A photograph or a feature story is like prairie fire over his acres. They can wipe out a territory for years, reducing him to hasty mustaches and expensive hair dyes when he chooses to return.

To the disgust of many, repeated exposure has recently forced some of the great pool hustlers into displaying their incredible abilities before a succession of television cameras and neat spectators who rarely ever breathe for fear of disturbing their cool and should be giving exhibitions themselves.

For the young man who would be hustler the world is still an oyster, round the way Columbus expected, populated the way Barnum estimated. All the aspirant would do is practice. If Jim Ryun runs 14 miles every day you have an idea of the task before the man who would hustle him, and somewhere there is one who will.

A novice hustler's lessons in his craft are necessarily expensive. There are no professionals to correct weaknesses on the practice greens, no trade schools offering scholarships and air-conditioned mothering. He must plunge in over his head and sink until he begins, slowly, to ride to the surface, the green gradually fading from behind his ears. When he has begun to recover his tuition fees from the established hustlers—when he can hustle the hustler—he is on his way.

As in any profession of pride there are regulations governing the hustler's conduct. Some are ill-defined, pliable to purpose; others are definite and dogmatic. A milkman, on his day off, might soak the city champion but he is still a milkman as long as he insists upon gainful employment, contact with contemporary conformity.

Although the hustler's code insists upon purity of motive, no stigma is attached to entertainment for the client especially if he has already been shorn by specialties and has only carfare remaining to be claimed. Titanic Thompson, the celebrated golf hustler, not only hustled left or right handed and played with garden tools but between holes could accomplish such exotic feats as throwing the ace of spades 50 yards. Surely it cannot be done.

Almost any sport dependent upon the man versus man equation is susceptible to hustling. Most of them have been and are being. The principal requirement is that the game be widely played so that a hustler can establish year-around trade routes, slipping once or twice into a city without fear his reputation and previous coups have barricaded his bridges before him. A hustler can ill afford anything except success and fear nothing else either.

(New York's chess hustlers are a breed unto themselves. Not only do they subsist on the "starchy diet"—peanuts and small potatoes—they rarely venture beyond the sound of their own mating, realizing, perhaps, they would surely starve in the Appalachians long before they even tried to cross the bleak and chessless Middle Western deserts.

Shuffleboard's holy city is Peoria, Ill., where Caterpillar employees first broke the penny-ante barrier in the '30s, proving that man could survive in wasted lands entirely on the flick of his fingers. A nostalgic tournament that attracts the aforementioned Two Hundred is held in Peoria each spring, but the game long ago outgrew its birthplace. California is now the shuffleboard center of the United States, and the game's two most celebrated players come from Tennessee and Texas.

Glenn Young has been hustling for the past seven years. For a long time he thought of himself as only second best as he hustled harder and faster than most. His handicap is loyalty to his home town, Memphis, where competition is rare and pickings slim. The situation is comparable to assigning A. J. Foyt a Volkswagen for a race around the parking lot with the neighborhood housewives. Nevertheless, Young makes the best of his environment when he is at home: He has won $400 playing blindfolded, and has also won by using a borrowed walking cane—in the style of a cue stick, and by playing opposite-handed.

A tangible asset in Young's game is his genuine friendliness and an appearance of complete, almost cherubic, innocence as though the desire to win money would be the last thing on his mind; it, after all, being only a game. His weakness is reputed to be carelessness when he has been drinking. On the other hand he has been known to blunder about with a vodka bottle full of water in one fist, so you cannot always be certain the weakness is not just another strength in sly disguise.

Several years ago Young was one of the best all-around athletes in Memphis. He was advancing nicely up the St. Louis Cardinal farm system until two years in the Army damaged his abilities to run and throw and he began advancing nicely right back down the St. Louis Cardinal farm system.

For a short time afterward he was employed by the City of Memphis and it was during this time "messing around Archie's on Jackson Avenue one evening" that he began watching shuffleboard and the action among the bystanders—little men who had never been All-Memphis in two or three sports and never played a day in the Texas League—involved in the mystique of profit for the sheer fun of money.

Seated in another Jackson Avenue establishment called Ching Chong's, which is not a place where you can purchase Chinese food, Young agreed, on another day, to discuss his career, realizing, probably, he is already as well known as a hustler can get before he plunges over the edge and into public acclaim.

GLENN YOUNG: I decided I wanted to be a player. I quit my job with the city, that was seven years ago, and I started devoting full time to shuffleboard. A lot of guys just travel around the country playing shuffleboard and that's what gave me the idea, people coming through here. I played day and night for a couple of months and then I started hustling around town here. After about a year I started out on the road. I didn't have a bit of trouble. It didn't cost me much to learn. Everything I've done has always been easy for me and in a couple of months I was beating everybody in town. Two people who helped me a lot were a fellow they call Little Richard and an old cripple[d] fellow, Mister Bill Rosenthald, who had played up in Peoria back in the Thirties. Between the two of them they showed me how the game is supposed to be played. I set my goal to beat a man named Bob Strong. He'd been the best in Memphis. I could do it in two months. He's still the best in Memphis next to me.

Within the first year Young hustled himself right out of the Memphis league and was reduced to stunts and giving away points to stir up unenthusiastic competition. Given the hammer—the last shot—Young can spot an opponent the maximum handicap, 14 of the game's 15 points, and always win. Under the circumstances it is not so difficult to understand the reluctance of the opposition. His name became a bomb to drop around smoke-veiled tables.

"Hell," recalled a player at the Yale Hotel and Cafe, named for the Memphis railroad yards and not the New Haven establishment, "This guy walked in one afternoon and said he'd play the best player in the house for twenty-five dollars. That was me and I didn't have twenty-five dollars but we got it up between us. I've got him down 12 to 9 and there's no doubt I'm going to win, then this guy walks up and says 'by the way I don't think I've met you; I'm Glenn Young.' I didn't score another point."

The man is not entirely certain he was playing Glenn Young but figures he might as well have been.

Shortly after Young began playing he met the other hustlers as they drifted in and out of Memphis. All of them carried a small book of names and addresses, a sort of coast-to-coast bankbook for hustlers. Young soon had his own book and his own plans for career.

One name cropped up each time a new counselor hit the Tennessee-Arkansas bridge:

GLENN YOUNG: I've heard of Billy Mays all my life.

Mays, a Dallas resident when he is residing, is 39 years old and 22 years a suffleboard hustler. His wife can beat most men. Mays can beat all men, including Rock Hudson, the best of the celebrity players, but no longer including Glenn Young.

GLENN YOUNG: In my opinion he was the best player in the world. I've played Mays several times. The first time he beat me to death. That was when I first started playing. One year I flew to Dallas, Texas, to play him some and we just went back and forth. I thought if I ever got to where I could beat him consistently I'd just quit but now I'm not going to.... Billy Mays' wife is probably the best woman player I've ever seen. She plays men, doesn't ever play women, but a lot of women play. There's a little girl over in Fort Smith, Arkansas; we've made a lot of money together playing partners.

Young follows a deliberate, well-plotted route when he leaves Memphis and heads West. He travels first to Little Rock; then to Fort Smith; Tulsa;

Liberal, Kansas; Gallup, New Mexico; San Diego, and finally up the California coast to San Francisco. The territory east of Peoria is dead to shuffleboard hustling; the chess players can have it. One evening, on an old Jack Paar television program, a guest claimed to be a shuffleboard hustler enroute to Florida for the season. His testimony sent Young and half a hundred other hustlers into the peninsula but they could find no sign of life as they knew it and determined the man was either a fraud or speaking of the sissy shipboard game played amidst mothers and children.

Occasionally Young will veer off the beaten path into pockets of activity like the West Texas-New Mexico oil corner—Odessa, Big Spring, Hobbs— "where there's lots of money left for me to make yet." There is also sporadic activity in Nashville.

> GLENN YOUNG: There's quite a bit of action in Memphis but there'd be a lot more if the police would let you play. You can go to a golf course and gamble and go to a bowling alley and gamble but you can't play shuffleboard. . . . To people out in California shuffleboard is a big thing. To them it's just like paying off a loan. You never get a bad check out there. A lot of people take gamblers ridiculously. Out there they mean it. . . . There are places in California you can just pull your shoes off and play on the carpets. In Sacramento they play in a big armory and in Galveston they charge admission to see tournaments.
>
> Every board is different. No two boards are alike. There are slow boards and fast ones. What makes a good player is being able to adjust, beat people on their own board. An old boy in Memphis is real hard to beat on his own board but you get him off it and anybody can beat him.
>
> You very seldom run into trouble on the road. When you get to other places they know why you're there. They like to see good shuffleboard. There's more trouble in Memphis, Tennessee than any place I've seen. They've never seen good shuffleboard and they're not really gamblers to start with. When you do have trouble it's usually some guy sitting on the sidelines betting a dollar.

Young has heard stories, here and there, of people who have beaten him at his own game but he does not believe any of them and in the back room of Ching Chong's, surrounded by one of Jackson Avenue's loudest juke boxes and a number of fascinated females, he does not leave the impression of a man who expects to lose in the near future. A friend urges him to get up and win them some money and he promises to do that; a customer, ordered out of the place by a shouting woman, presumably representing management, departs by way of Young's table and invites him to a game elsewhere and he promises to do that too, later.

Later can mean almost any hour these days, although for years the games in Memphis were clandestine after 1 a.m. because of a vice squad enforced theory that a city ordinance prohibited mechanical amusement beyond that hour. Not until recently did some dedicated researcher discover there had never been such an ordinance. The discovery has to be beneficial to Young's health because until then he had been known to sleep on the board to retain possession from closing time until the next opening hours; by custom the board belongs to the last game's winner so long as he chooses to exercise the privilege and Young was rarely inclined to relinquish possession. Now places like the Freeway Inn on Lamar Avenue remain open until an hour that threatens sunburn and a place in the shuffleboard line is not so desperately sought.

Asked to name a likely successor, Young could not.

> GLENN YOUNG: A lot of them want to do it but nobody impresses me. Nobody wants to practice by themselves, to put in all the hard work. They want to win but they don't want to practice.... The left hand is the hardest to learn. That's the game—developing the left hand.... Lagging is a big part of the game too and that's where I think I exceed over anybody else anywhere—lagging. I can more or less place the weights anywhere anytime.

The shuffleboard environment—late hours, intense smoke, heavy drinking, hostile losers—is not conducive to community pride and occasionally not even community tolerance. Young, however, can make the game sound as though it is an old favorite at Sunnybrook Farm.

> GLENN YOUNG: Every time anybody comes to town the place is packed. No matter where I am people find me; they get me on the phone, and we have a game. I love to play. I've met a lot of nice people playing. I don't consider it a bad thing like some people would. I put my talent against somebody else's and I'm willing to bet on mine.

Young's richest series have been in Peoria where he won $4,100 in three days and in California where he won $2,100 in two days. He laughs at the legend of a $20,000 duel with Mays, backed by a Texas syndicate. Various accounts have him failing to raise the capital, winning all, losing all.

> GLENN YOUNG: None of that ever happened.... Shuffleboard right now is at the stage pool was a few years ago. They add a few tournaments every year; I'm going to try to hold one up in Tipton County myself. There's not that much prize money in a tournament but you get that many good players together and when you aren't playing in the tournament you go off somewhere else and get up a game. That's where the money is. I've never been beat in a legitimate game, maybe a game or two, but never in a session.... In another five years it's going to be a big thing.

In five years Young may well have gone on to his other interests. He is presently engaged in the improvement of already considerable bowling skills. Bowlers even now will find it prudent to avoid a short, stocky stranger with combed back hair and an extremely pleasant manner, especially if the stranger offers to bowl blindfolded or throw the jack of diamonds across all 48 alleys.

14. Cross My Palm with Silver: Fortunetelling as an Occupational Way of Life

CHARLOTTE R. TATRO

It is Sunday afternoon in a blue-collar neighborhood. The yard in front of a meticulously kept frame home is filled with cars. A billboard eloquently displays the palm of a large hand. Entering the front door, one finds himself in an attractive reception room. The walls are lined with chairs and benches filled with people watching TV, thumbing through movie magazines, and munching dime-store candy provided for their pleasure.

Male and female, black and white, old and young, dowdy and well-dressed, dirty and well-groomed, they patiently await their turns. Troubled and lonely, in need of friends and reassurance, or perhaps just from habit, grandparents, parents, and young adults with children in tow religiously come to this place on Sunday afternoons over a lifetime. There is some talking, a little laughing, and even a few testimonial remarks as the customers, or "38s," as some fortunetellers refer to them, eagerly anticipate their moment with Madame Marian, the fortuneteller.

The door to the private office opens. Madame Marian, an attractively dressed woman in her late fifties appears. She smiles in recognition to some of the regular customers and says, "Next?" A customer rises and enters the office, and for those in the reception room the wait resumes.

"Come in. Have a seat." Madame Marian indicates a chair in front of her executive-style desk. She then sits in a chair behind the desk.

As the customer enters the office, he is immediately attracted by the eyes in a china face of Jesus. They give the illusion of following the observer from the door to his chair and still seem to be staring at him. He also notices the crystal ball on the desk and the glass ash tray in the form of "open palms."

Madame Marian begins reciting in a sonorous voice:

The Lord is my shepherd;
I shall not want.
He maketh me to lie down in green pastures....

The "38" is mesmerized. After reciting the entire 23rd Psalm, Madame Marian proceeds to reveal "facts" about the customer's life that presumably only a fortuneteller or one endowed with exceptional gifts could know. The "38" listens intently. Madame Marian touches on subjects of universal interest—love, money, and health—as she rapidly recites her patter. The "38" nods in agreement, smiles in acknowledgment of a "fact" revealed, moves his body and shifts his eyes in response to the almost hypnotizing patter of the fortuneteller.[1] Madame Marian astutely detects the responses of the customer and intones her voice to emphasize statements that seem to be of special relevance to the "38." A few questions follow the patter and perhaps a little sleight of hand as Madame Marian seeks to reveal the customer's name and produce a picture of someone who wishes evil for the customer. A portion of the prearranged fee is collected, and the importance of the next weekly visit is stressed. A blessing is pronounced, and incense is sprayed over the client as he departs, making way for the next customer and a reenactment of the scene just completed.

On a rare occasion a car of "faithfuls" will request that Madame Marian come outside to a waiting automobile to bless an old or infirm family member. Such requests often result in advice to rush this family member to the local charity hospital.

Late in the evening Madame Marian may receive a phone call from one of her very few extremely wealthy clients. These clients are the only ones who have access to Madame Marian at times other than during office hours. If lonely, these clients may merely discuss the happenings of their day; when troubled, they may reveal to one not in their social circle such embarrassments as the loss of $100,000 on a foolish investment.[2]

BRIEF HISTORY OF FORTUNETELLING

Within societies throughout recorded history, there has been one who sought to foretell events in other people's lives. He has engaged in this activity because he believed himself to be endowed with unusual foresight or because he sought economic gain, power, and prestige from this activity.

Fortunetellers claim to reveal facts about a customer's past, present, and future in exchange for money. In the ancient past, itinerant fortunetellers often ran afoul of the law for too energetically separating a client from his

---

[1] Edward T. Hall, *The Silent Language* (Garden City, N.Y., Doubleday, 1959) stresses the importance of body language.

[2] Data for this research were collected by observations and communication with fortunetellers (a husband and wife) over a period of 20 years. During this period the researcher informally interviewed many fortunetellers who were associates of the husband and wife.

money. Nevertheless, questioning by legal authorities was avoided by the nomadic habit of these people. Present-day law officials are more likely to look into fortunetelling activities, especially those in which the practitioner separates the customer from large sums of money over a short period of time in exchange for questionable services or commodities. However, this practice is certainly not limited to fortunetellers.[3] Many economic activities fall within this category, and several are currently under investigation by both the governmental and private sectors in America.[4]

Fortunetelling emerged from among low-caste hindu exiles from India. These highly mobile people carried fortunetelling across the plateaus of Afghanistan and Persia into 'Syria and Egypt. From there the wanderers moved northward across the mountains of the Caucasus into the Balkans, Greece, Western Europe, and finally into America and Australia.[5]

These peoples are known as Romani (gypsy) or Didakai (half-breed gypsy).[6] The women tell fortunes or "dukker." In the past the Romanichais (gypsy women) would "dukker" for kitchen maids in exchange for a piece of silver from the master's house. (Silver has traditionally been recognized as a valuable commodity for quick bartering. Even today one notes the strong affinity for silver by those engaged in fortunetelling.) Gypsy men engage in economic activities other than fortunetelling. In the past they were horse dealers, tinkers, and scrap metal dealers; today some are involved in the related activities of automobile and furnace repair, roof and gutter repair, aluminum siding installation, and sign painting.

The norms specifying the work for the gypsy woman dictate that if she is to be a gypsy woman of worth to her man and her subculture, she must be a good fortuneteller—that is, get much money. Thus fortunetelling is part of the occupational norms for the gypsy subculture. However, since fortunetelling is not part of the occupational norms for any other segment of the population in the United States, those who do engage in this economic activity are practicing a deviant occupation.

An occupation is defined as deviant if the occupational goal or access to the goal involves one in behavior that violates societal norms. In the case of fortunetelling, the goal—that of attaining great wealth—is socially approved; however, socially acceptable means for attaining this goal within

[3] Clifton D. Bryant, "Feathers, Spurs, and Blood: Cockfighting as a Deviant Leisure Activity." Paper presented at the 34th annual meeting of the Southern Sociological Society Meeting, Miami Beach, Florida (May 6, 1971).

[4] Note, for example, the present investigation by the government of the franchising business or Ralph Nader's examination of the automotive industry.

[5] Charles Godfrey Leland, *Gypsy Sorcery and Fortune Telling* (New Hyde Park, N.Y., University Books, 1963), p. vii.

[6] For a glossary of Gypsy words, see G. E. C. Webb, *Gypsies: The Secret People* (London, Herbert Jenkins, 1960), pp. 183–89.

this occupational structure are blocked. Therefore, the fortuneteller resorts to illegitimate means.[7] By misrepresenting his power and taking advantage of the customer's ignorance and superstitions, he is violating norms and using socially unacceptable means to attain his goal.

Several sociologists have examined the relationship between cultural goals and means for attaining these goals. Durkheim noted that social conditions lead to "over-weening ambition." In an effort to satiate the "over-weening ambition" individuals violate the regulatory norms.[8] Similarly, Merton studied the patterns of disjunction between culturally prescribed goals and socially organized access to them by legitimate means.[9] The goal of attaining great wealth is culturally acceptable. However, access to legitimate means to satisfy this goal seem to be blocked for the potential fortuneteller, and he therefore resorts to illegitimate means, thus practicing a deviant occupation.

FORMS AND FUNCTIONS OF FORTUNETELLING

Laws regulating fortunetelling are passed by local authorities. Business licenses are granted for specific sums; however, these fees are "negotiable" in most cases. Contributing to the campaign of the right politician, soliciting votes for candidates through customers, or even such rash behavior as dropping $1,000 bills in alderman's trash cans ensure rapid delivery of "misplaced" licenses. After obtaining a local license (and sometimes before), fortunetellers become involved in one of several forms of this deviant occupation.

One form of fortunetelling is practiced by some night club entertainers. They engage in this occupation by answering written questions while on stage, answering questions in private conference, or pitching horoscopes. Since in certain areas fortunetelling is illegal, becoming a night club performer is one way to circumvent confrontation with the law enforcement officials. Often monetary reward for their work is limited to tips of "gratuity."

Another form of fortunetelling is practiced by the highly mobile "big score" operator. He seeks to relieve customers of large sums of money over a short period of time in exchange for questionable services. The "big score" operator is usually prepared to leave a particular location immediately if the law enforcement officials begin to inquire about his activities. Likewise, carnival, fair, and road-type fortunetellers are highly mobile. These fortune-

---

[7] Illegitimate means refers to those prescribed by the existing mores.

[8] Emile Durkheim, *Suicide,* trans. by J. A. Spaulding and George Simpson (Glencoe, Ill., Free Press, 1951), pp. 247–57.

[9] Robert K. Merton, *Social Theory and Social Structure* (Glencoe, Ill., Free Press, 1957), Chs. 4 and 5.

tellers usually gear their patter to revelation of the customer's entire life span. They plan to read for the customer only one time for the highest possible fee and to read for as many customers as possible within a limited time period. The gypsy fortuneteller also fits this pattern.

A third form of fortunetelling is practiced by ethnic group members. Generally these fortunetellers have strong outgroup consciousness, plan to see their customers only one time, and use gimmicks and trickery in their readings. In some cases they may actually be fronts for prostitution. These "one shot"[10] ethnic group operators may be gypsies or "rag heads." "Rag heads" is a derogatory term used by "white readers" to refer to dark-skinned people who drift into the lower-class neighborhoods of town and set up a fortunetelling business.

Finally, there are those fortunetellers who seek to read for an established clientele. These fortunetellers take the protective position of offering a satisfaction-or-money-back guarantee to their customers, thus minimizing legal entanglements. The economic well-being of these readers is dependent on their weekly return of customers. The customers are told that they must return weekly to attain relief from their many problems. These fortunetellers desire to be "established" members of a local community. Caucasians are referred to as "white readers," while Negroids are known as "fortunetellers." Since it is the Caucasian fortuneteller who is engaged in a deviant occupation, he is the main concern of the present discussion.

Over a lifetime an individual fortuneteller may practice fortunetelling in several forms—as a night club entertainer, a highly mobile "big score" operator, an ethnic group member, or an established member of a local community.

Why do people seek out fortunetellers? When needs are unfulfilled through expected channels in society, some people (often those in powerless minority groups) will turn to fortunetellers. Their unfulfilled needs are communicated to the fortuneteller for his help through natural or supernatural means. Examples are customers who experience poor health for undiagnosed or undiagnosable reasons, those involved in tumultuous romantic entanglements, or those undergoing unexplained economic reversals. To the troubled ones, the fortuneteller offers consolation. For the "true believer," the white reader may offer emotional support. Some clients seek out the fortuneteller as an anonymous confidant.[11] Often the young seek her out as

---

[10] "One shot" operators refers to those fortunetellers who expect to read for a customer only one time.

[11] When an attractive middle-aged woman discovered the sexual indiscretions of her politically well-known husband, she traveled to a nearby city and confided her unhappiness to a fortuneteller. The function performed by the fortunteteller for the customer remind the researcher of the relation between community members and the

a source of adventure and excitement. Some look to the fortuneteller as a source for knowledge about the unknown. For these latter customers, the fortuneteller serves to alleviate anxieties. In general, when other sources of help fail, the troubled seek help from those who profess to provide it.

SOCIAL RELATIONSHIPS

The white reader is busy with his clients from early morning until late night. His office is constantly filled with 38s. There seems to be little time to spend with family and friends. However, since money is a major motivation for this occupational activity and since having many customers represents receiving a great deal of money, the fortuneteller does not complain about his busy day. Usually this is the only way the reader has learned to make money, and since he has learned to enjoy spending what he makes, he cannot take time off for other activities. If he must be away from the office for a few days, a household servant or family member may meet with his customers and collect the prearranged fee for continued considerations by the fortuneteller. During their first encounter, the fortuneteller assesses the customer's problems and sets a fee of $100 or more to alleviate the "38" of his worries. This prearranged fee is usually based on "what the traffic will bear." The original fee is paid in weekly installments, and if counselling is continued, a new prearranged fee is established. On occasion a transient customer will enter, and a fee of $5 or $10 will be charged.

Within the extended family those who have not been so economically successful as the reader may seek to secure money, clothing, and vacations by virtue of their relationship with the fortuneteller. Yet those family members who have attained financial success outside the deviant occupation may show less inteerst in maintaining the family relationship.

Generally friendships between the customer and the white reader are not desired by the latter for he feels that his black or poor white customers who have failed financially are of lower social standing. He may also feel that the 38 is not so intelligent as he is. However, during World War II, when money was plentiful and uncertainty a part of daily life, army officers, their wives, and political officeholders visited fortunetellers, and readers sought to borrow prestige from their association with these high-status customers. During this period readers frequently opened offices in the city,

---

stranger in Georg Simmel, *The Sociology of Georg Simmel,* trans., edited, and with an introduction by Kurt L. Wolff (New York, Free Press, 1964), p. 404. "... he [the stranger] often receives the most surprising openness—confidences which sometimes have the character of a confessional and which would be carefully withheld from a more closely related person."

but after the war offices were moved into the home, and poor blacks and whites became the typical customers.

Likewise, friendships are not sought in the neighborhood where the fortuneteller lives and works, since he views his blue-collar neighbors as a threat to his striving for higher social status. The white reader does seek to interact with other economically successful white readers, however. In times of sickness and death, long distance calls and visits are exchanged between the families of fortunetellers. Often when stopping in a strange city, the visiting fortuneteller wlll call on the local fortuneteller.[12] Knowledge of readers in other cities may be brought to the fortuneteller through their mutual customers. Exchanges of letters and cards also keep them in touch with one another.

Fortunetellers avidly seek social contacts with various professionals, church members, and politicians. They hope for a "halo" effect with a concomitant status gain from these societal members with higher social standing. They might invite their veterinarian, their lawyer, their doctor, and their dentist to a birthday celebration. The food will be lavish and elegantly served. The professionals will be present. But return invitations are rare.

By donating large sums of money or performing unusual services for a church, fortunetellers and their families may expect full church acceptance. In fact, the fortuneteller may find himself on the finance committee as a result of his generosity. Likewise, his wife may be included in all the church activities.

Usually relationships between politicians and fortunetellers are solely one of economic exchange. A local politician may cultivate the friendship of the fortuneteller and request that the reader secure votes for him in exchange for his obtaining political favors for the reader. Often through their wealth, fortunetellers are able to support selected political leaders. During the politician's term in office, the relationship may offer the fortuneteller a status boost. If, however, the incumbent loses an election, the fortuneteller may experience a downward shift in status.

The fortuneteller may seek counsel of an attorney to ensure his avoidance of legal entanglements. He may also cultivate the friendship of a doctor to whom he can refer patients who need more than "spiritual" treatments.[13]

Fortunetellers may endeavor to improve their social standing in the

---

[12] Similarly Polly Adler, the well-known madame, recounts visiting madames when she traveled to cities throughout the United States. *A House Is Not a Home* (New York, Rinehart, 1953).

[13] One fortuneteller recounts his important role in syphilis control in his early career. He reports his vigilance in sending obviously infirm customers to a local doctor for treatment.

community by giving elaborate parties, joining lodges,[14] sending their children to respected private schools, securing church positions for themselves and their families, and by engaging in expensive recreational pursuits, for example, purchasing and displaying the largest boats at resort areas. One fortuneteller, seeking to borrow status from her social contacts, reported that she had become acquainted with Dorothy Kilgallen and other celebrities by appearing on the television program "What's My Line?"

Fortunetelling represents a case of achieved success not leading to higher future aspirations. Merit in the occupation is judged by economic success. When the summit is reached, the highest point in the career in the way of prestige has been reached. To receive higher status, the fortuneteller must leave this work. Usually past educational limitations prevent realistic hopes for higher occupational aspirations outside the chosen field.

Without doubt, a status hierarchy exists among fortunetellers. Those who have succeeded financially without being recognized as causing undue hardships to others are seen as having the highest status. They are usually the ones who are established members of local communities. The place in the status hierarchy of the fortuneteller who works in night clubs is related to the differential prestige awarded individual clubs. Those who read in high-prestige clubs rank higher in the status hierarchy than do those who work in low-prestige clubs. Mobile fortunetellers—the gypsy, big score operator, carnival, fair and road types, ragheads, and other ethnic group practitioners—are generally considered as having the lowest status. Among other societal members, fortunetellers are generally looked up to by those who are less well off financially and by those whose educational attainment is limited.

ENTERING THE OCCUPATION

People of all ages, both sexes, many religious backgrounds, and all races enter fortunetelling. Usually they are born into low-income families and find channels blocked to alternate occupations in which monetary rewards are adequate for their projected goals. Fortunetelling offers "opportunities for status competition and achievement to those persons who might be socially

---

[14] Men in the past have felt that membership in the Masonic Lodge was important to their social status. Since many men in deviant occupations could not secure membership in Caucasian lodges, they joined Negro lodges. Thus, they obtained the insignia which they could proudly display on their lapels. However, for those who did not seek this channel to satisfy their desire for social acceptance, there were the less prestigious lodges, i.e., the Moose and the Oddfellows which were not as select as Masons in electing members.

inept to some degree or without appropriate resources to compete for status in other areas."[15] Furthermore, fortunetelling requires only a modest investment of money, while the symbolic rewards are great.[16]

In the past reaching young adulthood in the lower-middle class led to termination of schooling and immediate assumption of a supporting role in the family. A man might work in a mining camp or cook in an all-night diner. A young woman might take up factory or sales clerk work.

When a socializing agent for a lucrative occupation is proximal, the stage is set for ambitious young people to enter into a new way of life—the way of the fortuneteller. A family member or a friend might recruit the young person. In one case an uncle recruited one niece and four nephews. The niece and nephews married and recruited the help of their mates. In one marriage in which both husband and wife are fortunetellers, the wife had learned fortunetelling during a previous marriage. She married a gypsy boy and even though she was a "gorgio" (nongypsy), her beauty[17] and natural abilities led to a very close relationship between her mother-in-law and herself, during which the mother-in-law taught the young girl to tell fortunes. She was extremely successful, first with her mother-in-law and later alone in her own tent and office location. After her gypsy husband died, the young woman called on a male reader in a town where she was visiting; they formed a partnership in a very successful business and subsequently were married.

The recruiting agent may plan for the novice to work with him. Perhaps the novice may consider entering the occupation only until his financial situation improves. However, once involved in fortunetelling, the reader usually will not part with such a lucrative source of income. One fortuneteller told me of his novel plan to legally enfranchise his business. Already he is involved with one such franchise.

To become deeply involved in fortunetelling, one must resolve any qualms as to the ethics of the activity. The solution to the ethical question often lies in developing the concept that the fortuneteller is a member of the service professions—medicine, psychiatry, and psychology. Furthermore, a dynamic personality—even what some would identify as "gall"—is necessary for real success. To become an established member of the local community, he must decide to accept fortunetelling as a career and to give up big score techniques.

[15] Bailey, op. cit., p. 23.
[16] Ibid.
[17] This fortuneteller showed the writer clips from a movie newsreel depicting her selection by Rudolph Valentino as a beauty queen in Toledo, Ohio.

SOCIALIZATION

For the white reader, learning the language and culture of fortunetelling, including voice intonation, meaningful questioning, careful listening, ambiguously stated responses, broad generalizations, common-sense assumptions about human nature, and a memorized patter ensures monetary success. Many use the style of the "cold reader," which employs no physical aids, thereby avoiding materials that might be used as tangible court evidence when trouble with the law enforcement officials arises. A favorite formula for this technique is an exploratory opening, followed by a character analysis and a consideration of the main subjects of human interest—love and money, dangers and dreams, friends and enemies, health and illness. Added to this might be a hint of mystery and advice. Or as one white reader reports, "Into your reading you must inject mystery, color, glamor, encouragement and hope."[18]

Developing special skills in casing a client enhances the success of the fortuneteller. He learns by experience to detect characteristics and mannerisms of different types of people. In casing a client, the reader finds out somthing about the client by observing his dress, his personal grooming (fingernails, for example), his eyes, jewelry or the absence of jewelry, and any club insignias. Furthermore, he closely observes the client's physical and verbal reactions to his broad general statements. From his assessment of these factors, the reader proceeds to work with his client.

The principle of "calculated vagueness" and the "technique of fishing" are indispensable elements to the fortuneteller's practice. "Calculated vagueness" is based on the premise that the human mind retains that which interests him and discards that which does not interest him. The exploratory opening, consisting of a short spiel, presents the customer with more information than he could possibly remember. This deluge of ambiguous statements also helps the fortuneteller revive the customer's interest after an awkward mistake or when handling a tough customer. Leland, in *Gypsy Sorcery and Fortune Telling,* records common statements representing the "calculated vagueness" principle:

> "You have been three times in great danger of death." Pronounce this very impressively. Everybody, though it be a schoolboy, believes, or likes to believe, that he has encountered perils. This is infallible, or at least it takes in most people. If the subject can be induced to relate his hairbreadth escapes, you may foretell future perils.

[18] Robert Nelson, *Pages from a Medium's Notebook* (Columbus, Ohio, Nelson Enterprises, 1939), p. 18.

"You have had an enemy who has caused you great trouble. But he—or she—it is well not to specify which till you find out the sex—will ere long go too far, and his or her effort to injure you will recoil on him or her."...Or, "You have had enemies, but they are all destined to come to grief." Or, "You had an enemy but you outlived him."[19]

Likewise, in *Pages from a Medium's Notebook,* the fortuneteller presents examples of typical patter showing "calculated vagueness":

"M[y] friend, I see that you come to me with a troubled mind—there are certain problems before you on which you seek counsel and a solution, and I am glad that you DID come to see me, for I feel that I can help you just as I have helped so many others."
There, I got off the first blast. Already, I have told the client something that was in her mind. I talk rapidly, so as not to allow her time to mentally digest what I have said.
"You strike me as a person who is not entirely satisfied with present circumstances—one that is handicapped and held back by circumstances beyond your control. You don't know which way to turn—you decide upon one course, then other factors pull at you, and you reverse your decision. You don't know just what to do...."
"There is another person—one you regard as a close friend, but at times your suspicions have been aroused. Secretly you wonder if this person is a true friend, or one who wishes you harm. I can see that there is reason for such suspicions...."[20]

The "technique of fishing" involves an ability on the part of the fortuneteller to lead his customer into unconscious admissions about his thoughts and behavior. Once this information is revealed, the fortuneteller merely repeats it to the customer in slightly different words. Meanwhile, the customer would swear that he has said nothing to the fortuneteller.[21]

Material objects such as spiritual symbols are often used in an effort to convince the customer of the fortuneteller's relationship to the supernatural. Religious statues and pictures of Christ and Mary are displayed in some offices; "holy water" is sometimes sprinkled upon the customer as he leaves the office. Other material objects were hidden radio equipment and concealed lights and chemical compounds. Mysterious talking parrots and other birds were also often a part of the culture surrounding this occupational group.

[19] Leland, op. cit., p. 182.
[20] Nelson, op. cit., pp. 22–24.
[21] W. L. Greshan, "Fortune Tellers Never Starve," *Coronet,* Vol. 27 (February 1950), p. 170.

In learning work roles the white reader understands the vital importance of advertising. He advertises on select radio stations, passes out handbills in his office and has them delivered door to door, and has classified advertisements printed in the newspapers. At Christmas and on his clients' birthdays he sends them greeting cards.

From his activities and his assessment of other's evaluation of them, the fortuneteller develops his self-concept of himself as one engaged in a deviant occupation. In working out his self-concept, the white reader is acutely aware of illegitimate activities by presumably law-abiding citizens. He develops an elaborate set of justifications and rationalizations to cope with his awareness of a negative public opinion and unfavorable public image of his occupation.

CAREER PATTERNS

There is no age limit on recruiting fortunetellers. The younger ones are more daring, more likely to concentrate on big-score reading. They are willing to go to "college" (jail) in an effort to "make a score"—to make a lot of money fast. One such effort at a big score involved several fortunetellers. The male reader worked out an elaborate plan whereby his wife was the "maid" in a wealthy widow's home. He scheduled a "spiritual" wedding with the widow and proceeded to relieve this older woman of a large sum of money. However, this situation not only led to friction in the marriage between the fortuneteller and his wife, but also led to a trip to "college" for the fortuneteller.

Generally speaking, the older reader desires security and a stable community-service image. He is willing to forego the score in order to have a regular sum of money coming in weekly. He has become settled in the community and does not want to be troubled by law enforcement officials. He wants his customers to be content so that they will not involve him in costly and bothersome legal entanglements. He has become "class conscious" and desires to associate with the "better members of the community."

The monetary rewards for the successful white reader are practically limitless. However, he must not gain material rewards too rapidly, because the legal forces in the community take a dim view of this practice. With his money the reader engages in conspicuous consumption. This consumption may include purchasing large completely equipped automobiles, expensive boats, fancy vacation homes, furs and fine clothing, jewels and precious metals. One wonders in the present changing society just how meaningful this pattern of conspicuous consumption will continue to be. Also, with the current rate of theft and murder, how safe is one who displays these items? It may be that the fortuneteller will have to find another means of expressing his economic success and make a different adjustment to his attempt to gain status.

After a person becomes involved in fortunetelling, other deviant behavior emerges. In the process of securing a license, bribes may be paid to local aldermen. Or the fortuneteller may declare himself to be a spiritualist minister in order to avoid the problem of licensing.

Strains are placed on the lives of the other family members when some in the family choose this occupational activity. For some family members the generous fortuneteller may open doors to technical and trade schools. However, for the child who might hope for upward social mobility, fortunetelling parents present few important socializing influences and few valuable professional contacts for his later life. Likewise, a home in which the fortunetelling business is an integral part may not be the kind of home to which he would wish to bring his school colleagues. Life may be lonely for the offspring in this type of environment.

Fortunetelling parents may be ambivalent about the career plans for their child. They may hope that with the "sacrifices" they have made to send the child to the best schools, he will become a famous surgeon or trial lawyer from whom they can borrow prestige. However, if he fails in these endeavors, they may demand that he become a reader so that he can have a type of economic security denied all but very few in American society. The young person, however, after being so well educated, may be reluctant to agree with his parents' desires concerning his future. These are just a few consequences of the status inconsistency inherent in this occupation.

WORK PLACE

As the form of fortunetelling varies, the work place may vary also. Mobile offices such as the fair tent or trailer are common. The mobile trailer provides the reader with a quick way to exit a location after a big score. In the past when big county fairs were the most important yearly event in the county, the tent of the fortuneteller may have represented the finest home in the area. Oriental rugs were placed on quickly-laid wooden floors assembled by the roughnecks, and trunks of fine china and sterling silver allowed the fortuneteller to eat her meals with elegance equalled by few customers. However, today this type of life has largely given way to the office in the home such as that of Madame Marian. If the husband and wife do not work together in this occupation and if the husband is the primary reader, he may choose to set up an office away from home, perhaps in the downtown area. This office may be elaborate, with a receptionist, one-way glass, rigged sign-in equipment, and two-way mirrors and radios; or the office may simply be a neat place with a desk and chairs and a separate waiting room.

SOCIAL CHANGE EFFECTS ON FORTUNETELLERS

With the lessening of the importance of the big local fair for the community, many fortunetellers abandoned the mobile fortunetelling booths and moved into houses in a town they liked. There urbanization and the depression were boons to the business. Urbanization brought in many people who could not cope with their new environment; they looked to the fortuneteller for help. During the depression, when many people were concerned about their future and insecure in their financial status, the demand for fortunetellers became even greater. Furthermore, the depression engendered an overall feeling of helplessness and hopelessness which encouraged the seeking of advice and comfort from the fortuneteller.

During World War II military and political leaders confronted with uncertainty sought help from readers. However, as the educational level of a society moves upward and as rational, secular, and cosmopolitan philosophies of life become more important, fewer people seek the help of the "poor man's psychologist." Finally, as children look more and more outside their homes for occupational role models, recruiting for this occupation may become more and more difficult. Thus, as the economic, political and social conditions in the country continue to change, the position of the fortuneteller in the society will likewise continue to change.

15. Medical Quackery as Deviant Behavior

JULIAN B. ROEBUCK

and

ROBERT BRUCE HUNTER

Quackery in the area of health care is a recognized form of deviant behavior in the United States, although there is no full agreement about what it constitutes. Because of the number of definitions and formal groups involved, a clear conceptual definition of medical quackery is unavailable. It follows that a corresponding theoretical frame of reference underlying quackery remains uncrystalized. Perhaps a typology of medical quackery is required along with corresponding theoretical frames of reference. In short the phenomena included within the concept of medical quackery appear too amorphous and diverse for the development of any general theory. Efforts pointing toward the development of middle-range theory are demanded.

This paper, on the basis of a review of the literature,[1] attempts the following: (1) to conceptualize an operational definition of several forms of medical quackery, i.e., to ascertain and refine the definition or definitions of medical quackery that are utilized by various formal social groups in their labeling and sanctioning procedures; (2) to evolve an empirical typology of deviant practices within the broader field of medical quackery, i.e., to ascertain boundaries delimiting qualitative differences among several orders of quackery. These two steps are prerequisite to the development of any hypothetical frame of reference for the study of medical quackery as a form of deviant behavior.

"Medical Quackery as Deviant Behavior," by Julien B. Roebuck and Robert Bruce Hunter is reprinted from *Criminology* Volume 8, No. 1 (May 1970) pp. 46–62 by permission of the publisher, Sage Publications, Inc.

[1] The review of the literature included medical historical works (e.g., Young, 1967), works by M.D.s (e.g., Cramp, n.d.), collections of medical sociological works (e.g., Jaco, 1958), authoritative popular works (e.g., Cook, 1958), articles from medical, scientific and health journals. Government, health association, and AMA reports, studies, and pamphlets were also utilized.

DETERMINANTS OF DEVIANT BEHAVIOR

Students of deviant behavior stress the importance of the labeling and sanctioning processes and social roles in determining who or what is deviant. The deviant is one to whom that label has successfully been applied; deviant behavior is behavior that people so label (see Becker, 1963:9). Formal social rules in our complex society are the creation of specific social groups. It is often the task of specialized formal bodies, e.g., administrative agencies, licensing bodies, the courts, professional associations, and the like to make and enforce rules. The labeling and sanctioning procedures of such formal bodies in the area of health care is our point of departure.

A review of the literature reveals five formal, rule-making, labeling, and sanctioning bodies within the broad area of medical quackery: (1) The American Medical Association, (2) federal agencies, (3) the scientific establishment,[2] (4) commercial associations,[3] and (5) state agencies. The activities of these five labeling and sanctioning bodies are primarily concerned with (1) spurious nostrums, (2) spurious devices, and (3) spurious treatments. This paper deals exclusively with practices related to these three forms of medical deviancy. We define these practices as deviant behavior within the broader area of medical quackery—they may or may not be illegal. Spurious nostrums are worthless, misrepresented, or harmful products purporting curative or alleviating properties, e.g., "Hadicol." Spurious devices are worthless, harmful, or defective machines or implements purporting to diagnose or treat disease, e.g., "Sonus-Film-O-Sonic" treatments for cancer and arteriosclerosis (see American Medical Association, 1968:11). Spurious treatments are based on medical and scientific systems of thought contrary to those accepted by the AMA or other affiliates of the recognized medical and scientific establishments.

The five formal groups operate at different labeling and sanctioning levels. Moreover, each is active in areas within the field of medical quackery. Degrees of agreement and disagreement exist among them, and these bodies rarely apply any common definitions of deviant practices. Many groups and individuals throughout the social structure are often unaware of the deviant labels imposed by these bodies. Some of these individuals and groups, even when aware of the deviant label, may reject the label and/or the affixed sanction. There are voluminous examples of deviant practices related to nos-

---

[2] The scientific establishment consists of general scientific publications, e.g., *Science, Scientific American,* and the like, and the specific publications of private health associations, e.g., the American Cancer Society, the Arthritis and Rheumatism Foundation.

[3] The commercial associations are represented by the National Better Business Bureau, a national organization with local offices in many major cities of the United States.

trums, devices, and treatments. These examples fall within the confines of three behavior models: practices related to the purveyance of fraudulent or misrepresented nostrums and devices, illegal and/or unorthodox health care practices by licensed healers, and unorthodox practices by medical doctors These three behavior models comprise the typology.

FRAUDULENT NOSTRUMS AND DEVICES

The sale of fraudulent or misrepresented nostrums and devices occurs frequently in four fields: (a) nostrums for incurable diseases, (b) general panacea-type or "pep-you-up" types of nostrums, (c) nutritional supplements and diet pills, (d) bogus healing and diagnostic devices.

Persons suffering from chronic, painful diseases, e.g., arthritis, or terminal diseases, e.g., cancer, prove lucrative targets for peddlers of dubious nostrums and devices. Frequently these products are advertised via the mass media and given an aura of respectability. Testimonials by famous people, projected medical and scientific images that are associated with spurious products, and mock experimental techniques are all used to entice straw-grasping sufferers of painful and/or incurable diseases.

ARTHRITIS "CURES"

Many sales of fraudulent cures for arthritis are buried in the sales records of multi-purpose drugs and remedies of small but numerous manufacturers that never receive national attention. There are approximately eleven million arthritics in the United States who have at least twelve hundred nostrums and devices available to them (see Walred, 1960:123–33). A survey made by the Arthritis and Rheumatism Foundation found that 79 percent of these arthritics regularly use one of the following: heat devices, analgesics other than aspirin, vibrators, special diets (Walred, 1960:68). Arthritis sufferers in the United States paid an estimated 425 million dollars in 1960 for these drugs and devices, and another 10 million dollars in fees for fraudulent and misrepresented treatments (Walred, 1960:67).

A recent example of a cancer nostrum is "Collodaurum," a colloidal solution of metalic gold in pure water, manufactured and distributed by the Kehlenberg Laboratory in Sarasota, Florida, under the direction of H. H. Kehlenberg. The report of the AMA Council of Pharmacy and Chemistry concluded that Collodaurum is worthless in the treatment of cancer. The FDA took action against Collodaurum in 1963 in Florida and won the case by "default and destruction" in 1965 (Walred, 1960:90).

The American Cancer Society, Inc. is the most active body in combating cancer quackery. It publishes a journal, *CA-A Journal of Cancer for Clinicians,* that includes current listings of spurious cancer cures.

"HADICOL" AND PINKHAM'S PRODUCTS

The most colorful medicine man of recent vintage is Dudly J. LeBlanc, a former Louisiana state senator, whose product, Hadicol, became a best seller and a household word. Hadicol consists of twelve percent alcohol, some B-complex vitamins, iron, calcium, phosphorous, diluted hydrochloric acid, and honey (see Young, 1967:317). Originally, LeBlanc claimed that Hadicol was an energizing tonic that had a therapeutic effect on most human ailments. During 1950 he grossed at least twenty million dollars within a sales area of twenty-two states. The FDA forced LeBlanc to stringently modify his advertising claims regarding Hadicol's therapeutic value e.g., removal of the claim that Hadicol cured asthma and cancer (Young, 1967:321). Additionally, the FDA forced LeBlanc to modify the advertising claims listed on the label of his product.

Lydia E. Pinkham's vegetable compound and its sister product, Lydia Pinkham's tablets, are good examples of nostrums that endure despite the FDA's proof of false advertising. Originally, Lydia Pinkham's compounds and tablets were advertised and sold as panaceas for all women's "female problems" and as general energy boosters. After passage of the 1906 "Pure Food, Drug, and Cosmetic Act," all curative advertising claims were dropped. The FDA forced six modifications in the advertising claims of these two products between 1920 and 1950. Lydia Pinkham's products are still on the market. Current advertising claims maintain that they relieve hot flashes and other symptoms associated with change of life, cramps, and monthly period distress. The Bureau of Investigation of the AMA has found all of these claims to be false (see Cook, 1958:87).

NUTRITIONAL AIDS AND DIET PILLS

The American Medical Association reports that phony nutritionists operate on the basis of four false claims: (1) Americans do not eat a balanced diet, (2) foods lose their nutritional value when processed, (3) the soil in the United States no longer is able to produce nutritional foods because of its saturation with chemical fertilizers, (4) foods are poisoned and lose their nutritional value because of the sprays and insecticides used on them (American Medical Association, 1967:12–13).

The AMA's (1967:12–13) booklet, "Facts on Quacks," states that nutritional loss in food processing is replenished through enrichment processes, that U.S. soil is adequately fertilized and does not suffer from nutritive depletion, and that malnutrition is not widespread in the United States. The point that foods are poisoned by sprays and insecticides is debatable.

Many drug companies advertise the necessity for the intake of multiple vitamins as a supplement to the deficient American diet. The AMA claims that multiple vitamins are potentially dangerous and are not acceptable substitutes for a well-balanced diet (Cook, 1958:72–73). Women are exceptionally vulnerable to nutritional advertising. One of the most commonly used over-the-counter remedies by women is the diet pill. Diet pills are of dubious value and in some cases are dangerous to health. The manufacturers of reducing pills claim the use of their products insures the loss of several pounds in a short time without personal sacrifice. Reports by the AMA and the FDA state that it is unhealthy to lose weight rapidly and that it is also unhealthy to frequently fluctuate body weight (*Today's Health,* 1968:82).

An example of a worthless and potentially harmful reducing agent is the "Kelpidine Reducing Plan" that purportedly reduces weight at the rate of three to five pounds a week, while at the same time permitting the dieter to eat anything he desires in reduced amounts (Young, 1967:290). "Kelpidine," a product containing kelp (seaweed) and iodine, claims to promote weight reduction, providing the user restricts his diet to a caloric intake of 800 to 1200 calories a day. Supposedly kelp adds bulk to a low calorie diet and iodine acts as an antifat substance.

Joseph J. Pinkus, the manufacturer and marketer of Kelpidine, was confronted with a mail fraud order by the Post Office Department in 1945 for passing fraudulent materials through the United States mail. Government testimony disclosed that iodine was of no value in treating obesity and that kelp did not reduce hunger pangs by adding bulk to the diet. The daily diet recommended by Pinkus was termed too rigid, and the loss of more than three pounds a week was considered dangerous. Pinkus sued for an injunction to prevent the fraud order from taking effect and won in the District, Circuit, and U.S. Supreme Courts on a technicality. (His attorneys had not been allowed to cross-examine witnesses in the original Post Office hearings. See Young, 1967:291.)

BOGUS HEALING AND DIAGNOSTIC DEVICES

Bogus healing and diagnostic devices vary from machines that supposedly cure arthritis to devices claiming to diagnose ailments at long range via electronic waves. Although bogus healing devices have a long history, the age of electronics ushered in a new era in device quackery. Electricity puzzles many people, and many uninformed attribute to it wonder-making properties.

One of the first and most important phony machinists was Dr. Abrams, M.D., who crossed from orthodox practice of medicine to the unorthodox (see Kaplan, 1968:70–72). He developed the idea that electrons vibrate at a different speed for each different disease. Abrams invented the Oscilloclast to measure electronic reactions (ERA). He claimed he could determine a person's age, sex, personality traits (and diagnose their ailments) by feeding either a drop of a person's blood or a sample of their hand writing into the

Oscilloclast. The AMA estimates that at least fifty imitations of the Oscilloclast were inspired by Abrams financial success (see Smith, 1968:46).

Another device used in bogus treatments was the Sonus-Film-O-Sonic that operated by attaching moistened, wire-connected pads to the body. Ear phones were then attached to transmit controlled audible energy to treat and soothe the patient. When the Sonus-Film-O-Sonic was taken apart by FDA inspectors, it was found that the machine emitted a useless low hum and contained a recording device that played "Holiday for Strings" to cure arteriosclerosis and "Smoke Gets in Your Eyes" to cure cancer (American Medical Association, 1968:12).

For several reasons, purveying fraudulent or misrepresented nostrums and devices is fairly safe from legal prosecution. Numerous nostrums and OTC remedies are sold, all of which have to be eventually tested by the FDA for safety, effectiveness, and truthfulness in advertising. Cease and desist orders are used short of criminal action. When criminal action is required the FDA turns the case over to the Department of Justice for prosecution. Cataloging and keeping accurate records on thousands of nostrums and "challenged devices" is a costly and time-consuming process. Gathering evidence for hearings and court cases also takes time. Actual court cases instigated by the FDA sometimes last for two to three years. The Post Office Department's power in this area is limited to surveillance of the mails.

ILLEGAL AND UNORTHODOX PRACTICES BY LICENSED HEALERS

Practices within this classification are based on a system of medical and scientific thought that is unacceptable to the scientific and medical communities. These unorthodox practices must be legally licensed by the state.

The diversity of opinion about the acceptance of unorthodox healing practices is best exemplified by the treatment given the two major unorthodox cults in the United States today: the osteopathic and the chiropractic. Although both are legal in most states the AMA refuses to grant either recognition as legitimate healing groups (see Rayack, 1967:109).

OSTEOPATHY

According to the AMA, if an osteopath practices osteopathy, he practices a cult system of healing, and voluntary professional associations with him are unethical. If he bases his practice on the same scientific principle as those adhered to by members of the American Medical Association, voluntary professional relationships with him should not be deemed unethical (see *Journal of the American Medical Association*, 1961:774–76). A former president of the American Osteopathic Association said that the only difference between osteopaths and medical doctors is that some osteopaths still believe in manipulative healing along with the use of drugs and surgery (see Mills, 1960:24). An osteopath is considered deviant or nondeviant by the medical profession on two bases: (1) Does he openly express a belief in manipulation as a treatment method? (2) Does he actually utilize manipulation as a treatment method?

Osteopathic education requirements are higher and their medical education is generally superior to that of the other unorthodox cults. Moreover osteopathy in principle and practice is swinging toward the AMA and the scientific establishment (Rayack, 1967:253).

Many other unorthodox healing cults are unwilling to change the direction of their practices toward the AMA point of view. The homeopathic, the naturopathic, and the chiropractic cults have steadfastly refused to compromise.

THE CHIROPRACTOR

Chiropractors constitute the largest cult in the United States (14,360 listed in the 1960 census). Chiropractors not only refuse to compromise their beliefs and practices in line with those of the AMA, but they consider chiropractory superior to orthodox medical practices (see Wardwell, 1963:216‒17). The chief source of friction between the chiropractors and the medical doctors is the claim of the chiropractors that they can cure any disease by manipulating the spine, without the benefit of surgery or drugs. According to the AMA, the chiropractors have denied all the medical breakthroughs and stuck to their hardline that only manipulating the subluxations of the spine will improve health. Some chiropractors do, however, use machines, enemas, and certain forms of psychotherapy. These "mixers" belong to the American Chiropractic Association that broke away from the parent International Chiropractors Association.

Chiropractors require only four years education. None of the eighteen schools accredited by the two chiropractic associations are accredited by recognized accrediting bodies. Further, of the 267 catalogue-listed faculty members of chiropractic colleges, 141 do not have recognized four-year degrees. Of the 126 who claim four-year degrees, 23 were not confirmed by their colleges (see American Medical Association, 1968:2–11).

Many unorthodox healers remain within the law but at the same time engage in behavior that would be considered deviant by orthodox healers. James Parker, a chiropractor, owns a chain of eighteen chiropractic clinics in Texas. He holds six practice-building seminars yearly under the auspices of his Parker School of Professional Success. At these well-attended seminars (6,000 at one in Ft. Worth), Mr. Parker instructs in the art of money making. In Mr. Parker's words, "at these sessions I intend to teach you all the gimmicks, gadgets and gizmos that can be used to get new patients." According to Parker, "enthusiasm is the yeast that raises the dough." He advocates a six-step method to success: (1) treat only chronics and not acutes, (2) frighten people away from scientific medicine by saying that it treats only the symptoms and that you treat the causes, (3) place a *Bible* in the reception room to instill confidence and build image, (4) lather love lavishly to make the patient feel well treated, (5) lure the patient in with a free first consultation, and (6) always check the phone book or city map to determine the patient's income-status area (American Medical Association, 1968b).

Unorthodox healing practices are tolerated by the legal structure until the legal limits of the cult are breached. Probably the best recent example of an unorthodox practitioner who overstepped the legal limits of his cult is Dr. Marvin Phillips, a chiropractor who was found guilty of the murder of eight-year-old Linda Epping in California (see *New York Times,* 1963:33). Linda's parents became concerned about a lump behind her eye and took her to the UCLA Medical Center where her illness was diagnosed as cancer. Surgery was advised. Dr. Phillips persuaded the parents to remove her from the medical center and place her under his care. He charged $500 in advance plus $239 for medicines. After three weeks of laxatives, enemas, and 124 pills a day, Linda's parents saw the tumor was much larger and discharged Dr. Phillips. Linda died four months later, and subsequently murder charges were filed on the basis that Phillips had misrepresented his healing capabilities and that he had contributed to the death of a patient by practicing medicine illegally. Dr. Phillips was found guilty of second-degree murder, but was later freed by the state Supreme Court on a legal technicality. The County Deputy Attorney retried the case and secured another conviction for second-degree murder. Another appeal is now pending (see Miner, 1968).

Cease-and-desist orders issued by the various state licensing agencies constitute the most frequently used control measures for illegal practices by licensed healers. A list of cease-and-desist orders released by the California Department of Public Health reveals that eight were issued to legal healers between December 26, 1961, and August 31, 1963. The report includes two chiropractors, one osteopath, three osteopath M.D.s and two medical doctors (see U.S. Senate, 1964:73).

Probably the most complete study of offenders charged in the court with some form of medical quackery comes from California. The California Bureau of Food and Drug Inspections prosecuted 66 medical quacks in criminal court between 1947 and 1957 (U.S. Senate, 1964:26–28). In 42 cases defendants were charged with violations that included either the illegal sale of nostrums or the illegal sale of misrepresented devices. Diseases that these nostrums and treatment devices supposedly cured or alleviated included all the ills of mankind. Cancer, heart disease, and arthritis were the most frequently listed diseases. Criminal charges brought against the 66 defendants included the sale of adulterated and misbranded drugs, false advertising, practicing medicine without a license, conspiracy to violate health and safety codes, operating a clinic without a license, grand theft, and petty theft. Fifty-nine of 66 defendants were convicted as charged; 4 were dismissed, and 3 were found not guilty. Of the 59 found guilty, 26 received fines ranging from $25 to $5,000 (median fine $200) ; 15 received fines and sentences (in all 15 cases, sentences were suspended) ; 13 received jail sentences (4 of these served time, the other 9 received suspended sentences or probation). Five other defendants who actually served time were sentenced accordingly: 1 was sentenced to 1 year on a road camp, 2 received 6 months in the county jail, and 1 received 360 days in the county jail.

Of the 66 defendants in this California study (1948–57), 13 were unorthodox healers (12 chiropractors, and 1 osteopath). Ten of the 13 were found guilty; 2 had their cases dismissed before sentencing, 1 was found not guilty. Of the 9 convicted, one received a cease-and-desist order, 4 received fines, 1 was sentenced, and 3 received a combination of fine and sentence.

The California study indicates, at least for the 66 under study, the extreme leniency of the courts toward medical quackery. Only 4 who were found guilty served time. Thirty-seven convicted offenders were fined.

The 13 unorthodox healers were dealt with more leniently than the rest of the group. Their mean fine was $150 less than the fine of all other offenders.

UNORTHODOX PRACTICES BY MEDICAL DOCTORS

Practices in this category include the utilization of M.D.s of fraudulent, harmful, or misrepresented nostrums and/or devices or treatments. The M.D. who engages in unorthodox practices is not only subject to administrative and legal sanctions but also to sanctions by the AMA. Since M.D.s enjoy greater prestige in the area of health care than any other group, they stand to lose more by unorthodox practices than any other group of violators.

The aforementioned Dr. Abrams represents a licensed physician who employed a phony machine to make money in the practice of medicine (American Medical Association, 1968a:5). Abrams was finally exposed when a doctor from Michigan sent him a drop of chicken blood to diagnose. Abrams returned a diagnosis of diabetes, malaria, cancer, and syphilis. After this incident, Abrams was challenged by a California doctor to test his machine under clinical conditions. Abrams refused, claiming that the medical profession had organized against him and was suppressing his practice. The *Scientific American* magazine investigated Abrams' machine and concluded that "at least it is an illusion, at worst it is a colossal fraud" (see Kaplan, 1968:72–73).

A recent example of an M.D. who utilized a harmful nostrum is Dr. Robert Liefmann, a Canadian physician (see Smith, 1963:83). He manufactured "Liefcort," a dangerous combination of hydrocortisone and female hormones, for the treatment of arthritis. Some Americans have reportedly died as a result of this treatment. The manufacture or importation of Liefcort is illegal in the United States.

Our final example illustrates the controversial nature of deviant practices by M.D.s. Dr. Steven Durovic, M.D., a Yugoslavian physician, claims to have developed a drug, "Krebiozen," for the treatment of cancer; he brought it to the United States in 1949. Since mid-1959, a modification of this drug called L.D. (Lipopolysaccharide C.) has been prepared and studied by Dr. Andrew C. Ivy, M.D., professor emeritus of the University of Illinois. Drs. Durovic and Ivy established the Krebiozen Research Foundation in Chicago, Illinois and have furnished Krebiozen to physicians who requested it for investigational use (see CA-A *Journal of Cancer for Clinicians*, 1966:62).

In September 1961, the Krebiozen Foundation gave the National Cancer Institute a sample of Krebiozen and an analysis of their data collected on 4,200 patients treated with Krebiozen. The NCI studied the data and asked for more detailed information. The Krebiozen Foundation then provided treatment files on 504 cases to the NCI. The NCI concluded that Krebiozen was an ineffective cure for cancer (CA-A *Journal of Cancer for Clinicians*, 1966:63). After a detailed study, the American Medical Association, on the basis of a study of 100 cancer cases treated with this drug, claimed that 98 had failed to improve (see Ridgeway, 1963:32).

In 1964 Drs. Durovic and Ivy were indicted on 49 counts for violation of the Food, Drug and Cosmetic Act, mail fraud, mislabeling, making false statements to the government, and conspiracy (see CA-A *Journal of Cancer for Clinicians*, 1966:64). The jury trial started in the U.S. District Court in Chicago, Illinois on April 29, 1965. On January 30, 1966, all defendants, including the Krebiozen Research Foundation, were found innocent. Krebiozen is still being distributed in Illinois but may not be shipped in interstate commerce. Dr. Ivy was forced to drop out of the AMA, which considers Krebiozen spurious. Proponents of Krebiozen and Drs. Ivy and Durovic have published favorable articles and one book on Krebiozen since 1963 (see CA-A *Journal of Cancer for Clinicians*, 1966:7 and Ridgeway, 1963:32).

There is prevalent in some quarters, the view that licensed M.D.s who engage in medical quackery are more immune to detection and punishment than other quacks. Dr. R. N. Grant, M.D., speaking to the U.S. Senate Sub-Committee in 1964, voiced this view. The AMA disavows jurisdiction over

M.D.s charged with quackery who do not belong to the AMA. The AMA holds that the state's licensing agencies assert that it is difficult to prosecute quack M.D.s because of the reluctance of M.D.s to testify against each other. State licensing agencies take the position that quack M.D.s should be prosecuted by the FDA. At least one FDA administrative official stated, "It is a painful problem and you wonder what is the proper solution for it" (see U.S. Senate, 1964:337).

SUMMARY

The health care norms of groups engaged in labeling and sanctioning deviant behavior in the field of health care and groups who receive health care are often at variance. The norms of subgroups within these two groups are also frequently at variance. False advertising of nostrums and devices is the most prevalent form of deviant practice in the area of medical quackery. The detection and control of medical quackery is weak. The suggested threefold empirical typology at a minimum delimits and defines specific areas of study within the amorphous field of medical quackery. These efforts mark the first endeavor in this direction. We are dealing with behavior similar to what H. Laurence Ross (1963:236–37) calls folk crime, e.g., traffic violations and white-collar crime. This subspecies of folk crime is characterized by light sanctions and social stigma. The stigma and sanctions generally result from a confusion of norms in this area. This conceptualization of folk crime may contribute to the development of a frame of reference essential to the explanation of medical quackery as a form of deviant behavior.

REFERENCES

American Medical Association (1968a) "Health quackery: devices." Chicago.
—— (1968b) "Health quackery: chiropractic." Chicago.
—— (1967) "Facts on quacks." Chicago.
Becker, H. S. (1963) *The Outsiders*. New York: Free Press.
CA-A *Journal of Cancer for Clinicians* (1966) "Unproven Methods of Cancer Treatment." New York: American Cancer Society.
Cook, J. (1958) *Remedies and Rackets*. New York: W. W. Norton.
Cramp, A. (n.d.) *Nostrums and Quackery and Pseudo Medicine*.
Dorman, G. D. (1968) "International Quackery." Speech to 4th National Congress on Health Quackery, Chicago, October 2–3.
Jaco, E. G. (1958) *Patients, Physicians and Illness*. New York: Free Press.
Journal of the American Medical Association (1961) "Osteopath: Special Report of the Judicial Council to the AMA House of Delegates." (September 16.)

Kaplan, J. (1968) "Dr. Abrams—Dean of Machine Quacks." *Today's Health* (April).

Mills, L. W. (1960) *Opportunities in Osteopathy.* New York: Vocational Guidance Manuals.

Miner, J. W. (1968) "Quackery and the Law." Speech to 4th National Congress on Quackery, Chicago, October 2–3.

New York Times (1963) "Murder through Fraud Case Stirs Dispute in California." (September 1).

Rayack, E. (1967) *Professional Power and American Medicine: The Economics of the American Medical Association.* New York: World Publishing.

Ridgeway, J. (1963) "AMA FDA and Quacks." *New Republic* (November 9).

Ross, H. L. (1963) "Traffic Law Violations: A Folk Crime." *Social Problems* 8 (Winter).

Smith, R. L. (1968) "The Incredible Drown Case." *Today's Health* (April).

—— (1963) "The Hucksters of Pain." *Saturday Evening Post* (August 24).

Today's Health (1968) "AMA FDA Rap Diet Pill Fad." (April).

U.S. Senate (1964) Special Committee on Aging, Frauds and Misrepresentations Affecting the Elderly. Hearings before Sub-Committee, 88th Congress, 2nd Session, Part 1, San Francisco, January 13. Washington, D.C.: U.S. Government Printing Office.

Walred, R. (1960) *The Misrepresentation of Arthritis Drugs and Devices in the United States.* New York: Arthritis and Rheumatism Foundation.

Wardwell, W. I. (1963) "Limited Marginal and Quasi-Practitioners," in H. E. Freeman et al. (eds.) *The Handbook of Medical Sociology,* Englewood Cliffs, N.J.: Prentice-Hall.

Young, J. H. (1967) *The Medical Messiahs.* Princeton: Princeton Univ. Press.

16. Stripping for a Living:
An Occupational Study of the Night Club Stripper

JACQUELINE BOLES

and

A. P. GARBIN

In this chapter stripping is viewed as part of an exchange process: An individual performs a cluster of activities in exchange for goods and services.[1] The stripper's principal occupational activities involve taking off her clothes in a suggestive fashion for financial remuneration.[2] Stripping as is performed in contemporary America is a comparatively recent type of entertainment. Although it evolved from traditional burlesque, stripping did not constitute a part of that entertainment form until the late 1920s. Fraught with a variety of internal and external difficulties, burlesque responded by employing younger and more attractive girls who needed jobs because of the depression.[3] Soon it became standard for burlesque theaters to have two chorus lines— one for dancing and another for stripping. By 1932 most of the female stars practiced "bearing the breast to the audience."[4] In some respects this was the culmination of a trend—from the "theater" to "sex, nudity, and girls"— which had started in burlesque more than one-half century earlier. However, toward the end of the 1930s, burlesque houses felt the wrath of censors, and

---

[1] Frederick L. Bates, *The Structure of Occupations, Monograph II* (Raleigh, N.C., Center for Occupational Education, 1969).

[2] Other terms attributed the same meaning as strippers include *exotics* and *stripteasers.* However, the term *stripper* is used consistently in this paper because the subjects who participated in the study generally used this label in reference to their occupational group. Such female entertainers as "go-go" girls, "topless" dancers, and "bottomless" dancers are not strippers; they do not remove any clothes during their performances.

[3] Bernard Soebel, *A Pictorial History of Burlesque* (New York, Bonanza Books, 1956).

[4] Irving Zeidman, *The American Burlesque Show* (New York, Hawthorne Books, 1967), p. 142.

many strippers moved from burlesque to night clubs or strip clubs, where a majority of this occupational group is presently employed.[5] This article is primarily a descriptive consideration of selected occupational and occupationally related behaviors of strippers employed in one type of work setting —the night club.[6]

We propose not only to further the understanding of a low-prestige occupation about which little data exist[7] but also to contribute to the comparative study of occupations. According to Everett C. Hughes:

> Perhaps there is as much to be learned about the high prestige occupations by applying to them the concepts which naturally come to mind for the study of people in the most lowly kinds of work as there is to be learned by applying to other occupations the conceptions developed in connection with the highly valued professions.[8]

This should especially apply for occupations which are "primarily concerned with the creation of art forms or with the provision of entertainment,

[5] There is considerable discrepancy in the estimates available on the number of strippers in the United States. The range extends from 2,000 (Ann Terry D'Andre, *An Occupational Study of the Strip-Dancer Career*. Paper read at Pacific Sociological Association meetings, Salt Lake City, Utah [April 1965]), to 7,000 (Libby Jones, *Striptease* [New York, Simon and Schuster, 1967]). Basing his opinion on the number of girls he handles and the number of agents in the country, one agent interviewed indicated there are about 4,000 strippers.

[6] The data for the study were collected over a three-year period in a large southeastern city. There were nine night clubs in the city at which strippers performed; a few of the clubs employed some of the best known features. The interview (containing both structured and semi-structured items) and participant observation are the basic data-gathering techniques. Each interview lasted between three and five hours; at least two time periods were necessary to complete each interview. The interviews were conducted in a variety of settings: dressing rooms, apartments, hotel rooms, "after-hours" clubs, and restaurants. Gaining entré into the occupation was facilitated by the senior author's husband who had been in showbusiness and a local newspaperman who "covered" the night clubs for his column.

[7] Recent research on strippers include Skipper and McCaghy's study of burlesque strippers on the Eastern Wheel, D'Andre's paper on night club and burlesque strippers, and Salutin's study of burlesque strippers in Canada. James K. Skipper, Jr. and Charles H. McCaghy, "Stripteasers: The Anatomy and Career Contingencies of a Deviant Occupation," unpublished, 1970; "Stripteasing: As Sex Oriented Occupation," in James Hensilin (ed.), *The Sociology of Sex* (New York, Appleton-Century-Crofts, 1970); "The Stripteaser," *Sexual Behavior*, Vol. 1 (1971), pp. 78–87; D'Andre, op. cit.; Marilyn Salutin, "Stripper Morality," *Transaction*, Vol. 8 (1971), pp. 12–22. There have also been a few popular books on strippers such as Libby Jones, *Striptease* (New York, Simon and Schuster, 1967) and Arthur H. Lewis, *Carnival* (New York, Trident, 1970). Lewis' book is of especial interest because it deals partly with "kootch broads" (i.e., girls who work in "girlie shows" or "kootch shows" at carnivals).

[8] Everett C. Hughes, *Men and Their Work* (Glencoe, Ill., Free Press, 1958), p. 49.

recreation, information, or aesthetic satisfaction for the public."[9] Along with stripping, the "aesthetic and entertainment situs" includes ballet dancers, professional musicians, and movie actresses. A paucity of empirical research exists on occupations belonging to the "aesthetics and entertainment situs,"[10] particularly in the entertainment sector.[11]

A cross-cultural survey of secondary sources suggests that professional entertainers often tend to be associated with deviance.[12] The relationship of the occupation of stripping to deviance is heightened by: (1) the ancillary roles many strippers are expected to perform (for example, "hustling" drinks [asking customers to buy them drinks]); (2) their association with other deviants (for example, prostitutes, pimps, and gamblers), both within the work setting and as members of the night people's subculture; and (3) the structure of the occupation itself, which is conducive to certain kinds of deviance such as lesbianism.[13] Consequently, this paper also contains information relative to an occupation situated within a legitimate and important occupation situs, but is ascribed either marginal legitimacy or recognized as deviant by a substantial proportion of the population including legal authorities.[14] The approach used in this article views occupational and occupation-

[9] Richard T. Morris and Raymond J. Murphy, "The Situs Dimension in Occupational Structure," *American Sociological Review*, Vol. 24 (1959), p. 233. Entertainment is part of what Morris and Murphy described as the occupational situs of "aesthetics and entertainment." A total of 10 situses were delineated by these authors. In essence, occupational situs represents a classification of occupations by societal function. The situs classification divides occupations into horizontal groups of theoretically equal status ranges that form occupational families in terms of primary work functions.

[10] In this chapter only the word *entertainment* is used to refer to this situs.

[11] Some of the research dealing with entertainment has been reported by Sidney Wilhelm and Gideon Sjoberg, "The Social Characteristics of Entertainers," *Social Forces*, Vol. 37 (1958), pp. 71–76; Robert A. Stebbins, "Class, Status, and Power among Jazz and Commercial Musicians," *Sociological Quarterly*, Vol. 7 (1966), pp. 197–213; Marcello Truzzi, "The Decline of the American Circus: The Shrinking of an Institution," in *Sociology in Everyday Life* (Englewood Cliffs, N.J., Prentice-Hall, 1968), pp. 314–22; and Howard S. Becker, *Outsiders: Studies in the Sociology of Deviance* (New York, Free Press, 1963).

[12] Jacqueline Boles, *The Night Club Stripper: A Sociological Study of an Occupation*. Unpublished Ph.D. dissertation, University of Georgia, Athens, 1971.

[13] For a discussion of lesbianism among strippers, see Skipper and McCaghy's selection in this book, Ch. 8.

[14] Skipper and McCaghy ("Stripteasing" and "The Stripteaser," op. cit.) report a sample of 75 college students held a negative stereotype of strippers, associating such words as *lower class, immoral,* and *prostitutes* with them. Additional evidence of the negative stereotype held toward strippers is furnished in another study (Boles, op. cit.). Using the semantic differential scale, 124 college students rated strippers as individuals and also stripping as an occupation. In general, the occupation was evaluated lower than the individuals within the occupations. The students characterized the occupation as "degrading," "useless," "unrewarding," "unattractive," "insecure," "boring," and "dirty." However, they did judge the occupation to be "vital,"

ally related behavior of the stripper as a process consisting of three basic dimensions: antecedants, social relations and an action process, and consequences. Data are presented that will acquaint the reader with some of the more important facets of these dimensions, including entrance into the occupation, socialization, satisfaction and dissatisfaction with work, and work-related reference-group orientations. Throughout this paper intraoccupational comparisons are made between two types of night club strippers: features and house girls. Features have "star-billing," work under contract for limited periods of time at a number of clubs and other work organizations, and travel from city to city. House girls are not under contract and work for only one club in the city where they live. Previous related research is also compared with the results of the present investigation.

WORK SETTING AND WORK ACTIVITY

At the time of the study, a night club or strip club was the place of employment for the 51 strippers—26 features and 25 house girls—who provided data for this paper. Night clubs cover an extremely wide range, extending from fairly exclusive supper clubs and hotels, with very adequate night club facilities, to establishments at the other extreme, which are commonly referred to as strip joints or toilets. A substantial majority (85 percent) of the strippers preferred the night club to other types of work settings (burlesque theatres, carnivals, and ship cruises) ; private parties were the least preferred. Features and house girls prefer clubs for different reasons. Features prefer nightclubs because of the greater opportunity they provide. They point to the fact the big clubs in Las Vegas are now using strippers. Secondly, they like the "better class of audience" that patronize certain clubs. House girls, on the other hand, prefer clubs primarily because of the better class of audience. They also like the "atmosphere" in the clubs, staying in one place, and the shorter hours. Both features and house girls dislike private parties (e.g., stag party or smoker) the most because of the customers who were generally described as "dirty old men." As one stripper expressed it, "I can get away with more if they're (customers) are young; I don't have to strip completely, but with old men I have to go all the way."

A comparison of night club status systems revealed the existence of basically similar status hierarchies. At a complex level of differentiation, the status hierarchy may be briefly enumerated as follows: (1) the manager or owner of the club; (2) the feature or the stripper who has star billing; (3)

"pleasurable," and "exciting." The students considered the strippers themselves to be "ambitious" and "liberal." Interestingly, they did not rate the strippers as "stupid" or "bad."

the band leader; (4) the co-feature; (5) the house girls and members of the band; (6) the master of ceremonies and other acts; (7) "go-go" girls, hatcheck girls, and hostesses; (8) bartenders; and (9) waitresses. Obviously, the status hierarchies of the smaller clubs deviate from the above description. However, this is a consequence of a less differentiated division of labor, rather than differences in the relative positional status levels.

The types and content of the stripper's work activities vary greatly, depending upon a multiplicity of factors. In general, the strippers' work roles can be performed in three spatial areas: the stage, the floor, and outside the club. The specific content of any given stripper's act depends upon such diverse factors as the size of the club and stage, the city in which the club is located, and the number of performers composing the show. For example, many of the girls—especially the features—specialize in acrobatics or tasseltwirling, which they may be forced to modify if the stage area is limited. In some cases the amount of clothing a girl removes during her act depends upon local laws; there are "strong" cities where the strippers are permitted to "flash" (lower the G-string to expose the pubic area) or go completely nude. Furthermore, certain kinds of behavior, such as "floor work" (working on the floor or the stage or some horizontal platform simulating a bed or couch), caressing one's body or simulating intercourse, may be legal in one city and illegal in another. Carnival "kootch shows" undoubtedly work the most suggestively; they often allow members of the audience during the "blow-off" (second show for the same audience for which additional money is charged) to view the girls pubic area, sometimes with the aid of a flashlight. In general, if a club has only a few strippers and no other acts, the duration of each stripper's act is lengthened. Most clubs in the city where this research was done have three shows each night, opening around 9:00 P.M. and closing at 2:00 A.M. "Go-go" girls usually fill-in between acts. Considerably more time is spent by the stripper—dancing, posing, and "kidding around with the audience." (One common way of "kidding around with the audience" is for the stripper to squat on her haunches and bobble up and down while talking and joking with the customers seated around the stage.) Proportionally less time is spent stripping and teasing.

Strippers often work roles on the "floor," that is, where the audience is seated. The fact that girls who work in clubs mingle with the audience is one of the major differences between clubs and burlesque theatres. For instance, the house girls may be asked to substitute as bartenders, hostesses, or waitresses. When strippers are not performing, both the house girls and the features are expected to remain in the club and sit at the bar for the purpose of "decorating the club." In addition, the house girls and frequently the features are expected to sit with the customers at their tables. In the city where this study was undertaken, all but one of nine night clubs required strippers to accept drinks from the customers and also to "hustle" drinks when necessary.[15] In all the clubs the girls were also allowed to make arrangements for "hooking," that is, to make dates for prostitution.

On occasion, strippers are expected by the club owner to engage in certain extraclub activities: (1) A feature may be required or "requested" to engage in publicity stunts (for example, jumping into a public fountain "to cool off" or riding a horse down a principal street of the city, or kissing a famous ballplayer while the game is in progress); (2) house girls are often required to engage in publicity activities (for example, distributing door passes on the street); and (3) in at least two of the clubs, the strippers had to pay a percentage of the money they made "hooking" to the club managers.

ENTERING THE OCCUPATION

In discussing the general societal attitude toward the stripper, Salutin wrote:

> The public nudity, the portrayal of orgasm and masturbation, the open and public enjoyment of eroticism is something most people have been trained to condemn or even to fear. It represents a devaluation of their sex values....
> Strippers are viewed as "bad," then, because they strip away all social decorum with their clothes. They taunt the public with their own mores by teasing them and turning them on.[16]

Strippers are cognizant of their "low" standing in society—that the public views them as "bad." Since stripping can be classified as a deviant or improper occupation,[17] it is especially important to understand some of the career processes by which girls become members of this occupational group.

Personal and social variables are usually represented among the multiple factors effecting occupational choice. Consequently, this discussion begins with data relative to such characteristics as sex, race, nationality, age, ordinal position, socioeconomic background, education, residence, and family background.

All the 51 strippers were females, although one was transexual. However, males are not excluded from being strippers. Two clubs in the

---

[15] Strippers distinguish between "hustling" (i.e., soliciting drinks) and just accepting drinks when offered. Some of the subjects approve of the latter, but disapprove of the former, for as one girl remarked, "I can always buy my own drinks; I've never had to ask a man to buy me a drink."

[16] Salutin, op. cit., p. 15.

[17] Ned Polsky, *Hustlers, Beats and Others* (Chicago, Aldine, 1967).

community of our investigation did feature male strippers. Furthermore, there is a relatively new trend in which both males and females perform in certain stripping acts.

All the women interviewed were Caucasians. Four of the girls (all features) were foreigners; the remainder were native Americans. An agent mentioned in an interview that foreign girls were exceptionally popular and in great demand as strippers. On the other hand, he said it was quite difficult to "book" Negro girls.[18] This may explain partially what appears to be an underrepresentation of blacks among the stripper occupational group.[19]

Although the age range of the strippers extends from 18 to 53, the median age for the features is 24.5; the median age for the house girls is 23.0. The age range of the burlesque girls interviewed by Skipper and McCaghy was 19 to 45, 21 out of 35 girls (60 percent) were between 20 and 30 years of age.[20] Slightly less than half of the girls in our study were first-born children; a significantly higher percentage (89 percent) of the Skipper-McCaghy sample were first-borns.

With reference to socioeconomic background, three-fourths of the house girls' fathers were blue-collar workers; three-fifths of the features' fathers pursued blue-collar jobs. Four of the 26 features had one or both parents in show business, and none of the house girls came from what could be described as a show-business family.[21] In terms of educational achievement, about half of the house girls and two-thirds of the features were high school graduates. In general, Skipper and McCaghy's subjects seem to have slightly higher socioeconomic backgrounds and educational achievement levels.

Roughly the same proportion of strippers, about 90 precent, in the Skipper-McCaghy study and in the present research reported having been born or reared in cities of 100,000 or more.

Although the number of house girls from broken families is quite high (14 out of 26), the features do not appear to have a disproportionate rate (8 out of 26). In contrast, Skipper and McCaghy reported "at least 60 percent of the girls came from broken homes, or unstable homes, where they received little attention and affection."

[18] The interview with this agent was interrupted by a telephone call from an irate club owner. Mistakenly the club owner was upset because he thought the agent had sent him a black stripper.

[19] The absence of blacks in the sample cannot be explained solely by the location of the city in which the data were collected. Skipper and McCaghy ("Stripteasing," op. cit.) viewed the performances of 110 strippers in 10 major cities scattered throughout the United States and indicated that they had observed only two black strippers.

[20] Skipper and McCaghy, "Stripteasers," op. cit.

[21] Of the 17 strippers who participated in D'Andre's study (op. cit.) four came from show-business families.

In discussing an occupation that essentially involves the sensual exhibition of as much of one's body as the law will permit, the strippers' physical measurements are relevant. Skipper and McCaghy presented comparative data on the body measurements of the strippers in their sample, a group of Playboy Playmates, and a sample of American women between the ages of 20 and 30. The results suggest that strippers are taller, heavier, have larger hips and more developed busts. Specific information on body measurements was not collected in our research. However, observation of strippers reveals a wide range of "shapes and sizes," (particularly among the house girls.) Skipper-McCaghy and D'Andre also stress the wide variations in body types among strippers. A "modal body type" is not evident. Bust size is no longer limited to natural endowment. Over half of the girls in this study as well as that of Salutin have had silicone inserts placed inside the breasts ("boob jobs"), thereby increasing its size, sometimes to truly astronomical proportions. Only one girl revealed she had actually become a stripper because of the size of her bust; the girl was a size 48. She went into stripping at the encouragement of her grandmother, a former entertainer, who told her, "It would be a pity to waste a pair of boobs like yours."

Some of the strippers (primarily features) seemed very concerned about the appearance of their bodies. For instance, one girl would no longer strip to her G-string because her abdomen bore stretch marks. Other girls (primarily house girls) seemed to show little interest in the appearance and care of their bodies. An attempt was made to determine if the strippers' concern for their bodies might be manifested indirectly in the form of adherence to particular dietary and/or exercise regimentations. Many of the girls, obviously, did not have the "need" for such programs. However, it was evident that by most standards six or seven of the girls (all house girls) were overweight. Not one of these girls was involved in any sort of program aimed to achieve a reduction in weight.

As a group, the strippers were fastidious in choosing their costumes and accessories. They placed a great emphasis upon hair style, the exaggerated use of eye makeup, and elaborate display of lip and facial coloring.

Based on the above data, no conclusions can be reached concerning a pattern of personal-social characteristics that may have predisposed the girls to seek out the stripping occupation. However, certain other patterns emerge when additional data are considered.

As was also found by D'Andre,[22] practically all the subjects were in some form of show business before becoming strippers. This is characteristic of all the features with the exception of two. The features' previous show-business activities included chorus-line dancers, "straight men" in burlesque, and theatrical actresses. One of the two features with no previous show-business experience had been "picked up" in Las Vegas by a man who not only became her husband but also "made" her a stripper. The other girl had won a beauty contest and attracted the attention of an agent who in turn encouraged her to become a stripper.

Each of the features started in show business having contacts with individuals who were either in show business themselves or introduced them to show-business personnel. More specifically, the persons responsible for recruiting the features into show business were as follows: parents[23] or husband (60 percent) dance teachers (20 percent); and girl friends employed in show business (20 percent).

Seventy percent of the house girls had previously been "go-go" girls; another 20 percent had been working in clubs as waitresses, B-girls, or hostesses. Most of the house girls (75 percent) were recruited by either boy or girl friends who had some type of connection with individuals in the entertainment world. A fairly typical example of this patter is illustrated by this account: "I met this guy at a party. I started dating him, and I finally ended up living with him. His brother managed the _____ Club. He got me a job as a 'go-go' girl in the Club. Next thing I knew he turned me out [started me in prostitution]."

A few of the girls were recruited by employees of Clubs who suggested to the girls they might find the club a desirable place of employment. Two girls walked into the clubs and asked for jobs; one of these girls was responding to a newspaper advertisement.

Previous employment in another facet of show business must be considered important for a variety of reasons. First, it indicates most of the girls had the opportunity to learn some of the norms peculiar to entertainment-show business. Second, it provided these girls with the experience of performing before an audience; additionally, many of them had previously appeared scantily clothed. Third, the girls were members of a subculture and had reference groups that would be less inclined to view strippers and stripping in a negative manner compared to the viewpoints of the broader society or other subcultural groups. The opinions of significant others in the strippers' lives are generally more highly esteemed than the general sociocultural evaluation.

For most of the strippers, crucial career decisions were associated with

---

[23] There were at least three families in which two or more members were involved in the stripping occupation in some way. For example, one of the families consisted of the mother who managed clubs and carnival shows and her two daughters and younger sister who were strippers.

a "crisis situation" or a "crisis period." In the case of the features the crisis is related primarily to the girl's entertainment-oriented career, for example, those who had been stranded in a city where a legitimate show in which they were actresses folded. Stripping would have been the only entertainment-type job available to them at the time.

A crisis also affected the occupational histories of practically all of the house girls. In contrast to the features, however, the crises were more personal and transpired before their initial entry into show business. Nearly half of the house girls indicated they had just gotten a divorce prior to entering show business. As one of these girls revealed: "My marriage broke up and I was tired of the wife and mother bit; I wanted a whole new life." About one-third of these subjects cited an unexpected need for a large amount of money. Other house girls mentioned factors such as a dramatic break with parents or feeling that "the old life was empty or boring."

Although a few of the strippers deviate from this pattern, most of them became strippers at a time when they were having much financial stress. Often, the girl's support responsibilities included a husband or male companion and children. All the previous studies have also stressed that money was the principal motivating force inducing the stripper to enter—and continue—stripping. The choice of stripping as a livelihood was made with the knowledge that more money could be made stripping than would be possible in a more "legitimate" occupation. To quote one of the interviewees: "I had to work and the only other job I could get was a barmaid or waitress. I could make much more money stripping."

Slocum suggested that a continuum of rationality characterizes occupational decision-making, with decisions ranging from the purely impulsive to fully rational.[24] On the whole, the data reveal the career decisions of practically all the strippers may be classified toward the nonrational extreme. The decision to become a stripper was not the culmination of a requirement-benefit evaluative process in terms of which stripping was compared with other occupational alternatives. The only exception to this statement appears to involve economic remunerations, which *were* considered in a comparative sense by the subjects. Perceived monetary rewards were apparently ascribed great importance by the girls because most of them were experiencing financial pressures. Underlying this decision-making process is the presupposition of approval by the respondent's significant others. Such approval was readily obtainable because of the nature of their reference groups. Furthermore, the previous jobs held by the girls were similar in some respects to stripping and so they could view the stripping occupation as an acceptable alternative.

[24] Walter L. Slocum, *Occupational Careers* (Chicago, Aldine, 1966).

SOCIALIZATION

Once a girl becomes a stripper the effectiveness with which she performs her occupational roles is dependent upon mastery of work skills, learning the code of ethics that guides her occupational behavior, and internalizing an ideology justifying the appropriateness of the work activity.

The occupational socialization of strippers can be categorized in terms of "pre-job" and "on-the-job." Pre-job socialization experiences having some relationship to stripping are of two basic types: professional training in dancing or music and employment in some other facet of show business. All of the 26 features claimed formal study in dancing; 24 of them had held a show-business occupation prior to becoming a stripper. One-half had been dancers (chorus dancers) and one-quarter actresses. Fifteen of the 25 house girls acknowledged professional dance training, and the rest had some training in music or dramatics; 17 of the house girls had worked as "go-go" girls.

On-the-job socialization ranges from situational factors (for example, a stripper being ill necessitating, at least in the view of management, the instantaneous induction of a girl into stripping without benefit of training) to extreme factors in which a girl is carefully trained prior to stripping publicly. An example of the first type was witnessed by one of the writers. The manager came back to the dressing room and told one of the "go-go" girls that she was going to have to strip. The girl protested at first but finally agreed to do it. She then turned to the oldest stripper and said, "Well, what do I do?" The oldest stripper replied, "In the first set take off one glove and dance around; in the second set take off your gown and both panels; in the third set take off the other glove and your bra and strip pants.[25] A costume was assembled by the donations of separate items by three different girls, and the novice was ready to strip. She walked on stage, performed, and returned to the dressing room, appearing visibly shaken by the experience. She sat for a few minutes and then shuddered saying, "I couldn't take my strip pants off." One of the strippers responded, "Don't worry; that will come."

Some strippers, mostly features, receive extensive training in stripping before they perform before an audience. Many of the features had been trained in "kootch shows" by people whose job is specifically to train strippers. Some of the big carnivals like the Royal American and the James E. Strates Shows have very elaborate girl shows. These shows employ people who train neophyte chorus girls and strippers. The girls will be given a job in the chorus of a girl show and taught a few basic dance steps. Her instructor will then assist the girl in framing an original act that is compatible with her

---

[25] The order of removal given in this example does not necessarily apply to all strips. In the above example the novice was instructed to leave one glove on until the last set because "it looks sexier to just wear one glove."

personality. Further, a feature has a "gimmick," that is, a specialty with which she becomes identified. Some illustrations of "gimmicks" are: fans as made famous by Sally Rand; the imaginary lover; an "Eve" act with a Boa Constrictor; the sultan (a man from the audience is dressed with a turban and taught to belly dance) ; and a trained bird removing the clothes from the stripper and carrying them away. Sometimes the agent or husband will be her coach and act as a publicity agent—designing brochures, planning publicity stunts, and arranging for the stripper to appear on local talk shows. All of the girls interviewed in the study had role models, strippers whom they admired and to some extent imitated.[26]

All strippers must acquire certain work skills that include the ability to project or "sell" oneself to the audience (considered as important as the originality of the "gimmick") ; the tease (an essential aspect of stripping that entails the removing of one's clothes in a sexually provoking manner) ; "tricks of the trade" (for example, before going on stage wetting the bottom of their shoes to keep from slipping.) ; how and in what order to take off one's clothes; and how to deal with customers. The hostile (or apathetic) audience represents a special threat to the stripper, and she has evolved various means to cope with stressful situations. Strippers prefer verbally to deter men who start to interfere with their acts. Almost without exception, they use several "stock" insults when the situation dictates. A "line" one stripper used to "put down" male members of the audience is, "Hold onto that drink—it's the hardest thing you will be holding all night." In addition, they learn to cope with hostile members of the audience. One stripper, for example, returned backstage and reported how she dealt with a hostile female: "I shook my ass and boobs in her face; that fixed her."

Besides acquiring certain job skills, the stripper must learn her occupation's code of ethics. Although the code is not formalized, it is a fairly consistent set of norms that apply to the stripper's relations with the work organization, the customers, and other strippers. Certain expectations that appear fundamental to the stripper's relations with the work organization include: The stripper must report for work on time; if for any reason a stripper must be absent from work, she is expected to send a substitute; the stripper must respect the manager's decision about the position her name occupies in the billing. Most features have their billing specified in their contracts

Certain rules also pertain to the maintenance of social distance between

[26] All but one of the girls interviewed by Skipper and McCaghy ("Stripteasers," op. cit.) indicated they did not have role models. Salutin (op. cit.) revealed that the strippers who participated in her study did have role models. This discrepancy may be explained by the variation in the measurement items used. In our study the respondents were asked to identify the stripper each admired and to enumerate the characteristics that were the basis for their admiration.

the stripper and her audience. As an illustration, the stripper is not expected to allow the customer to "cop a feel," that is, to touch or grab her while she is on stage. Many of the girls also mentioned, "Never accept a date for less than $50. They said this in a "kidding on the square" vein. Several girls, when starting to work at one particular club, were told not to accept a "date" for less than $50. Besides charging for intercourse, some of the girls charge for allowing the customers to "cop a feel" while sitting at the customer's table. One girl reported making $75 one night by allowing a customer to feel her breast at $5 a feel.

A diversity of norms pertain to the stripper's relations with other strippers. The most important is that a stripper must never "badmouth" (criticize) another stripper to a customer.[27] Other norms are: Do not make a play for a stripper's husband; do not steal another girl's "gimmick" or dance-step; and do not imitate another girl's wardrobe.

Strippers seem to learn an ideology that revolves around the major functions of service, education, and entertainment.[28] The strippers, especially the house girls, feel they are performing a therapeutic service for men, in particular, and a protective service for society, in general. Most of them say their performances permit the men watching to fantasize about having intercourse with them, thus providing a therapeutic function by relieving sexual tension. Many of the girls believe there would be more sex crimes if it were not for strip shows. There is a tendency for both house girls and features to believe they provide educational instruction and information for women in attendance at the club. Surprisingly, several strippers reported they had been approached by women seeking advice on becoming more seductive and sexy. The entertainment function is mentioned primarily by features. Almost without exception, features see themselves as entertainers whose major contribution is the same as other members of show business.

Strippers realize they have a negative societal image. In the words of one of them: "They (the public) look down on us as a bunch of whores." The major function of the stripper's occupational ideology is to protect her from this negative stereotype by justifying the occupational activity, in terms of its functional aspects for society. Nevertheless, the stripper is confronted constantly with situations that reflect negative valuations. Sometimes women in the audience yell "whore." Frequently men assume the stripper is a prostitute and will proposition her; a rejection is generally construed as an indication that sufficient money was not offered. One stripper said, "When a guy asks me how much I charge, I say, 'How much does your mother

[27] Salutin (op. cit.) also found that this was a norm among burlesque strippers.
[28] Skipper and McCaghy ("Stripteasing" and "The Stripteaser," op. cit.) also reported that burlesque strippers expressed a similar ideology.

charge?' " The extent to which strippers accept their "lowly" stereotype is difficult to ascertain. Approximately half of the features and one-third of the house girls flatly denied its validity, pointing out that most strippers are wives and mothers like other women. They often expressed contempt for other women and their "holier than thou" attitude. As one said, referring to secretaries and teachers, "They do all kinds of things we wouldn't think of doing and they pretend to be so much better than we are." A stripper at one of the clubs was invited to an "orgy" which was held at the penthouse suite of one of the finest hotels in the city. She was so incensed at the behavior of the participants that she regaled everybody in the club for days about the "disgusting, sickening, and degenerate behavior of the phony, rich bastards" who attended the party.

About half of the strippers accepted the stereotype as being partially true; however, they denied any moral imputations. They felt that what people do is their own business and that an individual's sex life, in particular, is nobody's business but his own.[29]

Strippers defend themselves from negative evaluations in other ways. Strippers often "kid themselves and stripping." One evening a stripper in the dressing room was giving the other girls a "teasing" demonstration. She performed an elaborate routine of taking off her stocking, while making lewd remarks and risque gestures. The other strippers clapped and laughed; with much bravado and enthusiasm they strongly encouraged her to exaggerate the performance. Strippers also objectify (treat as objects without feeling) audiences in about the same manner as they feel audiences objectify them. Some girls show absolutely no emotion in their faces as they perform, feeling they are denying the audience what it desires most—affectivity and responsiveness. Some strippers have rather unique ways of "getting back" at the audience. One girl, for instance, keeps count of the number of times men in the audience, "who are trying to be so cool, miss ashtrays (with their cigarettes) or the table with their drinks."

SATISFACTIONS AND DISSATISFACTIONS

Once a girl becomes a stripper, the extent of her occupational adjustment depends partially on the rewards and dissatisfactions she perceives as emanating from that occupation. Rewards can be categorized as extrinsic and intrinsic. Extrinsic rewards include money, prestige, and job security; intrinsic rewards include psychic benefits such as creativity and ego satis-

---

[29] Skipper and McCaghy ("Stripteasing," op. cit.) found roughly the same percentage of respondents who either accepted, rejected, or partially accepted the negative stereotype attached to their occupation.

faction. In general, and more for the house girls than the features, the occupation of stripping permits few rewards, extrinsic or intrinsic, except income. All the girls cited money as the most important inducement to become strippers and the most important reward. House girls' salaries average from $150 to $175 each week, plus any additional money they can make "hustling drinks" or "hooking."[30] The salaries of the features range from $450 to $2,000 a week, with an average of $525. Apparently, money represents the principal incentive for the girls to remain in stripping, for it is not likely that any of the strippers interviewed would be able to make more money in any "more legitimate" work.

Job security is extremely tenuous. A house girl does not have a contract with the club where she is employed, and she can be fired "on the spot." In fact, one club owner fired all of his house girls one night as they reported for work because "he was in a peeve." The feature usually has a contract for a two-week engagement ("gig") with one club, but she is often not booked up more than two or three months ahead. In addition to two interview sessions, the senior author spent eight hours with perhaps the best known feature in this country. The major concern she expressed was the need to complete her tour schedule for the next six months. During this eight-hour period, she made seven long-distance telephone calls to agents in an effort to realize this end.

Within show business or society as a whole the occupation of stripping is accorded limited prestige, at best. As one stripper explained, "We are the bastard step-child of show business." Jessor and Donovan reported that strippers were given the least favorable rating of 10 occupations, including sales clerk, artist model, and professional gambler.[31] A sample of 124 undergraduate students were asked to rank 10 female-oriented occupations in order of desirability. Stripping was rated ninth, just above prostitution.[32]

In response to the question, "What do you like best about stripping?" features answered, dancing" (40 percent), "entertaining" (30 percent), and "just being a part of show business" (20 percent); house girls identified the

[30] The range of fees charged for an act of prostitution extends from $50 to $150, with a preponderance of fees being at the lower extreme. The city where this study was conducted is probably somewhat atypical in that strippers generally do not get a percentage of the price of every drink she hustles. Instead, the girl is encouraged by management to get the customer to give her money for sitting at his table; the girl is allowed to keep all this money.

[31] Clinton Jessor and Lewis Donovan, "Nudity in the Art Training Process: An Essay with Reference to a Pilot Study," *Sociological Quarterly*, Vol. 10 (1969), pp. 255–71.

[32] Boles, op. cit. Interestingly, the students rated "go-go" dancers higher in desirability than strippers. However, the strippers themselves rated "go-go" dancers as less desirable.

"atmosphere of the club" (45 percent), "entertaining" (30 percent), and the remaining 20 percent of the responses were highly varied. On the surface, "dancing" and "entertaining" appear to be activities that provide some intrinsic satisfactions to many of the strippers; however, each should be examined more closely.

Although most of the strippers, particularly features, have had either training or experience in dancing, dancing *per se* does not actually constitute an important segment of most acts; the tease and the strip are far more important. Even those girls who are good dancers rarely have the opportunity to dance to the maximum of their ability.[33]

Generally, the feature strippers view themselves as entertainers and consider the entertainment function as part of their ideology. There are certain factors, however, that mitigate against their ability to maintain their identities. As one house girl stated it: "We're here to sell booze and sex." Additionally, it is difficult for a stripper to maintain the identity of an entertainer because she is often required to perform work activities she considers antithetical to the role of an entertainer.

> When we're up on the stage, we're entertainers and then we come off stage and sit with the customers, and we're not special anymore. You know an entertainer has to be special; she can't be like the girl next door. Sitting with the customers takes away all the glamour.

D'Andre suggests this same type of explanation as to why some of her respondents preferred the burlesque theatre to the night club. In burlesque the "performer is always on a stage, separated by a (physical-social) barrier between herself and the patrons."[34] Thus, night club strippers are not only prevented from maintaining their social distance from the customers and thereby promoting their special status as entertainers, but they must often deal with the apathy and hostility of the audience. This attitude serves as a reminder of the general valuation the public has of them.

The occupational hazards and potential sources of job dissatisfaction associated with stripping abound. For instance, most strippers do not have health insurance. The American Guild of Variety Artists (AGVA) offers health insurance, but the stripper must have been a union member for five years before she is eligible. Actually, most of the house girls do not even belong to the union, but all of the features do. Any effectiveness of AGVA in protecting and representing the interests of strippers is questionable. None of

---

[33] "Go-go" dancing is very different from the type of dancing (or movements) associated with stripping. With little doubt, "go-go" dancing is more strenuous and probably more difficult.

[34] D'Andre, op. cit.

the AGVA members in this research believe their union protects and represents their interests adequately. They enumerated a variety of experiences to support their contentions. For example, the union has done nothing to improve the quality of the girls' dressing rooms; most dressing rooms are small, poorly lighted, dirty and inconveniently located. Further, some club owners assign duties to which the stripper might object, regardless of whether she received extra remunerations, or which she would be willing to do for additional money. To keep their jobs, two girls were required to accept "dates" with a judge and a newspaper reporter. At another club, employment depended upon the house girls distributing advertisements to passers-by on the street. None of these girls received money for those extra services.

The possibility of physical danger is always eminent. The kinds of associates a stripper may have enhances the potentiality that they might physically threaten her. For example, a stripper was knifed by a pimp who "would not take no for an answer." Strippers work late hours and often go home alone; many strippers have been followed home by men. The possibility of danger also arises from interaction between the stripper and a member of the audience. Strippers take precautions to avoid confrontations between themselves and overzealous customers, but sometimes to no avail. One of the researchers witnessed a stripper cutting a male customer with a broken glass when he persisted in climbing up on the stage.

Legal involvement represents another type of occupational hazard. One girl is being sued by her former mother-in-law to gain custody of a child, claiming the stripper is an unfit mother. Strippers frequently experience arrests for violating local statutes prohibiting "lewd and obscene dancing" which are usually misdemeanors. Actually, the stripper may intentionally incur the attention of the vice squad to gain publicity. There is also the danger of arrest for "soliciting." All of the workers in the clubs watch for the police, especially the vice squad. Members of the vice squad come into the clubs disguised as "ordinary customers." If any of the employees recognizes a policeman, he gives the signal and the "hustling" and "soliciting" come to a halt. One club has a red light installed behind the bar which is turned on when an employee has spotted a policeman.

Other occupational hazards pertain to the area of physical health. Falling during the performance is a real danger and a concern to most strippers. Tassel twirling tears down breast tissue. Acrobatic dancing with rolls can lead to the development of lumps on the breast. "Boob jobs" can cause unpleasant aftereffects for as long as a year, although silicone inserts are generally used today and are believed to be safe. The girls also complain of rashes from frequent shaving of pubic hair.

Compared to most other occupational practitioners, certain work roles ("hooking") pursued by some strippers and their associates (pimps and gamblers) increase the chances they will be involved in crimes of violence.

During a three-year period in the city where data was collected, two strippers were indicted for murder; one was murdered.

Trying to maintain a marriage and a family is a major problem. Salutin writes movingly about the marital difficulties strippers face—for instance, problems may arise because most of them support their husbands or male companions[35] Of the features interviewed, all but four were married; one was single, one was separated, and two were divorced. Most of their husbands did travel with them and lived on their wives' income. The difficulty of this kind of situation is illustrated by this statement from a stripper who traveled with her husband.

> _____ and I get on each other's nerves. We both sit around the hotel all day with nothing to do but get on each other's nerves. And of course, I'm making the money. If he could just find something to do on his own, things would be better between us.

At the time of the interviews, 30 percent of the house girls were married, 30 percent were divorced, 20 percent were single, and 20 percent were separated. Many of these girls also encountered difficulties with maintaining a marriage. For instance, two of the girls had married men who started them in prostitution. Several experienced marital difficulties because they worked at night and their husbands worked during the day. Additionally, a few of the girls complained about jealousy on the part of their husbands.

One-half of the features and two-thirds of the house girls had children. Three of the features had their infant children with them while on tour; the problems of traveling with small children are many. For example, a feature called one of the writers during the middle of the night for assistance in locating a doctor for her sick baby.

WORK-RELATED REFERENCE GROUP ORIENTATIONS

Each person assumes the perspectives of several reference groups. One's work represents an especially significant form of social participation. Consequently, the work-related reference groups to which a stripper identifies affect the standards she uses to evaluate her behavior. Her feelings toward herself (self-image) reflect the appraisals of membership and reference groups or at least her imagination of these appraisals.[36] The concepts of localism and cosmopolitanism have been used to differentiate between two basic types of

---

[35] Salutin, op. cit.

[36] B. F. Mannheim, "Reference Groups, Membership Groups and the Self-Image," *Sociometry,* Vol. 29 (1966), pp. 265–70.

actors' orientations.[37] Their application should prove fruitful in furthering understanding of the strippers' orientations.

Distinctions in the usage of locals and cosmopolitans were made by Gouldner in a study of faculty members at a small liberal arts college.[38] The term *locals* referred to those faculty members high in loyalty to their employing organization, lowly committed as to specialized role skills, and more probably using an inner reference group orientation. In contrast, *cosmopolitans* described those with limited loyalty to the work organization, highly committed to specialized role skills, and more probably using an outer reference group orientation. Generally the house girls are locals; the features tend to be cosmopolitans.

An example of the allegiance a house girl had for the employing organization is evident by her evaluation of the "go-go" girls in the club where she was performing.

> Go-go girls are good for the club. We used to have a comedian who worked in between shows, and most of the customers got up and left during his act; now, they stay for the next show. This way we do better business and have better crowds. We have the best club in town now.

Further indication of loyalty to the employing organization is suggested by the responses to the question. "What is your favorite club?" Most house girls named the club where they were presently employed. Conversely, none of the features expressed any particular allegiance to the club where they were performing. Because night club features work at a specific club for only a limited period, under most circumstances it is difficult for them to develop a sense of identity and loyalty to the club. However, all the features did mention favorite clubs that were invariably located in Las Vegas, Miami, or New York. They preferred night clubs high in prestige, managed by competent personnel, and employing "good" bands. House girls preferred certain clubs primarily because of the "class" of customers that frequent the club; the club represented "the only club I know"; and "I have friends here."

In particular, the house girls valued the friendships they developed with other employees. The intermittent requirements of their jobs, (especially during periods when the clubs were frequented by few customers) provided ample time and opportunity for the house girls to interact with co-workers

[37] Robert K. Merton, *Social Theory and Social Structure* (Glencoe, Ill., Free Press, 1957); Alvin W. Gouldner, "Cosmopolitans and Locals: Toward an Analysis of Latent Social Roles: I," *Administrative Science Quarterly*, Vol. 2 (1958), pp. 281–306.

[38] Ibid.

and evolve meaningful informal group relationships. The limited time spent by a feature stripper in any given city made it almost impossible for her to develop stable friendships while she was on tour. In addition, the feature's higher status negated the likelihood that she would become an integral part of the informal work group at any particular club.

Other researchers have presented data suggesting that more than half of all strippers engage in homosexual relations.[39] This possible fact was not specifically examined in our study. However, unstructured conversations with several of the study's subjects lead us to believe that homosexuality was not only a common occurrence, but that it was tolerated, if defined as an unacceptable behavioral pattern.

Many of the house girls did admit to having what might be described as paternal or maternal relationships with their club managers, who had been responsible for initiating them into stripping and continued to "watch over" them. Almost half of these girls also had sexual relationships with club managers/owners.

Various aspects of the work environment (for example, the glamour and atmosphere, a "classy" audience) were specified often by the house girls as important positive considerations for the rating they accorded their present clubs. Job requirements were also cited with some regularity. For instance, some of the girls favored their present places of employment because they were not expected to perform work other than that directly associated with stripping.

Considering the nature of the data gathering and measuring techniques used in this study, the extent to which the house girls are committed to the employing organization can be only roughly approximated in a comparative manner. However, the house girls do identify more closely with their clubs than either their occupations, or their occupational situs, or any other work-related group. The features do not identify with their work organizations, and they identify more closely with their occupations, compared to house girls. Few, if any, of the house girls were oriented toward the entertainment situs. For example, only a few belong to AGVA, and none of the house girls belong to any other show-business organizations (for example, Variety and Screen Actors Guild). Not only did none of the house girls read such show-business magazines as *Variety, Showcase,* or *Amusement Business,* but several of them were unaware of their existence. Among this group of strippers, no one aspired for another entertainment-oriented occupation. Additionally, of the 12 girls having retirement plans, no one anticipated an area of work even remotely related to show business.

The features as a group are oriented toward the entertainment situs

39 Skipper and McCaghy, "The Stripteaser," op. cit.; Salutin, op. cit.

which represents an "outer reference group." All but three were also members of other show-business organizations as well as AGVA. All but two also read magazines regularly which are related to showbusiness. In response to the question, "Have you ever considered doing anything other than stripping?" all of the features indicated another occupation within the entertainment situs, such as legitimate actress, singer, or movie star. As one feature expressed it, "I've made one movie already (*The Night They Raided Minsky's*), and I hope to make more because that's really what I want to do." Further, all but three of the features preferred another entertainment-oriented occupation as a means of making a livelihood. Finally, all but one of the features having retirement plans, had made such plans around some facet of show business. As an example, one feature reported, "I am planning to own and operate a theatrical costume shop."

The relevancy of informal work groups for the house girls is not restricted to the club, for many on-the-job relationships extend into their extrawork situations. The house girls were members of what one of them described as the "night people"—individuals who, because of the nature of their jobs, not only work at night but are also free to "socialize" at night, or more correctly, during the early hours of the morning. Three late-night restaurants and two "after-hours" clubs (open and serving liquor illegally after 2:00 a.m.) were the meeting places of the night people. The interaction of the house girls with other night people represents to some extent a continuation of reward-seeking behavior similar to that manifested by their involvement in the informal work group. The atmosphere of the restaurants and clubs is casual and relaxed—the night people are among their own. They go to "unwind." "When I get through with the last show I'm still high; I'm still keyed up. If I went home, I couldn't sleep. I have to unwind. Besides, I'm hungry. I've done three shows, and you know I move a lot."

Involvement in the night people's subculture also provides some of the participants alternative means for status acquisition; table hopping is a favorite pastime. The number of people one knows is a measure of prestige among the night people. One stripper said, "Its really great to walk into the _____ (restaurant) and know everybody there; I go from table to table and everybody says 'Hi, _____', and boy, my date knows I'm really in."

Significantly, the involvement of the house girls in the night people's subculture brings them together with other individuals who are generally congenial and supportive—who "understand them." Schneider, referring to the informal work groups of industrial workers, makes the point, "The group provides channels for a flow of conversation, the exchange of ideas, the communication of attitudes, and the sharing of values."[40] In other words,

---

[40] Eugene V. Schneider, *Industrial Sociology,* 2nd ed. (New York, McGraw-Hill, 1969).

membership and involvement as a night person enhances the possibility of a stripper having some of her personality needs met which otherwise might not be. The night people's subculture provides many of the house girls with increased security—psychological, economic, and even spiritual—and acceptance and recognition. All of the house girls work without contracts, and most do not have a work association to which they can appeal. Hence, it is crucial for them to keep abreast of possible job opportunities. The night people function as a citywide network of contacts whereby its members continually hear about job vacancies. The night people also enjoy easy and convenient access to a minister who counsels them and holds a religious service for them at 2:30 a.m. one morning a week.

Generally, the features did not participate in the night people's post-work gatherings. Unless she has a traveling companion, much of the traveling feature's free time is actually spent in semi-isolation in her hotel room, watching television, writing letters, and talking to friends on the phone. About half the features travel with male companions—legal or common-law husbands who often act as personal managers and reduce the loneliness which plagues the touring stripper. Some features travel with female companions who are in some cases their lovers and also act as personal managers.

Further evidence of the importance of work colleagues and night people to the house girls was gathered by asking the respondents to "list their five best friends by occupation." "Other house girls" headed the list, followed by service workers, including waitresses, bartenders, cigarette girls, and club hostesses. The third most frequently mentioned category was housewives; these were friends who lived in the same apartment complexes as did the house girls. "Other show people" was the next category identified—these were local entertainers such as "go-go" girls and musicians. Two of the house girls mentioned specifically that their best friends were prostitutes; however, most of the strippers identified as best friends were also prostitutes, at least on a part-time basis. All but one of the 17 unmarried house girls were living with a member of the night people subculture (one lived with a "go-go" girl; one lived with a pimp; another lived with a professional gambler; and another shared an apartment with a full-time prostitute).

Features not only desire but attempt to participate in entertainment-oriented, occupational subcultures. Although data on this subject are limited, certain impressions were derived that serve as a basis for some tentative conclusions.

Most of the features had families and kinship ties that facilitated involvement in an entertainment subculture. For example, most of the married features' husbands were also in show business of some kind. That this is not unique to these subjects is suggested by the fact that at least three other strippers are married or have been married to movie stars. These marriages were mentioned frequently and pointed at with pride by many of the features. Nearly half of the 26 features also have relatives in show business with whom they communicate regularly. In addition, several of the features have literally "grown up" in show business. One feature was both surprised and pleased upon learning that one of the authors spoke carnival slang and knew several people in outdoor show business. Another feature had spent several months in Las Vegas and volunteered a variety of accounts about the movie actors with whom she had "partied." She also talked animatedly about the Hollywood stars she had met on talk shows and shared much inside gossip about them. All of the features who had scrapbooks insisted that the researcher look through the scrapbook before beginning the interview. If she had a picture of herself with somebody in legitimate show business, she pointed it out: "See, there I am with _____."[41] In general, however, not many of the features participate actively in the occupational subculture of entertainers in legitimate show business. Furthermore, if they do participate, the intensity of their friendships is probably limited. In response to the question asking for a list of best friends, other feature strippers were cited most often. At a distant second came other show people such as singers, "carnies," comedians, and choreographers.

In the final analysis, there are few Lily St. Cyrs, Gypsy Rose Lees, or Sally Rands who have the "privilege" of interacting with and gaining acceptance by the top entertainment stars. Feature strippers are usually restricted to associations with the lesser talented and lower prestigious members of the entertainment world. Although features take the entertainment situs as a reference group, it is neither a concrete nor an interactional group for most of them, but an aspirational reference group. It is understandable why most features (all but two) indicated they would like "fame and success" before retiring from stripping. Such explanations as, "I want to become a household word" and "I want to be a center-fold in *Playboy*" were given as clarification of the words "fame and success." Most of the features preferred approval by such stars as Bob Hope (as opposed to a famous stripper), for the approval of such a famous entertainer would make credible the possibility that the feature was also an entertainer.

The house girls express some loyalty to their employing organization and little or no commitment to the occupation of stripping. In addition, the house girls have inner reference groups at their places of employment and among the night people in their community; these reference groups are both concrete and interactional. They are membership groups. The subjects did

[41] An agent recounted his conversation with a feature whom he had just booked into Las Vegas: "She was thrilled with the booking. She thinks this is her chance to break into legit show business, but I told her, 'Listen honey, where else can you make five bills a week working for 45 minutes a night?' "

not aspire to pursue other types of show business occupations, nor were they oriented to a broader occupational situs. Generally, they did not perceive themselves as entertainers, nor did they view stripping as a "career." In fact, most of the house girls expressed a definite preference for marriage and housekeeping roles.

Whether these girls would quit stripping, should the economic necessity to work be removed, remains an empirical question. At least three house girls had married financially successful men. In each case the girl returned to stripping after a short period of retirement. One of the girls who went back to work said, "I miss the club. I was lonely without my friends. You know while I was pregnant I made some strip pants and stuff and sold them around the clubs." These girls missed their membership groups and not participating in the night people's subculture. Their work had taken on meanings other than economic.

17. The Carnival as a
Marginally Legal Work Activity:
A Typological Approach to Work Systems

PATRICK C. EASTO

and

MARCELLO TRUZZI

Until recently the North American carnival has received little sociological attention. Indeed, prior to 1970 very few works dealt with the carnival in what might be called a sociological perspective.[1] On the other hand, the carnival has enjoyed (and sometimes suffered) widespread attention in the popular literature.[2] This is evidenced by the large number of articles, essays, books and even exposés dealing with the life and work of "carnies."

The more recent sociological interest in the carnival has been focussed in two specialty areas of our discipline. First, Bryant has argued the carnival may be viewed as a complex organization and work culture, and that as such sociologists of work or occupations have good reason to be interested in the carnival social system.[3] Second, we have argued elsewhere that the carnival

Copyright © 1972 by Patrick C. Easto and Marcello Truzzi. Paper read at the Annual Meetings of the Southern Sociological Society, New Orleans, Louisiana, April 1972.

[1] See especially: John F. Cuber, "Patrons of Amusement Parks," *Sociology and Social Research*, Vol. 24 (1939), pp. 63–68; Wittold Krassowski, "Social Structure and Professionalization in the Occupation of the Carnival Worker," unpublished Master's Thesis, Purdue University, 1954; and Patricia A. Nathe, "Carnivals, Also Fairs, Circuses, and Amusement Parks: A Historical Perspective," unpublished Master's Thesis, School of Criminology, University of California, Berkeley, 1969. The major historical work is: Joseph McKennon, *A History of the American Carnival,* unpublished manuscript, xerox, 1972, 588 pp.

[2] See the bibliography at the end of this paper for some of the more interesting popular references.

[3] Clifton D. Bryant, "Sawdust in Their Shoes: The Carnival as a Neglected Complex Organization and Work Culture." Paper read at the Annual Meetings of the Southern Sociological Society in Atlanta, Georgia (April 1970).

represents a subculture wherein sociologists concerned with stratification and prestige systems may find a fertile testing ground for some of their hypotheses. In addition, the carnival "language" was introduced and we suggested that linguists interested in the development of argot or cant might learn much from the carnival.[4]

This paper is an attempt to introduce the carnival to students of work and deviant behavior. Beginning with a definition and brief history, we describe the work organization of the carnival with a view toward classifying it as a marginally legal work system. Finally, we offer some speculation about the "deviant" character of carnival life.

Good data on carnivals are not readily available. Bibliography as we have already noted are quite diffuse and often unreliable. Outside of the sociological investigations noted, the major source of information on the carnival is *Amusement Business* magazine.[5]

Although our review which follows relies heavily upon the bibliographic materials cited and upon numerous interviews with carnival workers, the bulk of our data relies upon participant observation. It must be noted, however, that the ratio of participation to observation is weighted heavily on the side of participation. Thus like Nels Anderson and his now almost classic work on homeless men, our scholarly interest in the carnival developed after spending several years of involvement in that millieu.[6] We draw therefore upon our experiences and our memories after they have been formed through our participation. Though we do not feel that this seriously distorts our perspective, it does mean that many things might have been observed which were not thought to be important. Thus, data is still unavailable to us on many important aspects of the carnival world.

DEFINITION AND SCOPE OF CARNIVALS

A precise definition of the carnival is not a simple task. A typical dictionary definition is: "an entertainment with side shows, rides, games and refreshments, usually operated as a commercial enterprise." Yet, at any one time, any of these elements can be missing. It is far easier to define a carnival by example. The three major features of a carnival are (1) riding devices, (2)

---

[4] Patrick C. Easto and Marcello Truzzi, "Towards an Ethnography of the Carnival Social System," in Joseph G. Jorgensen and Marcello Truzzi (eds.), *Anthropology of American Life* (Englewood Cliffs, N.J., Prentice-Hall, 1974). A brief version of this same paper appeared as "Carnivals, Road Shows, and Freaks," *Society*, Vol. 9, No. 5 (March 1972), pp. 26–34.

[5] Sometimes called the "bible" and virtually always by its former name, "The Billboard," *Amusement Business* is the trade journal. See especially the 75th Anniversary Issue, Vol. 81, No. 52 (December 1969).

[6] Nels Anderson, *The Hobo* (Chicago, University of Chicago Press, 1923).

shows or exhibits, and (3) concessions. Riding devices include the familiar merry-go-round (considered by some to be a necessary element in the definition of a carnival), the ferris wheel, the tilt-a-whirl, and many others which constitute the "major"[7] rides. In addition to these major rides, there are the "punk rides" which cater to small children such as the boat rides, miniature train, and tank ride.

There are also a wide variety of shows and exhibits. These include presentations of performers (as in girl shows and freak shows), animals (wild life and rare or freak animals), or interesting objects (wax figures, historical objects, even dead people as in the case of preserved freak embryos like a two-headed baby). Almost without exception, however, the largest show on the carnival midway is the freak show or "ten-in-one."[8]

Concessions include a wide variety of both games and refreshment operations. There are two major types of games: "flat-stores" and "hanky-panks." The "flat-store" refers to those concessions which are strictly gambling operations where the probability of winning is rarely on the side of the patron. Examples would include the "swinger," a game where the customer swings a small bowling ball in such a fashion as to knock over a small bowling pin; the "roll-down," where the customer spills a number of marbles down a runway filled with numbered depressions; the "six-cat" where the object is to toss three baseballs and knock over two large catlike dolls. The other type of game, the "hanky-pank," typically rewards its patron with a prize each time he plays. Typical hanky-panks are the fish-pond, the ring-toss, and dart throwing games. The crucial distinction between the flat-store and the hanky-pank is whether the customer is rewarded each time he plays.

In the minds of many of the public, carnivals are equated with circuses. Though a limited degree of intersection between the carnival and circus worlds exists (that is, there are a few people in the carnival world who have worked on circuses and vice-versa), they are very separate and very different social and cultural worlds. Within the outdoor amusement industry itself, circus personnel are generally ranked higher in the overall stratification system. Circus people often "look down" upon carnival people. The circus has been defined as a "traveling and organized display of animals and skilled performances within one or more circular stages known as rings before an audience encircling these activities."[9] Thus the circus is perceived

---

[7] Throughout we use elements of carnival argot set off by quotation marks. If the meaning is not clear from the context, we define it for the reader.

[8] So called because the patron usually sees 10 attractions in the one show.

[9] Marcello Truzzi, "The Decline of the American Circus: The Shrinkage of an Institution," in M. Truzzi (ed.), *Sociology and Everyday Life* (Englewood Cliffs, N.J., Prentice-Hall, 1968), pp. 312–22.

as an extension of theater by its members. The carnival is perceived by carnival and circus people as having very different origins and connections from street fairs and the world of gambling. The carnival is primarily an entertainment which seeks the participation of the customer in contrast to the more passive viewer of the circus.

Secondly, carnivals differ from circuses in terms of the economic relationship between the management and workers. In the circus, virtually all personnel work indirectly or indirectly (through a chain of authority) for the owner. The carnival, in contrast, is comprised of an owner-operator who, though he may own a majority of the various attractions, enters into contracts with independent ride, show and concession owners in order to enlarge his midway.[10] These economic arrangements are often highly informal; thus, a recent issue of *Amusement Business* showed an advertisement by the Coleman Brothers Shows stating that "many of our contracts are represented by handshake only."[11]

A third distinction between the circus and the carnival is that the carnival (unlike most circuses) frequently changes its size and content during the working season. It is not unusual for independent ride, show, and concession owners to "book with," that is join, several different carnivals during a season. The advertisements published weekly in *Amusement Business* facilitate such moves, and this is one reason for the importance of this periodical in the carnival world.

Unlike circuses, which have been declining in number since the turn of the century,[12] carnivals have shown a great increase over the years. Some early data based on route lists published in 1934 by the *Billboard* showed an increase from 1902. This listing showed 17 carnivals known to be in operation in 1902 growing up to 119 in 1934.[13] Though we do not have data for years 1934–1970, an examination of the number of carnivals submitting route lists for 1969 showed 163 carnivals, a further increase.[14]

The route list data above, however, do not accurately reflect the true number of carnivals for any given year. In part, this is due to the fact that carnival owners do not always submit their route lists for publication. In addition, they may not have the entire season "booked." Writers on carnivals vary in their estimates, usually stating that between 300 to 500 carnivals are

[10] An exception is the Royal American Shows which is reported to be entirely owned by one operator.

[11] *Amusement Business,* op. cit., p. 69.

[12] Truzzi, op. cit.

[13] *Amusement Business,* op. cit., p. 135.

[14] Ibid., pp. 171, 174, and 176–77. The view that carnivals in general have declined is argued by Nathe, op. cit., pp. 25–38. This difference seems to be largely the result of her definition of carnivals as including fairs and amusement parks, both of which seem to have been in decline.

currently operating in the United States. But the problem is largely a definitional one. As an editor of *Amusement Business* recently summarized the problem:

> The...[number] is elusive. Nobody knows. Estimates range from around 800 to thousands, and the larger number is frequently correct. That is because whenever the...independent owner with two or three rides sets up for business he has a carnival. The following week he may tag along as part of a larger show, paying a percentage as an independent operator. But this week, if his name is Pinson, he has every right to call his little display "Pinson's Mighty Grand Spectacular Exposition Shows."[15]

The size of the audience played to, the sheer number of carnivals and the complexity of social organization hinted at in our definition should function to create interest in the carnival for the sociologist. Assuming such interest we turn to a more complete description.

HISTORY

Since lengthy historical descriptions of the carnival and its origins exist only a brief presentation will be made here.[16] While it is possible to trace the origins of carnival into antiquity, the North American Carnival may be traced to the World's Columbian Exposition at Chicago in 1893. It was here that a number of concessionaires realizing the disastrous financial effects of slim attendance met to consider their common fate. This meeting is regarded as the "first attempt to pool the interests of showmen."[17] Two important decisions resulted from this meeting. First, the concessionaires decided that while it was one thing to have a fair, it was quite another to put it over. Accordingly, they induced a prominent Chicago clergyman to denounce the exposition because of a particularly suggestive dance being exhibited on the midway. The clergyman's denouncement was quickly picked up by both the local and national media, and as a result, attendance figures soared. Everybody, it seemed, wanted to see "that dance."

The second decision resulting from that meeting was to move the

---

[15] *Amusement Business,* op. cit., p. 55.

[16] See, for example, David Braithwaite, *Fairground Architecture: The World of Amusement Parks, Carnivals and Fairs* (New York, Praeger, 1968); Thomas Frost, *The Old Showman and Old London Fairs* (London, Chatto and Windus, 1881); William F. Mangels, *The Outdoor Amusement Industry* (New York, Vantage, 1952); and Samuel McKechnie, *Popular Entertainments Through the Ages* (New York, Frederick A. Stokes, 1932).

[17] This section is taken largely from a comparable section on carnival history in *Amusement Business,* op. cit., p. 135.

assembled attractions to various cities. At first showmen assembled their attractions on already existing fairgrounds. One of the first was at Syracuse, New York, but proved unfruitful. The point to keep in mind however, is that the idea of the carnival had been born. Later that same year Frank C. Bostock assembled a collection of attractions on Coney Island which could be referred to as the first carnival. Utilizing the talents of Joseph and Francis Ferari, he put together a traveling street fair. This was the first attempt to actually make portable a group of attractions and is therefore considered the first carnival.

At first these early carnivals moved by horse-drawn wagons, but by 1914 the Smith Greater Shows was moving by truck. In terms of progress since 1914, consider the above discussion in the light of a current advertisement in *Amusement Business* by the Royal American Shows.

> Today Royal American travels on 80 double-length railroad cars, the world's largest private train, loaded with 145 massive pieces of equipment. Reflecting the public's change in taste and demands for thrills, the midway features more than 50 rides and attractions and seven under-canvas shows. Royal American has grown in height (tallest ride is 103 feet), length (over a mile long midway) and capacity (12.5 million annually).[18]

CARNIVAL WORK ORGANIZATION

Carnival work is organized along four general lines and for the most part the status or prestige hierarchy overlaps these divisions. Specifically, we can identify an administrative division; the independent ride, show or concession owners; the performers, and the workers.

The administrative level consists of the carnival owner and several other administrative-type roles. The show owner and his administrative assistants arrange the seasonal route at conventions, decide upon acquisitions like new riding devices or shows, and determine the carnival's needs with respect to "booking" other attractions for various "spots" or locations throughout the season. In addition to these long range decisions are the administrative problems associated with managing a moderate to large scale business organization.

The number and type of administrative personnel varies from carnival to carnival but usually include:

1. A "lot man" whose task it is to precede the carnival to a given city or town and decide where to place the various rides, shows and concessions. This role requires that its incumbent be well versed in the technical aspects

[18] Ibid., p. 8.

of the various attractions, since he must know precisely how much area is required by the rides, shows and concessions. For example, the octopus riding device requires a circular area of approximately 100 feet whereas the "ten-in-one" might require 110 feet of midway frontage. The reader can appreciate the difficulty of this task by recalling that mile long midway advertised by the Royal American Shows.

2. The "patch" is a role that can best be described as a kind of legal advisor. His work involves patching up in a public relations sense (but more often financial sense) any carnival-related complaints held by town or city officials. Based on our experience and interviews with carnies, it appears as though in the majority of cases these officials are simply paid off (bribed). In addition to activities of this type, the patch is called upon to settle grievances like a concessionaire "beating a mark" without giving his patron the much sought after stuffed animal; or even more critically, placating local law enforcers when it is discovered that one or more of the strippers are in fact, female impersonators.

3. "The ride superintendent" is a kind of grand mechanic whose responsibility involves maintaining not only the riding devices but the tractor-trailer units which move them. On a large truck-moved carnival these responsibilities are formidable. For example, the Blue Grass Shows moves each week in forty tractor-trailer units. The task of maintaining the trucks as well as the equipment moved in them falls upon the shoulders of this role incumbent.

This brief discussion of the administrative division is, of course, far from complete. Moreover, it neglects to point up the fact that on many carnivals we might discover the assistant manager doubling as the patch; or the lot man serving as "advance man," a role involving "papering" a city with placards announcing the carnival's arrival.

Another major division of labor in carnival work organization is comprised of the independent ride, show and concession owners. Here we find individuals who own one or more major riding devices, shows of one kind or another or perhaps several concessions. They "book" with a carnival owner for all or a portion of the season, paying either a percentage of their gross (as in the case with rides and shows) or a flat rate called the "privilege" (as is the case with concessions). As we have already noted this group is responsible for the changing character of carnivals as they move from week to week, and these "independents" often book with several different carnivals during a season. To some extent the existence of this group is the result of the increasing cost of a major ride. The newer rides (the double ferris wheel, for example) are so expensive that several individuals often form a corporation in order to purchase only one ride. It is important therefore that they only "book" the larger, high income-producing fairs. In order to do this they must join different carnivals through a season, since no one carnival owner has a monopoly on the better fair locations.

Still another level of work organization consists of the performers. In discussing this group Krassowski distinguished three types of shows wherein the performers are likely to work: freak shows, thrill shows, and girl shows.[19] While these three types are more or less self-explanatory we would note that the thrill show category would include everybody from a motorcycle rider in the "Motor-drome" to illusion show performers in the currently popular "Ape-girl" illusion.

A final division consists of what might be called the workers. But this is a highly differentiated level. For example, among those who operate the riding devices we find foremen and second men. The foreman's task involves responsibility for "upping and downing or sloughing" (assembling or dissembling) the ride to which he is assigned. The second man is simply his assistant. Generally the latter is less experienced and is paid less, whereas the former sometimes receives a bonus for staying with a carnival the entire season. In a recent interview with a carnival owner, it was learned that one of his foremen earns a bonus amounting to 2 percent of the ride's gross at the end of the season. This in addition to this weekly wage of $150 per week.[20]

Another example of a carnival worker is the concession agent. These individuals operate the flat-stores and hanky-panks. In some cases they are paid like salesmen in that they receive a weekly wage plus a commission, whereas in another instance we might discover an agent on straight salary. However, we should note that there is a greater distinction among "concessionaires" than simply the manner in which they are paid. "Flatties" (those who operate the straightforward gambling concessions) are sometimes looked down upon by hanky-pank operators because the hanky-pank operators feel themselves to be more legitimate since they give a "prize everytime." What is more, we have often heard performers suggest that flatties are nothing more than common thieves and that they (the entertainers) at least give the suckers something for their money. A final note should be added concerning flat stores. The number of these concessions is very often limited by carnival owners, not because of a shortage of persons with the requisite skills, but that the rigged or "gaffed" character of their games tends to keep the patch very busy.

---

[19] Krassowski, op. cit., p. 20.
[20] Interview with C. C. Groscurth, owner of the Blue Grass Shows at the Michigan State Fair, September 1971.

The work organization of the carnival therefore, is highly differentiated. What is more, patterns of social interaction often coincide with these divisions of labor. That is, it is not unusual to hear a performing family admonish their children for playing with the children of a "roughie" or ride boy. However, counteracting this tendency is the carnival ideology that "we're all in the same boat" which is a recognition of the fact that carnies are usually, if not always, seen as deviant by the community in which they are temporarily located. A far more typical admonition would involve sanctioning a carnie child for playing with a "sucker punk."

Having introduced the notion of deviance let us now ask about the extent to which the carnival work system may be properly referred to as deviant.

THE CARNIVAL AS A MARGINALLY LEGAL WORK SYSTEM

In addition to confusing the carnival world with the circus, the public more often than not perceives the carnival as a deviant group. The reasons for this attribution of deviance are many and not entirely irrational. Let us examine some of the work activities within each division of carnival labor with a view toward understanding the tendency on the part of the public to label the carnival as a deviant group.

One of the groups that the public comes into contact with most frequently is the ride operators (foremen and second men). Since this group typically recruits its members from the lower and working classes, it often manifests the class behavior of its non-carnival class counterparts. Accordingly, it is not unusual for the public to detect evidence of heavy alcohol use, cleanliness norms not shared by the patron, and public use of profanity. Since the public sees the ride operator as shouldering great responsibility (at least when their children ride the device) it is easy to understand the attribution of deviance to this group.

Concession agents as a group are likely to earn the deviant label since the public perceives their games as rigged, and this perception is more accurate. For example, the hanky-panks which offer "a prize everytime" are accused of being so designed that it is virtually impossible to win a large prize; whereas the flat stores are accused of outright robbery. Concerning the legitimacy of these attributions of deviance, it can be noted that the public's perceptions are rooted in experience since the "prize everytime" awarded by hanky-panks typically involves a small very inexpensive novelty item (called "slum" by carnies), and in fact it is very difficult to win a large prize. Take as example a typical hanky-panky like the "duck pond," where the object of the game is to select a small plastic duck from several floating in a circular tank. Here, there simply are no ducks whose numbers correspond to a large prize.[21]

Concerning flat-stores it can be truthfully said that the patron's experience is very likely, if not always going to involve losing money.[22] In short, through often complex technological devices flat stores are rigged in favor of their operators.

Even the "guess your age—guess your weight" concessions which are not rigged in any manner, have a built-in benefit for their operators. When the patron selects the type of prize he is playing for (the bottom, middle or top shelf) it turns out that nothing on these shelves costs the operator more than the price to the patron for playing. Thus, even when the operator "loses" (fails to guess the patrons' age within two years, or his weight within three pounds) he wins, because the prize selected by the "winning" patron costs the operator less than what the "mark" has payed to play. The public attribution of deviance to concession agents is therefore not unfounded.

The performers by virtue of their various acts are likely to be perceived as deviant. For example, most carnival patrons have difficulty understanding the psychology of a person who punctures his or her body with pins and needles for pay (the "human pin cushion"), or a person who each day eats a number of razor blades and light bulbs ("the man with the iron stomach"). Indeed, we might hypothesize that one way in which the public rationalizes these performances is to believe that they are "faked" in some way. The truth is that they are not.

In addition to "freaks" of the type described above, we might also note the patron's difficulty in understanding how females can display their bodies for wage as is the case in the girl shows. While there are noncarnival counterparts to this situation (topless barmaids, dancers) this public incomprehension would increase if the patrons were made aware of the fact that sometimes the "barker" who convinced them to enter the girl show is the star stripper's spouse.

Other performances which are likely to be labeled deviant are the wild man, or "geek" shows as they are called by carnies. Here the performer dons a costume of animal skins, sometimes wears a long haired wig and sits in a pit-like box with snakes and lizards of various types. The "show" as it were, consists of patrons walking to the edge of the pit and peering over the edge

[21] It should be noted, however, that a duck whose number does correspond to a large prize can very easily be slipped into the tank by the operator through a hole in the back of the tank should the game's legitimacy be questioned by a local law enforcer.

[22] Re: the carnival hustling process, see Nathe, op. cit., Appendix B, pp. 41–42. Re: carnival games in general, see John Scarne, *Scarne's Complete Guide to Gambling* (New York, Simon and Schuster, 1961), pp. 456–523.

at the performer as he or she handles the snakes and lizards. In some cases the "geek" will remove the head of a snake by biting it, an act which is quickly seen as deviant. While the animal-eating geek show is becoming increasingly rare, the public still tends to view these wild man performances as deviant in character.

Finally, with the administrative level, we could hypothesize that if the public was made aware of the activities of the "patch" they would probably apply the deviant label. But if the public knew of the work activities of the "patch", they would also learn a great deal about some of the work activities of local public officials. Recall that one of the major responsibilities of the "patch" is to make "pay-offs" to local officials.

This brief catalogue of carnival work activities has been drawn together with a view toward shedding some light upon the public attribution of deviance to the carnival world. As such we believe it stands as a reasonably good example of how labeling theory has helped us to understand why carnies often wear the deviant label.[23] However, by reconceptualizing our observations we think this catalogue of work activities has implications for the development of a general typology for work systems.

It can be seen that one way to classify these work activities is to ask about their relationship to legal norms.[24] For example, some of these activities could clearly be called deviant *vis-a-vis* legal norms (flat stores, the patch, alcoholism), yet recalling our description of the work activities of the "advance man" or "lot man" we see that we could refer to other activities as conforming to legal norms (at least they do not violate legal norms). On the other hand, many of the work activities just cited violate community norms (i.e., non-legal norms in the form of folkways, customs and mores). For example, cleanliness norms, exhibiting one's body for pay, eating potentially dangerous objects, "freak" shows and the like. Beginning with these two types of norms, we would like to develop a typology for work systems in terms of the entent to which the activities associated with them either deviate or conform to community and legal norms. Concerning justification for using such an approach we would cite Howard S. Becker in his well known work on marijuana users and dance musicians, where he notes that the work activities of certain occupational groups are often seen as

---

[23] Re: the limits of labeling theory, see Edwin M. Schur, "Reactions to Deviance: A Critical Assessment," *American Journal of Sociology,* Vol. 75 (1969), pp. 309–22; and Don C. Gibbons and Joseph F. Jones, "Some Critical Notes on Current Definitions of Deviance," *Pacific Sociological Review,* Vol. 14 (1971), pp. 20–37.

[24] Re: problems in the definition of legal norms, see Jack P. Gibbs, "Definitions of Law and Empirical Questions," *Law and Society Review,* Vol. 2 (1968), pp. 429–46; and his earlier "Norms: The Problem of Definition and Classification," *American Journal of Sociology,* Vol 70 (1965), pp. 586–94.

deviant despite the fact that the work is often entirely in accord with the legal norms. Talking specifically about dance musicians, he observes:

> Though their activities are formally within the law, their culture and way of life are sufficiently bizarre and unconventional for them to be labeled as outsiders by more conventional members of the community.[25]

In taxonomic form therefore, the dance musician work system would fit into a cell representing the intersection where work activities conform to legal norms, yet are deviant when compared to community norms. Indeed, it might prove fruitful to use Becker's concept of the "outsider" to analogously represent work systems as well as persons who have been labeled deviant.[26] The taxonomy in Figure 17.1 is presented not only to explore this avenue but in hopes that it can lead us to see other possibilities.

Work Activities
in relation to
Community Norms

		Deviant	Conforming
Deviant Work Activities in Relation to Legal Norms		Deviant Work System	"Vigilante" Work System
Conforming		"Outsider" Work System	Conforming Work System

Figure 17.1. A Typology for Work Systems

Looking at the three remaining cells in our taxonomy we see that the notions of the deviant work system and the conforming work system could be placed in the upper left and lower right hand cells respectively. Here the deviant work system would involve a social organization whose work activities are deviant not solely in legal terms, but also deviant *vis-a-vis* community

[25] Howard S. Becker, *Outsiders* (New York, Free Press, 1963), p. 79.
[26] Three levels of possible discussion seem apparent: deviance of the actor, deviance of a social role, and deviance of an organized system of roles. Our concern here is with the last.

norms. The conforming work system on the other hand, is one whose work activities lie within the framework of both legal and community norms. The upper right hand cell in our taxonomy defines a work system whose activities are deviant in terms of legal norms, yet conforming with respect to community norms. Having delineated these logical possibilities and placed some familiar concepts into them, let us ask about some examples.

The "outsider" work system of the dance musician has been the focus of a major work by Becker and needs little elaboration here. We would suggest however, that other work systems that operate within the framework of legal norms yet are sometimes in violation of community norms, could be placed into this taxonomic category. Some likely examples might be the work systems of taxi-drivers and hotel bell-hops (unless, of course, some of the work activities associated with these systems do in fact deviate from legal norms—a point to be considered below). The deviant work system normally contains members whom Polsky has called "career deviants," actors for whom "illegal activity . . . constitutes . . . [their] regular job."[27] Typical studies of such workers would include Sutherland's early discussion of the professional thief,[28] Maurer's study of pickpockets,[29] the discussion of armed robbers by Roebuck and Cadwalleder,[30] and Polsky's work on pool hustlers.[31]

There is a vast literature which both defines and describes the social structure of various careers, jobs and occupations within conforming work systems. Hall's work on the medical profession,[32] Whyte's investigation of waitresses,[33] and Peter Berger's collection of articles dealing with several different occupations[34] present examples of work systems that violate neither legal nor community norms.

The final cell in our taxonomy represents a work system whose activities are classifiable as deviant in terms of legal norms yet conform to community norms. For want of a better name, we have termed this the "vigilante" work system since extra-legal organizations seeking to implement the local com-

[27] Ned Polsky, *Hustlers, Beats and Others* (New York, Doubleday, Anchor Book edition, 1969), pp. 93–94.

[28] Edwin Sutherland, *The Professional Thief* (Chicago, University of Chicago Press, 1937).

[29] David W. Maurer, *Whiz Mob* (New Haven, Conn., College and University Press, 1964).

[30] Julian Roebuck and Mervyn Cadwalleder, "The Negro Armed Robber as a Criminal Type," *Pacific Sociological Review,* Vol. 4 (1961), pp. 21–26. Also see Werner Einstadter, "The Social Organization of Armed Robbery," *Social Problems,* Vol. 17 (1969), pp. 64–83.

[31] Polsky, op. cit.

[32] Oswald Hall, "The Stages of a Medical Career," *American Journal of Sociology* 53 (1948), pp. 327–36.

[33] William F. Whyte, "The Social Structure of the Restaurant," *American Journal of Sociology* 54 (1949), pp. 302–10.

[34] Peter L. Berger (ed.), *The Human Shape of Work* (New York, Macmillan, 1964).

munity's notions of justice represent a good example of this form. Thus, an organization like the Ku Klux Klan might do illegal acts with the general consent of the local population. However, less dramatic work systems might also act as examples, including, to a degree, such operations as bootlegging or bookie rings which constitute illegal practices that everyone might condone except for the few persons commissioned to enforce the law. There would seem to be some evidence that within many a college campus community the sale of marijuana may be an example of such legal deviance which is not contrary to the local norms. Comparatively little work has been done on the type of work organization designated by this final cell of our taxonomy, but it represents a form of special interest for any developing theory of deviance.

As we noted in our earlier description some carnival work activities may be classified as deviant in terms of legal norms, whereas others might be called deviant with respect to community norms. At the same time, many carnival work activities conform to both types of norms. For example, it might be argued that with the exceptions noted above, the majority of carnival work activities conform to legal norms. Laws defining the circumstances under which individuals or groups of individuals may form corporations, legal restrictions placed upon the preparation and serving of foodstuffs, various local codes defining the proper uses and distribution of such necessities as electricity and water, and even trade union contracts are conformed to in the carnival work system.

In a similar manner, while many of the work activities cited violate community norms, many other aspects of carnival life do not do so. Carnival children are encouraged to do well in school, and in cases known to the writers, are encouraged to attend colleges and universities. Moreover, those carnival families comprising the middle and upper levels of work organization (independent ride, show or concession owners; performers; and the administrative level) typically manifest many "straight" middle class values and behavior patterns. For example, during the winter months when carnies return to their home communities, it is not unusual to find them participating in a wide range of community activities. One interesting case involves a stripper who participates heavily in her local Parent-Teacher Association during the winter months. Needless to say, her summer occupation is unknown to her colleagues.

What we find therefore in the carnival work system is a mixture of conforming and deviant work activities in relation to both legal and community norms. With this mixture of conformity and deviance in mind, let us return to our typology with a view toward classifying the carnival as one of several different types of work systems.

It is clear that the carnival can not be called a conforming work system. Such a designation would imply that all carnival work activities conform to both legal and community norms—a situation not supported by our observations. In a similar manner, the mixture of conforming and deviant work activities in the carnival prevents us from placing it in the deviant work system category. Such a decision would imply that all carnival activities are deviant with respect to both legal and community norms.

To categorize the carnival as an "outsider" work system, we would have to find that carnival work activities are conforming in a legal sense but deviant *vis-a-vis* community norms, and categorizing it as a "vigilante" work system would mean the reverse. Since our observations reveal a mixture of conformity and deviance with respect to both types of norms, we must conclude that the carnival does not accurately reflect either an "outsider" or "vigilante" work system.

It can be seen that underlying our difficulty in categorizing the carnival as one of the several types of work systems in our taxonomy is the interesting mixture of conforming and deviant work activities. This is so regardless of the type of norm employed in the assessment of conformity and deviance. This mixture of deviance and conformity suggests an expansion of our original taxonomic categories.

Whenever the work activities associated with a particular work system neither fully conform nor fully deviate from either legal or community norms, we might refer to that social organization as a marginally legal work system.[35] While this term might seem to imply that the majority of work activities associated with a marginally legal work system are illegal, this is not our intention. This balance represents a continuum, and the problem of precisely defining the ratio of legal to illegal work activities shall not be examined here. Rather, let us return to our typology with a view toward modifying it to take account of marginally legal work systems. Figure 17.2 suggests the placement of the marginally legal work system relative to the other types we have discussed.

Figure 17.2 centrally places the marginally legal work system as neither fully conforming nor fully deviating from legal norms. The same is true of conformity or deviance relative to community norms. Since the concept of the marginally legal work system takes account of a work system whose activities manifest a mixture of conformity and deviance with respect to both legal and/or community norms, we now have a taxonomic category into which we can meaningfully place the carnival.

Figure 17.2 would suggest that rather than existing as a type of work system separate from others included in the original typology, the marginally legal work system actually represents a combination of the characteristics associated with the other work systems. The marginally legal work system shares characteristics common to the deviant, "outsider", "vigilante," and conforming work systems.

[35] We thank Clifton Bryant for first suggesting this term to us.

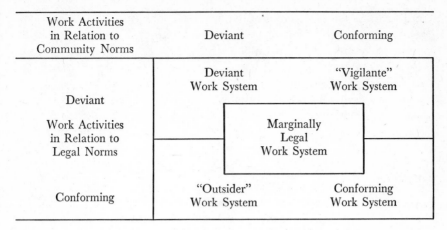

Figure 17.2. A Typology for Work Systems

As a marginally legal work system, the carnival represents a combination of characteristics common to other work systems, but the relationships can be quite complex. Visualizing our original taxonomy (Figure 17.1) as a mapping, we can see that the placement of a marginal system can vary in its location. Thus, as in Figure 17.3, it can, for example, predominantly reflect deviance from legal norms (Position A) or deviance from community norms (Position B).

Variations of placement of the marginally legal work system can exist

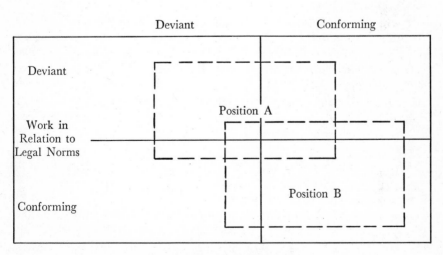

Figure 17.3. Variations in Marginal Work Activities
in Relation to Community Norms

according to the different ratios of deviance and conformity to both types of norms. Carnivals exhibiting most possible variations have existed empirically at one time or another. Historically, the American carnival has moved as a marginally legal work system from an earlier position represented by Position A to Position B in Figure 3.

If it proves possible to quantify the ratios of deviance and conformity to legal and community norms, the shape as well as the position of the cell we call the marginally legal work system will take on additional meaning.

SELECTED ADDITIONAL BIBLIOGRAPHY ON THE AMERICAN CARNIVAL

Anonymous
  1949   "I'll Gyp You Every Time." *The Saturday Evening Post* 222 (September 17):24.
Boles, Don
  1967   *The Midway Showman.* Atlanta: Pinchpenny Press.
Carrington, Hereward
  1913   *Sideshow and Animal Tricks.* Kansas City: A. W. Wilson.
Clausen, Connie
  1961   *I Love You Honey, But the Season is Over.* New York: Holt, Rinehart and Winston.
Dadswell, Jack
  1946   *Hey There Sucker.* Boston: Bruce Humphries.
De Belle, Starr
  1946   *Dictionary of Midway Slang: Webster Was a Sucker.* Cincinnati: Billboard Publications.
Doc and the Professor
  1939   *Hurry, Hurry, Hurry: A Handbook of the Modern Carnival Midway.* Providence: Pyramid Publishers.
Gibson, Walter
  1946   *The Bunco Book.* Holyoke, Mass.: Sidney Reader.
Gresham, William Lindsay
  1948   "The World of Mirth." *Life* 25 (September 13):142.
  1953   *Monster Midway.* New York: Rinehart and Co.
  1960   "Its Magic is the Magic of Life." *New York Times Book Review* 65 (March 13):34-35.
Holtzman, Jerry, and Harry Lewiston
  1968   *Freak Show Man.* Los Angeles: Holloway House Publishing Co.
Jones, John Paul
  1947   "Carnival Comes on Cat Feet." *Christian Science Monitor* Magazine Section (July 26):5.

Klein, Frederick C.
1969 "Step Right Up: How 'Heels' Shapiro Makes a Tidy Living Off a Carnival Game." *The Wall Street Journal* (Tuesday, September 30):1.

Kobler, J.
1953 "World's Biggest Show: Royal American Shows." *Cosmopolitan* 135 (November):78‒93.

Lewis, Arthur H.
1970 *Carnival.* New York: Trident Press.

Mannix, Daniel P.
1948 "Strange People." *True* (September):34.
1951 *Step Right Up.* New York: Harper and Bros.
1958 "Sex on Sawdust." *Playboy* (June):17.
1961 "Two-legged Fox of the Midway." *True* (July):46.
1964 "A Rare Look at Rare People." *True* (January):60.

Maurer, David W.
1931 "Carnival Cant: A Glossary of Circus and Carnival Slang." *American Speech* 6:327–37.

Millstein, Gilbert
1952 "Carnie Biz—Bigger than Ever." *New York Times Magazine* (May 18):22.

Mockridge, Norton
1970 "Carnival." *The American Way* (New York: American Airlines) (May):8‒21.

Poling, James
1953 "Sawdust in Their Shoes." *The Saturday Evening Post* 225 (April 11):32‒33, 102‒03, 105 & 107.

Skardon, James A., and Arthur Shay
1957 "Carny" Kids. *Coronet* (December):148‒57.

Time
1956 "The Last Individualists." *Time* 68 (August 30):38‒39.
1959 "No More Rubes." *Time* 72 (September 29):41‒42.

Zinser, William K.
1967 "A Lot of Quarters." *Look* 31 (September 5):18.

V

ILLEGAL OCCUPATIONS AND WORK SYSTEMS

Deviant Vocations

Rich man, poor man, beggar man, thief! All societies except those with the most rudimentary division of labor frequently have persons whose vocational pursuits are in violation of formal norms and are therefore deviant if not illegal. Krause has suggested that such deviant or illegal occupations may be articulated into those that render some service to their clientele, even if in violation of the norms, and those that are essentially "predatory upon the public."[1] Prostitution or bookmaking are examples of the former, while thievery or extortion are illustrations of the latter.

One might argue that many "professional" criminals also render a service (albeit illegal) to a clientele. The "contract" killer and career political assassin kill impersonally, at the specific request of someone who pays their fees. Many burglars and thieves steal on order, delivering specified goods to a "fence" who, in turn, passes them on to customers at prices under those of comparable merchandise that is not "hot." Social scientists have essentially neglected the study of our clandestine economy based on stolen goods. A significant segment of our population may well depend in some degree on access to stolen goods as a means of maintaining a satisfactory level of living. Professional murderers and thieves may depend on and service a clientele, who have no other means of effecting their goals through legitimate channels. In *The Godfather*, for example, one father came to Don Corleone and sought revenge for his raped and dishonored daughter, when the police and district attorney failed to effect punishment appropriate to the crime. In parts of West Africa secret societies operate to obtain revenge illicitly for their members and as an expeditious means of collecting debts, using fear and force to accelerate the collection process. The "hatchet man" of the Chinese tongs in our country at the turn of the century served much the same function, affording individuals an illegal means of obtaining justice or maintaining some degree of social equilibrium through extranormative channels. As Krause puts it, "The *latent* function of most illegal occupations lies in their ability to handle the unsolved problems (premarital pregnancy,

[1] Elliott A. Krause, *The Sociology of Occupations* (Boston, Little, Brown, 1971), p. 279.

sexual frustration in marriage) which may burden individuals within the existing social system."[2]

George Ritzer makes the point that "most deviant occupations are free occupations; that is, they do not exist in formal organizations."[3] In large measure this is true, although he does mention criminal organizations such as the Costa Nostra. We must not overlook the smaller work systems such as abortion "mills," brothels, clandestine bookie "joints," and after-hours clubs which function as mechanisms of mass evasion for the violation of the closing laws.[4] But admittedly in large measure the deviant occupational member is a self-employed practitioner who presumably enjoys the gratifications and challenges of American free enterprise at its most elementary level.

While the economically and socially lower classes are perhaps the most victimized by various kinds of exploitive illegal occupations, at the same time, the illegal occupations may offer job opportunities that would not otherwise be available to persons of this social level. Criminal occupations may offer opportunities for survival and mobility as opposed to the alternative of idleness and starvation. The "moonshiner" often produces illegal whiskey because it may be the only way he can support his family. Some illegal pursuits are far from lucrative, yet they often still appear economically attractive to persons who are culturally deprived and occupationally inept. In other cases certain deviant occupational enterprises may offer exceptional economic rewards and therefore have extraordinary appeal to persons with aspirations of wealth and no practical licit means of implementing such a goal. A young attractive female, for example, who yearns for a luxurious lifestyle, but has no talent to catapult her into stardom and no prospective wealthy husband may become a high-priced call girl. Krause states:

> Schoolteachers with expensive tastes ... these are the ones who will choose prostitution ... as [a] career. But in general, the lack of economic opportunity for women and the dull exploitative jobs in factories and offices available to them, at present as well as in the past, have been a powerful factor predisposing them toward prostitution and related occupations.[5]

Illegal skills are like any other occupational skills, and some individuals are the recipients of occupational inheritance. A young mountaineer may

[2] Ibid., p. 290.

[3] George Ritzer, *Man and His Work: Conflict and Change* (New York, Appleton-Century-Crofts, 1972), p. 275.

[4] For a detailed description and analysis of the operations, clientele, and functions of an After-Hours club, see Julien Roebuck and D. Wood Harper, Jr., "The After-Hours Club: An Illegal Social Organization and Its Clients." Paper read at the Thirty-fifth annual meeting of the Southern Sociological Society, New Orleans, Louisiana (April 7, 1972).

[5] Ibid., p. 283.

follow in the occupational footsteps of his moonshining father, and the teen-aged son of the Mafia leader may be groomed to take over the responsibilities of his father's criminal leadership role. Girls are occasionally trained in the sexual arts by their prostitute mothers, and some criminal skills such as safe cracking and counterfeiting may be jealously guarded family secrets, accruing to the eldest son.

The exigencies of time and social circumstances have made deviant practitioners out of those in formerly legal pursuits (and vice versa), for norms and public values change with fickle regularity. What was a speakeasy during Prohibition may now be only a neighborhood bar, and the patent-medicine huckster of yesterday may be in violation of Federal Pure Food and Drug Administration regulations today. Some prostitutes are complaining that the loose morals of the young people today are hurting their business since many girls "give it away free." With attitudes about abortion undergoing rapid change, criminal abortionists may soon be a thing of the past since many doctors now legally perform abortion on demand.

Yet most illegal occupations are, in fact, true occupations. They often have history and rich tradition. They have structure and not infrequently have an elaborate attendant subculture. Individuals are selectively recruited as in conventional occupations. They are subjected to involved socialization processes, sometimes even of a formal nature. (Oliver Twist, if you recall, went to thieves' school.) Counterfeit money engraving is not an inherited skill, and quality fornication requires expertise not acquired through maturation alone. There are operant controls and career contingencies. Illegal practitioners, like members of regular occupations, exhibit craftsmanship values and pride in the product or service they render. Polly Adler, the famous brothel madame, had an allegedly justifiable reputation for what she termed "the quality of my establishment and consideration of my customers." People in deviant occupations develop distinctive work routines, esoteric skills, and occupational ideologies often unique to their calling. They have their career ups and downs, some succeeding and others falling short of "the big time." Like any line of work, theirs may on occasion be disaffective or stressful, if not otherwise dysfunctional. There are also unique hazards, risks, and pathologies attendant to their work. In the final analysis, however, where a particular kind of goods or services is demanded, (even if contraindicated by law and custom) there will inevitably be those who will supply it—and often with the aplomb and dedication of a professional.

THE PRODUCTION AND SALE OF MOUNTAIN DEW

Although some have suggested that the distillation of alcohol was originated by medieval European alchemists, in reality the practice was much older. Aristotle mentions it in his *Meteorology,* and there are accounts of distilled liquors being made from rice in China and Japan and from rice and flowers in India at least eight centuries before Christ.[6] Nevertheless, distilled alcoholic beverages have perhaps been more closely associated historically with Europe and America than other parts of the world.

The Mayflower and the other early vessels carrying the colonists also carried adequate supplies of alcoholic beverages, including distilled spirits.[7] The settlers made and imbibed spirits, and in Boston America had its first saloon by 1625. Later many prominent colonial leaders such as George Washington and Thomas Jefferson operated distilleries on their estates to produce whiskey for their own use.[8] By the early 1600s alcoholic over-indulgence had become something of a problem. At about the same time the colonies began to regulate alcohol manufacture, sale, and consumption.

One of the first serious challenges to the authority of our early federal government was the so-called Whiskey Rebellion of 1794.[9] Farmers of the upper Monongahela of western Pennsylvania raised grain and used the surplus to make rye whiskey. The distilled spirits were easier to transport than the grain itself, and the rye whiskey became a standard of exchange, interchangeable with money, throughout the region. Lacking the roads and adequate transportation for their crops, the settlers turned to whiskey-making as an economic necessity. Distilled spirits were compact and light in weight and thus an efficient medium in which to contain their grain crops.

In 1791 the government levied a tax on the whiskey, which was bitterly resented and resisted by farmers of the area. They assaulted federal officials who tried to collect the tax, terrorized local farmers who disclosed the location of stills to officials, and threatened an armed attack on the federal garrison in Pittsburgh. A volunteer federal army of 15,000 was raised and marched into the region, broke the insurrection, and captured some of the ringleaders. The power of the federal government to tax whiskey prevailed—although some Americans never accepted this fact.

In spite of excise taxes, laws, regulatory rules, government edicts, "revenuer" agents, national prohibition, and other assorted impediments and hinderances, a significant number of Americans have continued to pursue the ancient art and craft of whiskey-making in their own way without regard for statutory constraints.

---

[6] See Marshall J. Robb, *Scotch Whiskey* (New York, E. P. Dutton, 1951), p. 15.
[7] For a detailed history of distilled spirits see Jess Carr, *The Second Oldest Profession: An Informal History of Moonshining in America* (Englewood Cliffs, N.J., Prentice-Hall, 1972), especially Chapters One and Two.
[8] Ibid., pp. 11–15.
[9] See Margaret L. Coit, and the Editors of *Life, The Life History of the United States, Volume 3: 1789–1829—The Growing Years* (New York, Time Inc., 1963), p. 17.

Illicit whiskey-making, or moonshining as it is popularly known, has continued to flourish in this country for a number of reasons. Even until relatively recent times the problem of crop transportation to market has continued to exist in some isolated rural areas.[10] The roads were particularly bad in much of the southern Appalachian region through the 1920s and into the 1930s. In some places they are still nonexistent or pathetic in quality. In this region moonshining has tended to endure and flourish.

Alcoholic spirits have from the earliest history had medical properties ascribed to them. Controversy still continues about the actual therapeutic value of alcohol, but alcoholic beverages do often moderate or alleviate the *symptomatic* discomfort of medical disorders and infirmities. Liquor has historically served an important analgesic function for many of our isolated frontier, rural, and mountain settlers. Until the mid-twentieth century, physicians were not readily available, which caused the development of a substitute: folk medicine. It often involved so-called patent medicines, frequently highly laced with alcohol and morphine and home remedies which also depended heavily on pure corn whiskey for their effectiveness. The large number of wounded and disabled veterans from the American Civil War (and from the Spanish American War) plus the heavy child-bearing regimen of many rural women coupled with the erosive physical effects of hard work, the elements, and poor nutrition—all took their toll in terms of chronic ailments and discomforts calling for symptomatic reliefs, often from a jug of homemade whiskey.

In the early years of our country almost everyone, regardless of his economic or social station, drank homemade whiskey. In more recent times, however, as a commercial licit liquor industry has developed, the more affluent citizens have been able to afford licensed alcoholic beverages, but the poor have often had to resort to the "moonshine bootlegger" for their liquor supplies. Nontaxed homemade whiskey is cheaper than commercially distilled taxed whiskey by a significant margin. It may lack the subtleties of flavor and body and the uniform quality of commercial whiskey, but it is effective and cheaper; to bargain seekers moonshine is a most attractive package. Illicit whiskey-making also has flourished because it affords a supply of alcoholic spirits when not available through legal channels.

The term *moonshiner* often conjures up a rural or mountaineer type like Snuffy Smith. However, during Prohibition the great alcohol demand was urban, and the beer barons and booze lords established their breweries

---

[10] For an interesting account of an isolated community in the South that nurtured moonshining until recently, see Lynwood Montell, "Coe Ridge Moonshining: Social Evil or Economic Necessity." Paper read at the annual meeting of the Western History Association, Santa Fe, New Mexico (October 14, 1971).

and distilleries in the big cities. (Interestingly, federal law enforcement officials even today encounter illegal stills in urban settings, some gigantic in capacity, but the majority are smaller stills known as "nip joints." Urban dwellers also seem to have a taste for "white lightning.") No doubt some of the crime syndicate operations must have recruited distillers from the hills. In states that retained Prohibition after the repeal of the Volstead Act and in local-option counties that elected to remain "dry," persons who sold illegal whiskey were known as "bootleggers." Many such persons sold regular alcoholic beverages derived from legal production sources in other states. In some instances the bootlegging of regular federally taxed spirits was extremely big business. Mississippi, for example, during its dry days, imposed a "black market" tax on the illegal sale of such whiskey. Accordingly bootleggers would pay their black market tax to the state, and an "operating tax" in the form of bribes to local law enforcement officials and run their liquor business on a semi-open basis. Some areas in the deep South, for example, traditionally had "drive-in" bootleg establishments where the customer drove up in his car, blew his horn and got curb service. In some locales, bootleggers even listed themselves in the yellow pages (under thinly disguised business titles), offered home delivery, and proffered charge accounts to preferred customers. Only a few years back in one large southern metropolitan area, a well-known bootleg wholesaler announced his intention to retire late one fall. The local newspaper editorialized on his retirement and made a plea that he stay in business until after the yule season so as not to discommode his customers. In so doing, they argued, he could be performing a constructive community service.

The moonshiner, however, makes and often sells illicit whiskey. In spite of the very strenuous efforts of the government to suppress moonshining activity, it has never been entirely successful in doing so. In the late 1870s, for example, the commissioner of Internal Revenue reported that over the preceding four-year period, more than 4,000 stills had been seized or destroyed, and more than 7,000 persons arrested.[11] In the 1950s and 1960s, as many as 20,000 stills a year were being seized or destroyed, but even so, during this time an estimated 40 to 60 million gallons of non-tax-paid whiskey was being manufactured each year.[12] Admittedly in very recent years the government's war against moonshiners has been somewhat more successful.

Law enforcement techniques to locate and arrest moonshiners have become more sophisticated, employing airplanes, helicopters, and elaborate radio communication devices. The moonshiner, likewise, has also become modern in his approach to evading discovery and arrest. He too

[11] Ibid., p. 38.
[12] Ibid., p. 137.

makes use of walkie-talkie communication and may even fly over his own still to check its camouflage effectiveness. In some cases he has employed equally imaginative disguise techniques in his manufacturing process, for example, adding deodorant to used mash and even coloring it.[13]

Moonshining is a major illicit industry, employing perhaps more than 200,000 people ranging from "being professional sugar gatherers to craftsmen engaged in making the stills."[14] For most such illicit practitioners, however, their participation in moonshining is a spare-time occupation, an excellent way for some farmers, loggers, coal miners, and workers to "moonlight." Moonshine liquor is obviously profitable. Without the usual costs involved in taxes, overhead, advertising, licenses, rent or building, and fringe benefits, illegal whiskey is much less expensive than legal whiskey. The profit margin is considerable, and this no doubt attracts many to moonshining as an economically productive sideline. As one moonshiner was reported to have said, "You know, when a man's family is hungry, he'll make liquor or [do] anything to feed them."[15] Many moonshiners who have given up their trade voluntarily or been forced out by law enforcement pressures have ended up on welfare roles.

Moonshine, "pop-skull," "white lightening," "mountain dew," or whatever name it goes by is an alcoholic beverage with unique properties of taste and effect. Many people prefer it to legal liquor. Carr points out:

> First of all, millions of people really like it—swear by it, in fact. Long, habitual drinking of the dynamite-like liquid makes all other drinks seem childishly mild in contrast. To some laboring-class men, if a drink doesn't take the top of your head off, you've been cheated.[16]

Moonshiners themselves often seem quite partial to their own product, claiming it is superior to tax-paid whiskey. As one enthusiastically put it:

> "If I could walk into a liquor store and buy moonshine, I'd kick any guy who offered me the other kind. And I'd say seven out of 10 people around here feel the same way."[17]

Many people, particularly the isolated eastern mountain dwellers, have always harbored deep-seated resentment against government interference with their lives, including the taxing and regulation of whiskey manufacture and consumption. They fight back by continuing the practice of moon-

[13] Ibid., p. 139.
[14] Ibid., p. 141–42.
[15] Bob Cooper, "Moonshine Makin' A Dying Art," *Bowling Green,* Kentucky *Daily News.* (Sunday, October 18, 1970), p. 9.
[16] Carr, op. cit., p. 143.
[17] Cooper, op. cit.

shining. Local inhabitants are seldom, if ever, inclined to report such activities and are reluctant to cooperate with law enforcement officials. Juries made up of people from the region may be prone to acquit or levy mild sentences. Moonshining is a way of life for some in addition to being a clandestine occupational pursuit.

Moonshine, with all of its redeeming features, unfortunately also has several dysfunctional characteristics, often the result of bad craftsmanship in its manufacture. In addition to often tasting "raw and firey," moonshine can be potentially lethal. Practices such as carrying or storing moonshine in a galvanized can by the unknowledgeable has caused blindness for those who drink it. Some amateur moonshiners have been known to include lye, potash, or clorox in their product so that it will "bead" better and have a better "bite."[18] In the true spirit of craftsmanship, however, such practices are bitterly condemned by the "genuine" master-moonshiners. One, for example, said:

> [A] man ought to be put in a chain gang with a ball tied to him if he uses potash to make whiskey. 'Bout all you call that is low-down meanness. He ain't makin' it t'drink himself, and he ain't makin' it fit for anyone else to drink neither.[19]

A frequent practice in recent years is the use of automobile radiators as condensor coils in the absence of more appropriate equipment. Unfortunately, the lead salts from the radiator coils contaminate the whiskey and cause pain, blindness, paralysis, or death for the drinker. An estimated 30 to 40 percent of all moonshine whiskey has some concentration of lead salts.[20] Other moonshiners have on occasion used ether, paint thinner, rubbing alcohol, and even antifreeze to "enrich" their product. Lack of good petrochemical engineering knowledge can indeed be an ultimate hazard to the consumer. Quality control and cleanliness in manufacture is not, generally speaking in recent years, characteristic of the moonshining process. Insects, snakes, even rats have been known to be mixed up in the mash. At best, moonshine is "unique;" at worst it is a filthy poison. The moonshiner, like other men of commerce, has apparently been corrupted by greed and all too often has substituted quantity for quality.

The chapter in this Part is John L. Gordon's essay on moonshining in the Georgia mountains. He provides an elaborate account of the technology and procedures involved, but more importantly, he also affords an intimate

[18] Ibid.

[19] Buck Carver, "Moonshining as a Fine Art," in *The Foxfire Book* (Garden City, N.Y., Doubleday, 1972).

[20] Carr, op. cit., pp. 138–39.

glimpse of the life and mind of a moonshiner and his family. Doc, the moonshiner, is portrayed as sterotypical of the mountain dweller who moonshines for economic gains, to realize his creative capacity, and because, as Gordon puts it, "moonshining satisfies a fundamental craving of the mountain personality. Moonshining is action, it is thrills and it is the antithesis of the routine—it is frightfully unpredictable."

THE OLDEST PROFESSION

The shaman, or witch doctor, of paleolithic times, ancestor to today's minister and medical healers, was perhaps the oldest true "professional" in the sense of being a specialized practitioner. The prostitute was, however, apparently not far behind on the occupational scene. By neolithic times, prostitution was well established in the Mesopotamian city-states.

Prostitution apparently flourished in all of the early civilizations, and in fact was institutionalized as a component of religious ritual and offering. In Babylon, for example, all women customarily went once in their lifetime to the temple at Mylitta to prostitute themselves with a stranger as a religious offering.[21] In both Egypt and Phoenicia girls at one time or another in their lives were temple prostitutes. In other early societies, particularly in the Mediterranean region, prostitution was the customary method for "the daughters of the common people" to accumulate money for their marriage dowry. The Babylonian goddess of fertility was also the goddess of prostitution. Accordingly, various fertility ceremonies and *rites-de-passage* involved some kind of ritualized prostitution. Presumably economic prostitution grew out of the ritualized forms of religious prostitution.

By the Greek era there were elaborate houses of prostitution, even some state brothels, labeled *Dicteria*.[22] The prostitutes of such brothels were, in a sense, civil servants, even though they enjoyed a relatively low societal status and were deprived of most of their citizen's rights. Because of such treatment and some repressive laws, courtesans had formed themselves into corporations or unions for collective protection. Marriages were seldom based on love but were more often marriages of convenience and property or were arranged by families, and adultery with a married woman was sternly sanctioned. The brothels were viewed as a necessary evil for preventing adultery by affording an approved sexual outlet for married men.

Athenian prostitutes, like prostitutes today, ranged from the brothel inmate to the "streetwalker" to the semi- or part-time prostitute who was

---

[21] For a detailed discussion of this practice, see Fernando Henriques, *Stews and Strumpets: A Survey of Prostitution (Volume I, Primitive, Classical and Oriental)* (London, MacGibbon & Kee, 1961), pp. 121–22.

[22] See ibid., especially Ch. II.

connected with entertainment and provided sexual services on an ancillary basis to her other forms of entertainment.

In Rome the public baths were used for clandestine meetings with lovers and with prostitutes. In time many of the baths had become little more than brothels with washing and massage facilities. As with the Greeks, some prostitutes also offered dancing and musical instrumentation as allied talents.[23] Unlike Greece, however, there does not appear to have been any major development of religious prostitution. The abundance of women slaves in Rome and women of lower economic levels perhaps made the flowering of prostitution inevitable. But the rigid marriage laws and the sexual preoccupation flagrant in Roman religion, art and leisure no doubt nourished its growth.

In Europe up through the middle ages and into modern times prostitutes marched as camp followers, at the sides of the army. The famous song "Greensleeves" is about prostitute camp followers. The great cities of the continent have for centuries maintained their brothels, and prostitution has historically been very much an institutionalized part of European culture, tolerated as a desirable, if not necessary, component of the social enterprize.

In an earlier period in the United States prostitution was also viewed as something of a practical, albeit evil, necessity. The large waves of emmigrants inundating our shores were predominantly males, with minimal prospect of ever bringing women from the old country to be their wives. A high female mortality rate also added to the unbalanced ratio of males to females. In many of the isolated frontier and rural areas men were much in the majority, and frequently many of the male population never had the economic resources appropriate to marriage. The cowtown bordellos and the prostitutes' cribs in the ethnic ghettos were often the only sexual outlet available to significant portions of the male population. In addition, from the late 1800s until the 1920s (and even later in many regions), a common rationalization for prostitution was that it served a functional need in the face of the sexual Victorianism supposedly rampant in the land. Brothels were felt to afford a harmless outlet for male lust, and prostitution was viewed as a preferable alternative to rape and other sex crimes and depravity forced on "decent" women. Even today many still articulate such a sentiment. Prostitutes it would seem are especially fond of this rationalization. As one ex-madame echoed it:

> "I just wish they'd legalize prostitution," she said. "Honey, I'd donate money just to get things started. Be the best thing ever happened to this country. Save young fellas from forcing themselves on their girl

[23] See ibid., especially Ch. III.

friends. Save old men from getting involved with their secretaries. Save everybody from getting V.D. It would be great."[24]

In spite of the so-called social emancipation of women in recent decades, the general increase in sexual permissiveness and a more enlightened view of the female sexual urge, and the loss of the traditional rationalization, prostitution continues to thrive, both here and abroad. In Italy, for example, prostitution yields an estimated $3.4 billion per year.[25] In the sixteenth century, a census listed 20,000 prostitutes in Rome alone, and today 2,000 streetwalkers sometimes gather around soccer matches looking for clients. Although a 1958 law closed the brothels and technically outlawed prostitution, there are still approximately one million prostitutes in Italy—one in every 54 citizens. In Germany prostitution is such big business that one firm is offering to sell limited partnership shares in its chain operation. The money raised through the sale of these shares will be used for expansion purposes.[26] In France bordellos were outlawed after World War II, but streetwalkers filled the void. Today there are an estimated 35,000 regular prostitutes and 75,000 "part-time amateurs" in Paris alone.[27] Veneral disease rates are skyrocketing, and the streetwalkers are such a nuisance that some politicians are talking about legalizing brothels and having them managed by civil servants.

In the United States prostitution continues seemingly unabated by law enforcement pressures and undiminished in the face of widespread sexual promiscuousness. In some of the large cities the concentration of prostitutes has become so great that the police are being inundated by the frequent complaints of apartment house dwellers who find the prostitutes who live there are a decided nuisance. Their pique arises from the steady parade of clientele, some unsavory, to the prostitutes' apartments; the prostitutes' pimps who loiter, if not live, in the buildings; and the general noise and disturbance the prostitutes generate in the course of their business.[28] The prostitutes even walk the streets of the neighborhood "early in the morning, in time to catch [the] patronage of early rising construction workers."[29]

At one time prostitution was largely carried on either by independent

[24] George Vecsey, "I've Had a Wonderful Time. And I Feel Like I've Helped a Lot of People," *The New York Times* (Monday, December 27, 1971), p. 32.

[25] Charles W. Bell, "The Prostitution Boom in Italy," *The Washington Post* (Sunday, August 13, 1972), p. H14.

[26] Lorana O. Sullivan, "Love for Sale: Firm Operating Brothels Looks for Investors," *The Wall Street Journal* (Friday, December 31, 1971), pp. 1 and 13.

[27] "Bring Back the Brothels?" *Time*, Vol. 96, No. 19 (November 9, 1970), p. 30.

[28] Lesley Oelsner, "Prostitute Neighbors Vexing Tenants, Especially in Luxury Units," *The New York Times* (Sunday, August 22, 1971), p. 46.

[29] Eric Pace, "Operation Eros Seeks Eviction of Prostitutes," *The New York Times* (January 23, 1972).

streetwalkers or within brothels. Brothels ranged from shabby rooming houses in the slums, staffed by a handful of derelict women, to plush genteel mansions, offering a full complement of beautiful women. Many famous dixieland jazz musicians began their musical careers as piano players in New Orleans whore houses. Some brothels attained regional and even national fame (or infamy, depending on one's point of view) and could boast of having entertained celebrities and politicians of national prominence. The brothel often housed an elaborate work system, including cooks, maids, musicians, bouncers, prostitutes, and of course the madame who served as manager and general trouble shooter. Winick and Kinsie describe her job:

> A madam running a typical city brothel in the 1920s and 1930s carried many responsibilities: to make arrangements for opening the place, attract prostitutes and customers, effect working relationships with police authorities and customers, and otherwise run a complex business establishment. She also had to be sensitive to a client's special interests and know how to praise his choice of prostitute.
>
> Considerable tact was required to supervise a number of women competing with each other and working on a commission basis. The madam had to receive customers, encourage visitors to buy drinks, "show off" the prostitutes, collect and spend money, and keep records. She was the brothel representative who suffered punishment in case of a raid. If she were convicted and served time in prison, the brothel owner often paid her a fee for each day she was incarcerated. Although some madams regularly robbed clients who were too intoxicated to know what was happening, such behavior was infrequent.[30]

After World War II many brothels were slowly forced out of business by pressure and harassment from law enforcement officials, the high cost of "protection," and the changing tastes and requirements of the clientele. Many of the retired madams undertook to chronicle their occupational experiences, and a number of books, at least one movie, and innumerable television guest appearances resulted.[31] The brothel in time gave way to new patterns of prostitution. During World War II some imaginative entrepreneurs carried the brothel to the military camps in the form of a trailer, thus attempting to make the prostitutes as accessible as possible to the servicemen who might not be able to find transportation to nearby cities.[32]

---

[30] Charles Winick and Paul M. Kinsie, *The Lively Commerce: Prostitution in the United States* (New York, New American Library, 1972), p. 92.

[31] Among the better known autobiographies of brothel madames were Polly Adler, *A House is Not a Home* (New York, Popular Library, 1953) (made into a movie); Sally Stanford, *Madamehood as a Vocation* (G. P. Putnam's Sons, 1966); Stephen Longstreet, *Sportin' House* (Los Angeles, Sherbourne Press, 1965); and most recent, Pauline Tabor, *Pauline's* (Louisville, Touchstone, 1971).

[32] Winick and Kinsie, op. cit., p. 163.

One prostitute and her companion operated a pickup truck with covered sides as a rolling brothel.[33] In more recent and affluent times, private yachts have appeared as floating brothels.

The prostitute may increasingly be leaving the brothel for the hotel bar or to be a call girl, but she is not working alone. Rather, she is often part of a work system, involving concerted team effort. Her co-workers may include bell hops, cab drivers, bartenders, pimps, and even the attorney on retainer who will bail her out of jail when arrested.

In the past, as Winick and Kinsie point out, taxi dance halls and dance studios served as "covers for prostitution."[34] Newer guises include the ubiquitous "massage parlor," and the "escort service." Some massage parlors offer nothing but conventional massages (often of inferior quality) and some artificial companionship. Patrons are sometimes lured in by inaccurately perceived implicit promises of sexual gratification which are never realized. Other massage parlors do offer full prostitution services or, as an alternative, provide "local massages" (penis manipulation).[35] The escort service, or "rent-a-girl" system, purports to provide a female escort-guide for business-men who need female companionship for the evening. Many such services are "straight" and so are their girl employees; some girls may proposition their escorts as a means of picking up extra money.[36]

Prostitution is usually classified as deviant or criminal behavior, but it possesses all of the characteristics of an occupation, including a system of rewards, occupational recruitment and socialization, expected role behavior, structured relationships with clientele and colleagues, and mechanisms of control. Contrary to popular stereotype, prostitutes are not the victims of white slavery, and a great many of them apparently find their work sufficiently rewarding economically, if not intrinsically, to make a life's career of it. A year or so back the City Council in Detroit appropriated more than $150,000 in model cities' funds to rehabilitate prostitutes in the inner city. The money was to be used for job counseling and retraining. The program was cancelled after a year when not one single prostitute could be found who desired to be rehabilitated.

Prostitution is a lucrative vocation. Even brothel prostitutes today may

---

[33] Ibid.

[34] Ibid., p. 143–45.

[35] For an interesting documentary tape on the subject, consult "Relax, You're Going to Enjoy This!" (Berkeley, Pacifica Tape Library, 1972); see also Edward G. Armstrong, "The Massage Parlor Phenomenon." Paper presented at the forty-sixth annual meeting of the Virginia Social Science Association (April 28, 1973). For one of the few, albeit superficial, books on the topic, see B. J. Hurwood, *The Girls, The Massage & Everything* (Greenwich, Conn., Fawcett, 1973).

[36] See David Shaw, "Rentagirl: A Look at Escort Agencies," *Forum: The International Journal of Human Relations*, Vol. 1, No. 12 (September 1972), pp. 50–53+.

charge $15 or $20 per "trick." Streetwalkers may charge even more, and the call girl may even command prices up to several hundred dollars for an all night "date." The prostitute, however, is not "working" all the time and must accordingly price her services sufficiently high to cover her nonwork time. She also has extraordinary expenses—for example, tips, payoffs, court fines, lawyer fees, medical bills, beauty shop cost, and clothing expenses.

Prostitutes may have to offer a wide variety of sexual services, some bizarre even by pathological standards. Her repertoire includes oral and anal sex in addition to conventional coital sex. (Winick and Kinsie contend that "fellatio is the service now requested by most men.") In addition prostitutes may have to participate in a range of behavioral perversions such as beating or whipping the client or being beaten by the client (this practice is known as "dumpings"). Some prostitutes even specialize in "dumpings," exacting high fees and payment of any attendant medical or dental bills. Most prostitutes have limits however beyond which they will not go. As one expressed it:

> That time I went along with the customer. Other times I flatly refused. I refused to be covered with black shoe polish for one of Bea's Johns, despite his protests that it would come right off. I refused to wear a collar and leash and be led around an apartment and eat crackers from a dish on the floor, although I did consent to lead the John in that way, which partly satisfied him.[37]

Prostitutes also play something of a therapeutic and counseling role, in addition to offering sexual services. Some claim that many of their clients are as much interested in conversation and companionship as in sex, and in this sense many prostitutes claim that by providing therapy for married men, they are "holding marriages together." Some of the most economically successful prostitutes are the so-called "baby pros," often 10 to 15 years old who are in special demand by clients whose sexual proclivities include children.

The successful practice of any occupational specialty requires appropriate socialization. Occupational socialization, according to Gross includes both the transmission of skills and ideas, as well as a change of status.[38] The transmission of occupational skills includes, first, the teaching of regular technical skills. Prostitutes must be "turned out," or apprenticed. They must acquire a broad repertoire of sexual approaches and techniques. Included here are such concerns as sexual positions, practices, and responses. As James

[37] Virginia McManus, *Not for Love* (New York, Dell, 1961), p. 149.
[38] Edward Gross, *Work and Society* (New York, Thomas Y. Crowell, 1958), p. 128.

H. Bryan has pointed out, prostitutes must become familiar with oral genital sexual techniques, as well as appropriate orgasm control. He states, for example, "You teach them to French (fellatio) and how to talk to men."[39] Transmission of occupational skills also includes the learning of "tricks of the trade." Examples of this might include learning deceptive responses to the male clientele's sexual efforts, protecting themselves against venereal disease and pregnancy, gracefully obtaining their fee in advance from the client, and avoiding detection and arrest by law enforcement officers.

Finally, there is the necessity of acquiring social skills that will permit the prostitute to interact appropriately with clientele and fellow prostitutes. Here the prostitute acquires appropriate social graces and role behavior that permit her to pursue her trade effectively. Bryan reveals that

> Training may also include proprieties concerning consuming alcohol and drugs, when and how to obtain the fee, how to converse with the customers and occasionally, physical and sexual hygiene.[40]

Accompanying the transmission of skills is the acquiring of new ideas and values including a "professional" detachment or impersonality. Bryan points out, "There seems to be some encouragement not to experience sexual orgasms with the client, though this may be quite variable with the trainer."[41] Furthermore prostitutes, as part of their training, are taught to believe that

> ... people, particularly men are corrupt or easily corruptible, that all social relationships are but a reflection of a "con," and that prostitution is simply a more honest or at least no more dishonest act.than the everyday behavior of "squares." Furthermore, not only are "johns" basically exploitative, but they are easily exploited, hence they are, in some respects, stupid.[42]

The prostitute is taught to be exploitive because others will attempt to exploit her. Thus prostitutes, like other practitioners, develop a so-called occupational ideology or outlook relevant to the needs of their vocation, which better permits the practice of their trade, by allowing them a rationalization supportive of a satisfactory self-image.

The next essay in this Part is Mary Riege Laner's "Prostitution As An Illegal Vocation: A Sociological Overview." Surveying some of the major theoretical positions concerning prostitution as a social problem, she also

[39] James H. Bryan, "Apprenticeships in Prostitution," *Social Problems,* Vol. 12, No. 3 (Winter 1965), p. 293.

[40] Ibid., p. 293.

[41] Ibid.

[42] Ibid., p. 291.

examines the motivational elements for prostitution both in terms of practitioners and clientele. Exploring a variety of etiological factors involved in the vocation she concludes that "prostitution is a craft which can be practiced by some girls whose social and economic positions are marginal. . . ." It persists apparently because of a number of social functions it serves which are relevant to the "institutionalized regulation of sex expression" and "the role of woman in the social structure."

While prostitution may not be the oldest "profession," it would appear to easily qualify for the title of the most *durable* profession."

STEALING AS FULL-TIME WORK

Stealing can be a vocation. The New World has had a significant tradition of theft and pillage. The privateers, buckaneers, freebooters and other assorted pirates who roamed the Spanish main were "professional" thieves. A significant number of early settlers were criminals or the offspring of criminals. Some of the colonies were founded with convict colonists, and history tells us that persons were often given a choice of staying in prison or going to the New World. Presumably the settlers brought some criminal skills and vocational pursuits.

Land grabbers, timber pirates, and claim jumpers were all very much in evidence in frontier days and in subsequent times. Some of the early bank and train robbers were simply individuals who could neither find nor hold down a conventional job, and the derelicts who roamed the West after the Civil War were frequently persons with undistinguished and unsavory pasts and few legitimate skills. Some turned to commerce for a vocation and sold illegal whiskey and guns to the Indians. Still others, less imaginative, became highwaymen, rustlers, and hired gunmen.

Nor was crime confined to the frontier and boom towns. In the thriving metropolises of the East, crime was flourishing often under the protection of widespread political graft and corruption. The hordes of immigrants arriving daily were easy picking for financial exploitation, and petty larceny and swindles were endemic to the eastern ghettos. Criminals, particularly petty criminals, were often recruited from the ranks of the economically inept and the culturally deprived who could not effectively compete in the market place. Crime quickly took on social organization, particularly in the big cities, and thievery as usual often became the dominant gang norm. In response, new ethnic criminal gangs appeared both as protection devices and as a means of economic adaptation.

Statistics would seem to suggest that the United States has an inordinately high rate of crime in comparison with other western countries. A variety of factors may combine to produce a social climate conducive to criminal activities. Our economic system with its merchandizing impetus may tend to make certain kinds of crime too easy to commit and thus afford too favorable an opportunity structure. Branch banks and the "open" architecture of banks today makes the money appear more accessible and thus tempting to would-be bank robbers as well as customers. Most retail stores have effected "self-service" to maximize efficiency and minimize overhead. They also have a tempting large array of merchandise out and available for close examination and inspection. Burglary and shoplifting have reached alarmingly high rates in this country.

The high volume shopping-center commerce attendant to our urban sprawl has made necessary a heavy reliance on checks and credit cards rather than money. The problem is compounded by the high geographical mobility of our population and the extremely large number of persons trading at given stores. It becomes almost impossible to know the individual customer, and the rapid rate of customer processing renders ineffective efforts to identify customers who give checks or use credit cards for merchandise. As a result a whole new crime industry based on stolen credit cards has blossomed, and both "cold checks" (insufficient funds), and "paper hanging" (forged checks) have become endemic to retail trade today especially in some shopping centers.

With the burgeoning technology since the late nineteenth century and especially in this century, whole new vistas of opportunity for crime have opened up. There are newer things to steal, such as automobiles and television sets, and such possessions are not only easy to steal but easy to dispose of.

The television and other mass media are constantly portraying a compelling image of the "good life" which most usually has heavy emphasis on the material goods. Many individuals are accordingly motivated to seek to actualize such a high level of material lifestyle even by illegal means.

The career criminal appears to be made rather than born, although his actual path to a career of crime may be a circuitous one. As Krause points out, "the great majority of those with illegal occupations do not seem to have been juvenile 'gang' members." They may, however, have had an early history of brushes with the law, as suggested by a recent Associated Press story in the newspaper which told of a nine-year-old third grader who had a "criminal career" of 30 burglaries and break-ins. Other persons may not run afoul of the law until their teen years or young adulthood. In some instances other legitimate career avenues may be closed or difficult to actualize for the individual. The lower-income or culturally deprived young person may turn toward illegal pursuits as a career alternative because it seems like one of the few options open to him likely to afford him some degree of "success." The orientation of his family, peers, and neighborhood may be distinctively supportive of an illegal career by esteeming some persons involved in criminal activities and considering those who follow honest pursuits, "suckers." By hanging around places where criminals congregate, such as pool halls, or bars, the young person is exposed to criminal society, its culture, and its participants.[43] He may also be invited to participate. If apprehended for a minor crime, he may be imprisoned and thus be particularly vulnerable to additional socialization in the criminal culture, as a member of a total institution, a "captive" audience. If not apprehended, he may graduate by inertia to more serious offenses and ultimately become a career criminal by default.

Career criminals may begin their lives of crime early, shoplifting as youths, or they may enter the field relatively late in their adult life after encountering less than satisfactory success in their first and legal career. Embezzlers, for example, may take up their activities in middle age only when they become disenchanted with their bureaucratic career because it does not afford them the desired lifestyle and only when they are strategically located in terms of opportunity structure. A criminal may require special physical or mental abilities and an unusual combination of talents. Pickpockets may require extraordinary manual dexterity and timing, while the second-story man may need strength and agility and like solitary work. Confidence men ideally must have brains, imagination, self-confidence, and a persuasive conversational ability. Sometimes con men are even college men, but most con men agree that college or any formal education is not absolutely necessary to succeed in their field, rather only "to be specious."[44] Presumably the college-trained con men simply seek an easier means of "success" than climbing the difficult corporate ladder.

Criminal practitioners may well take "professional" pride in their work. Some counterfeiters have achieved international reputations, and some safe "crackers" and confidence men have a particular *modus operandi* so distinctive in quality and effectiveness that other criminals and knowledgeable law enforcement officials alike invariably recognize it. Those who render criminal services for a fee, such as the contract killer, may even demonstrate a kind of "professional ethics" in striving to provide full worth for the fee they receive.

The next reading in this section chronicles the life and work of a dedicated career thief. Niholas Pileggi in his article "The Year of the Burglar" tells of a professional career which in the words of Armand, the protagonist of the article, requires that you have "patience" and "dis-

---

[43] Ibid.

[44] See Robert Louis Gasser, "The Confidence Game," *Federal Probation,* Vol. IIVII, No. 4 (December 1963), pp. 45–54.

cipline almost above everything else." Armand, the inheritor of his European father's skills in theft, is essentially a society burglar. Each year he undertakes only a few big burglaries in wealthy homes. The rewards for such work are materially satisfying. Armand "earns" up to a quarter million dollars per year, owns expensive European automobiles, a cabin cruiser, and an art collection. He travels widely and loves to hunt and fish in his spare time. He is good at his trade and works hard at it to achieve perfection. He has what Pileggi terms "Old-World pride" in his craft. Burglary is big business. In recent years there have been in excess of 100,000 annually in New York City alone. Many are committed by rank amateurs, of course, and some of them are apprehended and convicted. The professionals, however, are usually not so inept. Armand, for example, after gaining admittance to an apartment with a lock pick, goes immediately to the bathroom and flushes the pick down the toilet. In this way, if arrested on suspicion, he will be carrying no pick and can, thus, not be convicted of "possession of burglar's tools," in the absence of more incriminating evidence. Using such ploys and strategies, Armand has and does avoid arrest and conviction for burglary. For the true professional like Armand, crime is part science and part art, part talent and part skill. It is a way of life as well as a livelihood.

Criminal activities, both those providing illegal services and the predatory variety, are as old as civilization itself. Work, whether legal or illicit, that has challenge, stimulation, intrinsic gratification, and most importantly, handsome economic rewards is bound to be attractive as a vocation. The attendant hazards and social disadvantages notwithstanding, it draws a large following of willing practitioners.

ANTI-OBSTETRICS AS DEVIANT MEDICAL SPECIALTY

Once upon an agrarian time, there was considerable benefit, both social and economic, attendant to large families. Many children meant manpower to work the farm and tend the flocks and perform the multiple and demanding household responsibilities. Children also represented protection—protection against physical hazard and harm and against the vicissitudes and exigencies of life and nature, old age and illness, economic endeavors, and the social enterprise. Children meant companionship and diversion in a rural routine often incipient in existence. Children were in some instances also a visible symbol of male virility: *maschismo*.

With the coming of industrialization, the economic worth of children began to decline, and children could less frequently make a direct economic input to the financial well-being of the family. The family had shifted from a unit of economic production to that of economic consumption. Every additional child simply consumed that much more, thus diluting the overall allocation to other family members. With the rise of living standards and a new awareness of the gratifications of relative affluence plus the proliferation of the mass media providing an ever-present image of the good economic life for invidious comparisons, the last bulwarks of justification for large families gave way.

Where marriages had once been unions of economic and productive convenience, they have increasingly become units of companionship and emotional gratification as well as social vehicles that allow the actualization of individualism, the expression of self, and the maximization of capability and potential. Excessive children are impediments to the realization of these goals. Children are time consuming and require attention and affection that might otherwise be available to the adult marital partners. The large family declined except in some rural areas where contraceptive sophistication was limited and among various religious and ethnic groups whose values proscribed contraception.

In spite of new and improved mechanical devices of contraception, and more particularly "the pill," many pregnancies are unplanned and many births are undesired. Some impending births are so undesired that means are sought to terminate the pregnancies. Because of deep-seated religious and ethical values, abortion was traditionally viewed as inappropriate behavior dysfunctional to the social enterprise and constituting the taking of human life. Consequently, laws prohibiting other than therapeutic abortion under rigidly defined circumstances were widely enacted and in many instances rigidly enforced.

Because of religious and social pressures, states enacted legislation prohibiting abortion outright or permitting it only under rigidly prescribed circumstances. Some of these anti-abortion statutes were enacted during the nineteenth century and had not been liberalized during the interim. Although a few states modified their laws on abortion somewhat over the past several decades, legal abortions were usually obtainable only under very extraordinary circumstances. By the mid 1960s, however, pressures for reform or liberalization of existing laws dealing with abortion were beginning to be brought to the surface. These pressures derived from several sources. Concern with the "population bomb" issue gave impetus to population control efforts. The thalidomide babies of the early 1960s brought vivid attention to the problem of children born with gross deformities or handicaps. This problem was particularly dramatized by Mrs. Sherri Finkbines' unsuccessful attempts to obtain a legal abortion in this country after she had taken thalidomide. The new sexual freedoms of the 1960s, a stand for liberalized laws on the part of the American Medical Association, the political posture of the young generation, and the movement for female equality all combined to set the stage for abortion reform. Some physicians, mostly of the younger generation, were beginning openly to provide abortions on request, thus inviting arrest and test cases. By the late 1960s, various states such as California, New York, and Hawaii, among others, had taken legislative steps that made legal abortion available under much relaxed circumstances. A series of court cases ultimately paved the way for a United States Supreme Court decision in the early 1970s that ruled that abortion in the early months of pregnancy is a matter to be decided not by the law, but rather by a woman. The Court further ruled that abortion after the first three months is also legal but subject to some limited state regulations. The result of the Court's ruling was the overturning of much existing state legislation and the substitution of liberalized laws on abortion in many states. Several states, for example, no longer require that a woman declare a reason for wanting an abortion. While some states still require proof of residence, six states do not and provide abortions for women from other states. Abortion is rapidly becoming a widespread and accepted gynecological surgical procedure. Until the late 1960s and early 1970s, however, abortion was a largely illegal procedure and tended to turn both patient and practitioner into outlaws. For the illicit practitioner or the medical doctor who illicitly practiced "anti-obstetrics," the legal risks were great, even if the economic rewards were attractive. In addition to legal hazards for the patient, however, others included social stigma; the possibility of criminal exploitation, through blackmail, for example; and most importantly, the danger of death, serious illness or mutilation, or permanent sterility.

Yet, for the pregnant female, there were often compelling reasons for abortion even if not provided for under statutory regulation. In some states a woman impregnated by rape could not legally be aborted. In other instances a woman who had reason to believe that her child might be born defective because of genetic factors or disease during pregnancy could likewise not secure a licit abortion. Women with serious physical and mental conditions were on occasions refused legal abortions. Requests for legal abortions on economic and social reasons were routinely rejected. More than 150,000 teen-aged and unmarried school girls become pregnant each year. It has been estimated that this figure will rise to more than 200,000 per year in the next decade. For the unmarried teenager, pregnancy with its enormous impact on family and peer relationships can be a highly disruptive and traumatic exigency. Clark Vincent has reported on married or divorced women who become pregnant by men other than their husbands.[45]

---

[45] Clark E. Vincent, "Illicit Pregnancies Among Married and Divorced Females," in Clark E. Vincent (ed.), *Human Sexuality in Medical Education* (Springfield, Ill., Charles C. Thomas, 1968), pp. 472–84.

Exact statistics are difficult to determine, but Vincent estimates that some 15,000 married women and 54,000 divorced women bear illicit children each year with the attendant social and marital impact. For the formerly married woman attempting to reestablish her life and with aspirations of remarriage, pregnancy can be equally stigmatic, disruptive, and traumatic. For some women an additional child may involve financial, social, and marital strains that would seriously threaten, if not destroy, her marriage.

In the face of such problems and pressures associated with bearing children in some situations and in view of the legal and social impediments to medically sanctioned therapeutic abortion, in previous times, large numbers of women sought means to terminate their pregnancies through criminal channels.

Prior to the recent court decisions and changes in the state laws, the criminal abortionists represented an unusually vivid example of an illegal occupational specialty and deserves detailed examination even though it is largely antiquated, if not essentially eliminated by legal reform.

Understandably, the exact number of illegal abortions obtained each year in this country before liberalization of the laws are extremely difficult, if not impossible, to estimate.[46] Some estimates have ranged from 200,000 to 1,200,000 illegal abortions per year. Contrary to some popular beliefs, the greatest number of abortions were performed on married women. As Germain G. Grisez has concluded:

> Single white women, especially former married ones, end a large part of their pregnancies with abortion, but the greatest part of all pregnancies occur in marriage, and the majority of the abortionists' clients undoubtedly are married women.[47]

Abortion was less frequent among the lower classes and the less educated than among women of higher socioeconomic and educational levels. Paul H. Gebhard and his associates have, for example, suggested, "As a rule induced abortion is strongly connected with status-striving."[48]

For social, economic, and marital reasons, married women have a considerable vested interest in determining the number of children they will bear. A failure in contraceptive method could have dramatic effect on lifestyle, career (or husband's career), the cohesion of the conjugal unit, and

[46] See Germain G. Grisez, *Abortion: The Myths, the Realities, and the Arguments* (New York and Cleveland, Corpus Books, 1970), especially pp. 35–42.

[47] Ibid., p. 54.

[48] Paul H. Gebhard, Wardell B. Pomeroy, Clyde E. Martin, and Cornelia V. Christenson, *Pregnancy, Birth, and Abortion* (New York, Wiley, 1958), pp. 180–81

social identity. Accordingly, criminal abortion offered an effective means of remedying such contraceptive failures. Some married women have had many abortions.

Relatively effective abortive procedures are known to many, if not most, primitive and peasant societies. In modern societies such procedures are a routine part of medical training. Therapeutic abortion is a relatively simple medical procedure if performed under sterile conditions. The risk of infection is perhaps the greatest hazard. Even though many physicians would be able and willing to perform abortion on demand, they are effectively prevented from doing so by legal and professional constraints. Therapeutic abortions performed in hospitals were, until recently, often done only after careful examination of the facts in the case and approval from an abortion committee and when clearly legal grounds were demonstrated. As with other illegal services, where there is demand, there will be supply.

To meet the significant demand for illegal abortions, a variety of persons began to perform the delicate surgical procedure with or without appropriate training. In addition to the women who manage to abort themselves, there appeared to be several categories of abortionists.[49] Some abortionists were simply amateurs who wanted to cash in on a lucrative business. They may have had little or no medical training. Included among such amateurs have been barbers, prostitutes, and even laborers. Unfortunately, their lack of medical knowledge made them particularly dangerous to their clientele. Some abortionists were simply "quack" doctors who attempted to pass themselves off as physicians even though they had little or no medical training. The abortions they performed may have been in addition to other medical services rendered, many of which were spurious. On occasion they even attempted to offer spurious abortions, pretending that some piece of electrical "apparatus" did in fact cause abortions. Not infrequently criminal abortionists had some limited medical training or experience—nurses, midwives, chiropractors, medical orderlies—that made their services seem plausible. Some of these people were drawn into abortion by the lure of quick profit, but apparently in some cases they became abortionists because they had been displaced from their original specialty. At one point in New York City during the Depression, for example, the New York City Department of Hospitals changed their policy to accommodate more uncomplicated maternity cases who formerly had been attended by midwives.[50] To maintain their licenses, midwives were required to attend a minimum of

---

[49] Jerome E. Bates and Edward S. Zawadzki, *Criminal Abortion: A Study in Medical Sociology* (Springfield, Ill., Charles C. Thomas, 1964), pp. 35–43.

[50] Ibid., p. 40.

at least four confinements per year, which they could no longer do. With their practices falling off and their incomes declining, many of them turned to criminal abortion to maintain their incomes.

The amateurs and "quack" doctors may have been so medically unknowledgeable about correct procedures to be used that they only accomplished to injure or kill the patient. The quasi-medical abortionists often used methods that were only partially effective such as uterine packing or the insertion of a sterilized rubber catheter into the uterus.[51] Such procedures sometimes do accomplish the expulsion of the fetus, but from time to time bizarre abortion procedures "involving the use of pastes, laminaria, voorhees bags, forced fluids, puncture, air pressure, and so forth" were reported. Dilation and currettage for abortion is seldom used except among physicians.

A significant percentage of all illegal abortions were performed by trained and licensed physicians. Some studies have suggested estimate. ranging from approximately one-fourth to three-fourths of criminal abortions were being performed by physicians. Some doctors apparently took up an abortion practice because of the extremely lucrative financial return, especially if they did not find conventional practice so economically rewarding as they had hoped. As Bates and Zawadzki describe it:

> After a period of struggle and vacillation, sometimes long, they often find their way into the abortion trade as they have long been aware that it offers an immediate opportunity to make an excellent living. Once the quick and easy tax-free dollars commence to flow in, pressures to remain an abortionist are reinforced and their rationalizations of their actions are often elaborated and extended.[52]

Some persons apparently do not have the social and psychological aptitude for successful medical practice and turned to abortion as a last resort. Sometimes a physician who was alcoholic or a narcotic addict and who had accordingly lost some of his practice may have seen abortion practice as a means of getting by and supplying his habit.

Some physicians were motivated by allegedly humanitarian reasons and spoke of performing a socially useful purpose.

Whatever the motivation, some physicians have obviously specialized in abortion, and many have had almost fantastic records in terms of the volume of criminal abortions performed. One is reputed to have performed 30,000 abortions without one death.[53] Some have reported performing up to 5,000

---

[51] Ibid., p. 50.
[52] Ibid., p. 37.
[53] Grisez, op. cit., pp. 48–49.

abortions annually. Dr. G. Lotrell Timanus of Baltimore claimed more than 5,000 over a period of years. He also claimed that patients had been referred to him by some 353 doctors.[54] A sympathetic physician may have directed a patient wishing an abortion to a "reputable" abortionist-physician. Timanus was ultimately arrested and convicted but received a relatively light sentence. He has been the subject of a television special and a successful book. He was also invited to participate in a Planned Parenthood Conference because of his "expertise" in the subject.[55] Sometimes the professional career of an abortionist was short. But apparently the "reputable" physician-abortionist may have, with the tolerance, if not tacit approval of legal auhorities and professional colleagues, enjoyed a long, and lucrative practice in "anti-obstetrics."

Abortion, however, like any other medical practice, often lends itself to a team approach. The physician may have been able to process and service his patients more effectively with ancillary personnel who could handle the secondary responsibilities such as clerical or contact. Abortion as a business venture also lends itself to a team approach in terms of maximizing profit by maximizing volume of business. Such abortion work systems were sometimes known as abortion "mills" or "rings." In regard to why abortion required such a work system, Jerome E. Bates has said:

> If the chief actor, the abortionist, is to run his establishment with the greatest possible efficiency and safety, he must have both business and medical assistants.... The mill is also "developed about a value or series of values." The chief value for the patients is a negative but nevertheless vital one from their standpoint, namely, the opportunity to have an unwanted pregnant condition terminated. The chief value for the abortionist and his staff is an opportunity to make a good many tax-free dollars quickly and with a minimum of effort. With these dollars a plethora of satisfying experiences may be purchased.[56]

Donald W. Ball provides a detailed inventory of the physical setting and the activities characteristic of one abortion mill as it existed prior to reform in the abortion laws, in "An Abortion Clinic Ethnography." In his analysis of the social aspects of the abortion process, Ball speaks of the strategies involved in the "rhetoric of legitimization." The rhetoric of the

[54] Ibid., p. 49.
[55] Ibid.
[56] Jerome E. Bates, "The Abortion Mill: An Institutional Study," *Journal of Criminal Law, Criminology, and Police Science*, Vol. 45, No. 2 (July–August 1954), pp. 157 and 168; For a patient's view of an abortion mill (albeit a small scale one) see Anonymous, "I Didn't Have the Baby, I Had an Abortion," in Clifton D. Bryant (ed.), *Social Problems Today: Dilemmas and Dissensus* (Philadelphia, J. B. Lippincott, 1971), pp. 182–90.

abortion clinic, he says, "operates to subvert the conventional world's view of abortion, and to generate a picture of legitimate activity." By neutralizing the deviant context of abortion within which the clinic operated, both patient and staff were better able to ward off threats to their identity and contributed to the legitimization of "anti-obstetrics" as a medical specialty with redeeming social function.

18. The Moonshiner:
Illegal Craftsman of the Georgia Mountains

JOHN L. GORDON, JR.

Doc is in many ways the stereotypical mountain man. Tall and lanky, he walks with an ungainly stride, and when sitting, he refuses to sit with his feet on the floor and his back upright. He twists his legs up over the chair's arms and turns his body sideways until he is in a comfortable position. Much of the time when Doc is not standing, he squats down like an athlete doing an extreme deep-knee bend. Feet flat on the ground, legs and body squashed into an "N" shape, Doc looks like some kind of contortionist. But this is a common position for many mountain people. Doc calls it the moonshine squat because he used to stoke the furnaces of his stills when sitting this way. Most people call it hunkering. Doc's face is long and gaunt, rounded out by a wiry beard which stretches from ear to ear. His eyes are crossed, and his hair is long, black, and straight. Doc always wears a hat of some sort and this strengthens his physical resemblance to the "ideal man" of the mountains.

The stereotype ends with physical resemblance, however, because Doc is most definitely *not* the tight-lipped, taciturn, and suspicious character of our mountain legends. His graciousness and hospitality are overwhelming, and he is always willing to talk about himself and his life. Doc became my close friend during the summer. He introduced me to many of his friends and, as long as I was with him, I never encountered any suspicion or hostility. Whenever Doc and I met someone he would say to them, "This here's John, he's a boy from down a' the University and he's up here a' larnin' the ways of people." A more concise definition of anthropology is hard to come by. . . .

Adapted from John L. Gordon, Jr., "Up Top Amongst None: Life in the Georgia Mountains," Parts One and Two, *The Georgia Review,* Vol. 24, No. 1 (Spring 1970), pp. 5–28, and Vol. 24, No. 2 (Summer 1970), pp. 183–99.

BUSTHEAD AND POPSKULL:
MOONSHINING IN THE MOUNTAINS

Mountain people divide all alcoholic drinks into three groups: beer, bonded liquor, and white liquor. White liquor is known to most people outside the mountains as either white lightnin' or moonshine, and its production is without doubt one of the distinguishing features of mountain subculture. Although moonshining and bootlegging are both very active industries in most of Georgia's and North Carolina's counties, it is only in the mountains that one finds moonshining as an openly discussed and openly publicized activity. News of moonshining in the Georgia Piedmont region, for instance, is usually limited to brief notices in the local papers telling the public of recent work by the State revenue agents. In the mountains, this is not the case. A tourist on State Highway 73 can see a genuine moonshine still on display for only twenty-five cents at the Kimsey Brothers Fruit Stand, and a similar still has been one of the most popular exhibits each year at the Muskogee County Fair. Furthermore, the first thing that usually comes to mind when someone mentions the mountains or mountain people is a mental picture of a bearded mountaineer with a long muzzle loading rifle squatting in front of his moonshine still. The beards and the muzzle loaders have long since disappeared, but making liquor remains a fundamental part of many mountain lives. Just as Indians make arrowheads, mountaineers make moonshine.

Moonshining has a long and vigorous history in the mountain region. The first documented evidence of the now classic meeting between the revenuer and the moonshiner is found in reports of the Whiskey Rebellion in 1791. The 178 years since this uprising have established the right of the government to regulate liquor manufacturing for tax purposes, but this has not lessened the spirit of moonshining mountaineers in the least. Making liquor is a game to them, a peculiar kind of game in which they stand to make a lot of money in a short and exciting time while faced with the constant possibility of having their entire enterprise destroyed. With its destruction, their backbreaking and meticulous work amounts to nothing. But it is a game, and because it *is* a game the moonshiners learn to accept defeats along with victories, and each time their still is "cut down" they gamely reorganize and start again with new equipment in a new place.

Among my informants I was fortunate in having both an expert moonshiner and an expert bootlegger. Doc Brown has been making liquor since he was eight years old. A master wood craftsman and sheet metal worker, Doc claims to have made both the smallest and the largest stills in the world. His biggest could hold more than three thousand gallons, and his smallest is a one-gallon rig which can be easily held in the hand. Doc has a license from the federal government to make these miniature stills for sale. Each is guaranteed to work, and the largest of the miniatures, a five-gallon still with furnace, pre-heater, and condenser sells for around $100.

Still technology, just like any other technology, has evolved through the years, and at its peak stillmaking was an art requiring great ingenuity and skill. This was in the heydey of moonshining; materials were the best, workmanship was thorough, and the product was superb. Today, unfortunately, much liquor is made not for the sake of the art but in order to make a fast buck. Quality control is obviously lacking and the result is a product that can often be deadly poisonous. The following description is of still technology at its height, and it is based on the word of a man with forty-two years experience in the field. Doc Brown comes from a long line of moonshiners. Both his father and grandfather were well known moonshiners in their day and Doc has carried on the tradition with a skill and ingenuity that are uncommon even in a community where moonshining is a well practiced art.

OPERATING A STILL

Many different varieties of stills have been invented; one of the most popular is the blocade or re-run still. It was this type of still that Doc was a specialist at constructing. The basic parts of a blockade still are: the still itself (the term "still" can refer to the entire unit as in "moonshine still" or merely to the metal container in which the mash is boiled), the furnance (which is built around the still), the cap and cap stem, the thump post and thump barrel, the headache piece, the pre-heater box and trough, the slide connections, the flake stand, and the condenser. After the still is constructed, the first step in the distilling process involves making the mash, or beer, which will be run through the still. Several different "recipes" for making the beer are used by various operators. Generally, to make the mash, the operator fills the still full of water and adds the proper amount of corn meal. The furnace is fired and this mixture of meal and water is cooked. It is unnecessary to connect any of the still's parts during this procedure. The boiling mixture is then drawn out of the still into barrels or into the box dug in under the slop arm. Corn malt and rye meal are then added to the cooked meal. This starts the mixture to "working." (The malt has the enzyme diastase which saccharifies the starch of the raw corn meal.) To obtain the corn malt the moonshiner often has to sprout and grind his own corn. This complicates the distilling process because it is a federal offense (just like moonshining itself) to grind sprouted corn. A miller who is a trusted friend is a necessity.

After the mixture has set for a day or so, it is stirred up again and sugar is added. Sugar increases the yield, but it is not used by all moonshiners because with its use the product is not considered "pure corn whiskey."

While the mixture is fermenting, a crust or cap forms on the surface. When the mixture works off, i.e., when the cap has disappeared, the beer is ready to run; the alcohol in the mixture has eaten off the crust.

When I asked Doc to give me his recipe for the mash, this is what he said:

O.K. John, you want me to give you a recipe how to make moonshine, so I can't write so I guess I'll just tell you how you do this and you can put it on your tape here. So the way you do that now you get your meal, you get your still and you put it in the furnace and you build a fare under it. So you fill it about two-thirds full of water, a fifty gallon still we'll say, a 'pacity fifty gallons. So you put a bushel a meal in it and you stir it up good with your scrape paddle. And you keep your fare under it and when it goes to boilin'—then, you cap it, with the cap, and the steam comes out the stem thar. You let it boil fifteen minutes. O.K., and then you draw it over in your boxes, now that's the box that's dug in under your slop arm where you make your beer. So you push your swab stick up and you draw your beer over into the box, ah, your meal or water you've cooked, and so you have your corn malt thar and on this 38 square box you put one-half bushel of dry corn malt and a gallon of rye meal. You stir it up good, and that's in the evening, or the morning, and you let it set about twelve to twenty hours and then you go back and stir it up good and you put about one hundred pounds of sugar on this box. Then you stir it up good and go back in about twelve hours and stir it up again. And then when it works off, you, ah—when it clears off like water on top—then you put it in your still and you go to runnin' it just like usual.

With the beer ready and the still parts connected, the operator can begin the run. A fire is built in the furnace and as the beer begins to heat, the operator must periodically stir the mixture to keep it from sticking to the bottom and sides of the still. A duck nest furnace of the type Doc builds, by recirculating its heat, is said to "burn its own smoke." This lessens the danger of discovery of the operation. After the beer has come to a boil, steam will begin to flow through the connections. From the still, steam goes through the thump barrel and headache piece into the pre-heater box. The thump barrel also contains beer, and the steam bubbling through the beer makes a deep thumping noise. The pre-heater contains a copper ring similar to the condenser. At the beginning of the run, beer is put in the box to cover the ring. Steam going through the copper heats the beer and when all of the beer in the still has boiled away, a trough is then placed between the heater box and the uncapped still. The gate on the box is opened and the pre-heated beer flows into the still. Because the beer is already hot, not as much time is lost waiting for the beer to boil. This makes the operation, therefore, almost continuous.

From the pre-heater box the steam goes into the flake stand. The flake stand, a wooden box similar to the pre-heater, contains the condenser. During distillation, water (usually from a nearby stream) runs through the box and condenses the steam into alcohol. The product trickles out the condenser stem and is caught in a bucket or barrel. A funnel inserted in the bucket or barrel contans a filter of charcoal wrapped in cloth which strains the fusel oils (a poisonous residue) out of the alcohol.

The first run will not likely produce any whiskey strong enough to "hold a bead." To check the strength or proof of the liquor, the operator fills a small bottle (called the proof vial) with the product and thumps the bottle in the palm of his hand. If the bubbles that rise remain steady, i.e., hold a bead, then the liquor is of proper strength. The product from the first run of a fifty gallon still should be about ten gallons of weak liquor. To start the next run, the still is drained and re-filled with fresh beer. The thump barrel is also emptied and the ten gallons from the first run, known as backings, are put in the thump barrel. On the second run the product will be much stronger because the steam is going through the alcohol in the thump barrel and being "doubled." The second run should produce a couple of gallons of good alcohol and around eight weak gallons. The weak gallons, as before, form the backings for the next run. This process is continued until all the beer is used.

Doc describes how he makes liquor:

> So the way you do, John, you make the mash, that's in boxes as we do back in the mountains. So you cook your meal and mash it up and you put your corn malt or anykind of malt you want to on it. Well, when your beer works off, it usually takes seventy-two hours on up to three or four days accordin' to how many hogs fall in it, and possums, so forth and so on. So anyway, John, now the way you do this, son, you fill up the still here with the beer and take the beer here and put it in this heater, it's a pre-heater, what it is, a double condenser, it's a quick way of makin' it. So why we invented this heater it's much faster and much easier, and while you rest you take off a keg of liquor and bring back a load of wood.
>
> So, haint nothing to it, and then you fill up the heater with beers. You got a trough over here in the flake stand, you run the water right down through hit, and so now what happens when it goes to boilin', you can use wood or coal or anything you want to, but we usually back in the mountains use wood, such as sourwood, fence rails, so forth and so on. So the way you do this now, when it goes to boilin', you cap it and you pour a couple a gallon of beer in your thump barrel to start off with. So then, when it goes to runnin' whiskey you take up a little proof vial we call it out there, under the condenser stem. And then you check it, you shake it down to a head and it gets down to about 100 proof then you stop an put the bucket, a bucket's usually what we use, or a tub, or a keg, or a barrel, and you change and catch the backins. Well the

backins is a low grade of whiskey, it's alcohol, and you catch 'em as long as it burns. The way you tell, when they get weak you throw 'em under the furnace and when they blaze, they still good. So you catch what backins you get there and then you go to changin' and you switch it from one to another. And then you pour, refill it back up and you start the same operation over and over again and again.

So, I have the names here on this little still, very 'cular names, they true. The names on these stills, here are the slop arm, that's where the slop comes out, we call it slop, after it's boiled down into whiskey then it goes back to make re-mash again. The slop arm is where you put the swab stick, a swab stick is a mallet or a forked stick with a tow sack wrapped on it, ever body that's ever made any whiskey knows what I mean. And then we come on up to the still, and the duck nest furnace is a new model furnace that burns its own smoke. So we used to make 'em old groundhog furnaces, two or three different ways you make furnaces. But we invented this duck nest furnace, it burns its own smoke, and the man won't see you—you know how it is—you gotta be careful when your makin' it, ah, I tried to be, seven times I learnt better.

So, the way you do it, go on down the cap stem on down into the headache piece, thump post go down in the barrel and thumps the backins into processed whiskey. And why they call it a headache piece, that's the one that goes up here, John, out of the thump barrel up here into the pre-heater, and it's the headache piece now, son, and the reason I know this *is* the headache piece, if you've drunk as much as this pop-skull I have, you'll find out exactly what I mean. Well, it goes on down and the water it runs into the slide connections, and the condenser is what condenses steam into alcohol. I'll tell you now about this condenser business, ah, we used to make 'em with old worms, coil worms, foil worms and all that. So my grandfather invented this condenser, it's a quick, easier way to make it. So the way the whole setup goes, the pressure, John, pushes the steam through this rotation, on through the thump barrel over into the pre-heater, right on down in the condenser. And the pressure, or the temperature, is about 480 degrees, so I've been told. And the pressure from this fare pushes it right on down and the steam goes right on through all these connections, right on down through the slide connections into the condenser, and the water condenses this into liquor—alcohol—and it comes out here at the money stick.

MAKING A STILL

Doc Brown has a special set of tools for making a still. Most of them are handmade, and two of them, the punch and the swedge, were handed down from his grandfather. The basic tools needed are soldering irons, punch and swedge, sheet metal cutters, an anvil, rivets, and a hammer. Doc's hammer was specifically made for use in still construction. The hammer head was made from a car axle; one end is for hammering and the other end is designed for "plumming the cap." The hammer is small and well suited for tapping rivets and shaping copper. Doc has three soldering irons, all identical and all made by inserting an iron rod into a wooden handle. In making his miniature stills, Doc uses a kerosene blow-pot to heat the irons. If this is not available, he will use an ordinary wood fire. The punch is used to make the rivet holes in the copper and the swedge is used to push the burr down on the rivet. The burr is like a washer. It fits on the shaft of the rivet and when the rivet is struck, the burr becomes permanently fixed in place.

The most difficult part of making a still is estimating the measurements for the various pieces. With a fifty gallon still, for instance, one would have to know the basic measurements which will produce a still that holds fifty gallons. Proportions then have to be calculated. The cap will have to be constructed so that it will fit the still, and so on with the other parts. The condenser must be of appropriate size to handle the steam coming through it.

Doc claims, in his usual manner, that he doesn't need to take measurements when cutting copper for a still. He has made so many stills and he is such a skilled craftsman that he knows how much copper to cut for each part. I imagine most other still makers would measure before cutting, but this remains an extremely complex process. No written instructions exist to tell a person how large each piece must be; so the still maker must ultimately rely on his experience and his innate sense of proportions.

After the still itself has been riveted together, the cap is made. As mentioned earlier, Doc has a special hammer for making the cap. To obtain the slight dome shape of the cap, a circular sheet of copper is placed on the ground and the worker takes his hammer and, starting in the center, he beats the copper in an ever-widening circle until he reaches the edge. This process is called "plumming the cap."

When the still is completed, it is transported to the place chosen for its installation. The place is usually as out of the way as possible. It must have a supply of water, however, and this limits the choice of sites somewhat. After the wooden parts of the still are assembled, the copper parts are inserted. Once in operation, the still is rarely shut down unless the operators fear a raid, and also, of course, if there is a raid. When Doc Brown was an active moonshiner the revenue agents would usually just cut down a still. This was simply a matter of chopping it up with an ax and leaving it in the woods. Too many enterprising moonshiners, however, managed to repair their chopped up stills and put them back in operation. The common method used today by the agents is dynamite. It rarely fails.

Why do mountain men make moonshine? "Money" is what *they* will tell you. Moonshining is a good way to make money in a hurry. But moonshining is a lot of back-breaking labor under terribly unfavorable conditions. Furthermore, it's downright dangerous. The captured moonshiner can at best expect to pay a large fine, and at worst he can find himself in jail for several years. Money? It's more than that. Moonshining satisfies a fundamental craving of the mountain personality. Moonshining is action, it is thrills, and it is the antithesis of the routine—it is frightfully unpredictable.

In north Georgia, numerous small textile plants have sprung up around mountain communities within the past ten years. These factories provide steady jobs with a good solid income for their employees. The work is mild and not very strenuous. With jobs of this sort available, it stands to reason that moonshining must have some appeal other than money. Why would a mountain man spurn a steady job with good pay in favor of an insecure, laborious activity? Precisely because that factory job is *routine*. Good pay, security, and pleasant working conditions can never obscure the fact that those jobs are just too damn boring! Mountain people are action-seekers. They live episodically and they live for adventure. Moonshining is for some of them the ultimate adventure....

DOC BROWN: A MOUNTAIN MOONSHINER AND HIS FAMILY

> If I could do it, I'd do no writing at all here. It would be photographs; the rest would be fragments of cloth, bits of cotton, lumps of earth, records of speech, pieces of wood and iron, phials of odors, plates of food and of excrement.
>
> James Agee, *Let Us Now Praise Famous Men*

People like Doc Brown are rare. Possessed with an extremely incisive and perceptive mind, Doc is acutely aware of the current state of world affairs and he is always willing to give his opinion on the latest political happenings in the state and nation. Doc loves to talk, and his favorite subject is himself. Not an overly humble person, he is always eager to tell how good he is at building stills or at acting as the comedian for Clay's country music show. In his younger days he was consumed with a curiosity about the world which could not be satisfied by remaining in the small mountain community of his birth. He traveled back and forth across the country so much that he can now claim to have "draw'd a payday in forty-seven of the [then] forty-eight states." A characteristic of Doc's personality is his inability to stay on the same job for more than three months. Many mountain men, like Doc, are apparently unable to remain on a job long enough for it to become routine.

Doc's most noted exploits are those connected with moonshining. He made his first still when he was eight years old and his encounters with the law since that time have been numerous. His skill as a sheet metal worker and master still craftsman are almost legendary. Today Doc has a strangely moralistic attitude toward moonshining. He sees his current status as a poor, partially disabled man as the result of his earlier days in moonshining. Even so, he is not ashamed to admit that he's been arrested seven times for making liquor. Whenever he talks about moonshining now, he always speak in terms of the evil that will result from it. In an area where, according to Tom Wolfe, "there is hardly a living soul in the hollows who can conjure up two second's honest moral indignation over 'the whiskey business,' " one wonders if Doc is really repentant about his moonshining. He could just be acting this way because he thinks that it's what the "outsiders" want to hear.

Doc was the second of four sons born to the wife of a small mountain farmer. He grew up on the farm, nestled in a cove between the mountains separating North Carolina and Georgia. Although life was rugged for the Brown family, Doc's mother was eager to provide her children with the latest comforts available. When speaking of his childhood, Doc always says that he was "born with a tit in his mouth."

Doc began his schooling at the customary age, but after six months he'd had enough of "Baby Ray was a boy," "Baby Ray had a dog," "See the dog run," and all the other exercises in the *Baby Ray Primer*. He quit school and helped his father with the farm work. By the time he was eight he knew enough about moonshining to make his own still. For the next forty-odd years Doc mixed extensive moonshining with extensive traveling.

By the summer of 1968 Doc had been settled down fairly peacefully for several years. He claims, at age fifty-one, to be too old and sick to have any desire to make moonshine or to travel anymore. His three oldest daughters are now married, while his only son and his youngest daughter still live at home. Family disputes occasionally occur between Doc and his wife and his children. At such times Doc usually swears that he is going to leave again—start traveling across the country as he did when he was younger. It's not likely that he'll carry through with these threats, however. His harsh life is beginning to take an early toll on his vigor.

Doc is employed now during most of the year (except for the winter months) as a handyman at one of Pikeville's two motels. He picks up the garbage daily, cuts the grass, and, when the maids don't come in, he even cleans up the rooms. He recently did all of the carpentry for an addition to the motel's restaurant and he also helped clear out the nearby woods so that campsites could be built. The pay is low, $1.25 an hour, but Doc claims it's the best job he's ever had. The motel owners take care of him and periodically raise his pay so that he will not leave them. They don't get terribly upset when a hangover keeps him away for several days. Doc's other income is from the monthly unemployment check he receives from the State. The check helps to pay the rent on his house, and he hopes that the government officials do not find out that he has a job now. The family can barely live on their total income as it is.

Doc is always willing to talk about his adventurous life, and in the following pages he summarizes his years as a moonshiner:

O.K., John, being I give you a recipe how to make the moonshine so I'm gon tell ya exactly how if you do what I've done for forty-two years, then I'm gonna show you where you wind up at. So I started makin' when I was eight years old, I made my first fifty gallon still and I capped my first still and took it over, me and my brother, he was six and me eight. So we've headed on down the road ever since, and I'll tell you what makin' whiskey mounts to. Hit'll put you in the pore house, hit'll put your health bad, cause you to lose friends, hit'll cause people to talk about yee, and hit'll cause you every headache in the world imaginable. And if you don't believe it, you try it, son. So I started out, thought, well, nothin' else to do back in them days only make whiskey. So, I was raised in a still house, nothing to brag about, but it's the facts. So, when I started out I thought I'd make some money, well we started makin' and makin' and makin', years and years.

Well when I was eleven years old I got caught, county sheriff caught me, and he took an alder brush and whipped my hind end, and that was it, that was the first trial I had. So when I was fifteen I got caught again. Well, when I was twenty I got caught again, so by that time I got in the peckerwood army—that's the CC camp—so I just quit makin' whiskey there for six months and I went in the CC camp and I come back out I said, well, I've quit makin' whiskey now I'm gonna see the world. So we started travelin', me and a boy we raised, so we went to travelin'. I made every state in the union, time after time, so I'd always get some where up in New York or California some place and get to thinkin' about the old mountains, how much money I'd make makin' whiskey. So I'd come back home, we'd start again, well, I got caught in 19 and 40, again. So, ah, I got out on probation—federal got me that time—got out on probation, so I went to New York, and I worked up there in New York three or four months. And they keep writin' letters, wantin' me to come back home, so I 'cided to come back and start makin' again. Well, I come back home and I joined back makin' whiskey again with my dad and brothers, and cousins and nephews and so forth and so on. So I signed up and got back in the CC camp, stayed three more months. Well, we 'cided we'd go back west, and we got our old guitars and we headed out, so we go'd to California and got a good job out there. And that time I had to register when I was in the CC camp, so the army, draft board called me. So I had to come back home and went down to Ft. MacPherson and they throwed me out.

Well, I headed back on the go again, so I went to Ohio and I worked up there awhile, and some of the boys, we all got together, and I bought me an old car, a better car than I had. And so we 'cided to all go to California, went to California and so I got a letter to come back to the draft board again. Back I come, so, I go'd up to Muskogee, the county seat of the county where I lived, and the old country doctor he zamined me that time, he turned me down. So I went back and I went to Maine. We went up in Maine and I got a job on a boat, and I got seasick before I got on it, didn't like the idea of gettin' out on the ocean, so I come on down the east, down to Baltimore and got me a job in a bar, me and Hub Dodson, a boy we raised, and a bunch of us, makin' music in the bar at night. So we played there awhile and got to thinkin' about the old moonshine back in the mountains, we come home, and bought us some copper and made a new still, with a bunch of sugar and stuff we started back again. Well, that was the last time I got caught, the Federal got me that time, last time I got caught by the Federal. So, I got out on probation again, and I went to work for the T.V.A. over at Fontana, N.C. and we worked over there a couple of months.

So I 'cided to go back to California and get rich again, and away we went again back to California. Went out there, and so, went right back to the same place in Oakland. And J. D. Todd up there at Muskogee, he was chairman of the draft board, so, he called me back again, to go again. So I came back that time, went down to Ft. MacPherson again. And they rejected me, turned me down. So I come back and I went back to Ohio, and so I worked up there about four or five months, got to thinkin' about the old moonshine again, and I come on back home and we put us up another outfit and I got caught again. So that made six times that I'd got caught, well, I got to goin' with his ol' heifer, Dorothy, the one I married, so I sorta got sweet on her and I married, ah, June, ah, it was May 31 I got married. I 'cided well aint nothing to do around here—I was driving a truck, hauling logs, first one thing then another, working for four dollars a day—and I 'cided, well I'll get rich, started back makin' liquor again. Well in 1947 they caught me again, and that made the seventh time they caught me. High sheriff over there in States County caught me, and so we go'd down to Hughesville and the judge he got sorry for me and he charged me $75 and five years expended sentence. And he told me if you ever get caught again you'll have to build twelve months, pardner. And I said, 'Thank you, sir,' and I walked out and I come on back home. And where they'd cut us down, they was about five boxes practically full of beer, and I told my brother, "Hell, they can't do nothing with us, let's go back and run it." So went back and it hadn't been forty-eight hours from the time the judge told me that, Ted Ballard walked in on us again, grinnin', and said, "Look like you boys is right at it," said, "you know what the judge told you." I said, "You know what he told you shuriff," and he sorta grinned. So I jumped the log and I aint seed Ted Ballard from that day till this. Never did hear anymore about it, so well I 'cided, better quit makin' whiskey. So I went to work drivin' a truck for construction companies and I worked there in the season of 1947. And I 'cided, well I can't make nothing at this, was just gettin' sixty-five cents an hour. So we come on back home and we started makin' whiskey, and they never did catch me anymore. But I'll tell you one thing, they cut me down and destroyed our place more times than a bicycle's got spokes in the wheel. And so in 19 and 54, I 'cided, well, I'll go west again. And I told my old lady I'd go west, so I tore out the still, and we had a bunch of whiskey and we sold hit and me an' Melvin Price we headed for the state of Washington.

So I went out there and got me a good job and worked out there about six weeks and got homesick for the family. So I come on back home and I'd been home about two months, my old lady she taken TB and had to go to Batty's State Hospital, TB sanitorum. And so we go'd down there and I got a job workin' down there for the state as a maintenance. And so she stayed there nine months and she got where she could come home and we came back. And in 19 and 55 then she broke down again, and so I go'd back down and hired in to get a job, and they called me up for a physical and so they found it on me. And so they put me to bed, and I stayed fourteen months, me and her together. And we got her discharge and come on home and we been on the go ever since, disabled to work. I couldn't get none of my social security, it was frozen under the old laws, so ah, I had to draw state welfare. And they've helped me raise my children up till now, still draw a little dab of money there.

I'm a' trying to work ever day, and do the best I can, John, it's rough. And you see the doctor told me that's exactly what was wrong, why I had bad lungs was exposure and all makin' moonshine. And so here I'm settin' on the county, ah, one foot on the grave and the other one in the bank, or on the bank and in the grave, I spoke it backwards. So that's exactly what makin' moonshine mounts to. And so I told you the recipe, and I'd advise nobody to not listen to what I tell em, for I'll tell you the reason why, I've had experence, and experence like that is a great education to anybody. So I'd advise reason why I know, where I'm at today, the condition I'm in, the anybody to not even think about makin' whiskey, for the simple shape I'm in, is something to think about. So I'm, as I said, I'm workin here and yanner tryin to keep from starvin' to death and so, ever time I look out the window the big kids are runnin' the little uns around the house to catch em, trying to eat em, and so 'at gets rough. And I'd advise anybody not to listen to that recipe for you see where it put me, and this is all true and I can prove it, ever word I told you is the facts, so that's not one tenth, or one thousandth of a tenth, of what I've done in the moonshine life. And I just thought I'd explain it to you and tell you what it means. I'm not ashamed of what I told you, I don't care if ever body in the world hears this tape. If they'll listen at it real good and take some knowledge to it, then they'll realize what makin' moonshine means to a human being. And so I'd advise anybody to never fool with it, not even think about it. Don't even drink, that's my trouble now, I drink too much. They one thing about it, I try to drink it all and you know it's impossible, you can't. And so I'm tryin to quit, I been quit now about a week and I hope I never drink anymore unless I'm with somebody or by myself. And so, John, I thought I'd tell you all this and it's been a pleasure tellin' you.

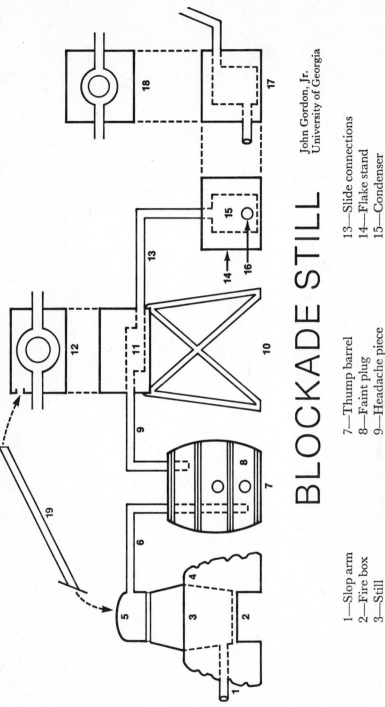

BLOCKADE STILL

John Gordon, Jr.
University of Georgia

1—Slop arm
2—Fire box
3—Still
4—Furnace (made of mud and stone)
5—Cap
6—Thump post

7—Thump barrel
8—Faint plug
9—Headache piece
10—Pre-heater box
11—Pre-heater coil
12—Pre-heater box (top view)

13—Slide connections
14—Flake stand
15—Condenser
16—Money stick (cond. stem)
17—Flake stand (side view)
18—Flake stand (top view)
19—Heater trough

19. The Year of the Burglar

NIHOLAS PILEGGI

"You must have patience. You must study. You must be disciplined," Armand said of his craft.

> Discipline almost above everything else. Once, I remember, I was in Palm Beach. I had finished upstairs and was checking the den when I saw a beautiful Parker shotgun. If you don't know shotguns—and they're my passion—let me tell you that this Parker was priceless. A collector's item. I couldn't just go out and buy it. I remember standing in that den. I had about $45,000 in cash and jewelry in my pocket, but the thing I really wanted was that shotgun. I could feel a burning for it inside my chest, but I knew if I took that gun it would jam me up. It would be my curse. So I left without it. Even after I got home, I remember, later that night, I was in bed and I kept thinking about that gun. It was like the devil to me that night. I almost got up and went back for it, but I didn't. That's what I mean by discipline.

Armand is a 34-year-old career burglar who makes between $125,000 and $250,000 a year for no more than six or seven carefully planned excursions into larceny. (While Armand is real, his name is not. It has been changed, along with some personal characteristics, to keep his identity secret.) He works alone, loves to hunt and fish and feels that the United States is going to the dogs. "You might laugh," he will say, "but I'm for law and order. What I do is my business. I don't hurt anyone, and anyway most of the people who lose stuff are insured, and I could tell you about the way they inflate their losses. But this mugging on the streets and the rapes and the way they have to coddle these creeps makes me sick."

A soft-spoken man, Armand has a complexion that is half natural olive and half winter sun. He has green eyes which, despite the open friendliness of an easy, big-toothed smile and healthy good looks, stare suspiciously down the sides of a long, thin nose. His hair is wavy, prematurely gray and razor-cut every two weeks for $15. He lives in a high-rent, five-room apartment in Manhattan behind a metal door fitted with a specially designed Swiss bolt lock that he altered himself to make it pick proof.

He owns two automobiles—a 1967 Ferarri and a 1968 Jaguar sedan—both registered in the name of his brother. His brother and sister, thanks to Armand, are now the proprietors of a profitable business, and any official who might ask about Armand is told they support him entirely. Armand has a doctor who swears that Armand has always been too anemic to work and, therefore, he has no social-security number and has never paid taxes. He did register for the draft, but was rejected because one of his legs is slightly shorter than the other. He claims that he would happily have served.

Armand is not married, has no steady girl friend and no close friends. He allows himself the luxury of hunting trips into Canada for big game like elk and caribou. He keeps a diesel cabin cruiser moored near New York which is equipped for deep-sea fishing. He prefers a long fruitless day fishing for swordfish to a day filled with catching smaller fish. He is rarely in New York during the winter months since he must follow his prospective victims on the rounds of their resorts. Armand collects paintings (he recently paid $18,000 for a Spanish artist's work), likes expensive restaurants and attends sports-car races. He also practices lock-picking every day, using the latest burglar-proof locks, which he buys from distributors and manufacturers around the world.

He was apprenticed at the age of 13 to his father, a stern, European master burglar. His instruction included the memorization of the service manuals and diagrams of locks and safe mechanisms from all of the major European and American lock companies. As a youngster, Armand spent hours dismantling and reassembling locks under the watchful eye of his father, who would shout, "No! Not that way!" or "Stop! Stupid!" whenever his son's fingers went stiff. At the age of 17 Armand was an accomplished pickman.

Pickmen, the élite of the burglary profession, are so named because they "pick" locks rather than kick in doors, drill out lock cylinders or jimmy windows. Once the craft is mastered, a pickman can open almost any key-operated lock by the delicate manipulation of a pick and tension bar—a pair of four-inch strips of thin metal the width of a hacksaw blade. By inserting his pick into a keyhole, Armand is able to release each of the lock's tumbler pins in turn while holding them open with the tension bar. It takes nimble and sensitive fingers. In spite of his compulsive daily practice, his early training and his continuous study of lock mechanisms, it can still take Armand up to a half hour to open some locks.

"Sometimes a man's fingers are just not right," he explains. "Sometimes its the weather. Things stick. You can't feel. It's different for everybody. It's not like you've got a key."

Armand's father also instructed him in the identification and appraisal of valuable stones and precious metal so that he would never be at the mercy of expert jewelers who trade in stolen gems. His discipline prevents him from taking anything other than cash and jewelry, no matter how tempted he might be. A guarantee of anonymity and his Old-World pride in his craft convinced him to discuss the refinements in what he calls "a dying art."

Besides practicing with picks and locks every day, Armand reads newspaper society columns, financial news, real estate pages and auction announcements. His intimate knowledge of the day-to-day life of anyone he plans to rob would be as shocking to the potential victim as the loss. Armand not only follows wealthy people to their resorts, but often chats with them, knows their habits and their jewelers. Much of his information comes from listening to gossip (he is an excellent gossip, filled with news about the famous and wealthy) and talking to doormen, maintenance men, maids and delivery men whose suspicions he allays with tactful questioning, cash and subterfuge.

> You can go up to a doorman, for instance, he said, and say you're a private detective and hand him $50. You can say that you're checking for the owner. Say you're checking on the guy's wife. He wants a divorce. You get chummy, you see, by giving the guy information, and then he's more likely to tell you when she has visitors. Maybe she goes out to meet her boyfriend. When does she go out? Is there a maid there all the time who I should talk to? Little by little, before you know it, a guy can have all the information he wants.

A professional must know as much as possible about security in various hotels. This, Armand feels, is much more important than knowing about the local police. His familiarity with resort hotels is extraordinary. He knows about closed-circuit camera locations, and he knows when and on what floors they are used. He knows the routes or "runs" of security personnel in these hotels, and he knows the personalities of those on duty, on standby, and what floors are favored with security. Armand knows that millionaires rate security checks every three hours. A career man, Armand explains, will choose only one out of seven or eight excellent burglary possibilities.

> The English are pigeons, he laughed. They're very careless with their jewels and their cash. They leave it all around their bedrooms. It's a shame there aren't more of them. The wealthy French are tight, and you can't get anything out of the rich Italians. When you're in Italy it doesn't even pay to score.

As part of his daily routine Armand not only keeps up with the comings and goings of wealth and society, but he maintains an elaborate mailing list and regularly sends hundreds of holiday cards and thank-you notes—innocent correspondence to maintain as many contacts as possible among his potential victims. He speaks Italian, Spanish and French and has gone to Berlitz to learn German. He knows food, is free with money and can discuss for hours the relative merits of Swiss hotels. He is a frequent escort of wealthy young ladies to whom he is the ne'er-do-well heir of a European exporting family.

Armand said his father always insisted that he maintain superficial friendships among socially prominent and aristocratic Europeans, who, in turn, would guarantee that he would be socially desirable to wealthy Americans. He will accept as many invitations to parties as he can in the hope of gaining access to private apartments and houses. Once inside, his eye misses nothing, for later he can barter information concerning valuables and their location with other burglars. If an apartment or a house has particularly valuable paintings, or stocks and bonds kept in a safe—all items Armand will not touch—he will pass that information on to other burglars for either a flat fee or a percentage of the take.

"Art guys," as he calls burglars who specialize in taking valuable paintings, "can wait. Especially if it's a private house. I know that stuff isn't going anywhere. It's just going to hang on that wall. In a few months all a guy has to do is go in there and take it."

Any one of Armand's burglaries might take a month in preparation. He recalls on one occasion dating a girl several times just to see the floor plan of her parents' apartment. On another occasion, he took a job as a messenger for more than a week until he was able to check out the possibilities of burglarizing a wealthy family in a particular East-side cooperative to which he had been unable to gain entrance socially.

"I made it my business to be a classy guy," Armand said, "It made it easier for me to move around."

By dealing with fences he knows, Armand claims to get 30 percent value on jewelry broken down right away—that is, jewels the fence removes from their gold-and-platinum setting soon after they are stolen. He says that in this way the stones, which are usually unidentifiable when loose, can easily be mixed in and passed along with legitimate stones. He will also get "an ounce count" on the gold and platinum settings. Later, after they are melted down, Armand receives from $15 to $20 on ounce for gold and platinum. Fences, he claims, are sometimes legitimate jewelers and sometimes shady travelers who move easily between continents with multiple passports and Swiss bank accounts. Armand also points out that a professional burglar never unloads all of his loot with one fence. It is not only a safeguard against anything like the arrest or robbery of the fence and the loss of an entire haul, but it also places the professional in a better bargaining position with the fence. "He knows you've got other outlets," Armand winked.

The professional also never keeps anything he takes as a souvenir or a gift. "When I want some jewelry," he snapped, "I buy it." American Express, Carte Blanche and Diner's Club credit cards, which can bring in $500 on the illicit market if turned over within 24 hours of the theft, are passed up by Armand. "The value in those cards is tremendous," he explained, "you could do $10,000 worth of damage with a really good card in a few hours. But the people involved are not all that reliable. A fellow would have to expose himself to people who are not professional about their work. It would be dangerous. He'd be dealing with addicts. Scared guys. They'd sell a fellow out in a minute."

Pickmen like Armand are always nervous men, according to Deputy Inspector Thomas Gleason of the New York City burglary squad. "They work under tremendous tension. They might look smooth and talk calmly," Gleason went on, "but you'll find that noise disturbs them. They live carefully regulated lives and the slightest thing will set them off. If they're on a job and a pick-resistant cylinder takes them too long they'll just take off. They are suspicious, superstitious and sick. They like to lose themselves. Even when they're married you will find that they have no real life. They have a tendency to move around a lot. They stay away from their neighbors. Their drivers licenses are always false. They use the names of guys in prison. When they're finally caught they are worn out inside. Right down to nothing. They've eaten up their own insides. They're hollow."

Driving south along Sixth Avenue Armand recalled the one time he had been arrested for burglary.

> It was in the Sherry Netherland during a weekday afternoon, and I had picked my way into the suite of an old couple. They were supposed to have lots of jewelry. As soon as I got in I went straight to the bathroom and flushed the pick down the toilet. That's 'flushing time' down the drain right there. You get caught with that pick and it's 'possession of burglar's tools.' Then I went through the bedroom and checked the stuff, but the jewelry wasn't worth more than a couple of thousand dollars. I looked some more and found a few hundred in cash. I just knew it was a bust. Something told me, so I left everything there and walked out of the suite. A little way down the hall two hotel detectives grabbed me. I was arrested for burglary, but there was no evidence. I didn't take anything and I didn't have a burglar's tool. I don't even carry a nail file, just for that reason. In court I claimed to have been invited up there by some girl in the lobby. I said the girl told me to go to the room if I wanted a "good time." When I got there the door was open, I told the court, and I went in. When I got tired of waiting I left and the two detectives grabbed me. Case dismissed!

Armand slammed his palms against the steering wheel and whistled triumphantly. "I never walked into that hotel again. Those two detectives are now at the Plaza."

The police, Armand admitted, do know him.

> They know everybody. They've got a line on everyone. The thing is just not to get greedy. Don't make trouble for them. Keep out of the way. I move a lot. Say the police knew one guy was a big hotel pickman. Well, he might not do more than one or two in any one town every couple of years. It doesn't pay for them to trail him day and night. You usually get that kind of police attention only when they've got the word that something is in the works. When that happens a guy had better leave town and give up his partners.

When Armand's $13,000 Ferarri slid into the Rockefeller Center garage it was about 8:30 P.M. on a busy Friday night. Three young attendants bolted forward immediately for the opportunity to park it, leaving a line of customers unattended.

"Live," Armand suggested to the young men as they opened the door and helped him out.

In New York, 1968 has been the year of the burglar. There were 113,372 burglaries reported in the first eight months of the year in comparison with 94,106 reported during the same period last year. They have become a prime subject of chatter along Manhattan's high-rent East Side (where more than 1,000 burglaries are committed every month) as well as in the low-cost housing developments in Brooklyn and Queens. Newspapers carry ads puffing "burglarproof" locks. Home alarm systems, which set off siren horns and flashing lights, are being installed at prices ranging from $500 to $10,000. Books entitled "How to Avoid Burglary, Housebreaking and Other Crimes" and "How to Defend Yourself, Your Family and Your Home" have been selling well, and similar books are due for publication. Burglary is becoming such a preoccupation with New Yorkers, in fact, that many are changing their patterns of living just in order to avoid it.

"Some people who don't even like little dogs go out and buy big ones," a burglar-squad detective said, shaking his head. "People move out of nice top floor apartments because they know burglars prefer the top floor where nobody'll pass them by on the stairway and the roof is near for escape. It's really a shame. I've seen some people who, rather than give up good garden apartments, have cluttered them up with so many chains, bolts and even barbed wire that it looks like they're living in Khesanh."

The overwhelming number of these burglaries, of course, are not committed by career pickmen like Armand. They are the work of unskilled or semi-skilled "door shakers," "kick-it-in men," "loidmen" and "creepers."

"I've got a taste. I've got to live, and you can't live without money. I like the numbers. I'll go $100 on a number. 'Yes sir,' 'No, sir,' that ain't living to me."

Richie is a 28-year-old kick-it-in man who dreams of some day making enough money to become a heroin pusher. He is currently on bail in connection with two burglary cases. "When you're kicking-it-in you're trying to live. You're not thinking about the police. I know the first time a policeman came up and said he's going to put me in jail I was scared, but he's been putting me in jail all my life. I'm not scared to go to jail anymore. Whitey made the jails for us."

Richie laughs a great deal while he is talking. He will flash his hands nervously before his face as though molding his phrases as he speaks. "The first time I was arrested a friend tripped on a silent alarm cord. You don't even know they're there. I used Legal Aid that time. I laid over five months in the Tombs waiting for bail. Next time I was grabbed was on West 90th Street. I was carrying a duffle bag with a crowbar, screw driver and hammer. A detective called me over to his car. 'Hey you.' he said, 'Commere. What you got in that bag?' Wow!" Richie laughed at the memory.

A "kick-it-in man" can be defined roughly as anyone who uses force to gain entry. He will use any device conceivable to open or break in a door. In narrow corridors the stoutest door can be forced open by the use of an automobile jack and wooden blocks wedged between it and the opposite wall. Most apartment doors in New York, however, are of such flimsy material that pressure from a small crowbar or screw driver is enough to spring them open. A kick-it-in man like Richie might be dressed as a U.S. Marine "looking" for an imaginary uncle whom he thought lived in the building. He may rent a grocery delivery bike and wear the kind of clothes worn by delivery men in that specific neighborhood. A kick-it-in man will hold a clip board, heft a ladder, have a pencil jammed behind his ear, lug a tool kit, carry a lunch pail and even deliver groceries he has just bought to get past a doorman. Detectives often find full boxes of abandoned groceries in the hallways of apartment houses that have been burglarized. Burglars working in teams of four to six often go on a job or "cable" with walkie-talkies and are often racially integrated so as to better blend into a particular neighborhood. Couples are favored as lookouts in large commercial jobs.

"On a cable you always need two spotters," Richie explained.

> You need one guy to be a spotter, say on the corner, and you need another guy nearby who watches the spotter. If the place has Holmes [a private burglar detective service that provides armed men who respond to alarm signals] you've got to be one eight minutes after you've kicked it in. I mean Holmes comes in like cowboys.
> You get started kicking-it-in when your landlady starts sweeping outside your door all day long. She starts saying if you don't come through with your back rent she's going to take your clothes. Sometimes

you've got to wait because you don't want to go on a cable with sick guys. Some guys just have to mess up a place or mess up anyone they find in a place. You don't want guys like that. But if you hold out too long or if you get cold feet, then nobody wants to hustle with you.

You go by the seasons. In clothes, people want the best. You get your alligators and sweater shirts. You get orders for color TVs. The stuff is stashed in a room, usually it's a furnished room where you pay $15 or $17 a week. Sometimes you've got a girl and she stores the stuff for you. I mean baby.

He began acting out both parts of the pantomime. "Let me stay. You want nice things. Let me keep this here a little bit. I mean baby a girl's gotta help a guy. Girls gotta help a man."

Pausing a moment to emphasize his last remark, he continued:

A girl might have a little more education. She's had a job. She can help a guy. She gets his clothes cleaned for him. He's sleeping between clean sheets. She makes him take showers. He doesn't have to knock himself out just living. A woman does this for a man, and now he might take himself a safe. Get himself $7,000. Give her $1,000. Take $600 or $700 and mess up with some of his friends. He doesn't have to kick-it-in again right away. He might even fix up with a white boy. They can do pretty good.

On a day you might get up early. Ten-eleven o'clock. Get out and get yourself some eggs. Go to the bar. That's where you meet. It's like your living room when you're hustling. "Hey man," somebody'll yell, "Tops is looking for you" or "Little Red said wait for him, he'll be back." I know he's got a cable. He's setting up a team. These bars cater to teams. Stickup men have their bars. All the boys in them are stick-up men. There are bars for boosters or shoplifters. Gambling bars. Dope bars. And there are bars where all the guys who are kicking-it-in go.

When you're working you just walk right on by the doorman. Most of them are old. They don't know what's going on. Man you know where *you're* going. You just keep moving. If he stops you you've just got the wrong address. That's all. Sometimes I'm downtown and I'll see a friend and he's working or delivering or something and I'll say I'm not doing anything anyway so I'll help him deliver. And we'll walk into a building together and check things out, and I'm looking all the time. If I get a good line I'll even rent a truck.

Mostly, though, you move through the rear. We're going in the back way all the time. As long as we stay off the main drag we're safe. It's the service entrances. The fire escapes. We know about back doors. Most people never question a black man walking through a service entrance. They kind of go together, he smiled. That was Whitey's idea, you know, sending us to the back door.

Inside you ring the bell to make sure the place is empty. Sometimes you can even phone them up. You check every place somebody might be hiding. Make sure you're safe. You go through bedrooms first. Good furs and things you can put it all in a laundry bag. Sometimes you can leave the bag on a nearby roof and come back for it later. Nobody thinks to look on a roof and nobody expects to see their mink coat rolled up in a laundry bag.

The big moment comes when you split that stuff. It's very important that nobody walks away unhappy. That's where all the woe comes from. You've got to split it all good and even. Right down the line. One shirt or a tie can get a man in jail. Man, cut the tie in half. Right down the middle. Get some scissors and cut that tie half and half. No beefs.

Burglars like Richie very rarely try each others' techniques. They are habit-prone and conservative. Commercial burglars, for instance, will almost never give up burglarizing stores and turn their attention toward apartments or houses. A burglar who is successful working the two-family houses in a specific Queens neighborhood will continue operating in that same area until he is either caught or frightened off. When Richie was kicking in an apartment he might travel by subway an hour to that area of the city in which he felt most at ease. Burglars are so predictable in their methods of entry, in fact, that police categorize them accordingly. The "door shaker," for example, the least experienced of all burglars, simply goes through the city's large apartment buildings and hotels (usually between 9:30 and noon) trying doors. He will continue trying doors until he finds one unlocked or even ajar. It does not usually take very long. According to a recent New York City Police Department morning-hour survey of Queens apartment houses, 25 out of 150 apartment doors were left unlocked.

The "loidman" considers himself much more skilled than the "door shaker." In reality, his skill is limited to slipping a strip of celluloid into a doorjamb and then opening the door by exerting enough pressure to pry back the spring lock. Spring locks, the kind that snap shut automatically, are very common in New York, and for that reason the "loidman" is the most common of all career burglars in the city.

The "cat" burglar is not the gem-stealing romantic of fiction and film. He is usually a commercial burglar. He is primarily interested in bolts of cloth, racks of furs and cases of expensive whiskey. Usually short, slight and agile, he is often occupied wriggling through transoms, grease ducts and skylight panels. His is a dirty job. He very rarely works alone. His task is usually to get inside the building and then open a rear door for the rest of his band.

The loot taken by these burglars is sold for a fraction of its original value. It is mostly sold in the city's poorer sections, in both white and Negro neighborhoods, around factories, bars and, increasingly, among the financially hard-presed, lower-middle-class white suburbanites struggling with time payments and mortgages. Portable television sets for $35 are apparently a great temptation to many New Yorkers, judging by the volume of stolen merchandise sold. A color television set sells for $50. A $7,000 mink coat will bring a burglar $250, and a brand new $200 suit right off the rack, may bring as little as $15 to the burglar who stole it.

"It's all a hustle," Richie laughed, when asked when he expects to quit burglary.

> I've got to pay my lawyer. I've got a nice place now. I pay $150 a month. Got four clean rooms and a doorman. But it's all a hustle. You've got to watch for yourself how you can. Everybody's got something going, and I've got mine. I remember once I'm standing talking there in the bar, talking to one guy who I know real well, and while we're talking another guy who is with him is over at my place kicking-it-in. The two of them had been by my place at a card game. They saw stuff they liked.
>
> I once got arrested because a friend caught me in his place. I remember I'd been there and I saw something I liked, and when he was away I got in. It was that I just wanted something. Even just a little bottle. I just had to bring something back. You're not thinking of your friend. You're not even thinking of the police. You're just thinking that you want something.
>
> Sure, I'd like to make a bundle and relax. Get about $25,000. Enough for an eighth of a kilo. Get a little investment. You can cut it and bag it and relax for a while. You've got it made.

20. Prostitution as an Illegal Vocation: A Sociological Overview

MARY RIEGE LANER

"Prostitution occurs in almost every human society," and "The greater the sexual freedom of women, the less prostitution."[1] With these two sentences, the authors of *Human Behavior: An Inventory of Scientific Findings* summarize what frequently has been called the world's oldest "profession." It might seem that anything beyond these statements is merely commentary. Yet prostitution and its practitioners have fascinated people for centuries, as the volumes on the subject in our libraries quietly attest. Persistent interest in this vocation has been displayed by both scientific and nonscientific writers, from humanistic, psychiatric, and sociological points of view, among others. This paper is an overview of prostitution as a vocation, compiled from sociological theory and data, and compares the sociological perspective with other perspectives. The picture that emerges is somewhat confusing and at times seems paradoxical. Confusion stems in part from varying value orientations, in part from the failure of some researchers to base their studies on hypotheses derived from a unified body of theory, and in part from the incomparability of sample populations. Paradox, however, is only apparent. Yet the seeming paradoxes involved in prostitution and in the personalities of prostitutes are to some degree responsible for the ongoing interest in this occupation.

Our focus is on current aspects of the occupation since its structure and functions have undergone some changes in recent decades. As Davis points out:

> ... during the present century, in industrial societies, a rise in feminine sex freedom has occurred, especially among the single, widowed, and divorced.... With the greater availability of ordinary women for sexual companionship, we should expect the role of the prostitute, in both

---

[1] B. Berelson and G. A. Steiner, *Human Behavior: An Inventory of Scientific Findings* (New York, Harcourt, Brace and World, 1964).

volume and status, to decline. This is what the available evidence seems to show.[2]

Not all investigators agree about what the evidence shows, however. Fairfield calls prostitution "an immense social problem,"[3] but Barry observes that while streetwalkers are decreasing in number, call girls are becoming more numerous. Organized prostitution, he states, "is not thought to be of significant proportions, and so far as the indigenous population is concerned, the police have it well under control."[4]

Davis, who also feels that prostitution is not a major social problem—in fact, that it has little influence on society—notes that

> the concern over prostitution is due to its being regarded as a vice... the degrading indulgence of natural propensities or appetites...reprehensible in itself, regardless of whether it has evil consequences.[5]

Not only do estimates of the seriousness of the problem of prostitution vary, but so do definitions of and typologies of prostitution. Pomeroy defines prostitution as

> sexual activity with partners who are more or less indiscriminately selected. She (or he) must make a sizeable portion of her (or his) living from this activity for some period of time.[6]

May expands the definition to emphasize three characteristic elements:

> ...payment, usually involving the passing of money, although gifts or pleasures may constitute equivalent consideration; promiscuity, with the possible exercise of choice; and, emotional indifference.[7]

Davis asserts that the prostitute is indifferent not only to sexual pleasure but to her partner as well. Selling and indifference reflect a pure commercialization of the sexual relationship, and this commercialization is what Davis calls "the prostitute's affront." Although researchers do not agree about whether the prostitute *is* indifferent, affrontery can be seen sociologically in terms of primary and secondary relationships. Some researchers

[2] K. Davis, "Prostitution," in R. K. Merton and R. A. Nisbet (eds.), *Contemporary Social Problems* (New York, Harcourt, Brace and World, 1961).

[3] L. Fairfield, "Notes on Prostitution," *British Journal of Delinquency,* Vol. 9, No. 3 (January 1959), pp. 164–73.

[4] J. V. Barry, "Prostitution: A Report from Australia," ibid., pp. 182–91.

[5] Davis, op. cit.

[6] W. P. Pomeroy, "Some Aspects of Prostitution," *Journal of Sex Research,* Vol. 1, No. 3 (December 1965), pp. 177–87.

[7] G. May, cited in Davis, op. cit.

state that the prostitute simulates a primary relationship with her client (or "trick" or "john") in a context which, under most other circumstances, would warrant only secondary relationship behaviors.[8] That is, her relationship with the client is not so intimate and involved as she pretends it is. Here, then, is a seeming paradox, in that the simulated intimacy (as well as the sexual service) is what the client seeks. In this sense, prostitution is a crime without a victim, since the "trick" is a party to the deception. He knows the prostitute is deceiving him, but wants to believe in the deception and so participates in maintaining it. Moreover, the better the prostitute is at pretending to be fully involved with the client (other things being equal), the more successful she is at her work.

But other things are not equal. For example, prostitutes are not all of the same type or status. Reckless classifies prostitutes into four main types listed here in decreasing status order: the unorganized professional prostitute, the call girl, the brothel prostitute, and the street or public prostitute.[9] (The first type has also been called "the outlaw broad" by Bryan indicating a prostitute who does not have, or is not working with, a pimp.)[10] An elaborate and somewhat anachronistic typology is provided by Minnis whose seven-level scheme subdivides prostitutes into groups she calls pony girls, call girls, B-girls, cruise girls, streetwalkers, the Arctic class, and the Negro class.[11] Greenwald reports a simpler three-tiered classification scheme as told to him by a call girl: At the top of the status heirarchy is the party girl (who is often also a model, actress, or chorus girl); then the hustler or hooker; and at the bottom of the ladder, the prostitute or whore.[12] Another typology is provided by Pomeroy which does not differentiate between status levels but rather between four types of interpersonal relationship. These are: female heterosexual prostitution (females being paid by males); male homosexual prostitution (males being paid by males); male heterosexual prostitution

---

[8] Mary G. Riege, "The Call Girl and the Dance Teacher: A Comparative Analysis," *Cornell Journal of Social Relations,* Vol. 4, No. 1 (Spring 1969), pp. 58–71.

[9] W. C. Reckless, *The Crime Problem* (New York, Appleton-Century-Crofts, 1955).

[10] J. H. Bryan, "Apprenticeship in Prostitution," *Social Problems,* Vol. 12, No. 3 (Winter 1965), pp. 287–97. While a common colloquial term for the prostitute is "hustler," Ross states that this term really indicates an adjunctive aspect of prostitution called "hustling" by those who engage in it in which the "sale of sex is regularly and frequently associated with extortion from and robbery of the clients." H. L. Ross, "The 'Hustler' in Chicago," *Journal Stud. Research,* Vol. 1, No. 1 (Fall 1959), pp. 13–19.

[11] Mhyra S. Minnis, "Prostitution and Social Class," *Proceedings of the Southwestern Sociological Association,* Vol. 13 (1963), pp. 1–6.

[12] H. Greenwald, *The Call Girl: A Social and Psychoanalytic Study* (New York, Ballantine Books, 1958).

(males being paid by females) ; and, female homosexual prostitution (females being paid by females). Pomeroy notes that the last two types are rare.[13]

WHAT MAKES SALLY RUN?

Goode has pointed out that many types of deviant behavior seem to attract explanations that activate a principle of psychological abnormality. Goode states:

> The sociologist legitimately raises a question as to what it is about American society which begets a personality abnormality explanation for marijuana smokers . . . homosexuals . . . unwed mothers . . . as well as a host of other deviant groups.[14]

Goode proposes that adopting a "medical" approach to the deviant and his behavior effectively neutralizes his moral legitimacy and the viability of his behavior and that constructors of such theories mirror the basic values of American society.

Psychoanalytically, prostitutes have been described as masochistic, of infantile mentality, unable to form mature interpersonal relationships, regressed, emotionally dangerous to males, possessing a confused self-image, aggressive, lacking internal controls, excessively dependent, and demonstrating gender-role confusion. Bryan, who reports these descriptions, criticizes them and, like Goode, suggests that a different perspective might be more useful—for instance, one focusing on the interpersonal processes that help define the deviant role, the surroundings in which the role is learned, and the limits upon enactment of the role. His own study of apprenticeships in prostitution follows this pattern, addressing itself to *how* entrance into prostitution is accomplished, and not concerning itself with *why*.[15] Pomeroy's study, however, obtained self-report data from a cross-status sample of prostitutes regarding why they became prostitutes and why they stayed "in the life." The overwhelming majority of his subjects answered in terms of money, although a large proportion stated that meeting interesting people was a factor; and a sizeable number indicated that fun and excitement or the sexual activity itself were inducements. Pomeroy concludes that, at least on the conscious level, "there are not the ubiquitous feelings of guilt and regret over their life of prostitution that many of the writers on this subject would have one believe."[16]

[13] Pomeroy, op. cit.
[14] E. Goode, "Marijuana and the Politics of Reality," in D. E. Smith (ed.), *The New Social Drug* (Englewood Cliffs, N.J., Prentice-Hall, 1970).
[15] Bryan, op. cit.
[16] Pomeroy, op. cit.

Fairfield also stresses the economic advantages of prostitution that enable women to earn more and to live better and easier than they could with other jobs. Further, Fairfield notes that through the pimp, the prostitute has a satisfactory emotional life, since the pimp acts as both protector and as a source of psychological stability.[17] Schulman, whose case histories of prostitutes support Fairfield's findings, also comments on a "basic sense of aloneness" and a "strong need for a sense of normalcy" as characteristic of prostitutes.[18] (If Schulman is correct, the reasons stated by Pomeroy's subjects for entering and staying in a life of prostitution seem somewhat paradoxical.)

Other writers mention a need for a sense of superiority—presumably to compensate for basic feelings of inferiority—as basic to the prostitute's personality. Schulman reports the case of a prostitute who equated herself with, and considered her work superior to, that of psychiatrists in their doctor-patient relationships. This girl not only felt that she was helping her clients in similar ways, but that she "was more successful" at it than were the psychiatrists to whom she had turned for help.

Greenwald points out that an additional function of the pimp's role in this regard, is providing the prostitute with someone to whom she can feel superior—not only because she is the breadwinner, but also because society holds that the one vocation lower than that of the prostitute is that of the pimp.[19] However, in direct contradiction to Pomeroy's self-report data, the call girls studied by Greenwald generally discounted financial rewards as a factor in their continuing a life of prostitution.

WHO'S TELLING WHAT TO WHOM?

Such discrepant findings can be attributed to the defensiveness (and thus the unreliability) of self-reports given by prostitutes. Stearn, for instance states:

> Frequently I found myself wondering about what a girl had told me. While many girls talked frankly, they were often self-deluded and overly concerned with impressing their audience.... For example, when a girl told me she hated men, it was apparent to me as a reporter that she was only telling me what set her off to advantage.[20]

Stearn's reporting, however, leaves unclear just what *is* apparent. He confesses: ·

[17] Fairfield, op. cit.
[18] I. Schulman, *The Roots of Fury* (Garden City, N.Y., Doubleday, 1961).
[19] Greenwald, op. cit.
[20] J. Stearn, *Sisters of the Night* (New York, Gramercy, 1946).

Almost any conclusion I reached about these girls was subject to change as I continued my research.... But despite the fact that they operate in many different ways, they have one common denominator, one essential quality that distinguishes them from other women—a profound contempt for the opposite sex.[21]

Later in his account, Stearn notes:

The behavior pattern did not vary from girl to girl—an underlying hatred of men...and above all, there was a consuming loneliness, marked by constant flights from reality.[22]

Stearn's psychologizing has cluttered his ability to interpret his own data since his conclusions are clearly unwarranted. Prostitutes hate men, he asserts. Yet they also tell him only what sets them off to advantage and are often self-deluded and are constantly fleeing from reality. Are they then deluded about their hatred of men? Is hatred of men real, or part of a flight from reality? Or does stating that they hate men set them off to advantage? Little or nothing can be learned from such reporting beyond the bias that Stearn brings to his "investigation."

Data collected by self-report *may* be unreliable, but it is also subject to the interpretation of the investigator. The investigator's orientation (or cultural biases), superimposed on the data, are sometimes not easily recognized by the reader and seldom explicitly stated by the writer.

Comparing Stearn's reporting with Masters and Johnson's observations is profitable. These researchers used prostitutes in their initial selection of subjects for study of the human sexual response. They worked with 118 female and 27 male prostitutes for the first 20 months of their program. Due to the high degree of mobility of this population, the sample was ultimately reduced to 8 women and 3 men who were consistently available.[23] They describe them as knowledgeable, as having obvious intelligence and the ability to verbalize effectively, and as being consistently highly cooperative. In fact, their helpfulness and

[21] Ibid.
[22] Ibid.
[23] Masters and Johnson did not include the interrogative material and experimental results derived from the prostitute population in their book *Human Sexual Response*. The decision to exclude this material was based on several factors: (1) the availability for study of nonprostitute population samples, more representative of the "norm"; (2) the migratory tendencies of the prostitute population, which discouraged the recording of individual study-subject response patterns over long periods of time; and (3) the varying degrees of pathology of the reproductive organs usually present in the prostitute population which precluded the possibility of establishing a secure baseline of anatomic normalcy. W. H. Masters and V. E. Johnson, *Human Sexual Response* (Boston, Little, Brown, 1966).

... suggestions of techniques for the support and control of the human male and female in situations of direct sexual response proved invaluable.... Ultimately many of these techniques have been found to have direct application in therapy of male and female sexual inadequacy and have been integrated into the clinical research programs.[24]

In short, the comparison leads to the conclusion that a moralistic value orientation can not only color interpretation of data, but may also influence the subjects being interviewed in such a manner that they may respond in terms of the interviewer's bias. The difference in findings may also be simply the result of differences between a subjectively studied small sample when compared with an objectively studied large sample observed over time.

WHERE AND WHY DOES IT BEGIN?

Many writers of various orientations have studied the etiology of prostitution. Barry believes that no *psychological* explanation satisfactorily accounting for prostitutes is ever likely to be formulated, although if carried far enough, such an enquiry might show that

so far as vulnerability to prostitution is concerned, a basic causative factor in most cases may be found in early childhood and may reside in unsatisfactory parent-and-child relationships.[25]

This is, of course, a *social* factor. Psychologists and psychiatrists have written about the importance of social factors in leading to a life of prostitution, even though such factors, strictly speaking, are not in their domain of interest. For example, a psychiatrist interviewed by Stearn suggests:

Past experiences may have tended to break down the prostitute's relationship to society or to make her feel that it had been broken down. In this way she is conditioned or made vulnerable to her environment. ... She may drift to a big city.... She takes a job and finds herself in a stratum of society which encourages prostitution. She is caught up in the hurly burly of an indifferent city where the individual seems insignificant and she has little or no saving tie of affection with her family or anything in her past.[26]

So far, so good. The girl is particularly vulnerable to her new environment since she is without the family and other social restraints that make

[24] Ibid.
[25] Barry, op. cit.
[26] Stearn, op. cit.

most of us conform. The analyst, however, oversimplifies and distorts in what follows. He states:

> Once she has openly renounced the standards of ordinary society, she is on her way to 'conforming.' She is a 'working girl' with stipulated hours and conditions, and she can look around and see a great company of colleagues. At last, she is no longer alone—she has become a member of society.[27]

Once again, it is profitable to compare such an impressionistic viewpoint with empirical findings. Bryan's study of call girls reveals that (1) prostitutes are highly distrustful of their colleagues, and their relationships with colleagues are marked by interpersonal conflicts, disloyalties, and mutual exploitation; (2) friendships are formed with clients, toward whom the prostitutes feel empathetic; (3) findings from ratings obtained through a Semantic Differential Scale indicate that call girls rate themselves as significantly more worthwhile than their colleagues, but do not differ significantly from their ratings of men, other women, or clients; and (4) clients were rated somewhat higher than were other call girls. Bryan concludes that the high self-esteem ratings obtained belie the psychiatric notion that the prostitute must be emotionally disturbed—at least on this indicator.[28]

Perhaps the most extensive discussion of factors leading to a life of prostitution has been that of Greenwald, although his social and psychoanalytic study was limited to an analysis of call girls.[29] (His findings may generalize to other strata of prostitution, but to date there is no empirical evidence to support such a generalization.)

Greenwald's subjects reported varied educational backgrounds, but the average was completion of high school. Marital history also varied, as did number of children. Eighty-five percent of the call girls studied were from middle-class backgrounds, with the remainder equally distributed between upper and lower classes. Previous job history was fairly uniform in that the subjects had all held positions that required little skill or training. Greenwald found what he called an "amazing similarity" in the family backgrounds of the call girls—not one came from a home where there was a permanent, well-adjusted marital relationship between the parents. Further, over 90 percent of his subjects reported feeling rejected by both parents, which Greenwald states

---

[27] Ibid.

[28] J. H. Bryan, "Occupational Ideologies and Individual Attitudes of Call Girls," *Social Problems,* Vol. 13, No. 4 (Spring 1966), pp. 441–50.

[29] Greenwald, op. cit.

helped give them the feeling of worthlessness which was so characteristic of the entire group. The open rejection caused them to feel
unwanted and unloved, and unworthy of being wanted or loved.[30]

Additionally, the process of identification with parents (through which
values of "right" and "wrong" are usually incorporated) was either thus
distorted or incomplete. Finally, Greenwald sheds light on an apparent
paradox: Is a primary motivator in entering and continuing a life of
prostitution money or is it not?

> [W]hile economic factors, such as a wish for a high income, may
> have had some influence on the girls' decisions to become call girls,
> these factors were apparently more useful to them as a way of rationaliz-
> ing their choice. They could deny the emotional problems that led them
> to becoming call girls by asserting that it was just for money.... The
> call girls, plagued with uncertainty about their acceptability as human
> beings, sought evidence of their feminine desirability in their occupation.
> This occupation gave them the opportunity to demonstrate to the world,
> and particularly to themselves, that men not only desired them but were
> willing to give financial proof of their desires.[31]

If Greenwald's findings are correct, the situation is not an either/or
one, but rather, there is a connection between need for feelings of personal
worth as desirable women and financial proof of that worth. These two
factors, combined with a rejecting parental background (and any other
chance factors that combine to reinforce feelings of worthlessness in the
girls' early lives) make prostitution a compelling, albeit illegal, vocation.
    Not all girls, however, can be call girls. In general, the younger, more
physically attractive, brighter girls start at the call girl level. Those less well
endowed along these lines enter the occupation in other strata, the least well
equipped at the streetwalker level.
    Given that the factors that make girls vulnerable to a life of prostitution
have been isolated, how does entry into the vocation begin? Bryan has described the standard structure of the apprenticeship period during which
the girl learns the general philosophy of the profession and some specifics
(usually not sexual) of interpersonal behavior with customers and colleagues.
The "recruitment" is usually done by other professionals, or by men connected with prostitution circles (for example, pimps). The novice receives
her training either from a pimp or an experienced prostitute (usually the
latter) under whose supervision she serves her initial two to eight months of

[30] Ibid.
[31] Ibid.

apprenticeship. The trainer assumes responsibility for arranging contacts and negotiating the type and place of each sexual encounter for the novice. Interpersonal techniques are learned at this time, which Bryan describes as consisting primarily of "pitches," personal and sometimes sexual hygiene, rules against use of alcohol or drugs while with clients, how and when to obtain fees, and specifics concerning sexual habits of particular customers. The primary function of apprenticeship, for the trainee, is building a clientele. The apprentice is socialized into her new role primarily by being immersed in the subculture of prostitution where she learns the trade through imitation as much as through explicit tutoring. During this time she becomes acquainted with others who form her role-set.[32] The role-set of the prostitute has been described elsewhere,[33] but is presented here in expanded form to include those members whose relationship with the prostitute is primarily symbiotic.

Sources of clients:
bellboys, bartenders, doormen, cabdrivers

Masseuses,   Pimp
hairdressers,
other personal   Other
services   PROSTITUTE   prostitutes

        Police

    Doctor(s)   Clients

                            Attorney

                          Figure 20.1

Examination of this diagram indicates the extensive need-dimension involved in the prostitute's role-set. Other members in turn need the prostitute, but the mode and depth of the need differs. For the prostitute whose pimp is a paid lover rather than a panderer, her need is for psychological support, while his is for her money. She needs sources of clients and must

---

[32] Bryan, "Apprenticeships in Prostitution," op. cit.
[33] Riege, op. cit.

"pay off" to get them, but these sources also obtain money from those they direct to the prostitute. Again, they need her only for money, unless being able to locate a prostitute for their own clients enhances their position. Police are a constant source of strain to the prostitute since her work is illegal. Even if they take her payoff money, she has no guarantee that she will not be arrested. She needs the doctor's services so that she can continue to function in her work. Abortions, venereal diseases, and other possible physical mistreatment effects are vocational hazards for the prostitute. She needs certain service personnel to maintain a required level of attractiveness. She needs an empathetic attorney who will make bond for her or accompany her to court, should she be arrested. All these services require rather high payment, sometimes higher than "normal" in view of the illegality of the prostitute's profession.

Relationships with other prostitutes are somewhat less than friendly.[34] Clients, however, in need of her services, support the prostitute's need for companionship and feelings of worth, and their fees enable her to support all those whom she must pay off.

Unfortunately for the prostitute, other members of her role-set will take her money, yet still disparage her occupational choice and her character. Thus, a life of prostitution is in a sense a vicious circle which spirals only downward. It is hazardous in terms of the law and of health. It is also psychologically hazardous since with increasing age and decreasing attractiveness always looming ahead, the prostitute is subject to an anxiety few other vocations produce. Given that one motivation for entering "the life" is an attempt to reduce anxiety about personal worth, a life of prostitution is not structured to alleviate that anxiety, except for relatively short periods.

In our current society (countermovements notwithstanding) the proof of worth is still to some extent found in the outward signs of success money can buy. There are few success stories among prostitutes. Some marry or take other jobs and leave "the life." Most others, never being able to fully satisfy their needs for feelings of worth, turn to alcohol and drugs for support. The combined effects of these supports, advancing age, and unattractiveness or illness connected with the services the prostitute provides move even those who start at the upper levels progressively down the rungs of the occupational ladder into the lower strata of the profession. This means progressively less money and progressively more hardship.

Investigators who have studied female delinquency have frequently commented on the crucial role that adequate cross-sex relationships, formed in early childhood and based on a successful relationship with the father or father-surrogate, play in the outcomes of delinquent or nondelinquent

---

[34] Bryan, "Occupational Ideologies," op. cit.

careers.[35] The best preventative of female delinquency (which usually takes the form of sexual misbehavior) or a life of prostitution might seem to lie in feelings of worth *as a female* developed early in the girl's life. But since prostitution exists as an occupation which appeals to those whose feelings of worth have not been adequately developed, we may ask profitably about those who form the other side of the equation—the clients of the prostitute.

According to Davis, discussions of the causes of prostitution usually overlook certain questions on the assumption that the sole question concerns the factors leading women to enter the business. But at least five separate questions might be asked. These concern (1) the causes of the *existence* of prostitution; (2) the causes of the *different forms* or *types* of prostitution; (3) the causes of the *rate* or *amount* of prostitution; (4) the causes leading some women *to enter,* and other women not to enter, the profession; and (5) the causes leading some *men to patronize* and others not to patronize, the prostitute.[36]

WHO BUYS?

The existence of prostitution and the causes for some men to patronize prostitutes are interconnected in a larger question: What is there about the nature of human society that causes it to give rise to and maintain an institution that it simultaneously condemns?

The answer may be found in Merton's analysis which points out that the persistence of deviant social structures can only be understood when their social functions (as well as dysfunctions) are taken into account.[37] The basic function of prostitution is to provide a primarily sexual service to people who either fail to meet the requirements of the more legitimate "market" or who exclude themselves from the larger market because they do not feel comfortable in it. The system is very flexible. Almost no one is turned away. Various mechanisms sift and sort "customers" and match them with "merchants" ready to sell them the services they want, whether it be strictly sexual encounter in one form or another, or a listening ear, or a combination of both.

Prostitution provides a source of revenue for a network of persons involved in the prostitute's role-set who may not only strive to sustain but also

[35] See, for example, A. K. Cohen, *Delinquent Boys* (Glencoe, Ill., Free Press, 1955); Gisela Konopka, *The Adolescent Girl in Conflict* (Englewood Cliffs, N.J., Prentice-Hall, 1966); M. G. Riege, "Parental Affection and Juvenile Delinquency in Girls," *British Journal of Delinquency* (April 1971).

[36] Davis, op. cit.

[37] R. K. Merton, *Social Theory and Social Structure,* rev. ed. (New York, Free Press, 1957).

to expand the practice of prostitution.[38] (The connection between prostitution and syndicated crime, for instance, has received considerable attention.) Prostitution also provides a service for the businessman in "entertaining" his customers, an adventure for the adolescent, an outlet for the single man (especially the physically unattractive one), and an outlet for the needs of the sexually abnormal. Since the transaction is essentially impersonal, prostitution can "free" the married man from emotional involvements and the possible scandal that might result from adultery with nonprostitutes. Prostitution to some extent "protects" ordinary women, particularly in places where large numbers of single men are concentrated (for example, military installations, migratory workers' camps). Prostitution may also function to sustain the sexual "conformity" of conventional women insofar as it reduces the pressure men might otherwise exert on them for nonconforming sexual behaviors. Finally,

> [T]he attempt of society to control sexual expression, to tie it to social requirements, especially the attempt to tie it to the durable relationship of marriage and the rearing of children, or to attach men to a celibate order, or to base sexual expression on love creates the opportunity for prostitution.[39]

[38] In the discussion that follows I am indebted to the excellent overview of the social functions of prostitution provided by S. K. Weinberg, "Prostitution," in *Social Problems in Modern Urban Society,* 2nd ed. (Englewood Cliffs, N.J., Prentice-Hall, 1970).

[39] Davis, op. cit.

21. An Abortion Clinic Ethnography

DONALD W. BALL

Traditionally, the study of deviant behavior, however defined, has suffered from a lack of primary data. Materials available to students of various forms of deviance have usually been, in some degree, removed from the actual phenomena under investigation. Thus all too often reports dealing with unconventional social behavior and/or its organization have been based on official statistics produced by variously concerned agencies and on self-reports by the apprehended violators of formal rules and regulations. Neither of these sources is likely to produce an unbiased sample of deviant actors, their actions, and the social organization of these phenomena.[1]

An alternative method of pursuing the study of deviance, one rarely utilized, is to develop contacts with unapprehended deviants themselves, i.e. to go directly to unconventional actors and their subcultures; it is only with such procedures that the natural context of deviance can be studied without the skewedness typical of the usual sources of data.[2] The report which follows is an effort of this alternative: an attempt to utilize actual direct contact with deviant actors in their natural habitat—in his case an abortion clinic—in

From Donald W. Ball, *Social Problems,* Vol. 14, No. 3 (Winter, 1967) pp. 293–300. Reprinted by permission of *The Society for the Study of Social Problems.* I am grateful to Stanford Lyman for his critical comments on an earlier draft of this paper, to Theodore Ravetz for help at various stages of the project, and to Carma Westrum Coon for clerical assistance. I cannot adequately express my debt of gratitude to the anonymous contacts and informants who made this study possible. Portions of this material were presented to the panel on Medical Sociology, Pacific Sociological Association meetings, Vancouver, British Columbia, April 7, 1966.

[1] The sources of bias in official statistics are too well known to require citation, e.g., differentials in organizational actions, variances in definitions, etc.; to deal with apprehended violators only is to study the *technically unskilled* and the *politically unconnected.*

[2] See the penetrating discussion of the ethical problems involved in this method by Ned Polsky, quoted in Howard B. Becker, *Outsiders* (New York, Free Press, 1963), pp. 171–72.

order to shed light on selected aspects of this relatively unstudied area of social life.[3]

More specifically, what follows is an effort to describe ethnographically certain aspects of a particular abortion clinic, especially as such data may illuminate the presentational strategies employed by an habitually deviant establishment in its dealing with a situationally deviant clientele.

For the clinic's staff, participation in an action legally defined as deviant, i.e. criminal abortion, is habitual; that is to say, it is regularly repeated on a routine, business-like basis. For patrons, however, participation is occasional, irregular, and frequently a once-in-a-lifetime engagement in this form of deviance. Most of them are members of otherwise law abiding cultures. Unlike the staff, their involvement in this deviant setting is not an aspect of a career, but an accidental consequence of an unwanted pregnancy.

In the context of the clinic, therefore, the deviant transaction ordinarily is enacted by two kinds of actors: those habitually involved in such exchanges, i.e. the staff; and those only situationally deviant, the otherwise conventional actors in their clinic-related roles as patrons. It becomes of some interest, then, to consider how the clinic manages and fosters impressions for this audience constituted of actors drawn from outside its habitually deviant, abortion-oriented sub-culture, and some of the characteristics of such strategies. Put another way, the focus herein will be upon techniques used by the clinic to key itself to the demands and expectations of a patronage drawn from the conventional culture.

Suffice to say, strictures of confidence prevent any elaborate discussion of method, problems of access, etc. Let it be noted, however, that the materials reported and interpreted herein are based upon: (1) sufficiently lengthy observation of a clinic's routine (exclusive of specifically medical procedures, which are not strictly relevant to the problem) to establish the patterns of its everyday functioning; (2) extensive interviews with a necessarily small number of patrons, some of whom were also observed within the clinic; and (3) limited discussions with some of the clinic's non-medical staff. Additionally, supplementary and confirmatory data have been drawn from interviews with individuals who have utilized other, similar facilities. Unfortunately, any more detailed methodological description would, not surprisingly, violate promises of anonymity guaranteed to the subjects involved; for similar reasons, no direct questions will be presented.[4]

---

[3] For a recent summary which demonstrates how little is known, see Edwin M. Schur, *Crimes Without Victims* (Englewood Cliffs, N.J., Prentice-Hall, 1965), pp. 11–16.

[4] For those interested in procedural minutiae as criteria of validity, the only answer can be: Go out and replicate using your own design. Though precise comparisons would not be possible, such confirmation or refutation would be most desirable.

BACKGROUND

The clinic studied is located, along with several like establishments, in a border town along the California-Mexico line. Its staff includes two practitioners or abortionists, ostensibly physicians, the younger of whom is in an apprentice relationship to the senior man; a practical nurse; a receptionist-bookkeeper; a combination janitress and custodian; a chauffeur-errand boy; and a telephone-appointments secretary.

As costs for such procedures go, the clinic is a relatively expensive one, with fees averaging $500 per abortion. The rate is somewhat less for other medical personnel and students, who are eligible for a discount, and more for persons desiring postoperative overnight observation, or else beyond the tenth week of pregnancy. In terms of finances, the clinic studied is probably representative of others catering to a middle and upper-middle class clientele.

In order to obtain a better picture of the establishment, a brief natural history of a typical involvement between clinic and patron is useful at this point.

Preliminarily, it should be recognized that the ideal-typical practitioner-patient model is not appropriate for the analysis of abortion. Like veterinarians and pediatricians, abortionists frequently have patients for whom financial, if not moral, responsibility is an aspect of the role of some other person, i.e. a client. For abortionists such clients include boyfriends, husbands, and parents. Along with persons such as accompanying friends, they comprise for the patient what might be classified as *supportive others;* persons attending the clinic along with the patient in order to provide psychological support and reinforcement in this crisis situation. Not surprisingly, it is rare for a patient to go to the clinic completely alone, without some morally supportive other. Thus, within the context of abortion, the typical practitioner-patient dyad usually becomes a triad, comprising practitioner, patient, and supportive other.[5]

After referral, usually by a physician, less often by friend or acquaintance, the patron makes original contact with the clinic by telephone. The typically tentative, noncommital, but implicitly urgent communication of the patron is immediately treated in a matter-of-fact manner by the telephone girl. In appropriate middle-class speech patterns she asks the length of the pregnancy, extolls the skills of the staff, sets up a tentative appointment, and discusses the fee and its mode of payment. Treating as routine the patron's problem helps minimize anxiety inherent in such situations. Parallel to this is a "medicalization" of the situation, also helping to disarm the patron

---

[5] In this discussion the general label *patron* will be used in reference to patients, clients, and supportive others, unless reference is spcifically limited to one of the roles in this category.

vis-à-vis the deviant nature of the proposed transaction; at all times, the terminology is that of conventional medicine and surgery. Later, ordinarily two or three days prior to the appointment, the patron again calls the clinic, this time to get confirmation of date and time.

Usually patrons spend the night before their appointment at a hotel or motel near the clinic. Early in the morning of the scheduled date they call the clinic once again, this time to get directions to the only then revealed place of rendezvous where they are picked up and transported to the clinic by one of the staff members in a large, late model station wagon.

It is at this time that patrons find that they are not alone in their dilemma as there are also several others picked up at the same time, filling the station wagon to capacity. Although propinquity might argue for it, there is little deliberate interaction among the patrons during the ride to the clinic, uncertainty effectively immobilizing them in this ambiguous situation.

Upon arrival at the clinic site, where the wagon and all related cars of the staff are hidden from street view, the patrons are ushered into a large, well furnished waiting room. The clinic itself resembles a roomy private home, both externally and internally in its nonmedical areas, and is located in a prestigious residential neighborhood.

Once in, the patrons find seats for themselves and settle into a waiting period of hushed expectancy. Conversation is limited to patients and their respective supportive others, i.e., to those previously known to one another. After a short interval of perhaps five minutes, the receptionist appears and calls out the name of the first patient. The pair, patient and receptionist, then retire out of sight of the remaining patrons and into the medical wing of the clinic.

The first stop in the medical wing is an office. After first explaining the procedure in explicitly medical terminology, the receptionist shifts to her bookkeeper role and requests the fee (in cash or traveler's checks) from the patient, frequently finding that it is being held by an accompanying supportive other still in the waiting room. Following this discussion and collection of the fee, the patient is then sent to a bathroom, well appointed in terms of luxury rather than gynecology, to remove her street clothes and put on a surgical gown. Once gowned, the patient is directed to the room where the actual abortion will take place.

Those specifically involved in the procedure include, in addition to the patient, the two practitioners, senior and apprentice, and a practical nurse. Although an anesthetic is administered, at no time is the patient allowed to lose consciousness; a necessity born of the possible need for quick removal in the event of visitation by legal agents. Immediately upon completion of the procedure the patient leaves the table and is sent to another room to rest for fifteen minutes to an hour and a half. Finally, after receiving medication and instruction regarding postoperative care from the receptionist, the patient and any supportive others are returned to the site of the original rendezvous and thus to their conventional worlds.

ANALYSIS

With this brief, oversimplified picture it is now possible to turn to more specifically sociological concerns: the aforementioned presentational strategies which make up what may be called, for the clinic, a *rhetoric of legitimization.*

Sociologically, a rhetoric is a vocabulary of limited purpose; that is to say, it is a set of symbols functioning to communicate a particular set of meanings, directed and organized toward the representation of a specific image or impression. Such vocabularies are not only verbal but also include visual symbols such as objects, gestures, emblems, etc.[6]

In the case of the clinic the rhetoric operates to subvert the conventional world's view of abortion, and to generate a picture of legitimate activity. Fundamentally, the question thus becomes: What techniques are utilized via this rhetoric to *neutralize* the context of deviance in which the clinic operates, so as to enhance parallels with conventional medical and social situations and thus derive a kind of "rightness" or legitimization?[7] How, in other words, are the setting and actions *qua* impressions manipulated to maximize the clinic's image over and above successful performance of its task and contradict the stereotypic stigma of deviance? Specifically, how does the clinic (1) minimize the possibilities of trouble with frightened or recalcitrant patrons; (2) generate the patron satisfaction necessary for referral system maintenance; and (3) present an image which will provide the most favorable self image or identity for the actors involved, whether patron or staff?[8]

---

[6] The concept of rhetoric as used herein is similar to but independent of the work of Kenneth Burke. As a theoretical point it should be noted that rhetorics are not necessarily the same thing as ideologies, although this may empirically be the case. The conceptual difference between the two is that rhetoric speaks to communication, both style and content, while ideology refers to perception and justification in terms of the ideologue's conception of the relevant portions of the world. It is quite conceivable that individual actors will utilize a rhetoric without any ideological convictions as regards its validity, but with a recognition of its pragmatic efficacy; and similarly, that ideological dedication does not automatically assume any developed rhetoric to attempt its maintenance or furtherance.

[7] Compare Gresham M. Sykes and David Matza, "Techniques of Neutralization: A Theory of Delinquency," *American Sociological Review* 22 (December 1957), pp. 664–70, where the analysis is individual rather than institutional; also Matza, *Delinquency and Drift* (New York, Wiley, 1964).

[8] The second and third problems are, in effect, special cases of the first. Minimization of trouble is not motivated by fear of patron complaints to legal agents, which would involve the complainants in admitting complicity, but by desire to maintain

For conceptual purposes, the clinic's rhetoric of legitimization may be treated by employing Goffman's delineation of *front* and its constituents of setting, appearance, and manner;[9] originally a framework for analyzing the presentation of self, it seems extendible to the strategies of establishments and institutions as well.

Essentially, front consists of those communications which serve to define the situation or performance for the audience: standardized expressive equipment including *setting,* the spatial/physical background items of scenery in the immediate area of the interaction; *appearance,* the sign-vehicles expressing the performer's social status or type; and those expressions which warn of a performer's demeanor, mood, etc., i.e. *manner.*

Examining each of these elements for evidence of how they are manipulated to make up a rhetoric will show the central themes and dimensions of the clinic's presentational strategies. Although the combination of the conceptions of rhetoric, neutralization, and front produces an admittedly loose theoretical scheme, the character of the data does not suggest the need for further rigor.

SETTING

A paramount feature of the clinic's rhetoric is its physical and spatial characteristics. Especially important for patrons generally is the stereotype-contradicting waiting room, the first impression of the clinic itself—and the dominant one for supportive others. The waiting room is likely to be the only room in which the supportive others will be present during their entire visit to the clinic, save the possibility of a short interval in the office if they happen to be holding the fee, a frequent occurrence, especially if the other is also a client.

Spatially, the waiting room is L-shaped and extremely large; approximately 75 feet long and 50 feet wide at the base leg. Its size is accentuated by the fact that most of the room is sunken about three feet below other floor levels. Fully and deeply carpeted, well furnished with several couches, arm chairs, large lamps, and tables, the room speaks of luxury and patron consideration, also implied by the presence of a television set, a small bar, and a phonograph, in addition to the usual magazines present in waiting-room situations.

---

referrals and enhance self images. Additionally, such minimization produces a smoother, easier work-flow for the staff; a similar rationale in conventional medical settings sometimes dictates the use of general anesthetics when, in terms of patient pain, locals would be adequate.

[9] Erving Goffman, *The Presentation of Self in Everyday Life* (Garden City, N.Y., Doubleday, 1959), pp. 22–30. This scheme formed the observational framework for data collection as well as a perspective for preparing the data.

Both the size of the room and the placement of the furniture function to provide private islands which need not be shared; space is structured so as to create withdrawal niches for each set of patrons. Couches and chairs are arranged along the walls of the room, maximizing distance between groupings and minimizing the possibilities of direct, inter-group eye-contact between the various patron-sets who, despite their shared problem and the recently experienced forced propinquity of the ride to the clinic, tend to keep their anxieties private. Thus, interaction among patrons in the waiting room is closed, confined to patients and their own accompanying supportive others only.

Turning to the medical wing: The picture is a far cry from the shabby and sordid image of "kitchen table abortion" drawn in the popular press; it is one of modern scientific medicine, and with it comes assurance to the patient. Once the patient has donned a gown, her next stop is the operating room, a designation used without exception by the staff. In addition to a gynecological table, the room contains familiar (to the lay patient) medical paraphernalia: surgical tools, hypodermic syringes, stainless steel pans and trays, bottles and vials enclosing various colored liquids, capsules, pills, etc.— props effectively neutralizing the negative stereotypes associated with abortion as portrayed in the mass media.

After the procedure has been completed, the patient is moved from the scientific arena of the operating room and back again into luxury. As is the waiting room, the rooms in which the patients spend their short period of postoperative rest are expensively furnished.

Ultimately, after resting, the patient returns to the waiting room and, for most, to supportive others, and receives a final postoperative briefing before being returned to the rendezvous site. Parenthetically it may be noted that throughout the entire episode piped-in music has pervaded every room in which patrons are present.

In terms of setting, the clinic presents itself as not unlike a small hospital albeit with a decorator-designed interior. For patient and supportive others the scenery and props have functioned to communicate an image of assurance and protection through the devices of cost and luxury along with scientific medicine, to minimize the deviant nature of the transaction, and to emphasize positive cultural values, thus efficiently counteracting the stereotypic image.

APPEARANCE AND MANNER

A widespread device for visibly differentiating various social categories or types is clothing.[10] Items of dress may function as insignia or uniforms to

---

[10] Mary Ellen Roach and Joanne Bubolz Eicher (eds.), *Dress, Adornment, and the Social Order* (New York, Wiley, 1965).

label the persons so garbed as members of particular social groups, occupations, etc. Such institutionalized symbols act as both identifiers and identities; to be attired in certain ways is to be a certain kind of person, not only in the eyes of the audience, but also in terms of the actor's perception of himself. Dress is an integral aspect of social identity.

So it is with the staff of the clinic: practitioners, patient, nurse—all wear the appropriate symbols, from the layman's point of view, of dress for surgically centered roles. White tunics are worn by the practitioners; the patient is surgically gowned; the nurse and even the janitress wear white uniform dresses. This element of the rhetoric is highlighted at the beginning of the procedure when both practitioners ostentatiously don surgical gloves, visibly emphasizing their, and the clinic's, concern with the necessities of asepsis. This ritualistic activity also serves to forcefully identify these actors in their roles as defined by the rhetoric.

The medical model is further underscored by the preoperative medical history which is taken and recorded upon a standard, multi-carboned form (the destiny of these duplicate copies is unknown). Actions such as this, along with dress, provide major modes of stressing the medical legitimacy of the clinic, its staff, and its task.

From the receptionist on up through the clinic's hierarchy, behavior, particularly verbal, emphasizes medical and professional aspects of the clinic's operation. Nowhere is this more apparent than in the area of vocabulary; it is strictly medical, with no effort either made or implied to speak down to the less knowledgeable lay patron. It is also noteworthy that at no time is the word abortion used in the presence of a patron; rather, it is referred to as the operation, the procedure, or as a D and C (dilation and curettage). Similarly, as noted above, the room in which the procedure takes place is at all times designated by the staff as the operating room.

Other elements of staff behavior which further the medical impression are (1) the postoperative consultation and medication which effectively contrast with the popular view of abortion as an "off-the-table-and-out" procedure, and (2) the presence of an apprentice practitioner and its obvious analogy, at least to the medically sophisticated, with a teaching hospital. For the patient, the teaching aspects of the senior practitioner's role help to generate confidence in his skill, a matter which is verbally reinforced by other staff members in their interactions with the patrons.

As with appearance, the manner of the staff is essentially directed toward the medical elements of the clinic's rhetoric; their demeanor is professional at all times, with one exception. This exception is the receptionist-bookkeeper, whose role is, by definition, outside the strictly medical aspects of the clinic. As a result, freed of the obligations of professional mien, the receptionist is able to interact with patrons in a reassuring and supportive manner; in effect, her presentation of the rhetoric is through expressive strategies, while the manner of other staff members is more instrumentally oriented.[11]

Before turning to the central themes engendered among the patrons by the clinic's rhetorical strategies, it may be well to at least take note of some flaws in the presentation, even though they may escape the usual patron's attention. These may be considered under the general rubrics of pseudo-sterility and miscellaneous delicts.

PSEUDO-STERILITY

Although ostentation is the rule as regards the emphasis of aseptic and antiseptic precautions, there are also omissions less readily obvious. It will be recalled that measures apparently designed to minimize infection and also at the same time maximize parallels with legitimate medicine included the wearing of tunics by the practitioners, their donning of surgical gloves prior to the procedure, and the display of the tools and paraphernalia of medicine and surgery in the operating room.

It should be pointed out that, aseptically, tunics are no substitute for full surgical gowns, that full precautionary tactics would also include such items as face masks, caps, etc.; and that it is highly irregular for an operating room to lack an autoclave (for the sterilization of instruments) and change-able covering for the table, and for surgical instruments to stand on display, exposed to the air for long periods of time. Additionally, it may be noted that the portion of the preoperative medical history which is taken by the senior practitioner is recorded by him after his elaborate display of putting on the surgical gloves—less than ideal practice for sterility.

These breaches of standard procedure suggest that much of what is passed to the lay patron as concern with asceptic and antiseptic practices is actually rhetoric, designed to communicate to the audience a standard of medical rigor which does not in fact exist.

MISCELLANEOUS DELICTS

Within this category are included additional practices at variance with the fostered impression.

Perhaps the most glaring of these is the lack of privacy afforded the patient in comparison with more conventional medical settings. The fact that patients are handled in groups, and moved and serviced in what in comparison with a hospital is a small and not systematically designed space, leads to a good deal of enforced contact between patients and staff involved in various stages of the process. Of necessity this leads to invasions of privacy,

---

[11] Excluded from this consideration is the telephone girl who is never in face-to-face interaction with her patrons but is also supportive in her demeanor.

at least as perceived by patients accustomed to more traditional medical situations. Thus, for instance, the room used as an office also doubles as a resting room, and a patient lying there for postoperative rest may suddenly find herself witness to a financial transaction as a later-scheduled patron pays the fee; the resting patient is thus treated, in effect, as an object, becoming, in Goffman's phrase, a non-person,[12] i.e., an actor not accorded the usual deferences given as minimal acknowledgements of a person's moral worth simply by virtue of that person's being human.

Also of interest is the function of the music, piped into every room including the one for the procedure. When the patrons first arrive at the clinic the music is quiet, soothing, and relaxing in style; but with the entrance of the first patient into the medical wing, the tempo and timbre increase. The volume of the music then operates to drown out any untoward sounds which might emanate from the medical wing and alarm those patrons still in the waiting room.

Another delict involves the marked contrast in vehicles used in picking up and returning patrons to the rendezvous. In keeping with the symbolism of cost and luxury presented to the prospective patron, the station wagon which brings them to the clinic is an expensive late model. By contrast, for the return to the rendezvous, which is not done en masse as in the initial pickup, and by which time presentational strategies are less necessary, the car driven by the chauffeur-errand boy is in an old, rather decrepit foreign sedan of low cost and questionable reliability.

Another item at variance with traditional medical procedures is the emphasis, especially by the practitioners, on the necessity of the patient's cooperation to assure the procedure's success. The patient is in effect invited, if not commanded, to become an active participant in the ongoing activity.[13] She is told, for instance, of the desirability of her concentrating on other matters, e.g., "think of something else and all will go smoothly and rapidly." This assigning an active role to the patient stands in marked contradiction to her objectification as regards matters of privacy, and implies expediency as a more central concern of the clinic's operation than is patient welfare.

Finally, it may be noted that though the practitioners are verbally represented by others on the staff as physicians, gynecologists in fact, no evidence of medical training in the form of certificates or diplomas is available for patron scrutiny.

---

[12] Goffman, *The Presentation of Self*, op. cit., pp. 151–52.

[13] See the discussion of the patient as basically helpless and passive in Talcott Parsons, *The Social System* (Glencoe, Ill., Free Press, 1951), pp. 439–47. An alternative approach is indicated in Robert Leonard's work. See his several papers in James Skipper Jr. and Leonard, *Social Interaction and Patient Care* (Philadelphia, J. P. Lippincott, 1965).

DISCUSSION

From this selective ethnographic description of various aspects of the clinic's front, two broad dimensions appear essential to its rhetoric of legitimization: (1) luxury and cost, and (2) conventional medical practices and procedures. It is these two themes which are emphasized in the clinic's efforts to neutralize its aura of habitual deviance before an audience of situationally deviant patrons drawn from the world of conventional culture. Thus, the rhetoric draws its vocabulary from meaningful and positive values of the patron's culture.

Within these two valued themes, four elements may be specified as contributing to the two broader dimensions of luxury and cost and conventional medicine: cleanliness, competence, conventionality, and concern for the patron.

Cleanliness and competence are both elements of the instrumental aspects of medicine. Albeit with significant flaws, unrecognized by most lay patrons anyway, the clinic's presentational strategies enhance these impressions, if not to the same extent their actualities. The obvious symbols of dress and equipment are presented to the patient in the medical wing of the clinic where anxiety and uncertainty are high. The symbols are readily recognizable and imply the conventionality of the situation; they provide, in effect, a set of familiar expectations drawn from past experience with legitimate medicine. In a similar allaying manner, the practitioner's skill and competence is repeatedly voiced by the staff from the time of the initial telephone contact until the beginning of the actual abortive procedure itself.

Conventionality here means a realization of the middle class values of most patrons. One of these values is, of course, a positive view of professional medicine, a view which the clinic attempts to exploit. Throughout the patron's experience with the clinic, parallels with this model are highlighted; but it is in another area that this element of the rhetoric functions most effectively.

This is the waiting room setting. The obvious expense, comfort, and general decor of this room are such as to disarm all but the most fearful and suspicious patron. This room and the first impressions it presents are such as to immediately link the clinic to the safe, known world of respectable middle class conventionality. In the process of this linkage, the clinic is, in the patron's perception, divorced from the usually illicit image conjured by abortion; if not rendered totally respectable, the clinic is at least brought within the context of the definitions and expectations of mundane, everyday experience. Because of its crucial location in the process, being the patron's first direct exposure to the clinic milieu, it is fair to say that this room is the most successful presentational strategy in the clinic's legitimizing rhetoric.

The comfort of the waiting room is but one of the forms of expression of concern for the patron which help to create a legitimizing presentation. Other strategies include the telephone girl's supportive routinization of the patron's problem at the time of the initial contact; the similarly solicitous demeanor of the receptionist; and the postoperative consultation. This involves not only the dispensing of drugs to facilitate the patient's convalescence, but also a brochure specifically detailing an expected course of progress and steps to be taken in case of complications.

By demonstrating concern, the clinic affirms its subscription to the values of its patrons, and thus asserts its basically conventional nature, i.e. the congruence of its operation with the norms of those upon whom its income relies.

All of these factors combine to help construct a rhetoric of legitimacy: a set of presentational strategies which allows the clinic to minimize problems inherent in typically anxious and fearful patrons, and thus to function more effectively; and in addition to generate the reputation necessary for an establishment of its kind, dependent upon referrals from physicians.

Additionally, whether manifest or latent, the rhetoric also has consequences for the identities of the actors involved. Both habitual deviants, the staff, and situational deviants, the patrons, are able to partake of the rhetoric so as to enhance their own self images. The rhetoric helps the staff define their participation in the clinic's habitually deviant activities, despite the occasional flaws, as involvement in a professionally operating establishment with the trappings of conventional medicine. For patrons, though they too are admittedly involved in a deviant situation, the rhetoric blunts this hard truth. By accepting the presentational strategies as part of the clinic's image, the patron is allowed to define the situation through the symbols drawn from his conventional everyday experience. Thus, for both patron and staff alike, the rhetoric allows for a minimization of the threat to identity which is built into their illicit transaction.

Unfortunately, the confidential nature of this research does not allow one of the usual canons of science to be met, i.e. that regarding exact replication; and no claim regarding the typicality of the clinic described herein can be made. Hopefully, however, the materials have shed some light on a relatively little known area of social behavior. Given the incidence of abortion, it may be hoped that similar analyses can be conducted by others.[14] Additionally, it may be suggested that the concept of rhetoric provides a useful tool for examining the dramas of social life, whether deviant or conventional, spontaneous or routine, unusual or mundane.

---

[14] A step in this direction is the dissertation (in progress) of Nancy L. Howell, "Information Channels and Informal Networks in the Distribution of Source Information," Department of Social Relations, Harvard University.

Index

431